intel

MCS®-8080/8085 FAMILY USER'S MANUAL

1986

Intel Corporation makes no warranty for the use of its products and assumes no responsibility for any errors which may appear in this document nor does it make a commitment to update the information contained herein.

Intel retains the right to make changes to these specifications at any time, without notice.

Contact your local sales office to obtain the latest specifications before placing your order.

The following are trademarks of Intel Corporation and may only be used to identify Intel Products:

> Above, BITBUS, COMMputer, CREDIT, Data Pipeline, GENIUS, i, Î, ICE, iCEL, iCS, iDBP, iDIS, I²ICE, iLBX, i_m, iMDDX,, iMMX, Insite, Intel, $int_e l$, int_elBOS, Intelevision, int_eligent Identifier, int_eligent Programming, Intellec, Intellink, iOSP, iPDS, iPSC, iRMX, iSBC, iSBX, iSDM, iSXM, KEPROM, Library Manager, MCS, Megachassis, MICROMAINFRAME, MULTIBUS, MULTICHANNEL, MULTIMODULE, ONCE, OpenNET, Plug-A-Bubble, PROMPT, Promware, QUEST, QueX, Ripplemode, RMX/80, RUPI, Seamless, SLD, UPI, and VLSiCEL, and the combination of ICE, iCS, iRMX, iSBC, iSBX, MCS, or UPI and a numerical suffix.

MDS is an ordering code only and is not used as a product name or trademark. MDS® is a registered trademark of Mohawk Data Sciences Corporation.

*MULTIBUS is a patented Intel bus.

Additional copies of this manual or other Intel literature may be obtained from:

Intel Corporation
Literature Distribution
Mail Stop SC6-59
3065 Bowers Avenue
Santa Clara, CA 95051

intel®

U.S. LITERATURE ORDER FORM

NAME: ______________________________

COMPANY: ______________________________

ADDRESS: ______________________________

CITY: ______________________ STATE: __________ ZIP: __________

COUNTRY: ______________________________

PHONE NO.: (______) ______________________

ORDER NO.	TITLE	QTY.		PRICE		TOTAL
☐☐☐☐☐☐☐ - ☐☐☐	________	____	×	____	=	____
☐☐☐☐☐☐☐ - ☐☐☐	________	____	×	____	=	____
☐☐☐☐☐☐☐ - ☐☐☐	________	____	×	____	=	____
☐☐☐☐☐☐☐ - ☐☐☐	________	____	×	____	=	____
☐☐☐☐☐☐☐ - ☐☐☐	________	____	×	____	=	____
☐☐☐☐☐☐☐ - ☐☐☐	________	____	×	____	=	____
☐☐☐☐☐☐☐ - ☐☐☐	________	____	×	____	=	____

Subtotal ____________

Add appropriate postage and handling to subtotal
10% U.S.
20% Canada

Your Local Sales Tax ____________

→ Postage & Handling ____________

Allow 2-4 weeks for delivery

Total ____________

Pay by Visa, MasterCard, Check or Money Order, payable to Intel Books. Purchase Orders have a $50.00 minimum

☐ Visa ☐ MasterCard Expiration Date ____________

Account No. ______________________________

Signature: ______________________________

Mail To: Intel Literature Sales
P.O. Box 58130
Santa Clara, CA
95052-8130

Customers outside the U.S. and Canada should contact the local Intel Sales Office or Distributor listed in the back of most Intel literature.

Call Toll Free: (800) 548-4725 for phone orders

Prices good until 12/31/86.

Source HB

Mail To: Intel Literature Sales
P.O. Box 58130
Santa Clara, CA 95052-8130

Table of Contents

*For complete data sheets on all microprocessor and peripheral products, refer to the Microsystem Components Handbook, Volume I & II. See inside front cover to order.

CUSTOMER SUPPORT

CUSTOMER SUPPORT

Customer Support is Intel's complete support service that provides Intel customers with Customer Training, Software Support and Hardware Support.

After a customer purchases any system hardware or software product, service and support become major factors in determining whether that product will continue to meet a customer's expectations. Such support requires an international support organization and a breadth of programs to meet a variety of customer needs. Intel's extensive customer support includes factory repair services as well as worldwide field service offices providing hardware repair services, software support services and customer training classes.

HARDWARE SUPPORT

Hardware Support Services provides maintenance on Intel supported products at board and system level. Both field and factory services are offered. Services include several types of field maintenance agreements, installation and warranty services, hourly contracted services (factory return for repair) and specially negotiated support agreements for system integrators and large volume end-users having unique service requirements. For more information contact your local Intel Sales Office.

SOFTWARE SUPPORT

Software Support Service provides maintenance on software packages via software support contracts which include subscription services, information phone support, and updates. Consulting services can be arranged for on-site assistance at the customer's location for both short-term and long-term needs. For complex products such as NDS II or I²ICE, orientation/installation packages are available through membership in Insite User's Library, where customer-submitted programs are catalogued and made available for a minimum fee to members. For more information contact your local Intel Sales Office.

CUSTOMER TRAINING

Customer Training provides workshops at customer sites (by agreement) and on a regularly scheduled basis at Intel's facilities. Intel offers a breadth of workshops on microprocessors, operating systems and programming languages, etc. For more information on these classes contact the Training Center nearest you.

TRAINING CENTER LOCATIONS

To obtain a complete catalog of our workshops, call the nearest Training Center in your area.

Boston	(617) 692-1000	London	(0793) 696-000
Chicago	(312) 310-5700	Munich	(089) 5389-1
San Francisco	(415) 940-7800	Paris	(01) 687-22-21
Washington, D.C.	(301) 474-2878	Stockholm	(468) 734-01-00
Israel	(972) 349-491-099	Milan	39-2-82-44-071
Tokyo	03-437-6611	Benelux (Rotterdam)	(10) 21-23-77
Osaka (Call Tokyo)	03-437-6611	Copenhagen	(1) 198-033
Toronto, Canada	(416) 675-2105	Hong Kong	5-215311-7

Introduction

1

CHAPTER 1
PART 1: INTRODUCTION TO THE FUNCTIONS OF A COMPUTER

This chapter introduces certain basic computer concepts. It provides background information and definitions which will be useful in later chapters of this manual. Those already familiar with computers may skip this material, at their option.

A TYPICAL COMPUTER SYSTEM

A typical digital computer consists of:

a) A central processor unit (CPU)
b) A memory
c) Input/output (I/O) ports

The memory serves as a place to store **Instructions,** the coded pieces of information that direct the activities of the CPU, and **Data**, the coded pieces of information that are processed by the CPU. A group of logically related instructions stored in memory is referred to as a **Program**. The CPU "reads" each instruction from memory in a logically determined sequence, and uses it to initiate processing actions. If the program sequence is coherent and logical, processing the program will produce intelligible and useful results.

The memory is also used to store the data to be manipulated, as well as the instructions that direct that manipulation. The program must be organized such that the CPU does not read a non-instruction word when it expects to see an instruction. The CPU can rapidly access any data stored in memory; but often the memory is not large enough to store the entire data bank required for a particular application. The problem can be resolved by providing the computer with one or more **Input Ports**. The CPU can address these ports and input the data contained there. The addition of input ports enables the computer to receive information from external equipment (such as a paper tape reader or floppy disk) at high rates of speed and in large volumes.

A computer also requires one or more **Output Ports** that permit the CPU to communicate the result of its processing to the outside world. The output may go to a display, for use by a human operator, to a peripheral device that produces "hard-copy," such as a line-printer, to a peripheral storage device, such as a floppy disk unit, or the output may constitute process control signals that direct the operations of another system, such as an automated assembly line. Like input ports, output ports are addressable. The input and output ports together permit the processor to communicate with the outside world.

The CPU unifies the system. It controls the functions performed by the other components. The CPU must be able to fetch instructions from memory, decode their binary contents and execute them. It must also be able to reference memory and I/O ports as necessary in the execution of instructions. In addition, the CPU should be able to recognize and respond to certain external control signals, such as INTERRUPT and WAIT requests. The functional units within a CPU that enable it to perform these functions are described below.

THE ARCHITECTURE OF A CPU

A typical central processor unit (CPU) consists of the following interconnected functional units:

- Registers
- Arithmetic/Logic Unit (ALU)
- Control Circuitry

Registers are temporary storage units within the CPU. Some registers, such as the program counter and instruction register, have dedicated uses. Other registers, such as the accumulator, are for more general purpose use.

Accumulator:

The accumulator usually stores one of the operands to be manipulated by the ALU. A typical instruction might direct the ALU to add the contents of some other register to the contents of the accumulator and store the result in the accumulator itself. In general, the accumulator is both a source (operand) and a destination (result) register.

Often a CPU will include a number of additional general purpose registers that can be used to store operands or intermediate data. The availability of general purpose registers eliminates the need to "shuffle" intermediate results back and forth between memory and the accumulator, thus improving processing speed and efficiency.

Program Counter (Jumps, Subroutines and the Stack):

The instructions that make up a program are stored in the system's memory. The central processor references the contents of memory, in order to determine what action is appropriate. This means that the processor must know which location contains the next instruction.

Each of the locations in memory is numbered, to distinguish it from all other locations in memory. The number which identifies a memory location is called its **Address**.

The processor maintains a counter which contains the address of the next program instruction. This register is called the **Program Counter**. The processor updates the program counter by adding "1" to the counter each time it fetches an instruction, so that the program counter is always current (pointing to the next instruction).

The programmer therefore stores his instructions in numerically adjacent addresses, so that the lower addresses contain the first instructions to be executed and the higher addresses contain later instructions. The only time the programmer may violate this sequential rule is when an instruction in one section of memory is a **Jump** instruction to another section of memory.

A jump instruction contains the address of the instruction which is to follow it. The next instruction may be stored in any memory location, as long as the programmed jump specifies the correct address. During the execution of a jump instruction, the processor replaces the contents of its program counter with the address embodied in the Jump. Thus, the logical continuity of the program is maintained.

A special kind of program jump occurs when the stored program "**Calls**" a subroutine. In this kind of jump, the processor is required to "remember" the contents of the program counter at the time that the jump occurs. This enables the processor to resume execution of the main program when it is finished with the last instruction of the subroutine.

A **Subroutine** is a program within a program. Usually it is a general-purpose set of instructions that must be executed repeatedly in the course of a main program. Routines which calculate the square, the sine, or the logarithm of a program variable are good examples of functions often written as subroutines. Other examples might be programs designed for inputting or outputting data to a particular peripheral device.

The processor has a special way of handling subroutines, in order to insure an orderly return to the main program. When the processor receives a Call instruction, it increments the Program Counter and stores the counter's contents in a reserved memory area known as the **Stack**. The Stack thus saves the address of the instruction to be executed after the subroutine is completed. Then the processor loads the address specified in the Call into its Program Counter. The next instruction fetched will therefore be the first step of the subroutine.

The last instruction in any subroutine is a **Return**. Such an instruction need specify no address. When the processor fetches a Return instruction, it simply replaces the current contents of the Program Counter with the address on the top of the stack. This causes the processor to resume execution of the calling program at the point immediately following the original Call Instruction.

Subroutines are often **Nested**; that is, one subroutine will sometimes call a second subroutine. The second may call a third, and so on. This is perfectly acceptable, as long as the processor has enough capacity to store the necessary return addresses, and the logical provision for doing so. In other words, the maximum depth of nesting is determined by the depth of the stack itself. If the stack has space for storing three return addresses, then three levels of subroutines may be accommodated.

Processors have different ways of maintaining stacks. Some have facilities for the storage of return addresses built into the processor itself. Other processors use a reserved area of external memory as the stack and simply maintain a **Pointer** register which contains the address of the most recent stack entry. The external stack allows virtually unlimited subroutine nesting. In addition, if the processor provides instructions that cause the contents of the accumulator and other general purpose registers to be "pushed" onto the stack or "popped" off the stack via the address stored in the stack pointer, multi-level interrupt processing (described later in this chapter) is possible. The status of the processor (i.e., the contents of all the registers) can be saved in the stack when an interrupt is accepted and then restored after the interrupt has been serviced. This ability to save the processor's status at any given time is possible even if an interrupt service routine, itself, is interrupted.

Instruction Register and Decoder:

Every computer has a **Word Length** that is characteristic of that machine. A computer's word length is usually determined by the size of its internal storage elements and interconnecting paths (referred to as **Busses**); for example, a computer whose registers and busses can store and transfer 8 bits of information has a characteristic word length of 8-bits and is referred to as an 8-bit parallel processor. An eight-bit parallel processor generally finds it most efficient to deal with eight-bit binary fields, and the memory associated with such a processor is therefore organized to store eight bits in each addressable memory location. Data and instructions are stored in memory as eight-bit binary numbers, or as numbers that are integral multiples of eight bits: 16 bits, 24 bits, and so on. This characteristic eight-bit field is often referred to as a **Byte**.

Each operation that the processor can perform is identified by a unique byte of data known as an **Instruction**

Code or **Operation Code**. An eight-bit word used as an instruction code can distinguish between 256 alternative actions, more than adequate for most processors.

The processor fetches an instruction in two distinct operations. First, the processor transmits the address in its Program Counter to the memory. Then the memory returns the addressed byte to the processor. The CPU stores this instruction byte in a register known as the **Instruction Register**, and uses it to direct activities during the remainder of the instruction execution.

The mechanism by which the processor translates an instruction code into specific processing actions requires more elaboration than we can here afford. The concept, however, should be intuitively clear to any logic designer. The eight bits stored in the instruction register can be decoded and used to selectively activate one of a number of output lines, in this case up to 256 lines. Each line represents a set of activities associated with execution of a particular instruction code. The enabled line can be combined with selected timing pulses, to develop electrical signals that can then be used to initiate specific actions. This translation of code into action is performed by the **Instruction Decoder** and by the associated control circuitry.

An eight-bit instruction code is often sufficient to specify a particular processing action. There are times, however, when execution of the instruction requires more information than eight bits can convey.

One example of this is when the instruction references a memory location. The basic instruction code identifies the operation to be performed, but cannot specify the object address as well. In a case like this, a two- or three-byte instruction must be used. Successive instruction bytes are stored in sequentially adjacent memory locations, and the processor performs two or three fetches in succession to obtain the full instruction. The first byte retrieved from memory is placed in the processor's instruction register, and subsequent bytes are placed in temporary storage; the processor then proceeds with the execution phase. Such an instruction is referred to as **Variable Length**.

Address Register(s):

A CPU may use a register or register-pair to hold the address of a memory location that is to be accessed for data. If the address register is **Programmable**, (i.e., if there are instructions that allow the programmer to alter the contents of the register) the program can "build" an address in the address register prior to executing a **Memory Reference** instruction (i.e., an instruction that reads data from memory, writes data to memory or operates on data stored in memory).

Arithmetic/Logic Unit (ALU):

All processors contain an arithmetic/logic unit, which is often referred to simply as the **ALU**. The ALU, as its name implies, is that portion of the CPU hardware which performs the arithmetic and logical operations on the binary data.

The ALU must contain an **Adder** which is capable of combining the contents of two registers in accordance with the logic of binary arithmetic. This provision permits the processor to perform arithmetic manipulations on the data it obtains from memory and from its other inputs.

Using only the basic adder a capable programmer can write routines which will subtract, multiply and divide, giving the machine complete arithmetic capabilities. In practice, however, most ALUs provide other built-in functions, including hardware subtraction, boolean logic operations, and shift capabilities.

The ALU contains **Flag Bits** which specify certain conditions that arise in the course of arithmetic and logical manipulations. Flags typically include **Carry, Zero, Sign,** and **Parity**. It is possible to program jumps which are conditionally dependent on the status of one or more flags. Thus, for example, the program may be designed to jump to a special routine if the carry bit is set following an addition instruction.

Control Circuitry:

The control circuitry is the primary functional unit within a CPU. Using clock inputs, the control circuitry maintains the proper sequence of events required for any processing task. After an instruction is fetched and decoded, the control circuitry issues the appropriate signals (to units both internal and external to the CPU) for initiating the proper processing action. Often the control circuitry will be capable of responding to external signals, such as an interrupt or wait request. An **Interrupt** request will cause the control circuitry to temporarily interrupt main program execution, jump to a special routine to service the interrupting device, then automatically return to the main program. A **Wait** request is often issued by a memory or I/O element that operates slower than the CPU. The control circuitry will idle the CPU until the memory or I/O port is ready with the data.

COMPUTER OPERATIONS

There are certain operations that are basic to almost any computer. A sound understanding of these basic operations is a necessary prerequisite to examining the specific operations of a particular computer.

Timing:

The activities of the central processor are cyclical. The processor fetches an instruction, performs the operations required, fetches the next instruction, and so on. This orderly sequence of events requires precise timing, and the CPU therefore requires a free running oscillator clock which furnishes the reference for all processor actions. The combined fetch and execution of a single instruction is referred to as an **Instruction Cycle**. The portion of a cycle identified with a clearly defined activity is called a **State**. And the interval between pulses of the timing oscillator is referred to as a **Clock Period**. As a general rule, one or more clock periods are necessary for the completion of a state, and there are several states in a cycle.

Instruction Fetch:

The first state(s) of any instruction cycle will be dedicated to fetching the next instruction. The CPU issues a read signal and the contents of the program counter are sent to memory, which responds by returning the next instruction word. The first byte of the instruction is placed in the instruction register. If the instruction consists of more than one byte, additional states are required to fetch each byte of the instruction. When the entire instruction is present in the CPU, the program counter is incremented (in preparation for the next instruction fetch) and the instruction is decoded. The operation specified in the instruction will be executed in the remaining states of the instruction cycle. The instruction may call for a memory read or write, an input or output and/or an internal CPU operation, such as a register-to-register transfer or an add-registers operation.

Memory Read:

An instruction **fetch** is merely a special memory read operation that brings the instruction to the CPU's instruction register. The instruction fetched may then call for data to be read from memory into the CPU. The CPU again issues a read signal and sends the proper memory address; memory responds by returning the requested word. The data received is placed in the accumulator or one of the other general purpose registers (not the instruction register).

Memory Write:

A memory write operation is similar to a read except for the direction of data flow. The CPU issues a write signal, sends the proper memory address, then sends the data word to be written into the addressed memory location.

Wait (memory synchronization):

As previously stated, the activities of the processor are timed by a master clock oscillator. The clock period determines the timing of all processing activity.

The speed of the processing cycle, however, is limited by the memory's **Access Time**. Once the processor has sent a read address to memory, it cannot proceed until the memory has had time to respond. Most memories are capable of responding much faster than the processing cycle requires. A few, however, cannot supply the addressed byte within the minimum time established by the processor's clock.

Therefore a processor should contain a synchronization provision, which permits the memory to request a **Wait state**. When the memory receives a read or write enable signal, it places a request signal on the processor's READY line, causing the CPU to idle temporarily. After the memory has had time to respond, it frees the processor's READY line, and the instruction cycle proceeds.

Input/Output:

Input and Output operations are similar to memory read and write operations with the exception that a peripheral I/O device is addressed instead of a memory location. The CPU issues the appropriate input or output control signal, sends the proper device address and either receives the data being input or sends the data to be output.

Data can be input/output in either parallel or serial form. All data within a digital computer is represented in binary coded form. A binary data word consists of a group of bits; each bit is either a one or a zero. **Parallel** I/O consists of transferring all bits in the word at the same time, one bit per line. **Serial** I/O consists of transferring one bit at a time on a single line. Naturally serial I/O is much slower, but it requires considerably less hardware than does parallel I/O.

Interrupts:

Interrupt provisions are included on many central processors, as a means of improving the processor's efficiency. Consider the case of a computer that is processing a large volume of data, portions of which are to be output to a printer. The CPU can output a byte of data within a single machine cycle but it may take the printer the equivalent of many machine cycles to actually print the character specified by the data byte. The CPU could then remain idle waiting until the printer can accept the next data byte. If an interrupt capability is implemented on the computer, the CPU can output a data byte then return to data processing. When the printer is ready to accept the next data byte, it can request an interrupt. When the CPU acknowledges the interrupt, it suspends main program execution and automatically branches to a routine that will output the next data byte. After the byte is output, the CPU continues with main program execution. Note that this is, in principle, quite similar to a subroutine call, except that the jump is initiated externally rather than by the program.

More complex interrupt structures are possible, in which several interrupting devices share the same processor but have different priority levels. Interruptive processing is an important feature that enables maximum untilization of a processor's capacity for high system throughput.

Hold:

Another important feature that improves the throughput of a processor is the **Hold**. The hold provision enables **Direct Memory Access** (DMA) operations.

In ordinary input and output operations, the processor itself supervises the entire data transfer. Information to be placed in memory is transferred from the input device to the processor, and then from the processor to the designated memory location. In similar fashion, information that goes from memory to output devices goes by way of the processor.

Some peripheral devices, however, are capable of transferring information to and from memory much faster than the processor itself can accomplish the transfer. If any appreciable quantity of data must be transferred to or from such a device, then **system throughput** will be increased by having the device accomplish the transfer directly. The processor must temporarily suspend its operation during such a transfer, to prevent conflicts that would arise if processor and peripheral device attempted to access memory simultaneously. It is for this reason that a **hold** provision is included on some processors.

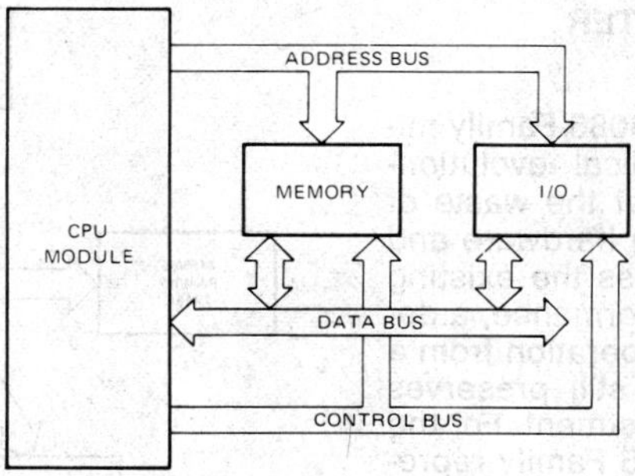

PART 2: INTRODUCTION TO THE 8085 FAMILY

THE 8085 FAMILY MICROCOMPUTER SYSTEM

The basic philosophy behind the 8085 Family microcomputer system is one of logical, evolutionary advance in technology without the waste of discarding existing investments in hardware and software. The 8085 Family provides the existing 8080 user with an increase in performance, a decrease in the component count, operation from a single 5-Volt power supply, and still preserves 100% of his existing software investment. For the new microcomputer user, the 8085 Family represents the refinement of the Intel 8080, along with a wealth of supporting software, documentation and peripheral components to speed the cycle from prototype to production. The same development tools that Intel has produced to support the 8080 microcomputer system can be used for the 8085 Family, and additional add-on features are available to optimize system development for the 8085 Family.

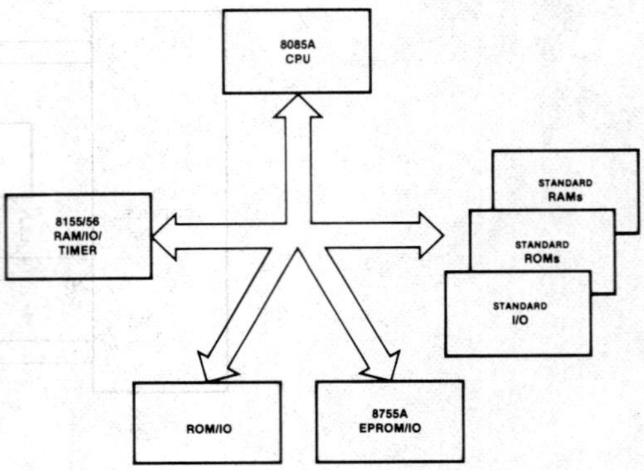

This section of the 8080/8085 User's Manual will briefly detail the basic differences between the 8085 and the 8080 families. It will illustrate both the hardware and software compatibilities and also reveal some of the engineering trade-offs that were met during the design of the 8085 Family. More detailed discussion of the 8085 bus operation and component specifications are available in Chapters: 2, 3, 4, and 5. The information provided in Chapter 1 will be helpful in understanding the basic concepts and philosophies behind the 8085 Family.

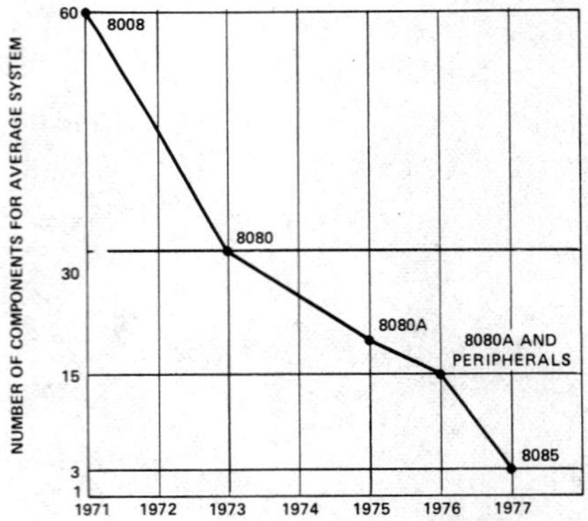

8-BIT SMALL SYSTEM COMPONENT COUNT 1971 – 1977

EVOLUTION

In December 1971, Intel introduced the first general purpose, 8-bit microprocessor, the 8008. It was implemented in P-channel MOS technology and was packaged in a single 18 pin, dual in-line package (DIP). The 8008 used standard semiconductor ROM and RAM and, for the most part, TTL components for I/O and general interface. It immediately found applications in byte-oriented end products such as terminals and computer peripherals where its instruction execution (20 micro-seconds), general purpose organization and instruction set matched the requirements of these products. Recognizing that hardware was but a small part in the overall system picture, Intel developed both hardware and software tools for the design engineer so that the transition from prototype to production would be as simple and fast as possible. The commitment of providing a total systems approach with the 8008 microcomputer system was actually the basis for the sophisticated, comprehensive development tools that Intel has available today.

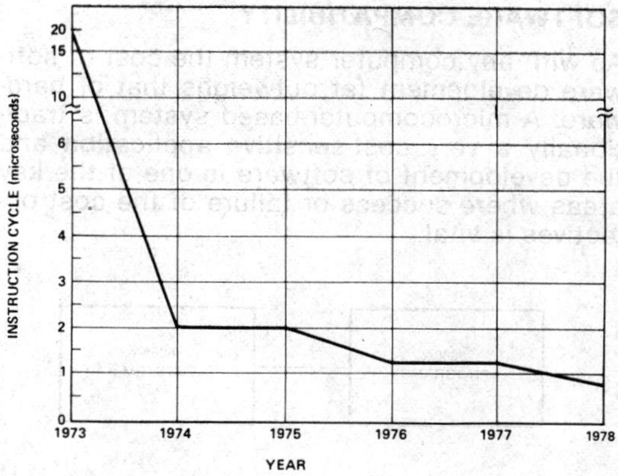

THE 8080A MICROPROCESSOR

With the advent of high-production N-channel RAM memories and 40 pin DIP packaging, Intel designed the 8080A microprocessor. It was designed to be software compatible with the 8008 so that the existing users of the 8008 could preserve their investment in software and at the same time provide dramatically increased performance (2 micro-second instruction execution), while reducing the amount of componenets necessary to implement a system. Additions were made to the basic instruction set to take advantage of this increased performance and large system-type features were included on-chip such as DMA, 16-bit addressing and external stack memory so that the total spectrum of application could be significantly increased. The 8080 was first sampled in December 1973. Since that time it became the standard of the industry and was accepted as the primary building block for more microcomputer based applications than all other microcomputer systems combined.

A TOTAL SYSTEMS COMMITMENT

The Intel 8080A Microcomputer System is an early example of Intel's total systems commitment. Beginning with the 8008 to the 8085A and beyond, Intel fully supports the user's needs from prototype system development through reliable, high-volume production. From MOS/VLSI peripheral components to resident high level systems languages (PL/M, Pascal), Intel provides the most comprehensive, effective solution to today's system problems.

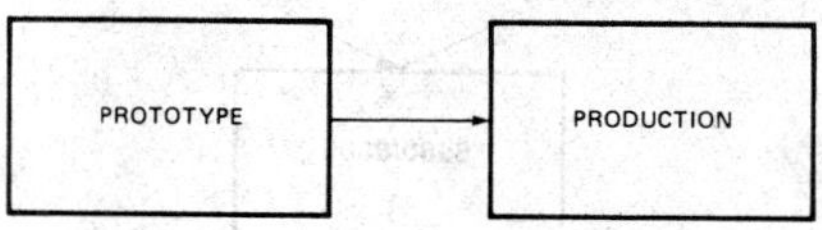

SOFTWARE COMPATIBILITY

As with any computer system the cost of software development far outweighs that of hardware. A microcomputer-based system is traditionally a very cost-sensitive application and the development of software is one of the key areas where success or failure of the cost objectives is vital.

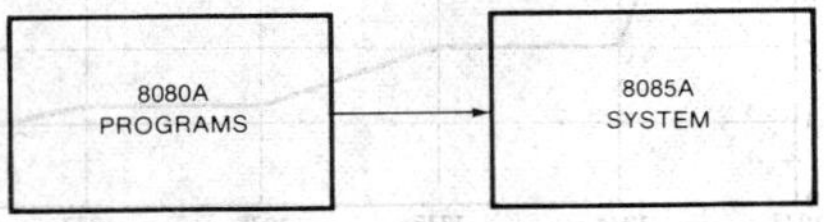

The 8085A CPU is 100% software compatible with the Intel® 8080A CPU. The compatibility is at the object or "machine code" level so that existing programs written for 8080A execution will run on the 8085A as is. The value of this becomes even more evident to the user who has mask programmed ROMs and wishes to update his system without the need for new masks.

PROGRAMMER TRAINING

A cost which is often forgotten is that of programmer training. A new, or modified instruction set, would require programmers to relearn another set of mnemonics and greatly affect the productivity during development. The 100% compatibility of the 8085A CPU assures that no re-training effort will be required.

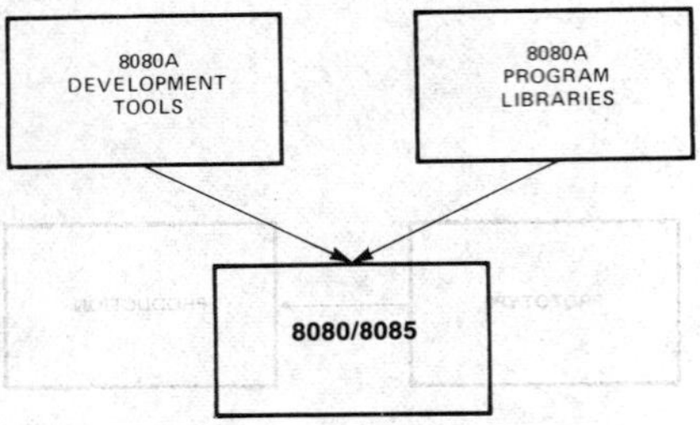

For the new microcomputer user, the software compatibility between the 8085A and the 8080A means that all of the software development tools that are available for the 8080A and all software libraries for 8080A will operate with the new design and thus save immeasurable cost in development and debug.

The 8085A CPU does however add two instructions to initialize and maintain hardware features of the 8085A. Two of the unused opcodes of the 8080A instruction set were designated for the addition so that 100% compatibility could be maintained.

HARDWARE COMPATIBILITY

The integration of auxiliary 8080A functions, such as clock generation, system control and interrupt prioritization, dramatically reduces the amount of components necessary for most systems. In addition, the 8085 Family operates off a single +5 Volt power supply to further simplify hardware development and debug. A close examination of the AC/DC specifications of the 8085 systems components shows that each is specified to supply a minimum of 400μA of source current and a full TTL load of sink current so that a very substantial system can be constructed without the need for extra TTL buffers or drivers. Input and output voltage levels are also specified so that a minimum of 350mV noise margin is provided for reliable, high-performance operation.

PC BOARD CONSIDERATIONS

The 8085A CPU and the 8080A are not pin-compatible due to the reduction in power supplies and the addition of integrated auxiliary features. However, the pinouts of the 8085 Family system components were carefully assigned to minimize PC board area and thus yield a smooth, efficient layout. For new designs this incompatibility of pinouts presents no problems and for upgrades of existing designs the reduction of components and board area will far offset the incompatibility.

8085 FAMILY SPECIAL PERIPHERAL COMPONENTS

The 8085 Family was designed to minimize the amount of components required for most systems. Intel designed several new peripheral components that combine memory, I/O and timer functions to fulfill this requirement. These new peripheral devices directly interface to the multiplexed 8085 bus structure and provide new levels in system integration for today's designer.

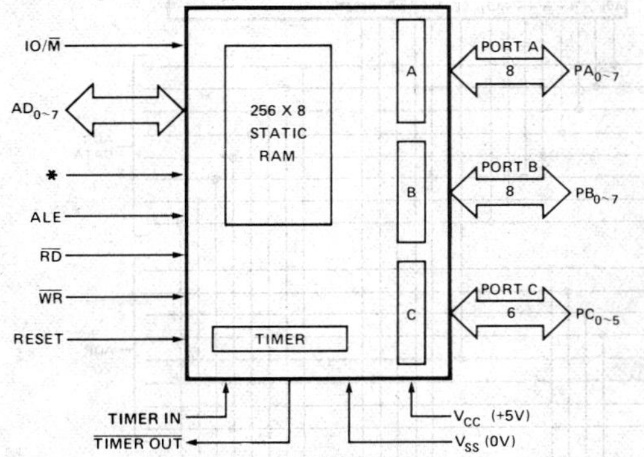

*: 8155 = $\overline{CE}$, 8156 = CE

8155/8156 RAM, I/O and Timer

- 256 bytes RAM
- Two 8-bit ports
- One 6-bit port (programmable)
- One 14-bit programmable interval timer
- Single +5 Volt supply operation
- 40 pin DIP plastic or cerdip package

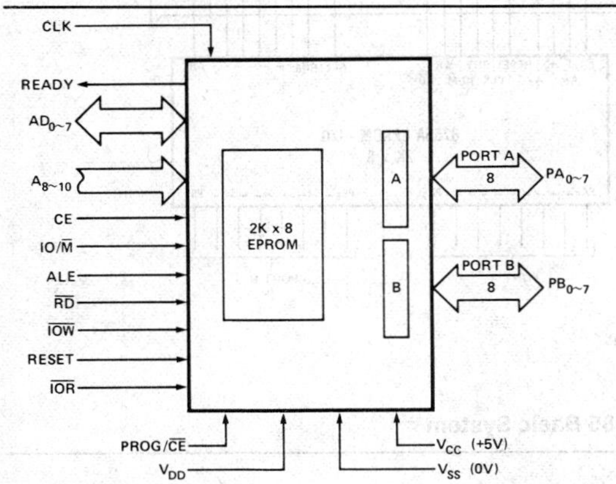

8755A EPROM and I/O

- 2K bytes EPROM
- Two 8-bit ports (direction programmable)
- Single +5 Volt supply read operation
- U.V. Erasable
- 40 pin DIP package

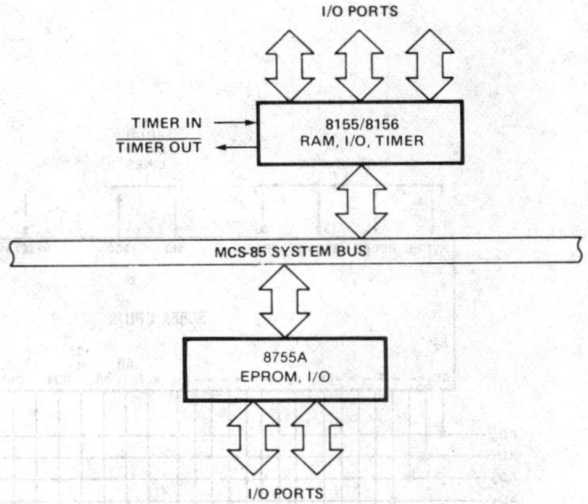

SYSTEM EXPANSION

Each of these peripheral components has features that allow a small to medium system to be constructed without the addition of buffers and decoders to maintain the lowest possible component count.

INTERFACING TO 8080/8085 PROGRAMMABLE PERIPHERAL COMPONENTS

The 8085 Family shares with the 8080 Family a wide range of peripheral components that solve system problems and provide the designer with a great deal of flexibility in his I/O, Interrupt and DMA structures. The 8085 Family is direclty compatible with these peripherals, and, with the exception of the 8257-5 DMA controller, needs no additional circuitry for their interface in a minimum system. The 8257-5 DMA controller uses a latch and some gating to support the multiplexed bus of the 8085.

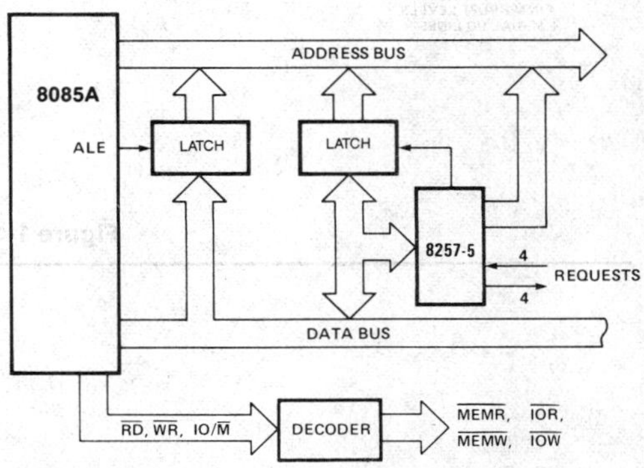

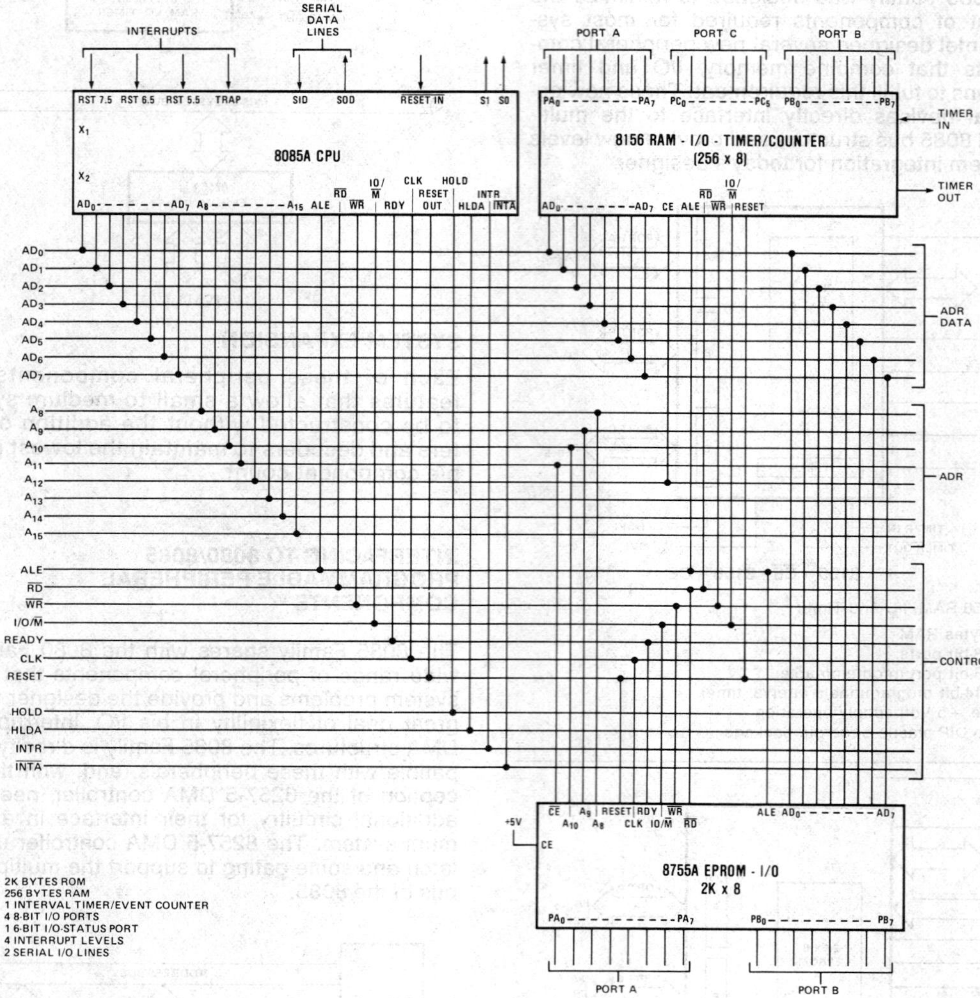

Figure 1-1. 8080/8085 Basic System

PROGRAMMABLE PERIPHERALS

The list of programmable peripherals for use with the 8085A includes:

8251A	Programmable Communications Interface
8253-5	Programmable Interval Timer
8255A-5	Programmable Peripheral Interface
8257-5	Programmable DMA Controller
8259-5	Programmable Interrupt Controller
8271	Diskette Controller
8273	Synchronous Data Link Controller
8275	CRT Controller
8279	Keyboard/Display Controller

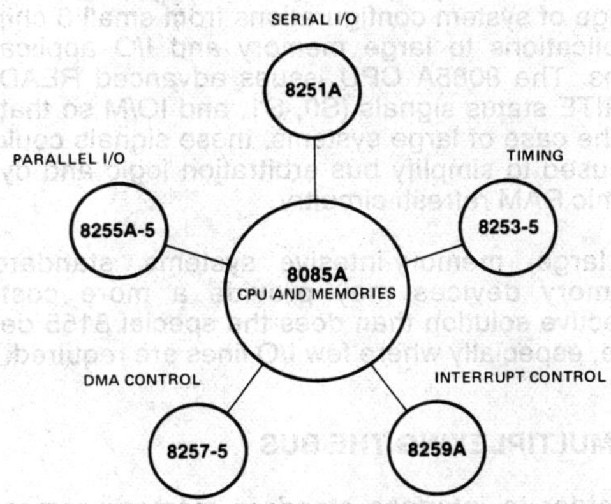

The 8080/8085 peripheral compatibility assures the designer that all new peripheral components from Intel will interface to the 8085 bus structure to further expand the application spectrum of the 8085 Family.

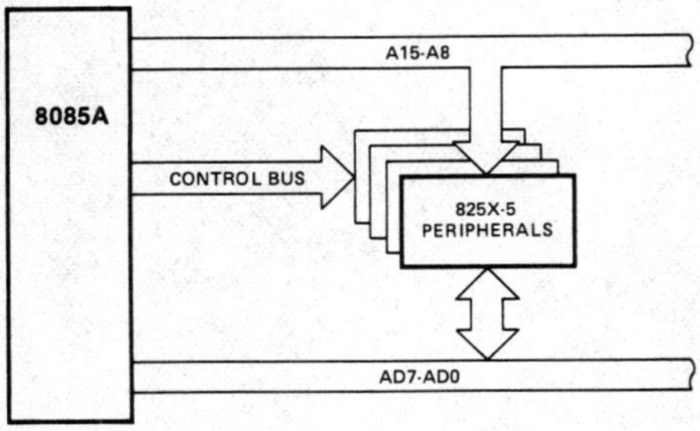

INTEFACING TO STANDARD MEMORY

The 8085 Family was designed to support the full range of system configurations from small 3 chip applications to large memory and I/O applications. The 8085A CPU issues advanced READ/WRITE status signals (S0, S1, and IO/M so that, in the case of large systems, these signals could be used to simplify bus arbitration logic and dynamic RAM refresh circuitry.

In large, memory-intesive systems, standard memory devices may provide a more cost-effective solution than does the special 8155 device, especially where few I/O lines are required.

DEMULTIPLEXING THE BUS

In order to interface standard memory components the 8085 bus must be "demultiplexed". This is accomplished by connecting a latch to the data bus and strobing the latch with the ALE signal from the 8085A CPU. The ALE signal is issued to indicate that the multiplexed bus contains the lower 8-bits of the address. This information is latched so that a full 16-bit address is available to interface standard memory components.

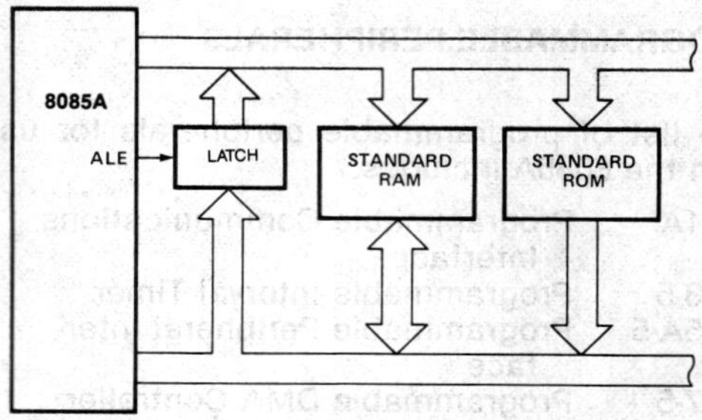

SYSTEM PERFORMANCE

The true benchmark of any microcomputer-based system is the amount of tasks that can be performed by the system in a given period of time. Increasing speed of CPU instruction execution has been the common approach to increasing system throughput but this puts a greater strain on the memory access requirement and bus operation than is usually practical for most applications. A much more desirable method would be to distribute the task-load to peripheral devices.

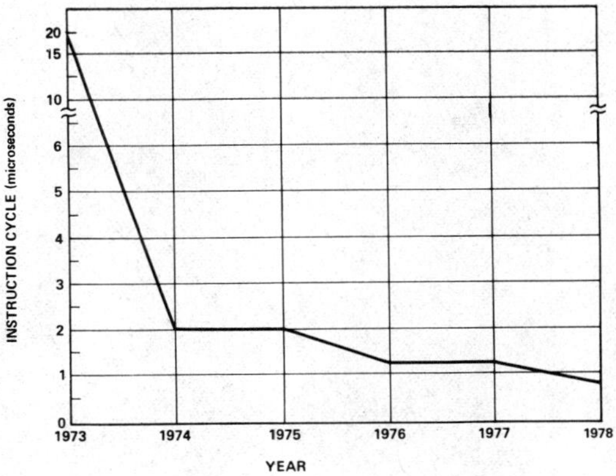

DISTRIBUTED PROCESSING

The concept of distributed task processing is not new to the computer designer, but unitl recently little if any task distribution was available to the microcomputer user. The use of the new programmable 8080/8085 peripherals can relieve the central processor of many of the bookkeeping I/O and timing tasks that would otherwise have to be handled by system software.

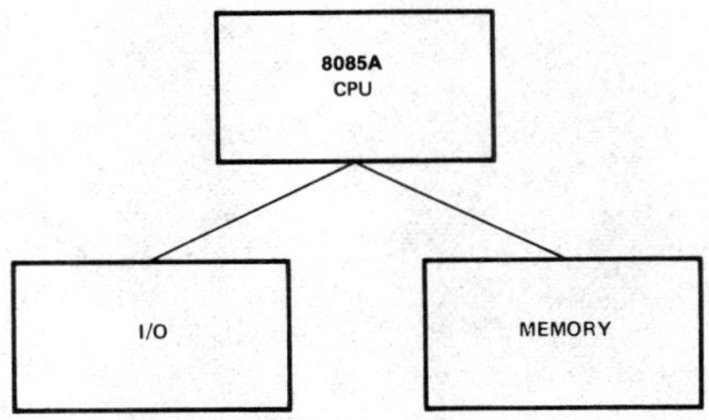

INSTRUCTION CYCLE/ACCESS TIME

The basic instruction cycle of the 8085A is 1.3 microseconds, the same speed as the 8080A-1. A close look at the 8085 bus operation shows that the access requirement for this speed is only 575 nanoseconds. The 8080 access requirements for this speed would be under 300 nanoseconds. This illustrates the efficiency and improved timing margins of the 8085 bus structure. The 8085A-2, a high-speed selected version of the 8085A with a .8 microsecond instruction cycle, provides a 60% performance improvement over the standard 8085A.

CONCLUSIONS: THROUGHPUT/COST

When a total system throughput/cost analysis is taken, the 8085 Family system yields a cost-effective, reliable, easy-to-produce system.

Functional Description 2

CHAPTER 2
8085A FUNCTIONAL DESCRIPTION

2.1 WHAT THE 8085A IS

The 8085A is an 8-bit general-purpose microprocessor that is very cost-effective in small systems because of its extraordinarily low hardware overhead requirements. At the same time it is capable of accessing up to 64K bytes of memory and has status lines for controlling large systems.

2.2 WHAT'S IN THE 8085A

In the 8085A microprocessor are contained the functions of clock generation, system bus control, and interrupt priority selection, in addition to execution of the instruction set. (See Figure 2-1.) The 8085A transfers data on an 8-bit, bi-directional 3-state bus (AD_{0-7}) which is time-multiplexed so as to also transmit the eight lower-order address bits. An additional eight lines (A_{8-15}) expand the 8085 Family system memory addressing capability to 16 bits, thereby allowing 64K bytes of memory to be accessed directly by the CPU. The 8085A CPU (central processing unit) generates control signals that can be used to select appropriate external devices and functions to perform READ and WRITE operations and also to select memory or I/O ports. The 8085A can address up to 256 different I/O locations. These addresses have the same numerical values (00 through FFH) as the first 256 memory addresses; they are distinguished by means of the IO/M output from the CPU. You may also choose to address I/O ports as memory locations (i.e., memory-map the I/O, Section 3.2).

2.2.1 Registers

The 8085A, like the 8080A, is provided with internal 8-bit registers and 16-bit registers. The 8085A has eight addressable 8-bit registers. Six of them can be used either as 8-bit registers or as 16-bit register pairs. Register pairs are treated as though they were single, 16-bit registers; the high-order byte of a pair is located in the first register and the low-order byte is located in the second. In addition to the register pairs, the 8085A contains two more 16-bit registers.

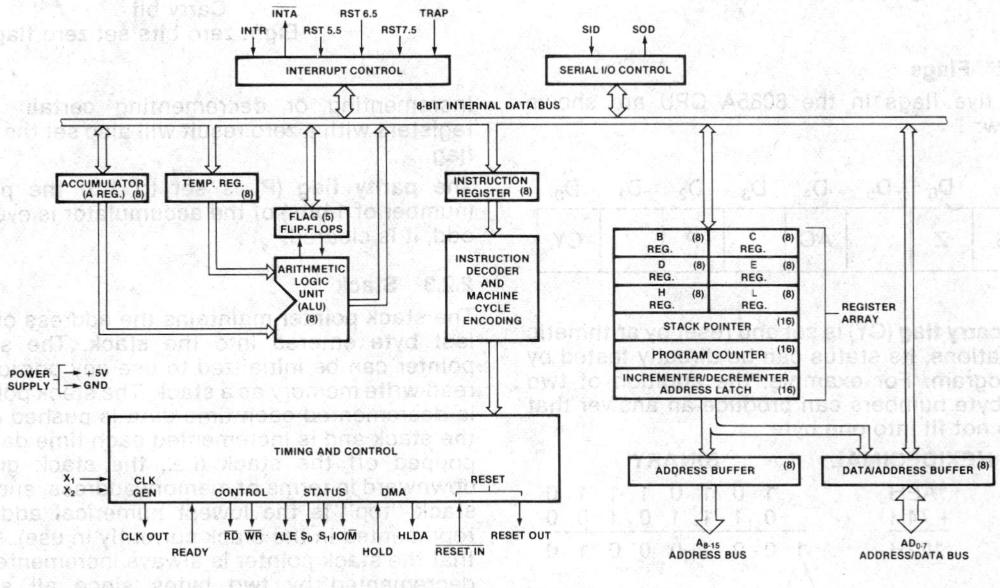

FIGURE 2-1 8085A CPU FUNCTIONAL BLOCK DIAGRAM

The 8085A's CPU registers are distinguished as follows:

- The **accumulator** (ACC or A Register) is the focus of all of the accumulator instructions (Table 4-1), which include arithmetic, logic, load and store, and I/O instructions. It is an 8-bit register only. (However, see **Flags,** in this list.)
- The **program counter** (PC) always points to the memory location of the next instruction to be executed. It always contains a 16-bit address.
- **General-purpose registers** BC, DE, and HL may be used as six 8-bit registers or as three 16-bit registers, interchangeably, depending on the instruction being performed. HL functions as a **data pointer** to reference memory addresses that are either the sources or the destinations in a number of instructions. A smaller number of instructions can use BC or DE for indirect addressing.
- The **stack pointer** (SP) is a special data pointer that always points to the stack top (next available stack address). It is an indivisible 16-bit register.
- The **flag register** contains five one-bit flags, each of which records processor status information and may also control processor operation. (See following paragraph.)

2.2.2 Flags

The five flags in the 8085A CPU are shown below:

D_7	D_6	D_5	D_4	D_3	D_2	D_1	D_0
S	Z		AC		P		CY

The **carry flag** (CY) is set and reset by arithmetic operations. Its status can be directly tested by a program. For example, the addition of two one-byte numbers can produce an answer that does not fit into one byte:

HEXIDECIMAL	BINARY
AEH	1 0 1 0 1 1 1 0
+74H	0 1 1 1 0 1 0 0
122H	1 0 0 1 0 0 0 1 0

Carry bit sets carry flag to 1

An addition operation that results in an overflow out of the high-order bit of the accumulator sets the carry flag. An addition operation that does not result in an overflow clears the carry flag. (See 8080/8085 Assembly Language Programming Manual for further details.) The carry flag also acts as a "borrow" flag for subtract operations.

The **auxiliary carry flag** (AC) indicates overflow out of bit 3 of the accumulator in the same way that the carry flag indicates overflow out of bit 7. This flag is commonly used in BCD (binary coded decimal) arithmetic.

The **sign flag** is set to the condition of the most significant bit of the accumulator following the execution of arithmetic or logic instructions. These instructions use bit 7 of data to represent the sign of the number contained in the accumulator. This permits the manipulation of numbers in the range from −128 to +127.

The **zero flag** is set if the result generated by certain instructions is zero. The zero flag is cleared if the result is not zero. A result that has a carry but has a zero answer byte in the accumulator will set both the carry flag and the zero flag. For example,

HEXADECIMAL	BINARY
A7H	1 0 1 0 0 1 1 1
+ 59H	+ 0 1 0 1 1 0 0 1
100H	1 0 0 0 0 0 0 0 0

Carry bit

Eight zero bits set zero flag to 1

Incrementing or decrementing certain CPU registers with a zero result will also set the zero flag.

The **parity flag** (P) is set to 1 if the parity (number of 1-bits) of the accumulator is even. If odd, it is cleared.

2.2.3 Stack

The stack pointer maintains the address of the last byte entered into the stack. The stack pointer can be initialized to use any portion of read-write memory as a stack. The stack pointer is decremented each time data is pushed onto the stack and is incremented each time data is popped off the stack (i.e., the stack grows downward in terms of memory address, and the stack "top" is the lowest numerical address represented in the stack currently in use). Note that the stack pointer is always incremented or decremented by two bytes since all stack operations apply to register pairs.

2.2.4 Arithmetic-Logic Unit (ALU)

The ALU contains the accumulator and the flag register (described in Sections 2.2.1 and 2.2.2) and some temporary registers that are inaccessible to the programmer.

Arithmetic, logic, and rotate operations are performed by the ALU. The results of these operations can be deposited in the accumulator, or they can be transferred to the internal data bus for use elsewhere.

2.2.5 Instruction Register and Decoder

During an instruction fetch, the first byte of an instruction (containing the opcode) is transferred from the internal bus to the 8-bit instruction register. (See Figure 2-1.) The contents of the instruction register are, in turn, available to the instruction decoder. The output of the decoder, gated by timing signals, controls the registers, ALU, and data and address buffers. The outputs of the instruction decoder and internal clock generator generate the state and machine cycle timing signals.

2.2.6 Internal Clock Generator

The 8085A CPU incorporates a complete clock generator on its chip, so it requires only the addition of a quartz crystal to establish timing for its operation. (It will accept an external clock input at its X_1 input instead, however.) A suitable crystal for the standard 8085A must be parallel-resonant at a fundamental of 6.25 MHz or less, twice the desired internal clock frequency. The 8085A-2 will operate with crystal of up to 10 MHz. The functions of the 8085A internal clock generator are shown in Figure 2-2. A Schmitt trigger is used interchangeably as oscillator or as input conditioner, depending upon whether a crystal or an external source is used. The clock circuitry generates two nonoverlapping internal clock signals, ϕ_1 and ϕ_2 (see Figure 2-2). ϕ_1 and ϕ_2 control the internal timing of the 8085A and are not directly available on the outside of the chip. The external pin CLK is a buffered, inverted version of ϕ_1. CLK is half the frequency of the crystal input signal and may be used for clocking other devices in the system.

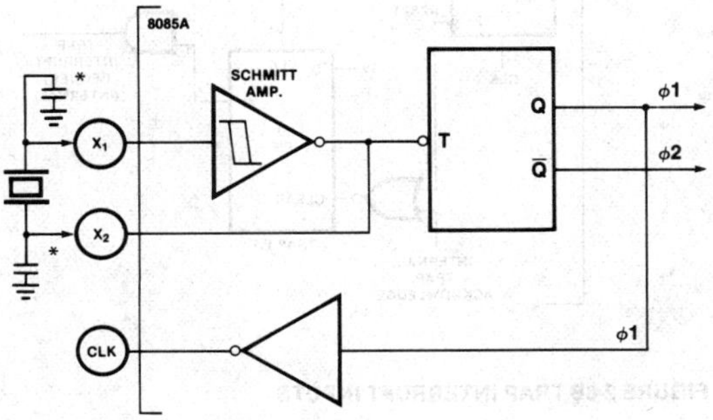

*EXTERNAL CAPACITORS REQUIRED ONLY FOR CRYSTAL FREQUENCIES ≤4MHz.

FIGURE 2-2 8085A CLOCK LOGIC

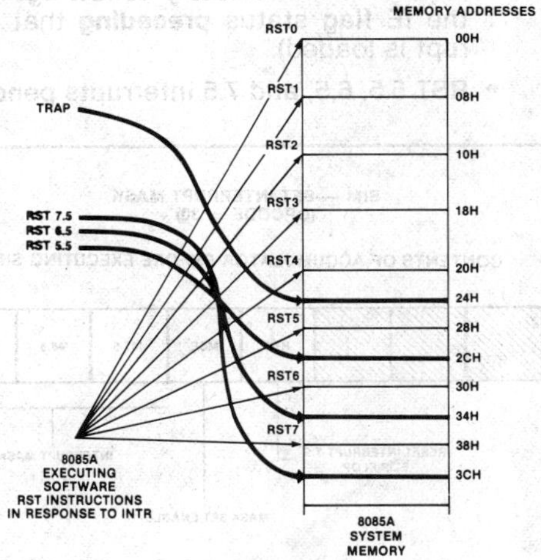

FIGURE 2-3 8085A HARDWARE AND SOFTWARE RST BRANCH LOCATIONS

2.2.7 Interrupts

The five hardware interrupt inputs provided in the 8085A are of three types. INTR is identical with the 8080A INT line in function; i.e., it is maskable (can be enabled or disabled by EI or DI software instructions), and causes the CPU to fetch in an RST instruction, externally placed on the data bus, which vectors a branch to any one of eight fixed memory locations (Restart addresses). (See Figure 2-3.) INTR can also be controlled by the 8259 programmable interrupt controller, which generates CALL instructions instead of RSTs, and can thus vector operation of the CPU to a preprogrammed subroutine located anywhere in your system's memory map. The RST 5.5, RST 6.5, and RST 7.5 hardware interrupts are different in function in that they are maskable through the use of the SIM instruction, which enables or disables these interrupts by clearing or setting corresponding mask flags based on data in the accumulator. (See Figure 2-4.) You may read the status of the interrupt mask previously set by peforming a RIM instruction. Its execution loads into the accumulator the following information. (See Figure 2-5.)

- Current interrupt mask status for the RST 5.5, 6.5, and 7.5 hardware status.
- Current interrupt enable flag status (except that immediately following TRAP, the IE flag status **preceding** that interrupt is loaded).
- RST 5.5, 6.5, and 7.5 interrupts pending.

RST 5.5, 6.5, and 7.5 are also subject to being enabled or disabled by the EI and DI instructions, respectively. INTR, RST 5.5, and RST 6.5 are level-sensitive, meaning that these inputs may be acknowledged by the processor when they are held at a high level. RST 7.5 is edge-sensitive, meaning that an internal flip-flop in the 8085A registers the occurrence of an interrupt the instant a rising edge appears on the RST 7.5 input line. This input need not be held high; the flip-flop will remain set until it is cleared by one of three possible actions:

- The 8085A responds to the interrupt, and sends an internal reset signal to the RST 7.5 flip-flop. (See Figure 2-6A.)

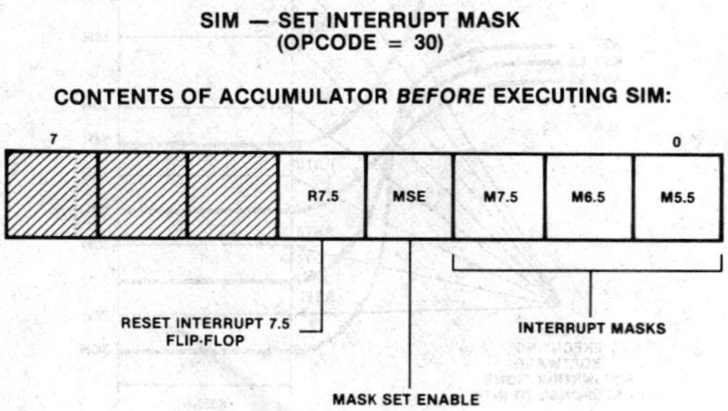

FIGURE 2-4 INTERRUPT MASKS SET USING SIM INSTRUCTION

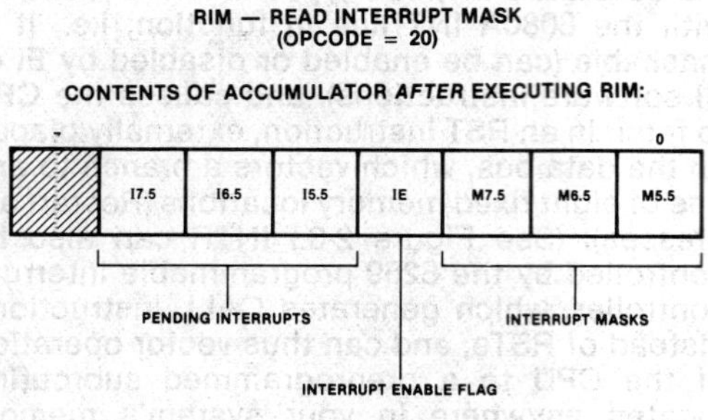

FIGURE 2-5 RIM — READ INTERRUPT MASK

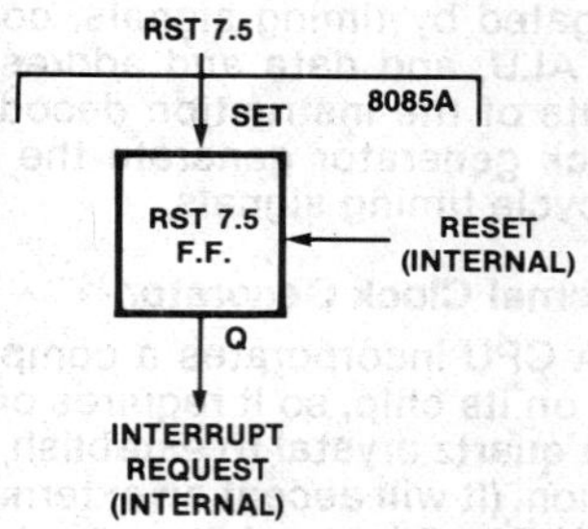

FIGURE 2-6A RST 7.5 FLIP FLOP

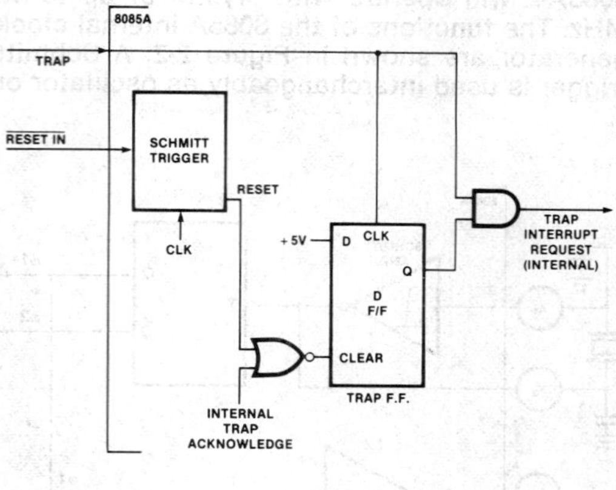

FIGURE 2-6B TRAP INTERRUPT INPUTS

FIGURE 2-6 RST 7.5 AND TRAP INTERRUPT INPUTS

- The 8085A, before responding to the RST 7.5 interrupt, receives a $\overline{\text{RESET IN}}$ signal from an external source; this also activates the internal reset.

- The 8085A executes a SIM instruction, with accumulator bit 4 previously set to 1. (See Figure 2-4.)

The third type of hardware interrupt is TRAP. This input is not subject to any mask or interrupt enable/disable instruction. The receipt of a positive-going edge on the TRAP input triggers the processor's hardware interrupt sequence, but the pulse must be held high until acknowledged internally (see Figure 2-6B).

The sampling of all interrupts occurs on the descending edge of CLK, one cycle before the end of the instruction in which the interrupt input is activated. To be recognized, a valid interrupt must occur at least 160 ns before sampling time in the 8085A, or 150 ns in the 8085A-2. This means that to guarantee being recognized, RST 5.5 and 6.5 and TRAP need to be held on for at least 17 clock states plus 160 ns (150 for 8085A-2), assuming that the interrupt might arrive just barely too late to be acknowledged during a particular instruction, and that the following instruction might be an 18-state CALL. This timing assumes no WAIT or HOLD cycles are used.

The way interrupt masks are set and read is described in Chapter 4 under the RIM (read interrupt mask) and SIM (set interrupt mask) instruction listings. Interrupt functions and their priorities are shown in the table that follows.

Name	Priority	Address (1) Branched to when Interrupt occurs	Type Trigger
TRAP	1	24H	Rising edge AND high level until sampled
RST 7.5	2	3CH	Rising edge (latched)
RST 6.5	3	34H	High level until sampled
RST 5.5	4	2CH	High level until sampled
INTR	5	(2)	High level until sampled

NOTES:
(1) In the case of TRAP and RST 5.5-7.5, the contents of the Program Counter are pushed onto the stack before the branch occurs.
(2) Depends on the instruction that is provided to the 8085A by the 8259 or other circuitry when the interrupt is acknowledged.

2.2.8 Serial Input and Output

The SID and SOD pins help to minimize chip count in small systems by providing for easy interface to a serial port using software for timing and for coding and decoding of the data. Each time a RIM instruction is executed, the status of the SID pin is read into bit 7 of the accumulator. RIM is thus a dual-purpose instruction. (See Chapter 4.) In similar fashion, SIM is used to latch bit 7 of the accumulator out to the SOD output via an internal flip-flop, providing that bit 6 of the accumulator is set to 1. (See Figure 2-7.) Section 2.3.8 describes SID and SOD timing.

SID can also be used as a general purpose TEST input and SOD can serve as a one-bit control output.

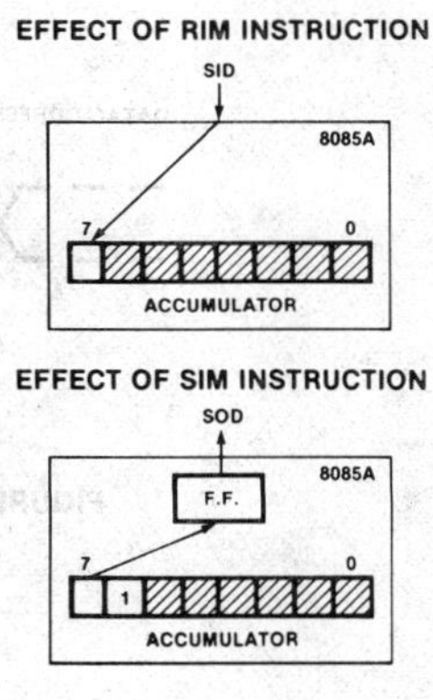

FIGURE 2-7 EFFECT OF RIM AND SIM INSTRUCTIONS ON SERIAL DATA LINES

2.3 HOW THE 8085 SYSTEM WORKS

The 8085A CPU generates signals that tell peripheral devices what type of information is on the multiplexed Address/Data bus and from that point on the operation is almost identical to the 8080 Family CPU Group. A multiplexed bus structure was chosen because it freed device pins so that more functions could be integrated on the 8085A and other components of the family. The multiplexed bus is designed to allow complete compatibility to existing peripheral components with improved timing margins and access requirements. (See Figure 2-8.)

To enhance the system integration of the 8085 Family, several special components with combined memory and I/O were designed. These new devices directly interface to the multiplexed bus of the 8085A. The pin locations of the 8085A and the special peripheral components are assigned to minimize PC board area and to allow for efficient layout. The details on peripheral components are contained in subsequent paragraphs of this chapter and in Chapters 5 and 6.

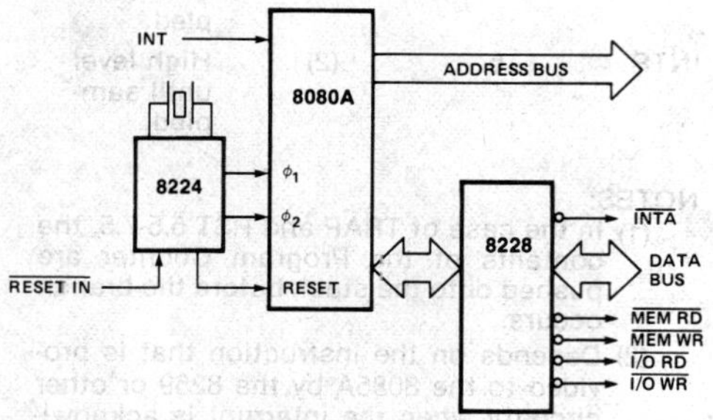

FIGURE 2-8A 8080 CPU GROUP

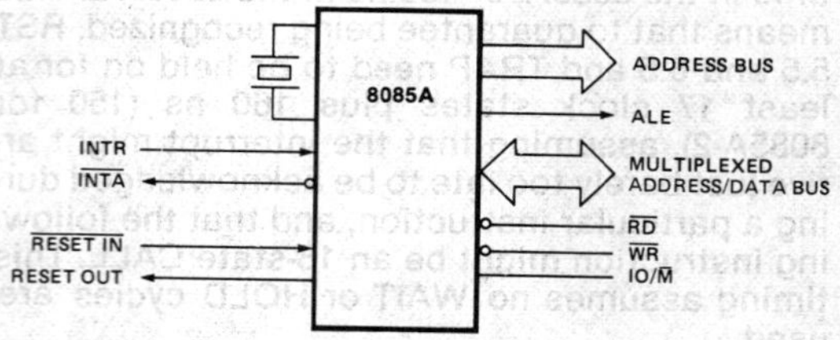

FIGURE 2-8B 8085 CPU/8085A (8080 COMPATIBLE FUNCTIONS)

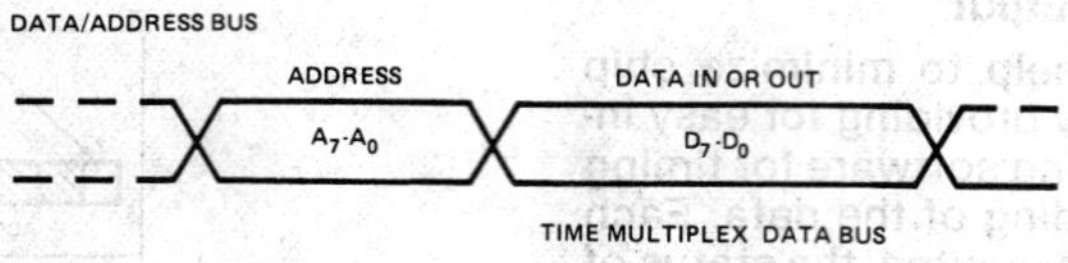

FIGURE 2-8C MULTIPLEXED BUS TIMING

FIGURE 2-8 BASIC CPU FUNCTIONS

2.3.1 Multiplexed Bus Cycle Timing

The execution of any 8085A program consists of a sequence of READ and WRITE operations, of which each transfers a byte of data between the 8085A and a particular memory or I/O address. These READ and WRITE operations are the only communication between the processor and the other components, and are all that is necessary to execute any instruction or program.

Each READ or WRITE operation of the 8085A is referred to as a machine cycle. The execution of each instruction by the 8085A consists of a sequence of from one to five machine cycles, and each machine cycle consists of a minimum of from three to six clock cycles (also referred to as T states). Consider the case of the Store Accumulator Direct (STA) instruction, shown in Figure 2-9. The STA instruction causes the contents of the accumulator to be stored at the direct address specified in the second and third bytes of the instruction. During the first machine cycle (M_1), the CPU puts the contents of the program counter (PC) on the address bus and performs a MEMORY READ cycle to read from memory the opcode of the next instruction (STA). The M_1 machine cycle is also referred to as the OPCODE FETCH cycle, since it fetches the operation code of the next instruction. In the fourth clock cycle (T_4) of M_1, the CPU interprets the data read in and recognizes it as the opcode of the STA instruction. At this point the CPU knows that it must do three more machine cycles (two MEMORY READs and one MEMORY WRITE) to complete the instruction.

The 8085A then increments the program counter so that it points to the next byte of the instruction and performs a MEMORY READ machine cycle (M_2) at address (PC + 1). The accessed memory places the addressed data on the data bus for the CPU. The 8085A temporarily stores this data (which is the low-order byte of the direct address) internally in the CPU. The 8085A again increments the program counter to location (PC + 2) and reads from memory (M_3) the next byte of data, which is the high-order byte of the direct address.

At this point, the 8085A has accessed all three bytes of the STA instruction, which it must now execute. The execution consists of placing the data accessed in M_2 and M_3 on the address bus, then placing the contents of the accumulator on the data bus, and then performing a MEMORY WRITE machine cycle (M_4). When M_4 is finished, the CPU will fetch (M_1) the first byte of the next instruction and continue from there.

State Transition Sequence

As the preceding example shows, the execution of an instruction consists of a series of machine cycles whose nature and sequence is determined by the opcode accessed in the M_1

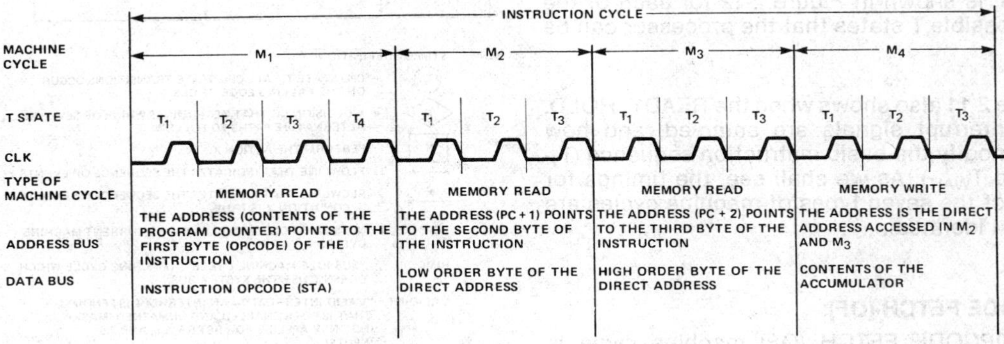

FIGURE 2-9 CPU TIMING FOR STORE ACCUMULATOR DIRECT (STA) INSTRUCTION

MACHINE CYCLE			STATUS			CONTROL		
			IO/$\overline{M}$	S1	S0	$\overline{RD}$	$\overline{WR}$	$\overline{INTA}$
OPCODE FETCH	(OF)		0	1	1	0	1	1
MEMORY READ	(MR)		0	1	0	0	1	1
MEMORY WRITE	(MW)		0	0	1	1	0	1
I/O READ	(IOR)		1	1	0	0	1	1
I/O WRITE	(IOW)		1	0	1	1	0	1
INTR ACKNOWLEDGE	(INA)		1	1	1	1	1	0
BUS IDLE	(BI):	DAD	0	1	0	1	1	1
		INA(RST/TRAP)	1	1	1	1	1	1
		HALT	TS	0	0	TS	TS	1

0 = Logic "0" 1 = Logic "1" TS = High Impedance X = Unspecified

FIGURE 2-10 8085A MACHINE CYCLE CHART

machine cycle. While no one instruction cycle will consist of more than five machine cycles, every machine cycle will be one of the seven types listed in Figure 2-10. These seven types of machine cycles can be differentiated by the state of the three status lines (IO/$\overline{M}$, S_0, and S_1) and the three control signals ($\overline{RD}$, $\overline{WR}$, and $\overline{INTA}$).

Most machine cycles consist of three T states, (cycles of the CLK output) with the exception of OPCODE FETCH, which normally has either four or six T states. The actual number of states required to perform any instruction depends on the instruction being executed, the particular machine cycle within the instruction cycle, and the number of WAIT and HOLD states inserted into each machine cycle through the use of the READY and HOLD inputs of the 8085A. The state transition diagram in Figure 2-11 illustrates how the 8085A proceeds in the course of a machine cycle. The state of various status and control signals, as well as the system buses, is shown in Figure 2-12 for each of the ten possible T states that the processor can be in.

Figure 2-11 also shows when the READY, HOLD, and interrupt signals are sampled, and how they modify the basic instruction sequence (T_1-T_6 and T_{WAIT}). As we shall see, the timings for each of the seven types of machine cycles are almost identical.

OPCODE FETCH (OF):

The OPCODE FETCH (OF) machine cycle is unique in that it has more than three clock cycles. This is because the CPU must interpret the opcode accessed in T_1, T_2, and T_3 before it can decide what to do next.

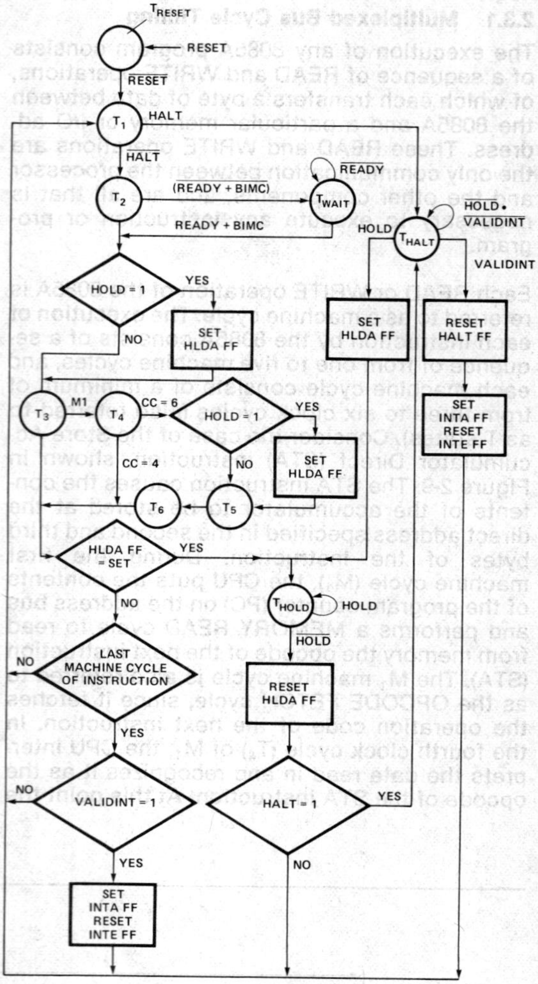

NOTE: SYMBOL DEFINITION

(T_x)	= CPU STATE T_x. ALL CPU STATE TRANSITIONS OCCUR ON THE FALLING EDGE OF CLK.
⟨X⟩	= A DECISION (X) THAT DETERMINES WHICH OF SEVERAL ALTERNATIVE PATHS TO FOLLOW.
[X]	= PERFORM THE ACTION X.
→	= FLOWLINE THAT INDICATES THE SEQUENCE OF EVENTS.
X →	= FLOWLINE THAT INDICATES THE SEQUENCE OF EVENTS IF CONDITION X IS TRUE.
CC	= NUMBER OF CLOCK CYCLES IN THE CURRENT MACHINE CYCLE.
BIMC	= "BUS IDLE MACHINE CYCLE" = MACHINE CYCLE WHICH DOESN'T USE THE SYSTEM BUS.
VALIDINT	= "VALID INTERRUPT" – AN INTERRUPT IS PENDING THAT IS BOTH ENABLED AND UNMASKED (MASKING ONLY APPLIES FOR RST 5.5, 6.5, AND 7.5 INPUTS).
HLDA FF	= INTERNAL HOLD ACKNOWLEDGE FLIP FLOP. NOTE THAT THE 8085A SYSTEM BUSES ARE 3-STATED ONE CLOCK CYCLE AFTER THE HLDA FLIP FLOP IS SET.

FIGURE 2-11 8085A CPU STATE TRANSITION

Machine State	Status & Buses				Control		
	S1,S0	$IO/\overline{M}$	A_8-A_{15}	AD_0-AD_7	$\overline{RD}$,$\overline{WR}$	$\overline{INTA}$	ALE
T_1	X	X	X	X	1	1	1†
T_2	X	X	X	X	X	X	0
T_{WAIT}	X	X	X	X	X	X	0
T_3	X	X	X	X	X	X	0
T_4	1	0*	X	TS	1	1	0
T_5	1	0*	X	TS	1	1	0
T_6	1	0*	X	TS	1	1	0
T_{RESET}	X	TS	TS	TS	TS	1	0
T_{HALT}	0	TS	TS	TS	TS	1	0
T_{HOLD}	X	TS	TS	TS	TS	1	0

0 = Logic "0"   1 = Logic "1"   TS = High Impedance   X = Unspecified

†ALE not generated during 2nd and 3rd machine cycles of DAD instruction.

*$IO/\overline{M}$ = 1 during T_4-T_6 states of RST and INA cycles.

FIGURE 2-12 8085A MACHINE STATE CHART

Figure 2-13 shows the timing relationships for an OF machine cycle. The particular instruction illustrated is DCX, whose timing for OF differs from other instructions in that it has six T states, while some instructions require only four T states for OF. In this discussion, as well as the following discussions, only the relative timing of the signals will be discussed; for the actual timings, refer to the data sheets of the individual parts in Chapters 5 and 6.

The first thing that the 8085A does at the beginning of every machine cycle is to send out three status signals ($IO/\overline{M}$, S1, S0) that define what type of machine cycle is about to take place. The $IO/\overline{M}$ signal identifies the machine cycle as being either a memory reference or input/output operation. The S1 status signal identifies whether the cycle is a READ or WRITE operation. The S0 and S1 status signals can be used together (see Figure 2-10) to identify READ, WRITE, or OPCODE FETCH machine cycles as well as the HALT state. Referring to Figure 2-13, the 8085A will send out $IO/\overline{M} = 0, S1 = 1, S0 = 1$ at the beginning of the machine cycle to identify it as a READ from a memory location to obtain an opcode; in other words, it identifies the machine cycle as an OPCODE FETCH cycle.

The 8085A also sends out a 16-bit address at the beginning of every machine cycle to identify the particular memory location or I/O port that the machine cycle applies to. In the case of an OF cycle, the contents of the program counter is placed on the address bus. The high order byte (PCH) is placed on the A_8-A_{15} lines, where it will stay until at least T_4. The low order byte (PCL) is placed on the AD_0-AD_7 lines, whose three-state drivers are enabled if not found already on. Unlike the upper address lines, however, the information on the lower address lines will remain there for only one clock cycle, after which the drivers will go to their high impedance state, indicated by a dashed line in Figure 2-13. This is necessary because the AD_0-AD_7 lines are time mulitplexed between the address and data buses. During T_1 of every machine cycle, AD_0-AD_7 output the lower 8-bits of address after which AD_0-AD_7 will either output the desired data for a WRITE operation or the drivers will float (as is the case for the OF cycle), allowing the external device to drive the lines for a READ operation.

Since the address information on AD_0-AD_7 is of a transitory nature, it must be latched either internally in special multiplexed-bus components like the 8155 or externally in parts like an 8-bit latch. (See Chapter 3.) The 8085A provides a special timing signal, ADDRESS LATCH ENABLE (ALE), to facilitate the latching of A_0-A_7; ALE is present during T_1 of every machine cycle.

After the status signals and address have been sent out and the AD_0-AD_7 drivers have been disabled, the 8085A provides a low level on $\overline{RD}$ to enable the addressed memory device. The device will then start driving the AD_0-AD_7 lines; this is indicated by the dashed line turning into a solid line in Figure 2-13. After a period of time (which is the access time of the memory) valid data will be present on AD_0-AD_7. The 8085A during T_3 will load the memory data on AD_0-AD_7 into its instruction register and then raise $\overline{RD}$ to the high level, disabling the addressed memory device. At this point, the 8085A will have finished accessing the opcode of the instruction. Since this is the first machine cycle (M_1) of the instruction, the CPU will automatically step to T_4, as shown in Figure 2-11.

During T_4, the CPU will decode the opcode in the instruction register and decide whether to enter T_5 on the next clock or to start a new machine cycle and enter T_1. In the case of the DCX instruction shown in Figure 2-13, it will enter T_5 and then T_6 before going to T_1.

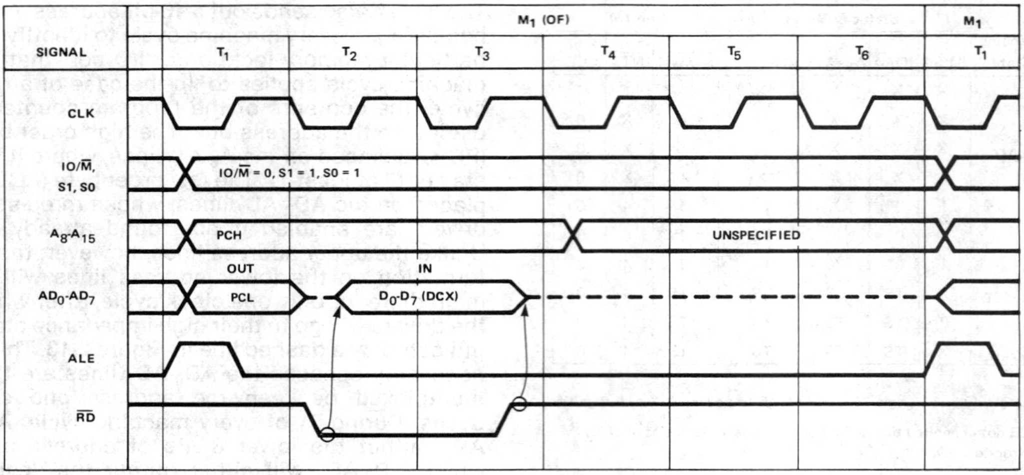

FIGURE 2-13 OPCODE FETCH MACHINE CYCLE (OF DCX INSTRUCTION)

During T_5 and T_6, of DCX, the CPU will decrement the designated register. Since the A_8-A_{15} lines are driven by the address latch circuits, which are part of the incrementer/decrementer logic, the A_8-A_{15} lines may change during T_5 and T_6. Because the value of A_8-A_{15} can vary during T_4-T_6, it is most important that all memory and I/O devices on the system bus qualify their selection with $\overline{RD}$. If they don't use $\overline{RD}$, they may be spuriously selected. Moreover, with a linear selection technique (Chapter 3), two or more devices could be simultaneously enabled, which could be potentially damaging. The generation of spurious addresses can also occur momentarily at address bus transitional periods in T_1. Therefore, the selection of all memory and I/O devices must be qualified with $\overline{RD}$ or $\overline{WR}$. Many memory devices like the 8155 and 8755A have the $\overline{RD}$ input that internally is used to enable the data bus outputs, removing the need for externally qualifying the chip enable input with $\overline{RD}$.

Figure 2-14 is identical to Figure 2-13 with one exception, which is the use of the READY line. As we can see in Figure 2-11, when the CPU is in T_2, it examines the state of the READY line. If the READY line is high, the CPU will proceed to T_3 and finish executing the instruction. If the READY line is low, however, the CPU will enter T_{WAIT} and stay there indefinitely until READY goes high. When the READY line does go high, the CPU will exit T_{WAIT} and enter T_3, in order to complete the machine cycle. As shown in Figure 2-14, the external effect of using the READY line is to preserve the exact state of the processor signals at the end of T_2 for an integral number of clock periods, before finishing the machine cycle. This "stretching" of the system timing has the further effect of increasing the allowable access time for memory or I/O devices. By inserting T_{WAIT} states, the 8085A can accommodate even the slowest of memories. Another common use of the READY line is to singe-step the processor with a manual switch.

2.3.2 Read Cycle Timing

MEMORY READ (MR):

Figure 2-15 shows the timing of two successive MEMORY READ (MR) machine cycles, the first without a T_{WAIT} state and the second with one T_{WAIT} state. The timing during T_1-T_3 is absolutely identical to the OPCODE FETCH machine cycle, with the exception that the status sent out during T_1 is IO/$\overline{M}$ = 0, S1 = 1, S0 = 0, identifying the cycles as a READ from a memory location. This differs from Figure 2-13 only in that S0 = 1 for an OF cycle, identifying that cycle as an OPCODE FETCH operation. Otherwise, the two cycles are identical during T_1-T_3.

A second difference occurs at the end of T_3. As shown in Figure 2-11, the CPU always goes to T_4 from T_3 during M_1, which is always an OF cycle. During all other machine cycles, the CPU will always go from T_3 to T_1 of the next machine cycle.

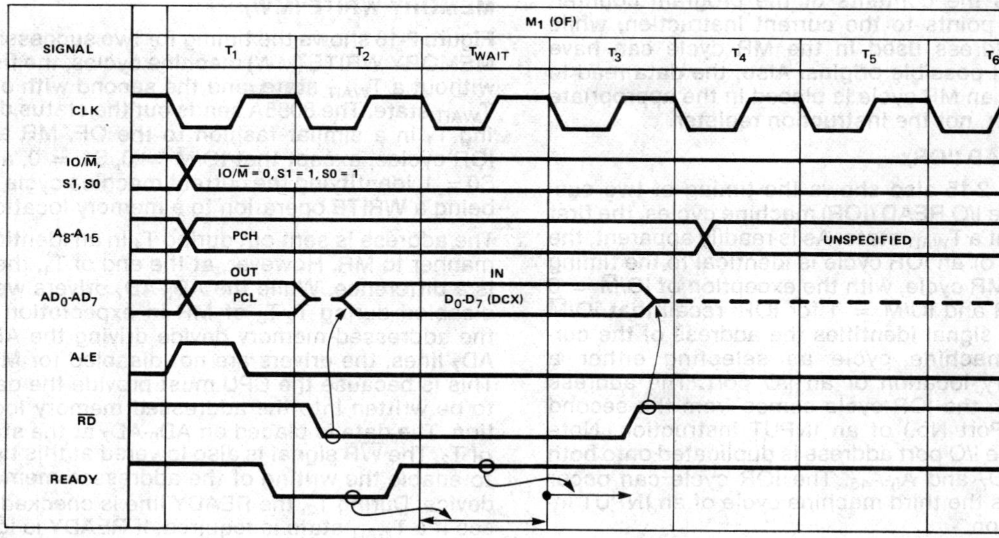

FIGURE 2-14 OPCODE FETCH MACHINE CYCLE WITH ONE WAIT STATE

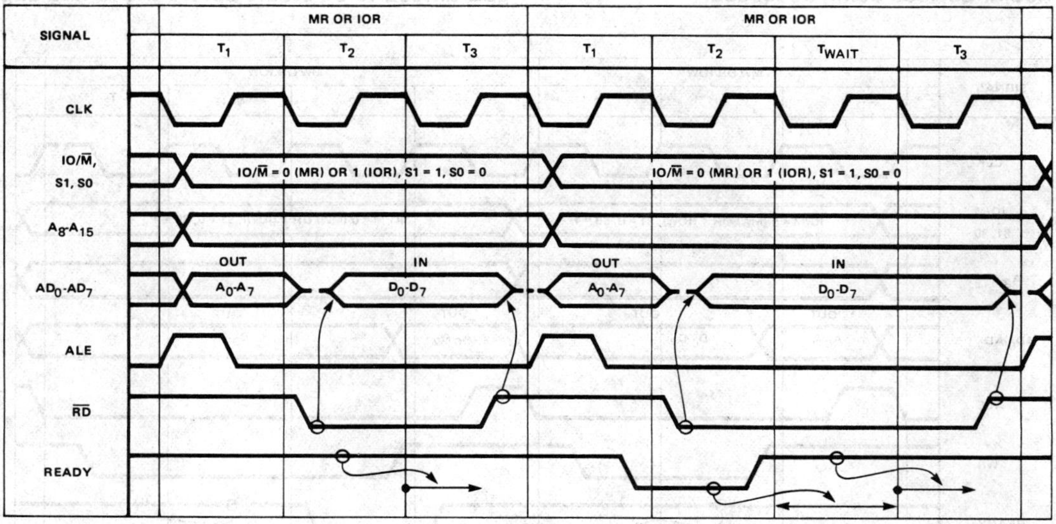

FIGURE 2-15 MEMORY READ (OR I/O READ) MACHINE CYCLES (WITH AND WITHOUT WAIT STATES)

The memory address used in the OF cycle is always the contents of the program counter, which points to the current instruction, while the address used in the MR cycle can have several possible origins. Also, the data read in during an MR cycle is placed in the appropriate register, not the instruction register.

I/O READ (IOR):

Figure 2-15 also shows the timing of two successive I/O READ (IOR) machine cycles, the first without a T_{WAIT} state. As is readily apparent, the timing of an IOR cycle is identical to the timing of an MR cycle, with the exception of $IO/\overline{M} = 0$ for MR and $IO/\overline{M} = 1$ for IOR; recall that $IO/\overline{M}$ status signal identifies the address of the current machine cycle as selecting either a memory location or an I/O port. The address used in the IOR cycle comes from the second byte (Port No.) of an INPUT instruction. Note that the I/O port address is duplicated onto both AD_0-AD_7 and A_8-A_{15}. The IOR cycle can occur only as the third machine cycle of an INPUT instruction.

Note that the READY signal can be used to generate T_{WAIT} states for I/O devices as well as memory devices. By gating the READY signal with the proper status lines, one could generate T_{WAIT} states for memory devices only or for I/O devices only. By gating in the address lines, one can further qualify T_{WAIT} state generation by the particular devices being accessed.

2.3.3 WRITE Cycle Timing

MEMORY WRITE (MW):

Figure 2-16 shows the timing for two successive MEMORY WRITE (MW) machine cycles, the first without a T_{WAIT} state, and the second with one T_{WAIT} state. The 8085A sends out the status during T_1 in a similar fashion to the OF, MR and IOR cycles, except that $IO/\overline{M} = 0$, $S1 = 0$, and $S0 = 1$, identifying the current machine cycle as being a WRITE operation to a memory location.

The address is sent out during T_1 in an identical manner to MR. However, at the end of T_1, there is a difference. While the AD_0-AD_7 drivers were disabled during T_2-T_3 of MR in expectation of the addressed memory device driving the AD_0-AD_7 lines, the drivers are not disabled for MW. This is because the CPU must provide the data to be written into the addressed memory location. The data is placed on AD_0-AD_7 at the start of T_2. The $\overline{WR}$ signal is also lowered at this time to enable the writing of the addressed memory device. During T_2, the READY line is checked to see if a T_{WAIT} state is required. If READY is low, T_{WAIT} states are inserted until READY goes high. During T_3, the $\overline{WR}$ line is raised, disabling the addressed memory device and thereby terminating the WRITE operation. The contents of the address and data lines are not changed until the next T_1, which directly follows.

Note that the data on AD_0-AD_7 is not guaranteed to be stable before the falling edge

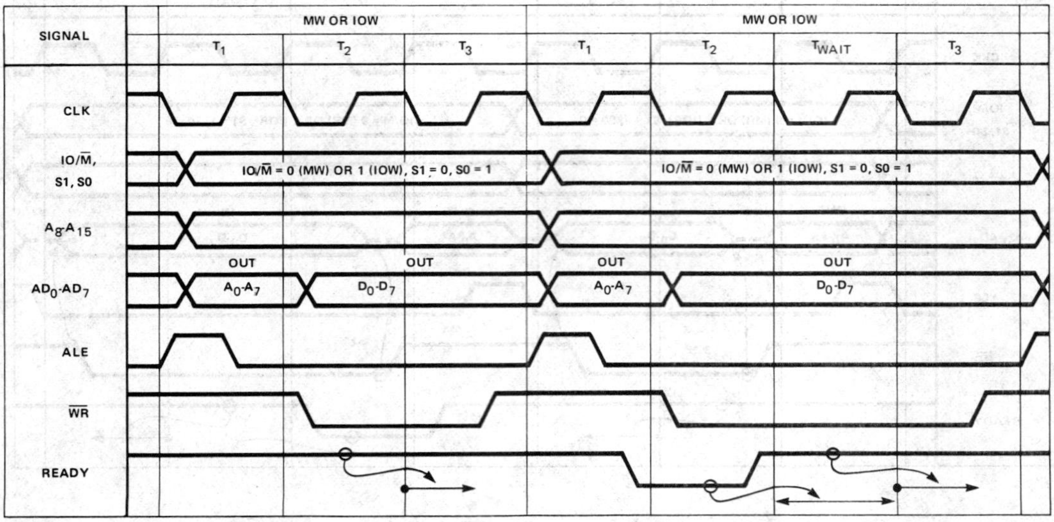

FIGURE 2-16 MEMORY WRITE (OR I/O WRITE) MACHINE CYCLES (WITH AND WITHOUT WAIT STATES)

of $\overline{WR}$. The AD_0-AD_7 lines are guaranteed to be stable both before and after the rising edge of $\overline{WR}$.

I/O WRITE (IOW):

As Figure 2-16 shows, the timing for an I/O WRITE (IOW) machine cycle is the same as an MW machine cycle except that IO/$\overline{M}$ = 0 during the MW cycle and IO/$\overline{M}$ = during the IOW cycle. As with the IOR cycle discussed previously, the address used in an IOW cycle is the I/O port number which is duplicated on both the high and low bytes of the address bus. In the case of IOW, the port number comes from the second byte of an OUTPUT instruction as the instruction is executed.

2.3.4 Interrupt Acknowledge (INA) Timing

Figures 2-17 and 2-18 (a continuation of 2-17) depict the course of action the CPU takes in response to a high level on the INTR line if the INTE FF (interrupt enable flip-flop) has been set by the EI instruction. The status of the TRAP and RST pins as well as INTR is sampled during the second clock cycle before $M_1 \bullet T_1$. If INTR was the only valid interrupt and if INTE FF is set, then the CPU will reset INTE FF and then enter an INTERRUPT ACKNOWLEDGE (INA) machine cycle. The INA cycle is identical to an OF cycle with two exceptions. $\overline{INTA}$ is sent out instead of $\overline{RD}$. Also, IO/$\overline{M}$ = 1 during INA, whereas IO/$\overline{M}$ = 0 for OF. Although the contents of the program counter are sent out on the address lines, the address lines can be ignored.

When $\overline{INTA}$ is sent out, the external interrupt logic must provide the opcode of an instruction to execute. The opcode is placed on the data bus and read in by the processor. If the opcode is the first byte of a multiple-byte instruction, additional $\overline{INTA}$ pulses will be provided by the 8085A to clock in the remaining bytes. RESTART and CALL instructions are the most

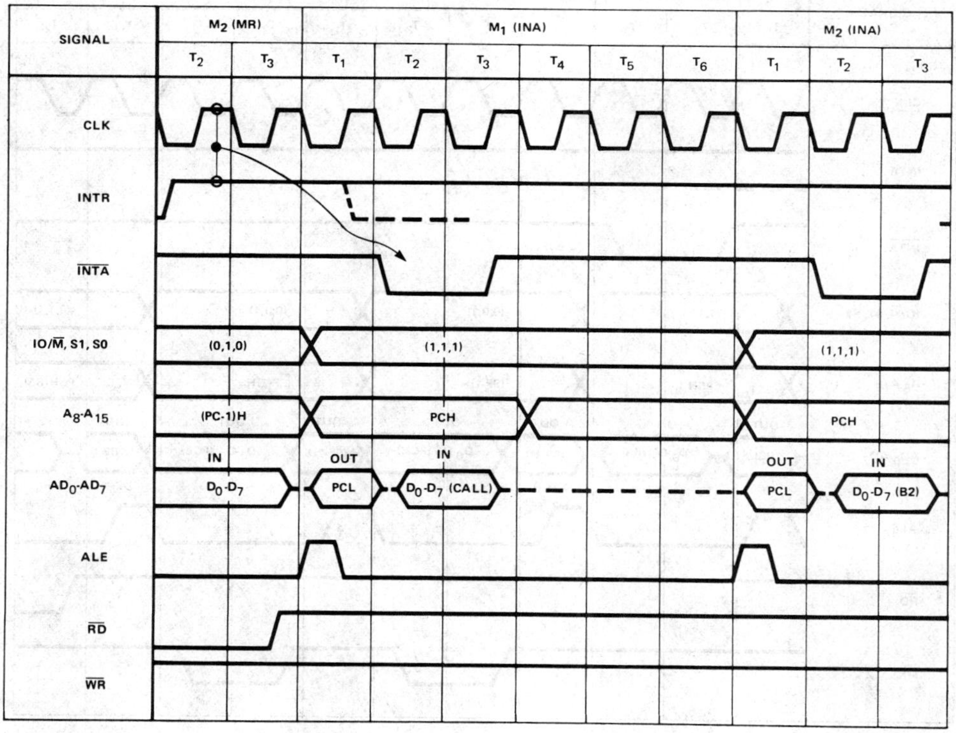

FIGURE 2-17 INTERRUPT ACKNOWLEDGE MACHINE CYCLES (WITH CALL INSTRUCTION IN RESPONSE TO INTR)

logical choices, since they both force the processor to push the contents of the program counter onto the stack before jumping to a new location. In Figure 2-17 it is assumed that a CALL opcode is sent to the CPU during M_1. The CALL opcode could have been placed there by a device like the 8259A programmable interrupt controller.

After receiving the opcode, the processor then decodes it and determines, in this case, that the CALL instruction requires two more bytes. The CPU therefore performs a second INA cycle (M_2) to access the second byte of the instruction from the 8259A. The timing of this cycle is identical to M_1, except that it has only three T states. M_2 is followed by another INA cycle (M_3) to access the third byte of the CALL instruction from the 8259A.

Now that the CPU has accessed the entire instruction used to acknowledge the interrupt, it will execute that instruction. Note that any instruction could be used (except EI or DI, the instructions which enable or disable interrupts), but the RESTART and CALL instructions are the most logical choices. Also notice that the CPU inhibited the incrementing of the program counter (PC) during the three INA cycles, so that the correct PC value can be pushed onto the stack during M_4 and M_5.

During M_4 and M_5, the CPU performs MEMORY WRITE machine cycles to write the upper and then lower bytes of the PC onto the top of the stack. The CPU then places the two bytes accessed in M_2 and M_3 into the lower and upper bytes of the PC. This has the effect of jumping the execution of the program to the location specified by the CALL instruction.

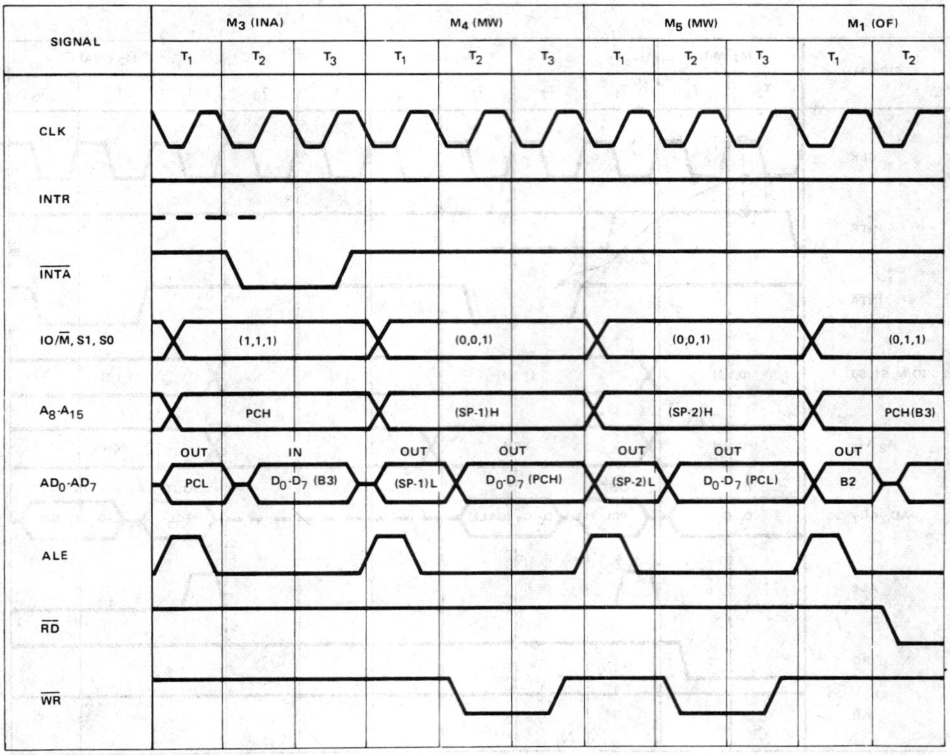

FIGURE 2-18 INTERRUPT ACKNOWLEDGE MACHINE CYCLES (WITH CALL INSTRUCTION IN RESPONSE TO INTR)

2.3.5 Bus Idle (BI) and HALT State

Most machine cycles of the 8085A are associated with either a READ or WRITE operation. There are two exceptions to this rule. The first exception takes place during M_2 and M_3 of the DAD instruction. The 8085A requires six internal T states to execute a DAD instruciton, but it is not desirable to have M_1 be ten (four normal plus six extra) states long. Therefore, the CPU generates two extra machine cycles that do not access either the memory or the I/O. These cycles are referred to as BUS IDLE (BI) machine cycles. In the case of DAD, they are identical to MR cycles except that RD remains high and ALE is not generated. Note that READY is ignored during M_2 and M_3 of DAD.

The other time when the BUS IDLE machine cycle occurs is during the internal opcode generation for the RST or TRAP interrupts. Figure 2-19 illustrates the BI cycle generated in response to RST 7.5. Since this interrupt is rising-edge-triggered, it sets an internal latch; that latch is sampled at the falling edge of the next to the last T-state of the previous instruction. At this point the CPU must generate its own internal RESTART instruction which will (in subsequent machine cycles) cause the processor to push the program counter on the stack and to vector to location 3CH. To do this, it executes an OF machine cycle without issuing RD, generating the RESTART opcode instead. After M_1, the CPU continues execution normally in all respects except that the state of the READY line is ignored during the BI cycle.

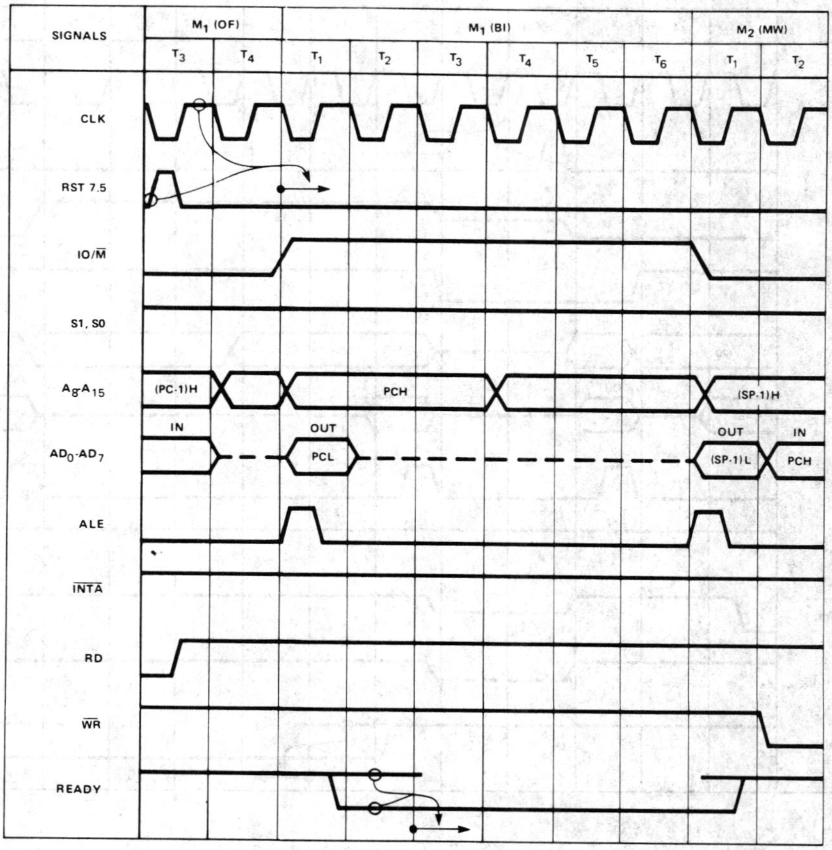

FIGURE 2-19 RST 7.5 BUS IDLE MACHINE CYCLE

Figure 2-20 illustrates the BI cycle generated in response to RST 7.5 when a HALT instruction has just been executed and the CPU is in the T_{HALT} state, with its various signals floating. There are only two ways the processor can completely exit the T_{HALT} state, as shown in Figure 2-11. The first way is for RESET to occur, which always forces the 8085A to T_{RESET}. The second way to exit T_{HALT} permanently is for a valid interrupt to occur, which will cause the CPU to disable further interrupts by resetting INTE FF, and to then proceed to $M_1 \bullet T_1$ of the next instruction. When the HOLD input is activated, the CPU will exit T_{HALT} for the duration of T_{HOLD} and then return to T_{HALT}.

In Figure 2-20 the RST 7.5 line is pulsed during T_{HALT}. Since RST 7.5 is a rising-edge-triggered interrupt, it will set an internal latch which is sampled during CLK = "1" of every T_{HALT} state (as well as during CLK = "1" two T states before any $M_1 \bullet T_1$.) The fact that the latched interrupt was high (assuming that INTE FF = 1 and the RST 7.5 mask = 0) will force the CPU to exit the T_{HALT} state at the end of the next CLK period, and to enter $M_1 \bullet T_1$.

This completes our analysis of the timing of each of the seven types of machine cycles.

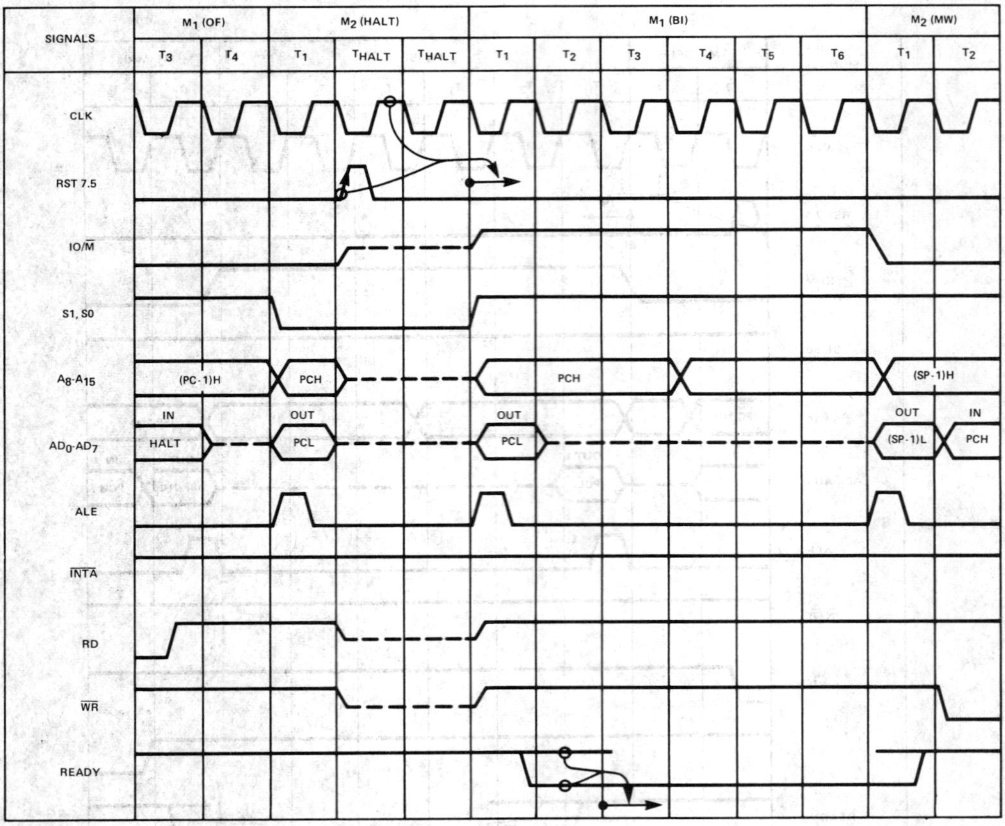

FIGURE 2-20 HALT STATE AND BUS IDLE MACHINE CYCLE RST 7.5 TERMINATES T_{HALT} STATE

2.3.6 HOLD and HALT States

The 8085A uses the T_{HOLD} state to momentarily cease executing machine cycles, allowing external devices to gain control of the bus and peform DMA cycles. The processor internally latches the state of the HOLD line and the unmasked interrupts during CLK = "1" of every T_{HALT} state. If the internal latched HOLD signal is high during CLK = "1" of any T_{HALT} state, the CPU will exit T_{HALT} and enter T_{HOLD} on the following CLK = "1". As shown in Figure 2-21 this will occur even if a valid interrupt occurs simultaneously with the HOLD signal.

The state of the HOLD and the unmasked interrupt lines is latched internally during CLK = 1 of each T_{HOLD} state as well as during T_{HALT} states. If the internal latched HOLD signal is low during CLK = 1, the CPU will exit T_{HOLD} and enter T_{HALT} on the following CLK = 1.

The 8085A accepts the first unmasked, enabled interrupt sampled; thereafter, all interrupt sampling is inhibited. The interrupt thus accepted will inevitably be executed when the CPU exits the HOLD state, even at the expense of holding off higher-priority interrupts (including TRAP). (See Figure 2-22.)

When the CPU is not in T_{HALT} or T_{HOLD}, it internally latches the HOLD line only during CLK = 1 of the last state before T_3(T_2 or T_{WAIT}) and during CLK = 1 of the last state before T_5(T_4 of a six T-state M_1). If the internal latched HOLD signal is high during the next CLK = 1, the CPU will enter T_{HOLD} after the following clock. When the CPU is not in T_{HALT} or T_{HOLD}, it will internally latch the state of the unmasked interrupts only during CLK of the next to the last state before each $M_1 \bullet T_1$.

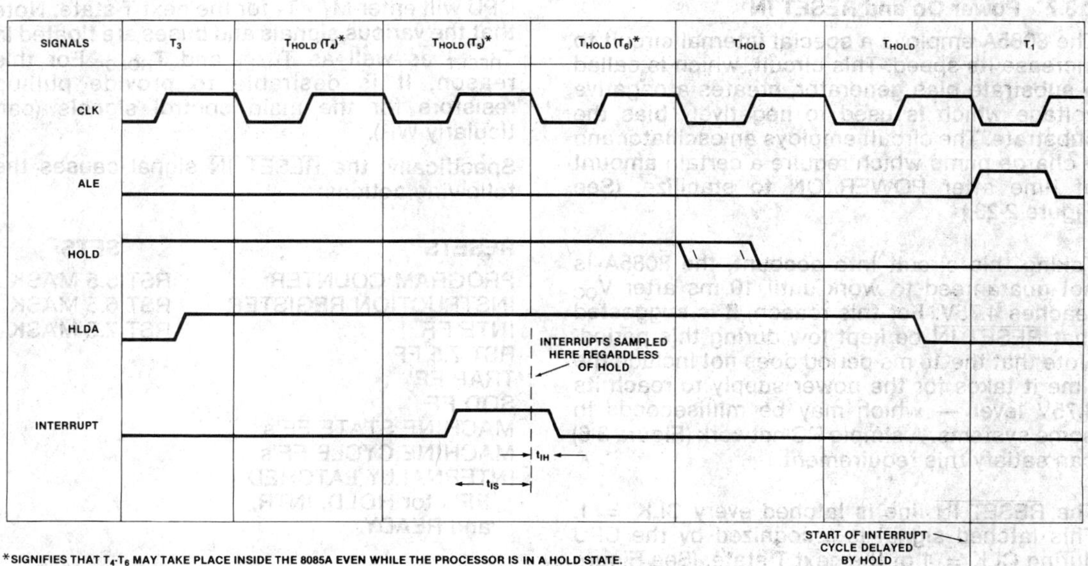

*SIGNIFIES THAT T_4-T_6 MAY TAKE PLACE INSIDE THE 8085A EVEN WHILE THE PROCESSOR IS IN A HOLD STATE.

FIGURE 2-21 HOLD VS INTERRUPT — NON HALT

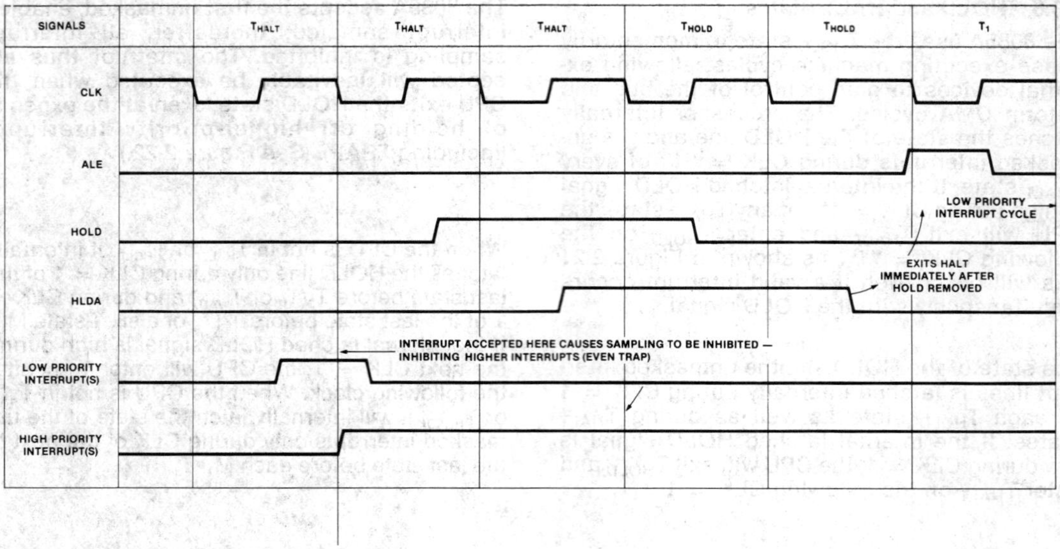

FIGURE 2-22 8085A HOLD VS INTERRUPTS — HALT MODE

2.3.7 Power On and $\overline{\text{RESET IN}}$

The 8085A employs a special internal circuit to increase its speed. This circuit, which is called a substrate bias generator, creates a negative voltage which is used to negatively bias the substrate. The circuit employs an oscillator and a charge pump which require a certain amount of time after POWER ON to stabilize. (See Figure 2-23.)

Taking this circuit into account, the 8085A is not guaranteed to work until 10 ms after V_{CC} reaches 4.75V. For this reason, it is suggested that $\overline{\text{RESET IN}}$ be kept low during this period. Note that the 10 ms period does not include the time it takes for the power supply to reach its 4.75V level — which may be milliseconds in some systems. A simple RC network (Figure 3-6) can satisfy this requirement.

The $\overline{\text{RESET IN}}$ line is latched every CLK = 1. This latched signal is recognized by the CPU during CLK = 1 of the next T state. (See Figure 2-24.) If it is low, the CPU will issue RESET OUT and enter T_{HALT} for the next T state. $\overline{\text{RESET IN}}$ should be kept low for a minimum of three clock periods to ensure proper synchronization of the CPU. When the $\overline{\text{RESET IN}}$ signal goes high, the CPU will enter $M_1 \cdot T_1$ for the next T state. Note that the various signals and buses are floated in T_{RESET} as well as T_{HALT} and T_{HOLD}. For this reason, it is desirable to provide pull-up resistors for the main control signals (particularly $\overline{\text{WR}}$).

Specifically, the $\overline{\text{RESET IN}}$ signal causes the following actions:

RESETS	**SETS**
PROGRAM COUNTER	RST 5.5 MASK
INSTRUCTION REGISTER	RST 6.5 MASK
INTE FF	RST 7.5 MASK
RST 7.5 FF	
TRAP FF	
SOD FF	
MACHINE STATE FF's	
MACHINE CYCLE FF's	
INTERNALLY LATCHED FF's for HOLD, INTR, and READY	

$\overline{\text{RESET IN}}$ does not explicitly change the contents of the 8085A registers (A, B, C, D, E, H, L) and the condition flags, but due to $\overline{\text{RESET IN}}$ occurring at a random time during instruction execution, the results are indeterminate.

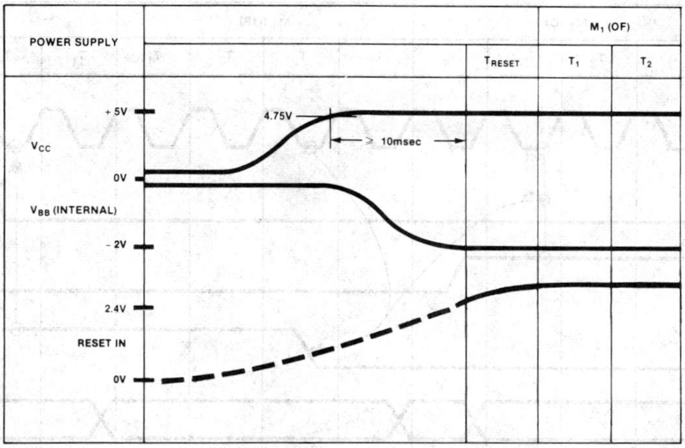

FIGURE 2-23 POWER-ON TIMING

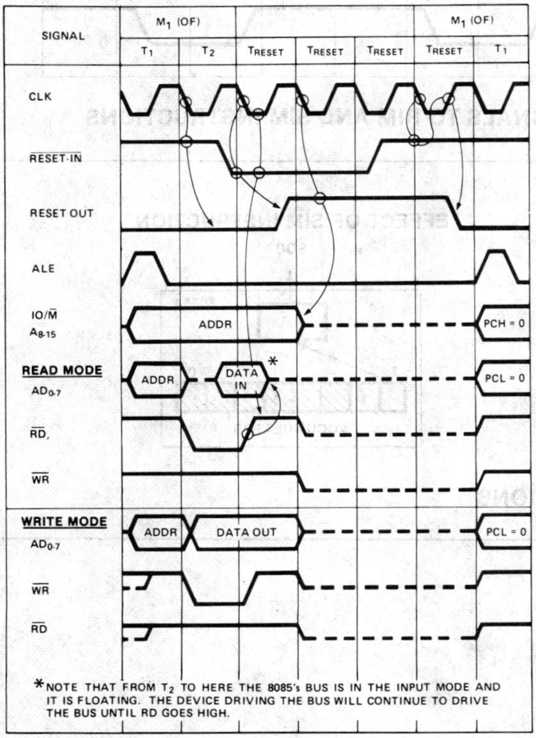

FIGURE 2-24 $\overline{\text{RESET IN}}$ TIMING

Following RESET, the 8085A will start executing instructions at location 0 with the interrupt system disabled, as shown in Figure 2-24.

Figure 2-24 also shows READ and WRITE operations being terminated by a RESET signal. Note that a RESET may prematurely terminate any READ or WRITE operation in process when the RESET occurs.

2.3.8 SID and SOD Signals:

Figure 2-25 shows the timing relationship of the SID and SOD signals to the RIM and SIM instructions. The 8085A has the ability to read the SID line into the accumulator bit 7 using RIM instructions. The state of the SID line is latched internally during $T_3 \cdot CLK = 0$ of the RIM instruction. Following this, the state of the interrupt pins and masks are also transferred directly to the accumulator.

The 8085A can set the SOD flip-flop from bit 7 of the accumulator using the SIM instruction. (See Figure 2-26.) The data is transferred from the accumulator bit 7 to SOD during $M_1 \cdot T_2 \cdot CLK = 0$ of the instruction following SIM, assuming that accumulator bit 6 is a 1. Accumulator bit 6 is a "serial output enable" bit.

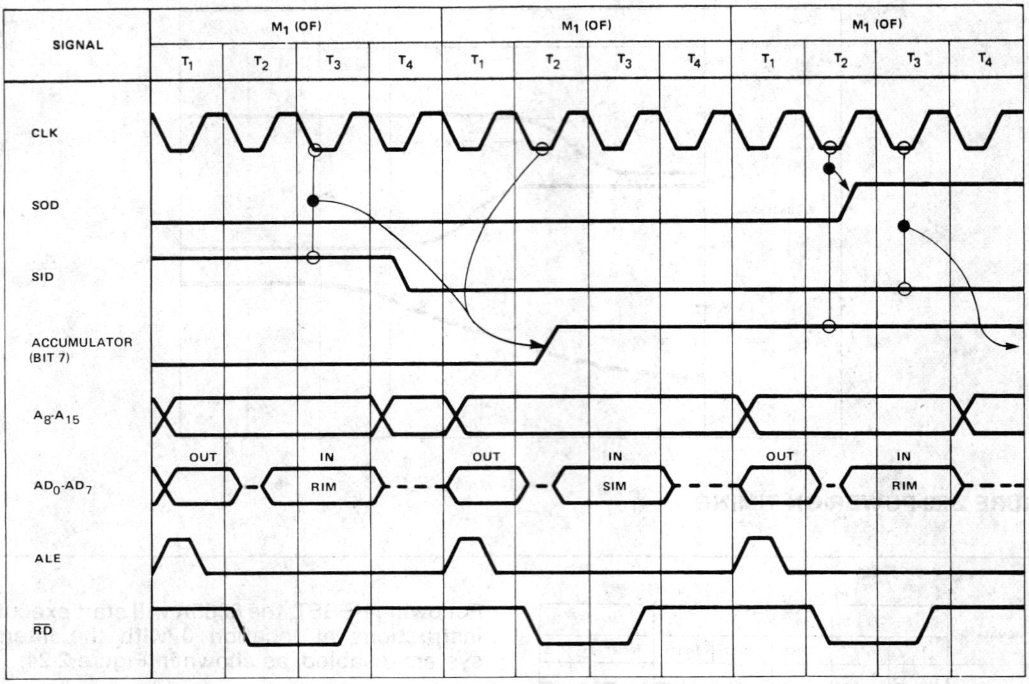

FIGURE 2-25 RELATIONSHIP OF SID AND SOD SIGNALS TO RIM AND SIM INSTRUCTIONS

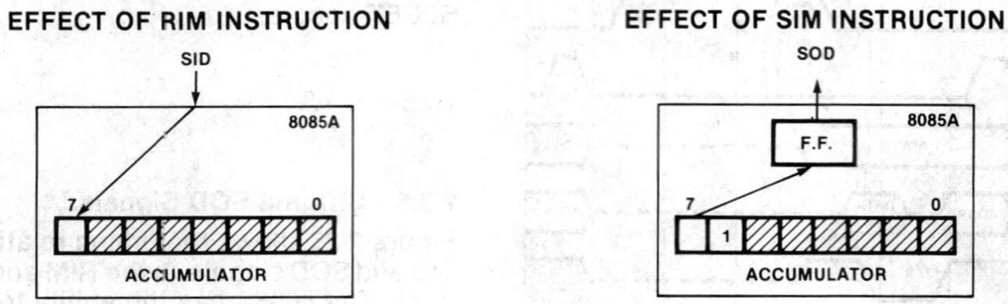

FIGURE 2-26 EFFECT OF RIM AND SIM INSTRUCTIONS

2.4 COMPARISON OF 8080 AND 8085 SYSTEM BUSES

This section compares the 8080 bus with the 8085 bus. Figure 2-28 details the signals and general timing of the two buses; the timing diagrams are drawn to the same scale (8080A clock cycle = 480 ns and 8085A clock cycle = 320 ns to facilitate comparison.

8080 System Bus

The 8080 bus is terminated on one end by the CPU-GROUP (consisting of the 8080A, 8224, 8228) and on the other end by the various memory and I/O circuits. The following figure shows the major signals of the 8080 bus.

8085 System Bus

The 8085 bus is terminated on one end by the 8085A and the other end by various memory and I/O devices. The 8085 bus may be optionally demultiplexed with an eight-bit latch to provide an 8080 type bus. The following figure shows the major signals of the 8085 bus.

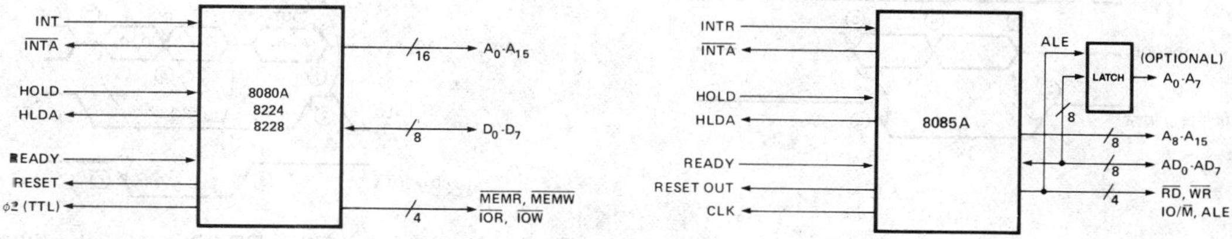

FIGURE 2-27 COMPARISON OF SYSTEM BUSES

MCS-80™ System Bus

SIGNAL(S)	FUNCTION
A_0-A_{15}	The 16 lines of the address bus identify a memory or I/O location for a data transfer operation.
D_0-D_7	The 8 lines of the data bus are used for the parallel transfer of data between two devices.
$\overline{MEMR}$, $\overline{MEMW}$, $\overline{IOR}$, $\overline{IOW}$, $\overline{INTA}$	These five control lines (MEMORY READ, MEMORY WRITE, I/O READ, I/O WRITE, and INTERRUPT ACKNOWLEDGE) identify the type and timing of a data transfer operation.
READY, RESET, HOLD, HLDA ϕ2 (TTL), INT	These signals are used for the synchronization of slow speed memories, system reset, DMA, sytem timing, and CPU interrupt.

MCS-85™ System Bus

SIGNAL(S)	FUNCTION
A_8-A_{15}	These are the high order eight bits of the address, and are used to identify a memory or I/O location for a data transfer cycle.
AD_0-AD_7	These eight lines serve a dual function. During the beginning of a data transfer operation, these lines carry the low order eight bits of the address bus. During the remainder of the cycle, these lines are used for the parallel transfer of data between two devices.
$\overline{RD}$, $\overline{WR}$, $\overline{INTA}$	These signals identify the type and timing of a data transfer cycle.
IO/$\overline{M}$	The I/O/$\overline{MEMORY}$ line identifies a data transfer as being in the I/O address space or the memory address space.
ALE	ADDRESS LATCH ENABLE enables the latching of the A_0-A_7 signals.
READY, RESET OUT, HOLD, HLDA, CLK, INTR	These signals are used for the synchronization of slow speed memories, system reset, DMA, system timing and CPU interrupt.

FIGURE 2-28 COMPARISON OF SYSTEM BUSES

8080 System Bus for READ CYCLE

The basic timing of the 8080 BUS for a READ CYCLE is as follows:

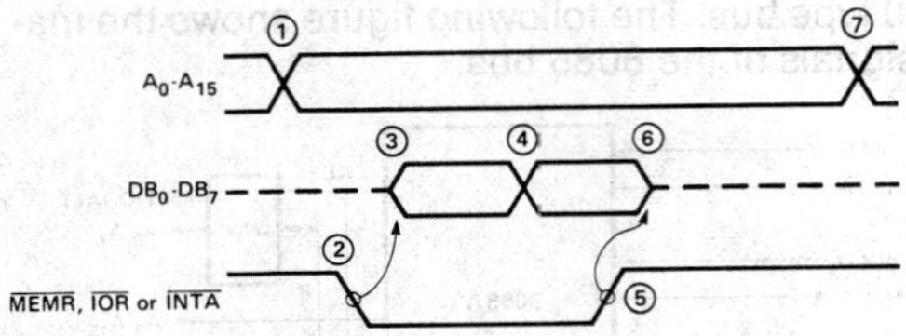

The 8080A first presents the address ① and shortly thereafter the control signal ②. The data bus, which was in the high impedance state, is driven by the selected device ③. The selected device eventually presents the valid data to the processor ④. The processor raises the control signal ⑤, which causes the selected device to put the data bus in the high impedance state ⑥. The processor then changes the address ⑦ for the start of the next data transfer.

8080 System Bus for WRITE CYCLE

The basic timing of the 8080 BUS for a WRITE CYCLE is as follows:

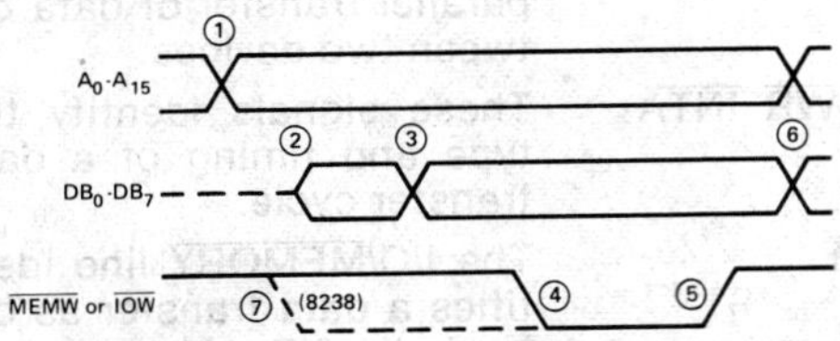

The 8080A first presents the address ①, then enables the data bus driver ②, and later presents the data ③. Shortly thereafter, the 8080A drops the control signal ④ for an interval of time and then raises the signal ⑤. The 8080A then changes the address ⑥ in preparation for the next data transfer. The advance write signal of the 8238 is also shown ⑦.

8085 System Bus for READ CYCLE

The basic timing of the 8085 BUS for a READ CYCLE is as follows:

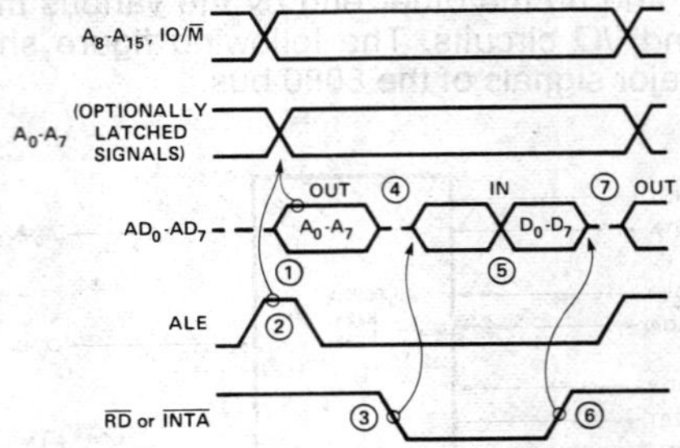

At the beginning of the READ cycle, the 8085A sends out all 16 bits of address ①. This is followed by ALE ② which causes the lower eight bits of address to be latched in either the 8155/56, 8755A, or in an external latch. $\overline{RD}$ is then dropped ③ by the 8085A. The data bus is then tri-stated by the 8085A in preparation for the selected device driving the bus ④; the selectd device will continue to drive the bus with valid data ⑤, until $\overline{RD}$ is raised ⑥ by the 8085A. At the end of the READ CYCLE ⑦, the address and data lines are changed in preparation for the next cycle.

8085 System Bus for WRITE CYCLE

The basic timing of the 8085 BUS for a WRITE CYCLE is as follows:

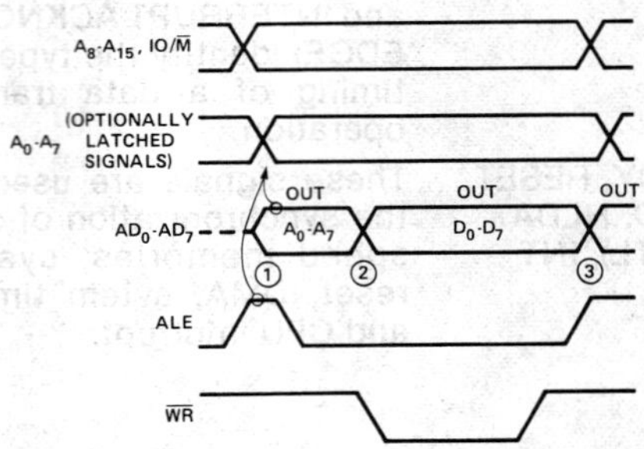

The timing of the WRITE CYCLE is identical to the 8085 READ CYCLE with the exception of the AD_0-AD_7 lines. At the beginning of the cycle ①, the low order eight bits of address are on AD_0-AD_7. After ALE drops, the eight bits of data ② are put on AD_0-AD_7. They are removed ③ at the end of the WRITE CYCLE, in anticipation of the next data transfer.

FIGURE 2-28 (Continued) COMPARISON OF SYSTEM BUSES

The following observations of the two buses can be made:

1. The access times from address leaving the processor to returning data are almost identical, even though the 8085A is operating 50% faster than the 8080A.
2. With the addition of a latch to the 8085A, the basic timings of the two systems are very similar.
3. The 8085A has more time for address setup to RD than the 8080A.
4. The 8080A has a wider RD signal, but a narrower $\overline{WR}$ signal than the 8085A.
5. The 8080A provides stable data setup to the leading and trailing edges of $\overline{WR}$ while the 8085A provides stable data setup to only the trailing edge of $\overline{WR}$.
6. The 8080A control signals have different widths and occur at different points in the machine cycle, while the 8085A control signals have identical timing.
7. While not shown on the chart, the 8080A data and address hold times are adversely affected by the processor preparing to enter the HOLD state. The 8085A has identical timing regardless of entering HOLD.
8. Also not shown on the chart is the fact that all output signals of the 8085A have $-400\mu a$ of source current and 2.0 ma of sink current. The 8085A also has input voltage levels of $V_{IL} = 0.8V$ and $V_{IH} = 2.0V$.

CONCLUSION:

The preceding discussion has clearly shown that the 8085A bus satisfies the two restrictions of COMPATIBILITY and SPEED. It is compatible because it requires only a latch to generate an 8080A type bus. If the four control singals $\overline{MEMR}$, $\overline{MEMW}$, $\overline{IOR}$ and $\overline{IOW}$ are desired, they can be generated from $\overline{RD}$, $\overline{WR}$, and IO/M with a decoder or a few gates. The 8085A bus is also fast. While running at 3 MHz, the 8085A generates better timing signals than the 8080A does at 2 MHz. Furthermore, the multiplexed bus structure doesn't slow the 8085A down, because it is using the internal states to overlap the fetch and execution portions of different machine cycles. Finally, the 8085A can be slowed down or sped up considerably, while still providing reasonable timing.

TO USE. The $\overline{RD}$, $\overline{WR}$, and $\overline{INTA}$ control signals all have identical timing, which isn't affected by the CPU preparing to enter the HOLD state. Furthermore, the address and data bus have good setup and hold times relative to the control signals. The voltage and current levels for the interface signals will all drive buses of up to 40 MOS devices, or 1 schottky TTL device.

The 8085A system bus is also EFFICIENT. Efficiency is the reason that the lower eight address lines are multiplexed with the data bus. Every chip that needs to use both A_0-A_7 and D_0-D_7 saves 7 pins (the eighth pin is used for ALE) on the interface to the processor. That means that 7 more pins per part are available to either add features to the part or to use a smaller package in some cases. In the three chip system shown in Figure 3-6, the use of the 8085A bus saves $3 \times 7 = 21$ pins, which are used for extra I/O and interrupt lines. A further advantage of the 8085A bus is apparent in Figure 3-7, which shows a printed circuit layout of the circuit in Figure 3-6. The reduced number of pins and the fact that compatible pinouts were used, provides for an extremely compact, simple, and efficient printed circuit. Notice that great care was taken when the pinouts were assigned to ensure that the signals would flow easily from chip to chip to chip.

System Operating and Interfacing 3

CHAPTER 3
8085A SYSTEM OPERATION AND INTERFACING

3.1 INTERFACING TO THE 8085A

The 8085A interfaces to both memory and I/O devices by means of READ and WRITE machine cycles, the timing of which are identical. During each machine cycle the 8085A issues an address and control signal, then either sends data out on the bus or reads data from the bus. Th 8085A may be performing a READ machine cycle, but what it reads could be a ROM, RAM, I/O device, peripheral device, or nothing.

There is no distinction between data, instruction opcodes, and I/O port numbers except the way the CPU interprets what it reads from the bus. If an opcode is what would logically appear on the bus, the CPU will treat as an opcode whatever does appear there; if an I/O port number is to be expected, what appears will be interpreted as a port number. The same is true for a WRITE cycle. The 8085A issues an address, data, and a control signal. Unless it is requested to WAIT (by use of the READY line) it will complete the cycle and proceed to the next. Regardless of whether there is a device present to accept the data, the CPU executes one instruction at a time, in sequence, until told to do otherwise. The program controls the sequence and nature of all machine cycles until an interrupt occurs.

There are two ways of addressing I/O devices in the 8085 system. If the IO/$\overline{M}$ output from the CPU is used to distinguish between I/O and memory READ and WRITE cycles, then that system is said to employ standard, or I/O-mapped, I/O. If IO/$\overline{M}$ is not so used, the CPU does not distinguish between I/O and memory, and its system employs memory-mapped I/O. Each method of addressing I/O has advantages and disadvantages.

3.2 MEMORY-MAPPED I/O

3.2.1 Advantages of Memory-Mapped I/O

Since the processor doesn't distinguish I/O from memory using this addressing scheme, you can take advantage of the larger instruction set that references the memory address space. Instead of only being able to transfer a byte of data between the accumulator and the I/O port (using INPUT and OUTPUT instructions), you can now program arithmetic and logic operations on port data as well as move data between any internal register and the I/O port. Consider the new meaning of the following instructions:

Examples:

MOVr,M	(Input Port to any Register)
MOV M,r	(Output any Register to Port)
MVI M	(Output immediate data to Port)
LDA	(Input Port to ACC)
STA	(Output from ACC to Port)
LHLD	(16-Bit Input)
SHLD	(16-Bit Output)
ADD M	(Add Port to ACC)
ANA M	(AND Port with ACC)

3.2.2 Disadvantages of Memory-Mapped I/O

While memory instructions may increase the flexibility of the I/O system, there are some drawbacks. Since I/O devices are now addressed as memory, there are fewer addresses available for memory. A common practice is to use address bit 15 (A_{15}) to distinguish memory from I/O. (See Figure 3-2 and accompanying discussion.) If $A_{15} = 0$ then memory is being addressed; if $A_{15} = 1$, I/O is being addressed. This particular scheme limits the maximum amount of memory that can be used to 32k bytes. A further disadvantage of memory-mapped I/O is that it takes 3 bytes of instruction and 13 clock cycles using the LDA or STA instructions to specify moving a byte of data between the accumulator and an I/O device, whereas the INPUT and OUTPUT instructions require only two bytes and 10 clock cycles. This is because the I/O address space is smaller (only 256 bytes) and therefore requires fewer bits to completely specify an address. A futher advantage of using the INPUT and OUTPUT instructions is that it allows the easy connection of the 8080 Family peripherals to the 8085 multiplexed bus. If you memory-map the 8080 Family peripherals to the 8085 bus, you must either latch the lower address bits or use a portion of the memory address space by connecting the chip selects and address lines of the ports to the unmultiplexed upper eight lines of the address bus.

3.3 ADDRESS ASSIGNMENT

3.3.1 Decoding

Besides memory-mapped I/O, another practice is to only partially decode the address bus when generating chip selects. Every device has a given number of unique addresses associated with it. The 8755A, for instance, has 2k bytes of EPROM and therefore has 2k addresses associated with the EPROM. Any one of these 2k addresses can be uniquely specified by a pattern on the 11 ($2^{11} = 2k$) address lines. However, since the 8755A must work with other devices in a system, it is not enough to simply specify the 11 bits; further bits of information must be used to locate the 2k bytes within the 65k address space. The 2k bytes within the 65k address space. The 2k bytes are located by the use of chip enable (CE) inputs to the 8755A chip. If the 8755A were to occupy the first 2k bytes of the memory address space, it would, strictly speaking, be necessary to decode the fact that A_{15}-A_{11} were all zeroes, and use that condition as a chip enable. Then the 8755A would be selected only when the address bus was less than 2k.

However, if other 2k blocks of addresses aren't being used, you may combine those addresses and not decode all of the upper five address lines for chip enables. In fact, in a small system you may need to decode only one bit of address, which is to say connect that bit of the address bus to the chip enable line of the 8755A. If you connect A_{11} to the $\overline{CE}$ line of the 8755A and tie CE to V_{CC}, then the 8755A would be selected whenever the memory address was less than 2k. (See Figure 3-1A.)

However, it will also be selected whenever memory locations 4k-6k, 8k-10k, 61k-63k (i.e., whenever bit $A_{11} = 0$) is addressed. If the programmer is aware of this, and if there are no other devices assigned to the other address spaces, then it may be an acceptable condition. Care must be taken, however, to ensure that at no time will two different devices be selected simultaneously. Whenever one device is selected, that memory address must deselect all other devices. If two devices are selected simultaneously for a READ operation, the electrical conflict on the bus may damage one or both parts. Note also that the address bus may reflect an undesired address during T_5, T_6 of an opcode fetch cycle and during address bus transitional periods in T_1 (this is illustrated in Chapter 2). Therefore, all memory and I/O devices must qualify their selection with $\overline{RD}$ or $\overline{WR}$, or the address on the bus at the falling edge of the ALE, so as to ignore all spurious addresses.

3.3.2 Linear Selection

Using and address bit as a chip select is referred to as linear selection. The direct consequence of linear selection is that you cut the available address space in half for each single address bit used as a chip enable. If this penalty is too high, you can always use an 8205 one-of-eight decoder. Also, some chips have multiple chip enables, which allows for some automatic decoding of the address. (See Figures 3-1B and 3-1C.)

One drawback to linear selection is that the memory addresses of the different parts are not contiguous. For example, if three 8755A's are addressed using linear selection, one might be located at 0-2k, the next at 6k-8k, and the next at 10k-12k. The programmer must recognize these page boundries and jump over them.

3.4 INTERFACING TO THE 8155/8156, 8755A

3.4.1 I/O Mapped I/O:

This section describes some of the techniques involved in connecting the 8085 combination memory and I/O chips to the 8085A as I/O devices.

Figure 3.1A shows one 8755A connected to the 8085A bus. (In the interest of simplicity, only the chip enable and IO/$\overline{M}$ lines are show; the other lines are connected as shown in Figures 3.6, 3.7 or 3.8.) Notice that CE is tied to V_{CC} and $\overline{CE}$ is connected to A_{11}. This is because after RESET the processor always starts executing at location 0. Since the EPROM normally contains the program, it must be selected when the address is all zeroes.

One consequence of the 8755A EPROM being selected by an all-zero address is that the I/O ports on the chip will be selected only when $A_{11} = 0$. This is because the I/O ports and the memory have common chip enables, therefore forcing the selection conditions of one onto the other. Furthermore, since the IO/M line of the chip is connected to the IO/M line of the chip is connected to the IO/$\overline{M}$ line of the 8085A, the port has I/O mapped I/O. The I/O ports can be accessed only by use of the INPUT and OUTPUT instructions; since these are the only instructions that cause IO/$\overline{M}$ to go high.

The boxes to the right of the chip in Figure 3.1A indicate the memory addresses and I/O Port numbers required to access the chip. As a result of the linear selection technique used, there are many "don't care" bits (marked by "X"s) in the address. While they don't affect the addressing of this device, they may affect other devices in the system, which would force them to be either ones or zeroes. Remember that two devices may not be

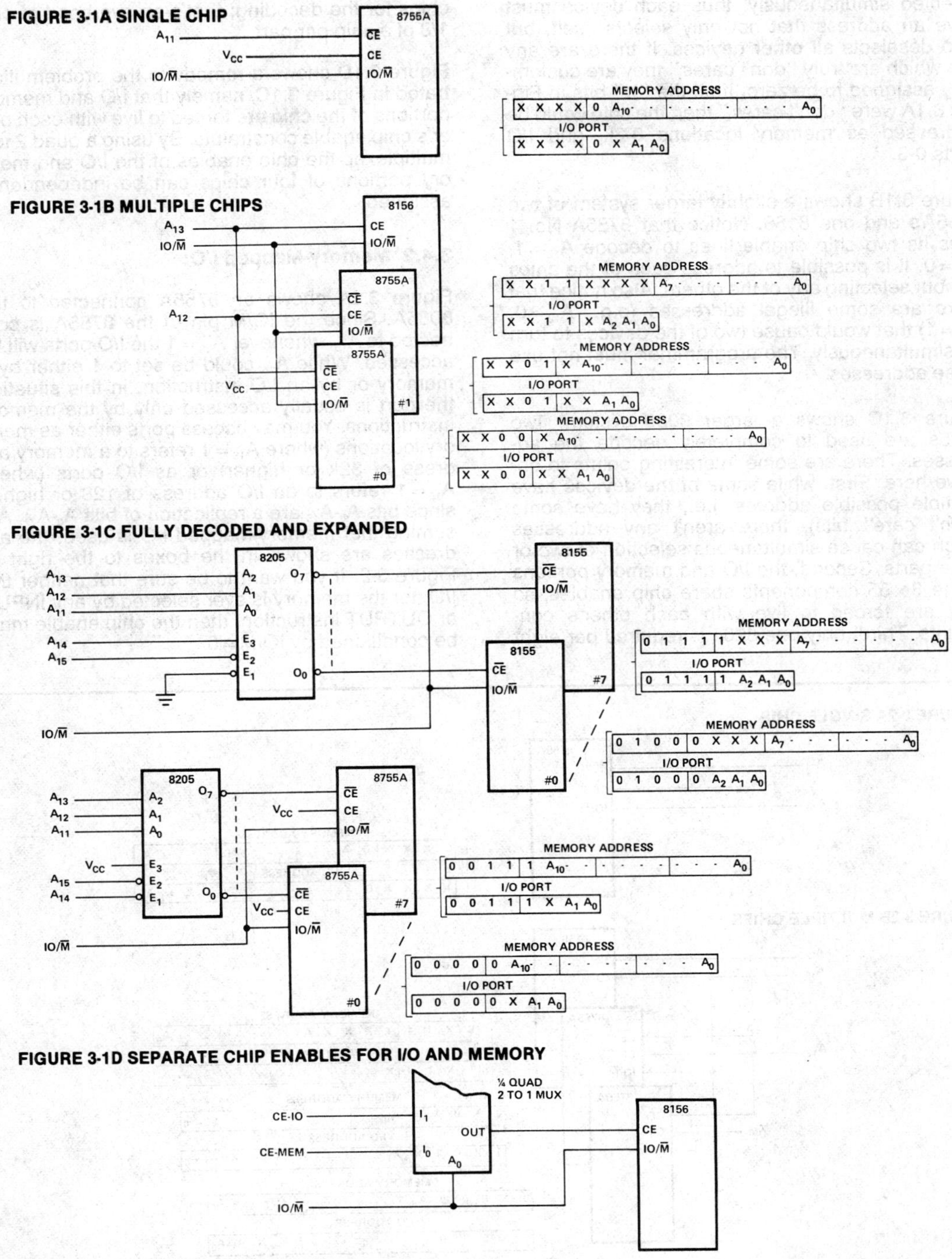

FIGURE 3-1 8085 PERIPHERALS WITH I/O MAPPED I/O

selected simultaneously; thus each device must have an address that not only selects itself, but also deselects all other devices. If there are any bits which are truly "don't cares," they are customarily assigned to be zero. If all the "X" bits in Figure 3.1A were "don't cares," then the chip could be addressed as memory locations 0-2k, and I/O Ports 0-3.

Figure 3.1B shows a slightly larger system of two 8755A's and one 8156. Notice that 8755A No. 1 uses its two chip enable lines to decode $A_{12}=1$, $A_{13}=0$. It is possible to address each of the chips without selecting any of the others. Also notice that there are some illegal addresses (e.g., $A_{12}=0$, $A_{13}=1$) that would cause two of the devices to turn on simultaneously. The programmer must not use these addresses.

Figure 3.1C shows a larger 8085 system. Two 8205s are used to completely decode the addresses. There are some interesting points to observe here. First, while some of the devices have multiple possible address (i.e., they have some "don't care" bits), there aren't any addresses which can cause simultaneous selection of two or more parts. Second, the I/O and memory portions of the 8 × 55 components share chip enables, so they are forced to live with each other's constraints. Third, only one 8205 is required per eight chips for the decoding; that's an overhead of only 1/8 of a chip per part.

Figure 3.1D shows a remedy to the problem illustrated in Figure 3.1C, namely that I/O and memory portions of the chip are forced to live with each other's chip enable constraints. By using a quad 2 to 1 multiplexer, the chip enables of the I/O and memory portions of four chips can be independently assigned.

3.4.2 Memory-Mapped I/O:

Figure 3.2A shows an 8755A connected to the 8085A. Since the $IO/\overline{M}$ pin of the 8755A is connected to A_{15}, whenever $A_{15}=1$ the I/O ports will be accessed. While A_{15} could be set to 1 either by a memory or by an I/O instruction, in this situation the port is usually accessed only by the memory instructions. You may access ports either as memory locations (where $A_{15}=1$ refers to a memory address of 32k or higher) or as I/O ports (where $A_{15}=1$ refers to an I/O address of 128 or higher, since bits A_8-A_{15} are a replication of bits A_0-A_7). Assuming that memory-mapped I/O is used, the addresses are shown in the boxes to the right in Figure 3-2. If you want to be sure that neither the I/O nor the memory is ever selected by any INPUT or OUTPUT instruction, then the chip enable must be conditioned by $IO/\overline{M}=0$.

FIGURE 3-2A SINGLE CHIP

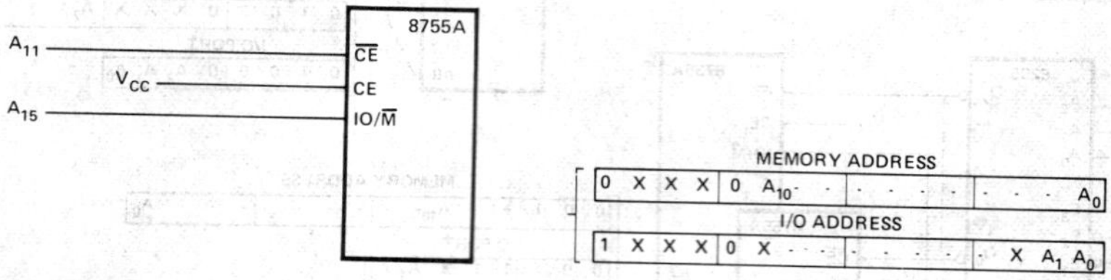

FIGURE 3-2B MULTIPLE CHIPS

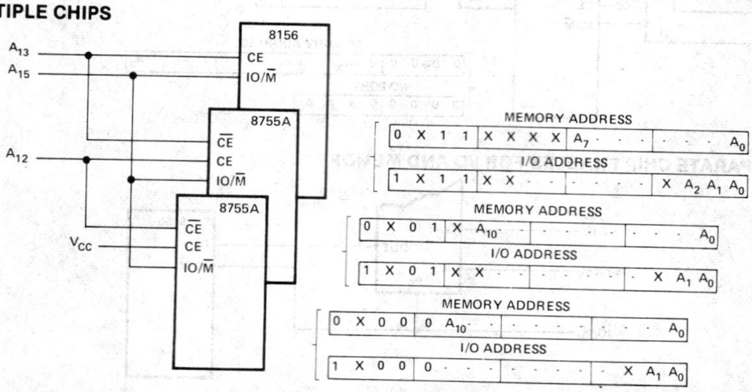

FIGURE 3-2 8085 FAMILY PERIPHERALS WITH MEMORY-MAPPED I/O

Figure 3.2B shows a somewhat larger system, also using memory-mapped I/O. As in Figure 3.1B care must be exercised to ensure that no two devices are accessed simultaneously. You can see that considerable memory address space is used up as a result of using memory-mapped I/O.

3.5 INTERFACING TO 8080 FAMILY PERIPHERALS

3.5.1 I/O Mapped I/O:

For want of a better name, the Intel 825x, 827x, and 829x series peripherals are referred to here as 8080 Family peripherals because unlike the 8155/56 and 8755A, they are compatible with the non-multiplexed 8080 system bus.

To interface to an 8080 Family peripheral, you must provide a constant address, a chip select, and $\overline{RD}$ or $\overline{WR}$. Since the upper address lines (A_8-A_{15}) of the 8085A are nonmultiplexed, they can be tied directly to the peripherals, as shown in Figure 3.3A To provide I/O mapped I/O, use either linear selection (keeping the I/O and memory addresses non-coincidental), or condition the chip selects $\overline{WR}$ with $IO/\overline{M} = 1$. Figure 3.3A shows a technique of gating the chip selects with $IO/\overline{M} = 1$, using an 8205. This technique also allows more I/O devices to be used than linear selection would. Note that this technique relies on the fact that the I/O Port number is copied onto A_8-A_{15} as well as A_0-A_7 during an INPUT or OUTPUT instruction.

Figure 3.3B shows an altenative approach to interfacing to 8080 Family components. By latching the lower 8 bits of address with a latch, and decoding the control signals with an 8205, you create an exact copy of the 8080 (8080A, 8224, 8228) bus. You may then use whatever circuits have been previously developed for the 8080. The total cost is one latch and one decoder.

3.5.2 Memory-Mapped I/O:

Exactly the same techniques used to memory map the 8085 Family apply to the 8080 Family I/O devices. Figure 3.4 shows an 8205 used to qualify the chip select of the I/O device with $IO/\overline{M} = 0$. Since the 8080 Family peripherals require nonmultiplexed address lines, linear select is not too useful unless the address lines are latched. This is because connecting both the chip selects and the address lines of the 8080 Family peripherals to A_8-A_{15} would deplete all the useful addresses very quickly.

3.6 INTERFACING TO STANDARD BUS MEMORIES

Standard bus memory devices are designed to be used with nonmultiplexed address and data buses. Interfacing to standard memories is very similar to interfacing to 8085 Family memories with the exception that A_0-A_7 must be latched. Once this requirement is met, all the tricks discussed earlier can be used. Since the address lines would eventually require buffering as the system size grew, the overhead of the latch again becomes negligible.

Figure 3.5 shows the interface of the 8085A to a large block of memory, specifically 16k bytes of ROM and 8k bytes f RAM. Besides the memories, the circuit requires only 2-1/6 other parts for logical gating. If 8080 Family I/O parts were used, the latch could be shared between the two groups, further reducing the gating overhead per IC. Sixteen 1k×4 RAMs and eight 2k×8 ROMs are used in this design. The data bus, address line 8-10, and control signals in this system all should be buffered. This applies to any system with the number of memory devices represented here.

Wherever two or more parts are paralleled on the same bus, they must be 3-state devices such as the 2148 RAM, 2716 EPROM, or 2732A EPROM, which have either an output disable (OD) input or multiple chip select (CS) inputs. To prevent bus contention, only one memory device may be output-enabled at a time in this configuration; the outputs of all others must be deselected during RD.

For additional information on interfacing standard memory devices, please read Section 2 of Appendix 1 and the Intel applications note AP-30 "Application of Intel's 5V EPROM and ROM Family for Microprocessor Systems" available from: Intel, Literature Dept., 3065 Bowers Ave., Santa Clara, CA 95051.

3.7 DYNAMIC RAM INTERFACE:

For interfacing the dynamic RAM, Intel makes a single-component dynamic RAM refresh controller, the 8202, which interfaces the 8085A to multiplexed-address-bus dynamic RAMs. The Intel 8202 provides the necessary refreshing for such dynamic RAMs, and also provides the control signals required for accessing, selecting, and address clocking. If allows for the use of the 8085A's full capabilitiy of 64k bytes of address space with no additional buffering devices. As with other standard memory interfaces, it is necessary to demultiplex the lower 8 bits of address from the multiplexed 8085A bus, AD_{0-7}.

FIGURE 3-3A DECODED CHIP SELECTS

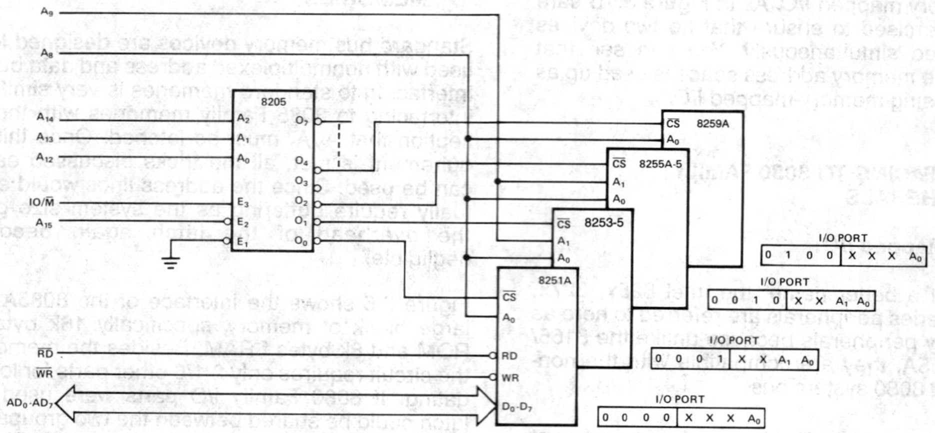

FIGURE 3-3B DECODED CONTROLS AND LATCHED ADDRESS (8080 TYPE BUS)

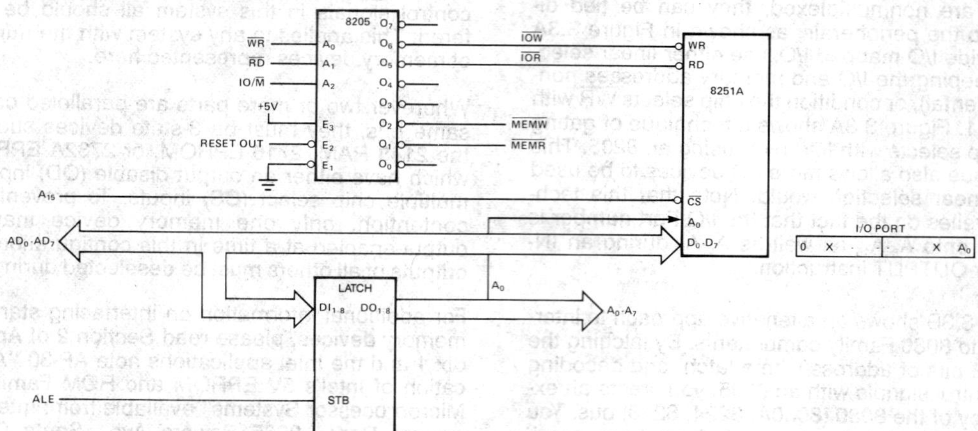

FIGURE 3-3 8080 PERIPHERALS WITH I/O MAPPED I/O

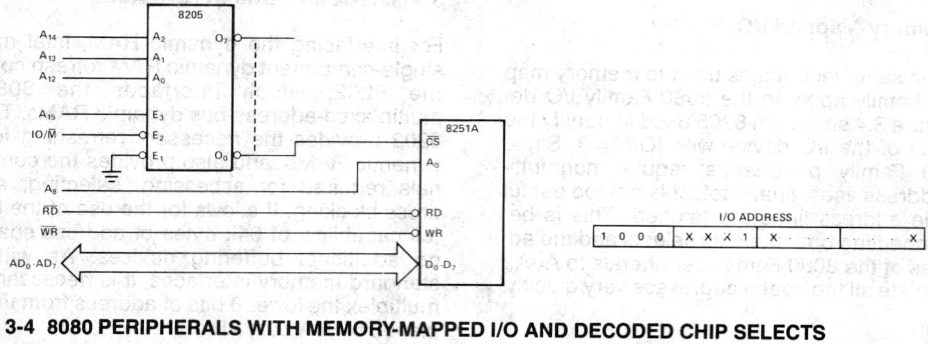

FIGURE 3-4 8080 PERIPHERALS WITH MEMORY-MAPPED I/O AND DECODED CHIP SELECTS

3.8 MINIMUM 8085 SYSTEM

The Schematics of Figure 3.6 depict a minimum system core. In actual use, some of the processor control signals (TRAP, INTR, and HOLD) would have to be terminated. Also, interface logic to external devices as well as more memory and I/O devices may be desirable. The first thing one notices about the system in Figure 3.6 is the scarcity of parts required to build this system. With a minimum of parts, we have constructed a microcomputer system that has the following functions:

PARTS

1 8085A
1 8755A
1 8156
1 Crystal
4 Resistors
1 Capacitor
1 Diode
1 +5 Power Supply

FUNCTIONS

1 CPU (Clock cycle ≤320 ns)
2048 Bytes of either EPROM or ROM
256 Bytes of RAM
38 I/O Lines
5 Interrupts
1 Programmable Timer/Counter
1 Crystal and Oscillator
1 Clock
1 Power-on Reset

By looking at the printed circuit layout of Figure 3.7, we can see that not only are there just 31Cs, but that the interconnection of these parts is extremely easy and provides a very dense layout. Especially notice the easy flow of the system bus on the solder side of the board.

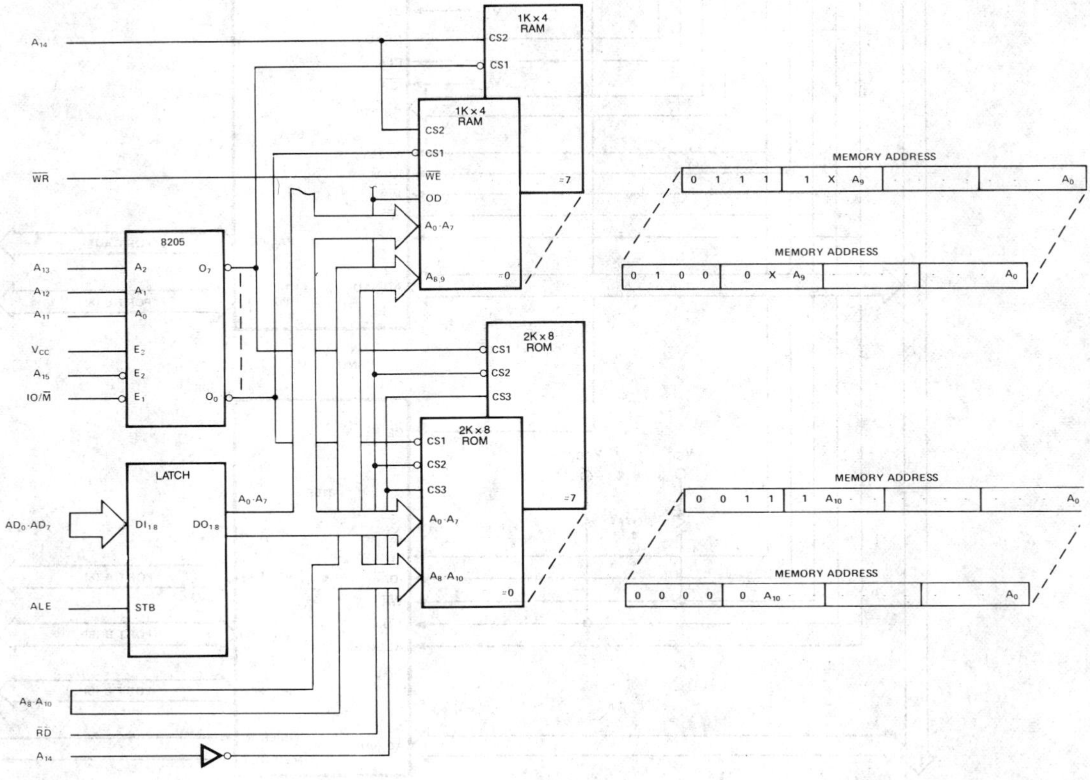

FIGURE 3-5 STANDARD MEMORIES WITH LATCHED ADDRESS AND DECODED CHIP SELECTS

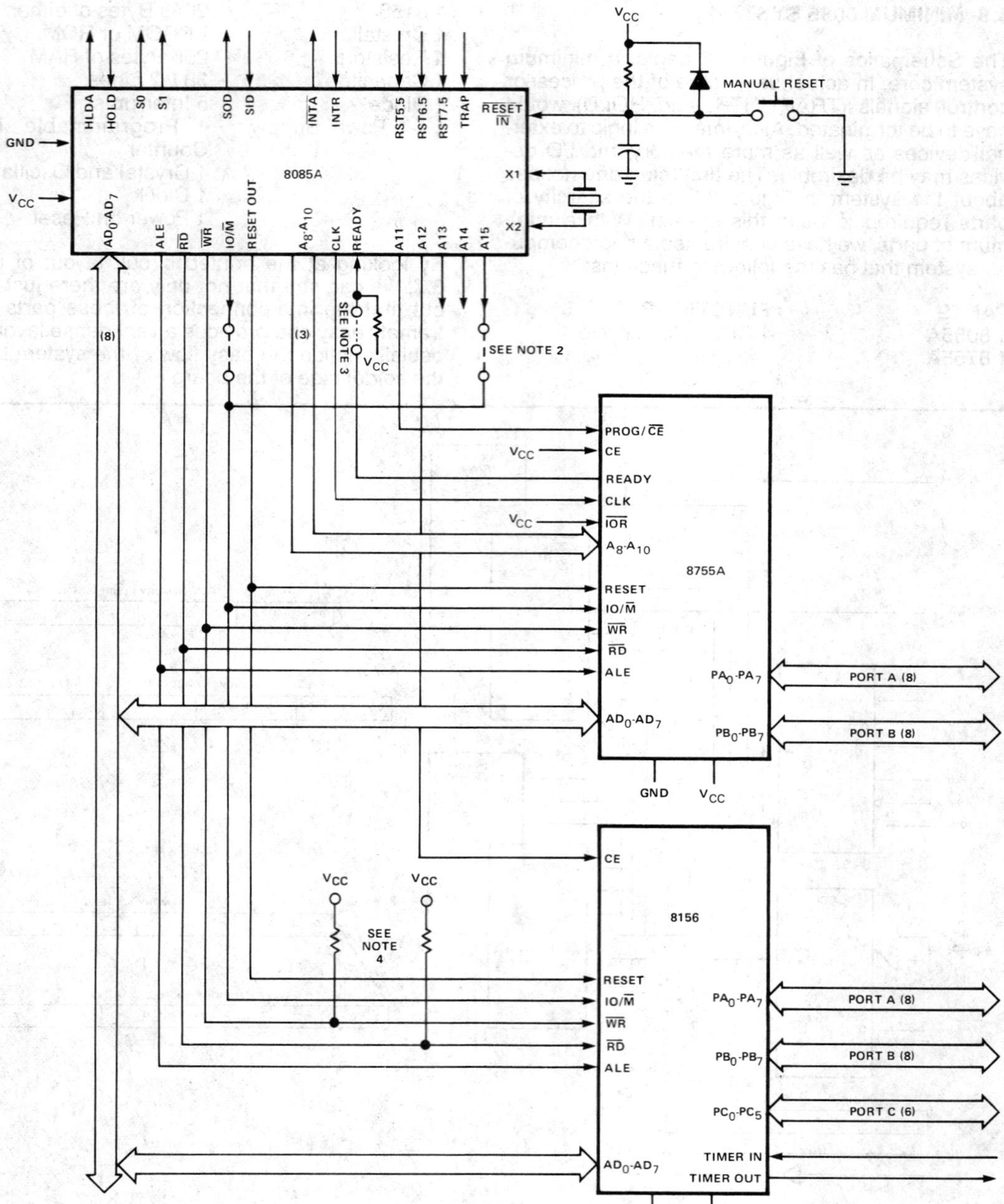

NOTE 1: TRAP, INTR, AND HOLD MUST BE GROUNDED IF THEY AREN'T USED.
NOTE 2: USE $IO/\overline{M}$ FOR STANDARD I/O MAPPING. USE A15 FOR MEMORY MAPPED I/O.
NOTE 3: CONNECTION IS NECESSARY ONLY IF ONE T_{WAIT} STATE IS DESIRED.
NOTE 4: PULL-UP RESISTORS RECOMMENDED TO AVOID SPURIOUS SELECTION WHEN $\overline{RD}$ AND $\overline{WR}$ ARE 3-STATED. THESE RESISTORS ARE NOT INCLUDED ON THE PC BOARD LAYOUT OF FIGURE 3-7.

FIGURE 3-6 MINIMUM 8085 SYSTEM

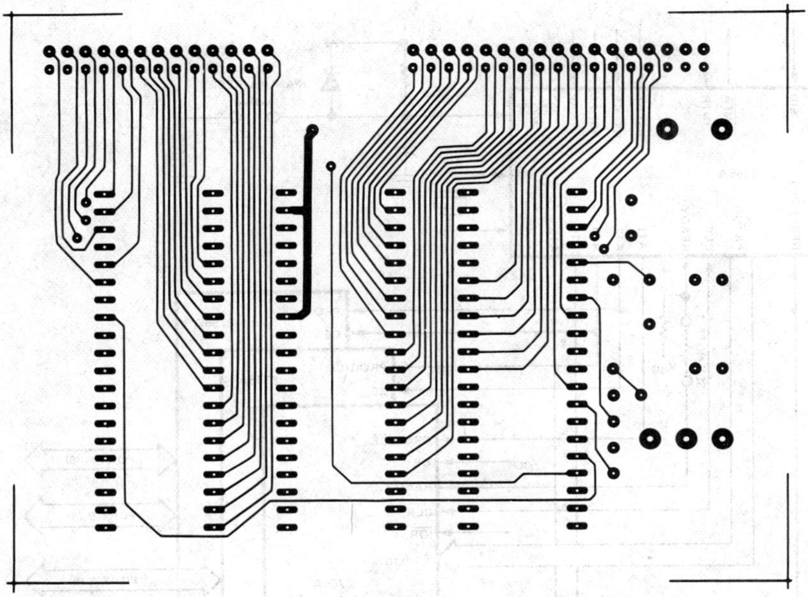

COMPONENT SIDE
SCALE: ≈1:1

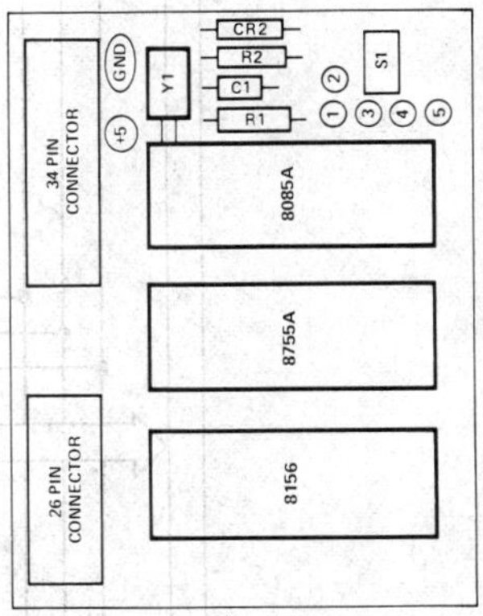

COMPONENT LAYOUT

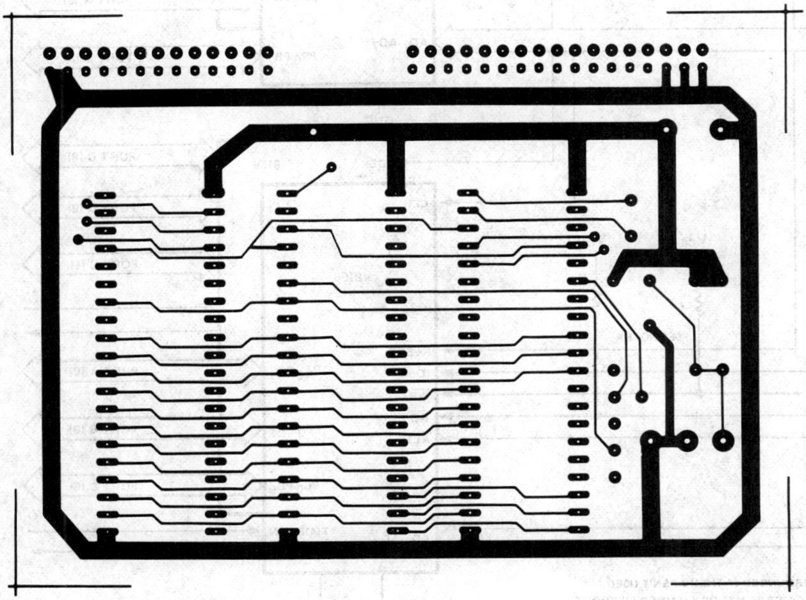

SOLDER SIDE
SCALE: ≈1:1

FIGURE 3-7 PRINTED CIRCUIT LAYOUT

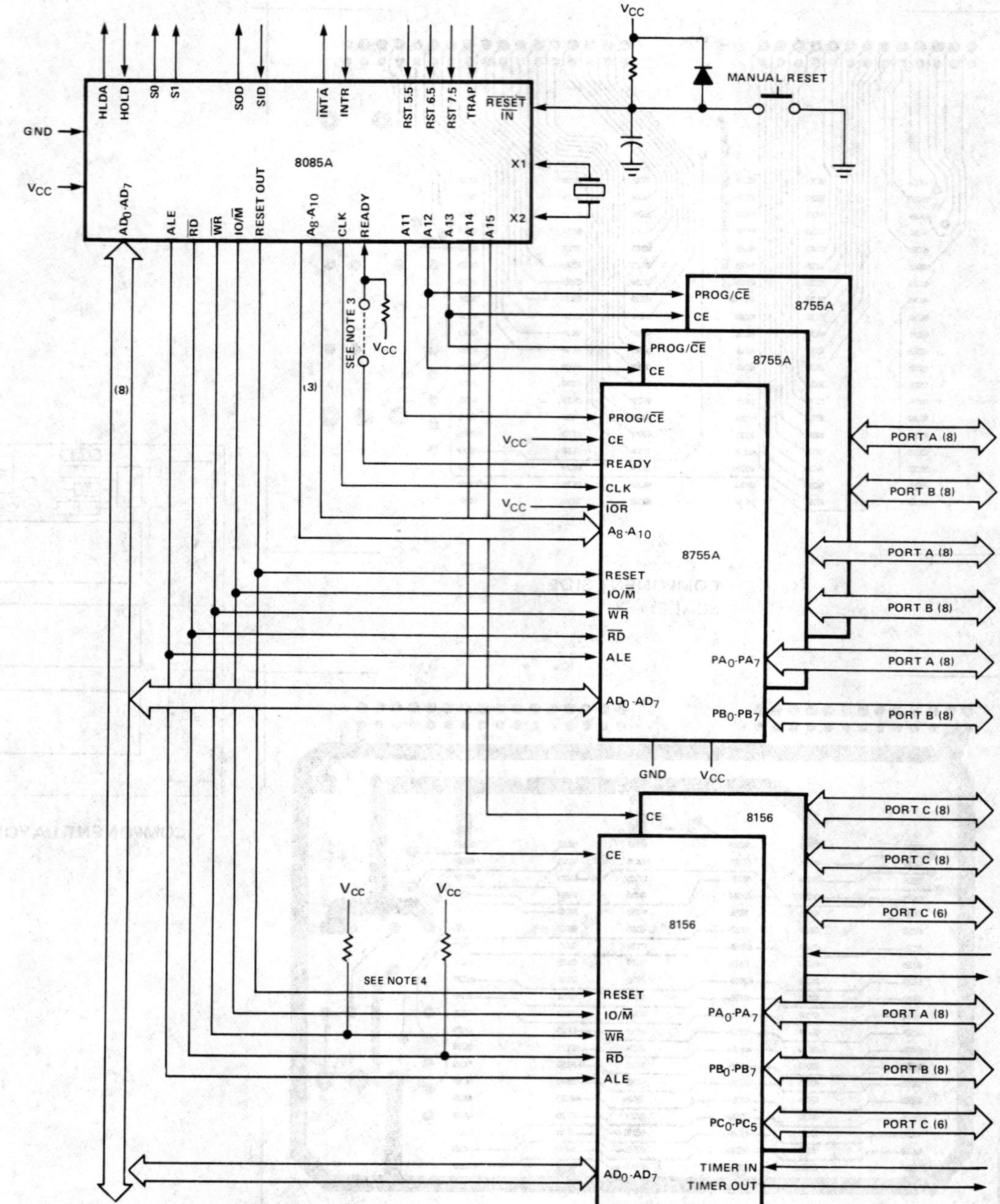

NOTE 1: TRAP, INTR, AND HOLD MUST BE GROUNDED IF THEY AREN'T USED.
NOTE 2: IN THIS CONFIGURATION, THE I/O CAN'T BE MEMORY MAPPED (WITHOUT EXTRA LOGIC) BECAUSE ALL OF THE ADDRESS LINES ARE IN USE.
NOTE 3: CONNECTION IS NECESSARY ONLY IF ONE T_{WAIT} STATE IS DESIRED.
NOTE 4: PULL-UP RESISTORS RECOMMENDED TO AVOID SPURIOUS SELECTION WHEN $\overline{RD}$ AND $\overline{WR}$ ARE 3-STATED.

FIGURE 3-8 EXPANDED SYSTEM

3.9 EXPANDED 8085 SYSTEM

Figure 3.8 shows the circuit Figure 3.6 expanded to its maximum size without the use of any extra logic. In an extremely small board area we can fit:

PARTS	FUNCTION
1 8085A	1 CPU (Clock cycle
3 8755A	≤320 ns)
2 8156	EPROM
1 Crystal	6144 Bytes
4 Resistors	512 Bytes RAM
1 Capacitor	76 I/O Lines
1 Diode	5 Interrupts
	2 Programmable
	Timer/Counters
	2 Serial I/O Lines
	1 Crystal and
	Oscillator
	1 Clock
	1 Power-on Reset

3.10 8085 SYSTEM WITH 8185

The 8185 1 K-byte static RAM chip is another multiplexed-bus component that insures that the most highly integrated systems can be built with 8085 Family components. Figure 3.9 shows a 4-chip 8085 system schematic with the following characteristics:

PARTS	FUNCTION
1 8085A	1 CPU
1 8185	EPROM
1 8156	2048 Bytes
1 8755A	1280 Bytes RAM
	38 I/O Lines
	5 Interrupts
	1 Timer/Counter
	2 Serial I/O Lines

The 8185 also has power-down capability. By connecting $\overline{CE}_1$ to IO/$\overline{M}$ from the 8085A the 8185 will be powered down during the I/O operations and Interrupt Acknowledge cycles.

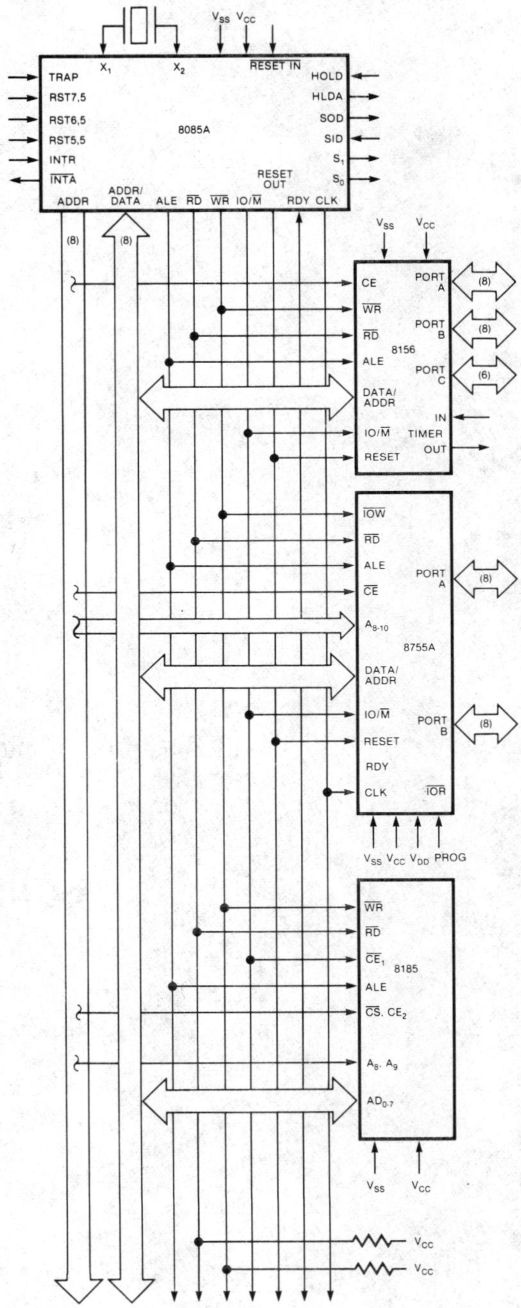

FIGURE 3-9 8085 SYSTEM WITH 8185

Functional Description

4

CHAPTER 4
8080A CENTRAL PROCESSOR UNIT

The 8080A is a complete 8-bit parallel, central processor unit (CPU) for use in general purpose digital computer systems. It is fabricated on a single LSI chip (see Figure 1-1) using Intel's n-channel silicon gate MOS process. The 8080A transfers data and internal state information via an 8-bit, bidirectional 3-state Data Bus (D_0-D_7). Memory and peripheral device addresses are transmitted over a separate 16-bit 3-state Address Bus (A_0-A_{15}). Six timing and control outputs (SYNC, DBIN, WAIT, WR, HLDA and INTE) emanate from the 8080A, while four control inputs (READY, HOLD, INT and RESET), four power inputs (+12v, +5v, −5v, and GND) and two clock inputs (ϕ_1 and ϕ_2) are accepted by the 8080A.

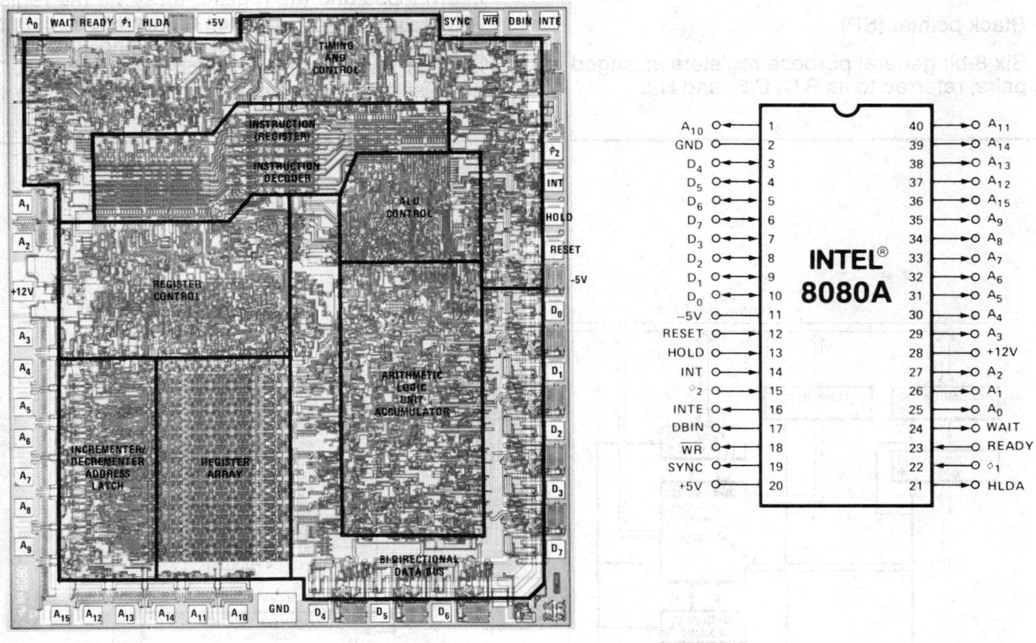

Figure 4-1 8080 Family Photomicrograph with Pin Designations

ARCHITECTURE OF THE 8080A CPU

The 8080A CPU consists of the following functional units:

- Register array and address logic
- Arithmetic and logic unit (ALU)
- Instruction register and control section
- Bi-directional, 3-state data bus buffer

Figure 4-2 illustrates the functional blocks within the 8080A CPU.

Registers:

The register section consists of a static RAM array organized into six 16-bit registers:

- Program counter (PC)
- Stack pointer (SP)
- Six 8-bit general purpose registers arranged in pairs, referred to as B,C; D,E; and H,L
- A temporary register pair called W,Z

The program counter maintains the memory address of the next program instruction and is incremented automatically during every instruction fetch. The stack pointer maintains the address of the next available stack location in memory. The stack pointer can be initialized to use any portion of read-write memory as a stack. The stack pointer is decremented when data is "pushed" onto the stack and incremented when data is "popped" off the stack (i.e., the stack grows "downward").

The six general purpose registers can be used either as single registers (8-bit) or as register pairs (16-bit). The temporary register pair, W,Z, is not program addressable and is only used for the internal execution of instructions.

Eight-bit data bytes can be transferred between the internal bus and the register array via the register-select multiplexer. Sixteen-bit transfers can proceed between the register array and the address latch or the incrementer/decrementer circuit. The address latch receives data from any of the four

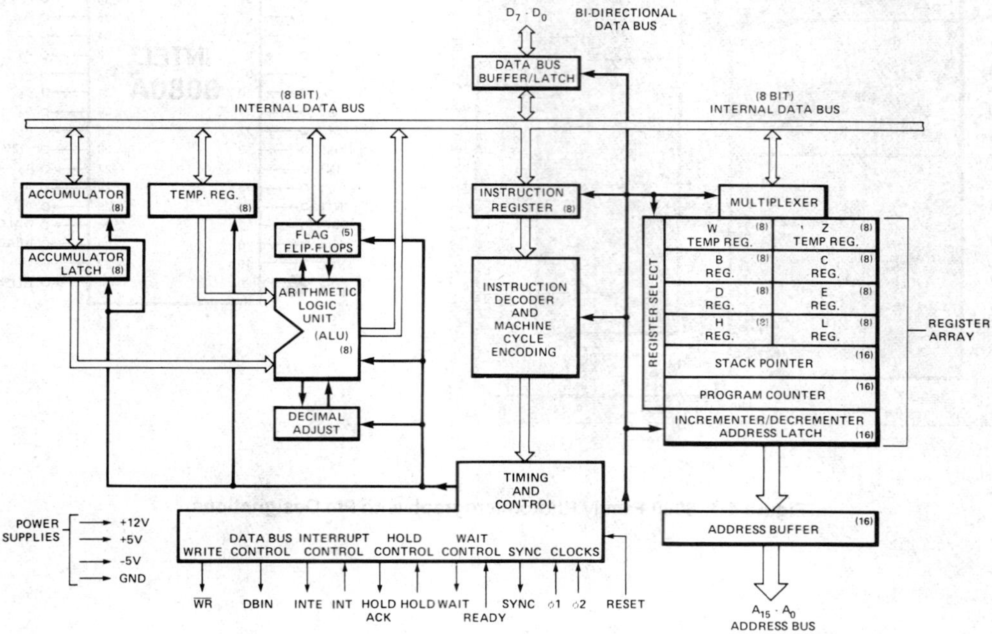

Figure 4-2 8080 Family CPU Functional Block Diagram

register pairs and drives the 16 address output buffers (A_0-A_{15}), as well as the incrementer/decrementer circuit. The incrementer/decrementer circuit receives data from the address latch and sends it to the register array. The 16-bit data can be incremented or decremented or simply transferred between registers.

Arithmetic and Logic Unit (ALU):

The ALU contains the following registers:

- An 8-bit accumulator
- An 8-bit temporary accumulator (ACT)
- A 5-bit flag register: zero, carry, sign, parity and auxiliary carry
- An 8-bit temporary register (TMP)

Arithmetic, logical and rotate operations are performed in the ALU. The ALU is fed by the temporary register (TMP) and the temporary accumulator (ACT) and carry flip-flop. The result of the operation can be transferred to the internal bus or to the accumulator; the ALU also feeds the flag register.

The temporary register (TMP) receives information from the internal bus and can send all or portions of it to the ALU, the flag register and the internal bus.

The accumulator (ACC) can be loaded from the ALU and the internal bus and can transfer data to the temporary accumulator (ACT) and the internal bus. The contents of the accumulator (ACC) and the auxiliary carry flip-flop can be tested for decimal correction during the execution of the DAA instruction (see Section 5).

Instruction Register and Control:

During an instruction fetch, the first byte of an instruction (containing the OP code) is transferred from the internal bus to the 8-bit instruction register.

The contents of the instruction register are, in turn, available to the instruction decoder. The output of the decoder, combined with various timing signals, provides the control signals for the register array, ALU and data buffer blocks. In addition, the outputs from the instruction decoder and external control signals feed the timing and state control section which generates the state and cycle timing signals.

Data Bus Buffer:

The 8-bit bidirectional 3-state buffer is used to isolate the CPU's internal bus from the external data bus (D_0 through D_7). In the output mode, the internal bus content is loaded into an 8-bit latch that, in turn, drives the data bus output buffers. The output buffers are switched off during input or non-transfer operations.

During the input mode, data from the external data bus is transferred to the internal bus. The internal bus is precharged at the beginning of each internal state, except for the transfer state (TW and T_3–described later in this chapter).

THE PROCESSOR CYCLE

An instruction cycle is defined as the time required to fetch and execute an instruction. During the fetch, a selected instruction (one, two or three bytes) is extracted from memory and deposited in the CPU's instruction register. During the execution phase, the instruction is decoded and translated into specific processing activities.

Every instruction cycle consists of one, two, three, four or five machine cycles. A machine cycle is required each time the CPU accesses memory or an I/O port. The fetch portion of an instruction cycle requires one machine cycle for each byte to be fetched. The duration of the execution portion of the instruction cycle depends on the kind of instruction that has been fetched. Some instructions do not require any machine cycles other than those necessary to fetch the instruction; other instructions, however, require additional machine cycles to write or read data to/from memory or I/O devices. The DAD instruction is an exception in that it requires two additional machine cycles to complete an internal register-pair add (see Section 5).

Each machine cycle consists of three, four or five states. A state is the smallest unit of processing activity and is defined as the interval between two

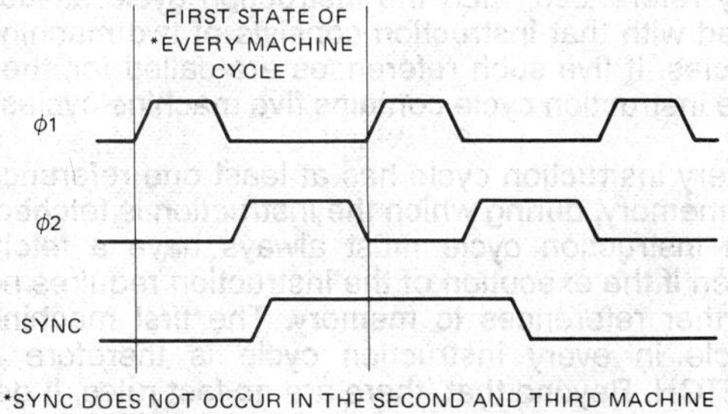

*SYNC DOES NOT OCCUR IN THE SECOND AND THIRD MACHINE CYCLES OF A DAD INSTRUCTION SINCE THESE MACHINE CYCLES ARE USED FOR AN INTERNAL REGISTER-PAIR ADD.

Figure 4-3 ϕ_1, ϕ_2 and SYNC Timing

successive positive-going transitions of the ϕ_1 driven clock pulse. The 8080A is driven by a two-phase clock oscillator. All processing activities are referred to the period of this clock. The two non-overlapping clock pulses, labeled ϕ_1 and ϕ_2, are furnished by external circuitry. It is the ϕ_1 clock pulse which divides each machine cycle into states. Timing logic within the 8080A uses the clock inputs to produce a SYNC pulse, which identifies the beginning of every machine cycle. The SYNC pulse is triggered by the low-to-high transition of ϕ_2, as shown in Figure 4-3.

There are three exceptions to the defined duration of a state. They are the WAIT state, the hold (HLDA) state and the halt (HLTA) state, described later in this chapter. Because the WAIT, the HLDA, and the HLTA states depend upon external events, they are by their nature of indeterminate length. Even these exceptional states, however, must be synchronized with the pulses of the driving clock. Thus, the duration of all states are integral multiples of the clock period.

To summarize then, each **clock period** marks a **state**; three to five states constitute a machine cycle; and one to five **machine cycles** comprise an **instruction cycle**. A full instruction cycle requires anywhere from four to eighteen states for its completion, depending on the kind of instruction involved.

Machine Cycle Identification:

With the exception of the DAD instruction, there is just one consideration that determines how many machine cycles are required in any given instruction cycle: the number of times that the processor must reference a memory address or an addressable peripheral device, in order to fetch and execute the instruction. Like many processors, the 8080A is so constructed that it can transmit only one address per machine cycle. Thus, if the fetch and execution of an instruction requires two memory references, then the instruction cycle associated with that instruction consists of two machine cycles. If five such references are called for, then the instruction cycle contains five machine cycles.

Every instruction cycle has at least one reference to memory, during which the instruction is fetched. An instruction cycle must always have a fetch, even if the execution of the instruction requires no further references to memory. The first machine cycle in every instruction cycle is therefore a FETCH. Beyond that, there are no fast rules. It depends on the kind of instruction that is fetched.

Consider some examples. The add-register (ADD r) instruction is an instruction that requires only a single machine cycle (FETCH) for its completion. In this one-byte instruction, the contents of one of the CPU's six general purpose registers is added to the existing contents of the accumulator. Since all the information necessary to execute the command is contained in the eight bits of the instruction code, only one memory reference is necessary. Three states are used to extract the instruction from memory, and one additional state is used to accomplish the desired addition. The entire instruction cycle thus requires only one machine cycle that consists of four states, or four periods of the external clock.

Suppose now, however, that we wish to add the contents of a specific memory location to the existing contents of the accumulator (ADD M). Although this is quite similar in principle to the example just cited, several additional steps will be used. An extra machine cycle will be used, in order to address the desired memory location.

The actual sequence is as follows. First the processor extracts from memory the one-byte instruction word addressed by its program counter. This takes three states. The eight-bit instruction word obtained during the FETCH machine cycle is deposited in the CPU's instruction register and used to direct activities during the remainder of the instruction cycle. Next, the processor sends out, as an address, the contents of its H and L registers. The eight-bit data word returned during this MEMORY READ machine cycle is placed in a temporary register inside the 8080A CPU. By now three more clock periods (states) have elapsed. In the seventh and final state, the contents of the temporary register are added to those of the accumulator. Two machine cycles, consisting of seven states in all, complete the "ADD M" instruction cycle.

At the opposite extreme is the save H and L registers (SHLD) instruction, which requires five machine cycles. During an "SHLD" instruction cycle, the contents of the processor's H and L registers are deposited in two sequentially adjacent memory locations; the destination is indicated by two address bytes which are stored in the two memory locations immediately following the operation code byte. The following sequence of event occurs:

(1) A FETCH machine cycle, consisting of four states. During the first three states of this machine cycle, the processor fetches the instruction indicated by its program counter. The program counter is then incremented. The fourth state is used for internal instruction decoding.

(2) A MEMORY READ machine cycle, consisting of three states. During this machine cycle, the byte indicated by the program counter is read

from memory and placed in the processor's Z register. The program counter is incremented again.

(3) Another MEMORY READ machine cycle, consisting of three states, in which the byte indicated by the processor's program counter is read from memory and placed in the W register. The program counter is incremented, in anticipation of the next instruction fetch.

(4) A MEMORY WRITE machine cycle, of three states, in which the contents of the L register are transferred to the memory location pointed to by the present contents of the W and Z registers. The state following the transfer is used to increment the W,Z register pair so that it indicates the next memory location to receive data.

(5) A MEMORY WRITE machine cycle, of three states, in which the contents of the H register are transferred to the new memory location pointed to by the W,Z register pair.

In summary, the "SHLD" instruction contains five machine cycles and takes 16 states to execute.

Most instructions fall somewhere between the extremes typified by the "ADD r" and the "SHLD" instructions. The input (IN) and the output (OUT) instructions, for example, require three machine cycles: a FETCH, to obtain the instruction; a MEMORY READ, to obtain the address of the object peripheral; and an INPUT or an OUTPUT machine cycle, to complete the transfer.

While no one instruction cycle will consist of more than five machine cycles, the following ten different types of machine cycles may occur within an instruction cycle:

(1) FETCH (M1)

(2) MEMORY READ

(3) MEMORY WRITE

(4) STACK READ

(5) STACK WRITE

(6) INPUT

(7) OUTPUT

(8) INTERRUPT

(9) HALT

(10)HALT INTERRUPT

The machine cycles that actually do occur in a particular instruction cycle depend upon the kind of instruction, with the overriding stipulation that the first machine cycle in any instruction cycle is always a FETCH.

The processor identifies the machine cycle in progress by transmitting an eight-bit status word during the first state of every machine cycle. Updated status information is presented on the 8080A's data lines (D_0-D_7), during the SYNC interval. This data should be saved in latches, and used to develop control signals for external circuitry. Table 4-1 shows how the positive-true status information is distributed on the processor's data bus.

Status signals are provided principally for the control of external circuitry. Simplicity of interface, rather than machine cycle identification, dictates the logical definition of individual status bits. You will therefore observe that certain processor machine cycles are uniquely identified by a single status bit, but that others are not. The M_1 status bit (D_5), for example, unambiguously identifies a FETCH machine cycle. A STACK READ, on the other hand, is indicated by the coincidence of STACK and MEMR signals. Machine cycle identification data is also valuable in the test and debugging phases of system development. Table 4-1 lists the status bit outputs for each type of machine cycle.

State Transition Sequence:

Every machine cycle within an instruction cycle consists of three to six active states (referred to as T_1, T_2, T_3, T_4, T_5 or $_W$. The actual number of states depends upon the instruction being executed, and on the particular machine cycle within the greater instruction cycle. The state transition diagram in Figure 4-4 shows how the 8080A proceeds from state to state in the course of a machine cycle. The diagram also shows how the READY, HOLD, and INTERRUPT lines are sampled during the machine cycle, and how the conditions on these lines may modify the basic transition sequence. In the present discussion, we are concerned only with the basic sequence and with the READY function. The HOLD and INTERRUPT functions will be discussed later.

The 8080A CPU does not directly indicate its internal state by transmitting a "state control" output during each state; instead, the 8080A supplies direct control output (INTE, HLDA, DBIN, WR and WAIT) for use by external circuitry.

Recall that the 8080A passes through at least three states in every machine cycle, with each state defined by successive low-to-high transitions of the ϕ_1 clock. Figure 4-5 shows the timing relationships in a typical FETCH machine cycle. Events that occur in each state are referenced to transitions of the ϕ_1 and ϕ_2 clock pulses.

Instructions for the 8080A require from one to five machine cycles for complete execution. The 8080A sends out 8 bits of status information on the data bus at the beginning of each machine cycle (during SYNC time). The following table defines the status information.

STATUS INFORMATION DEFINITION

Symbols	Data Bus Bit	Definition
INTA*	D_0	Acknowledge signal for INTERRUPT request. Signal should be used to gate a restart instruction onto the data bus when DBIN is active.
$\overline{WO}$	D_1	Indicates that the operation in the current machine cycle will be a WRITE memory or OUTPUT function ($\overline{WO}$ = 0). Otherwise, a READ memory or INPUT operation will be executed.
STACK	D_2	Indicates that the address bus holds the pushdown stack address from the Stack Pointer.
HLTA	D_3	Acknowledge signal for HALT instruction.
OUT	D_4	Indicates that the address bus contains the address of an output device and the data bus will contain the output data when $\overline{WR}$ is active.
M_1	D_5	Provides a signal to indicate that the CPU is in the fetch cycle for the first byte of an instruction.
INP*	D_6	Indicates that the address bus contains the address of an input device and the input data should be placed on the data bus when DBIN is active.
MEMR*	D_7	Designates that the data bus will be used for memory read data.

*These three status bits can be used to control the flow of data onto the 8080 data bus.

8080A STATUS LATCH

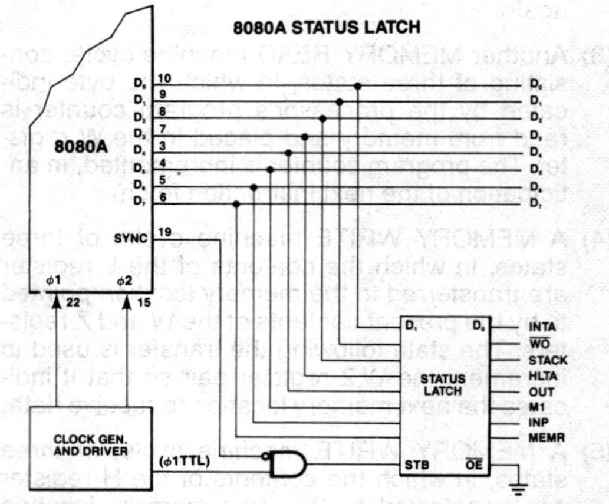

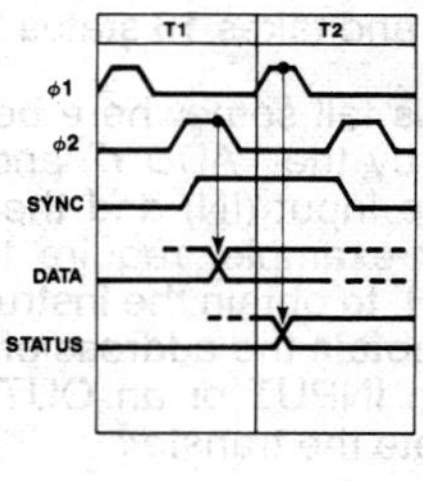

STATUS WORD CHART

TYPE OF MACHINE CYCLE

DATA BUS BIT	STATUS INFORMATION	① INSTRUCTION FETCH	② MEMORY READ	③ MEMORY WRITE	④ STACK READ	⑤ STACK WRITE	⑥ INPUT READ	⑦ OUTPUT WRITE	⑧ INTERRUPT ACKNOWLEDGE	⑨ HALT ACKNOWLEDGE	⑩ INTERRUPT ACKNOWLEDGE WHILE HALT
D_0	INTA	0	0	0	0	0	0	0	1	0	1
D_1	$\overline{WO}$	1	1	0	1	0	1	0	1	1	1
D_2	STACK	0	0	0	1	1	0	0	0	0	0
D_3	HLTA	0	0	0	0	0	0	0	0	1	1
D_4	OUT	0	0	0	0	0	0	1	0	0	0
D_5	M_1	1	0	0	0	0	0	0	1	0	1
D_6	INP	0	0	0	0	0	1	0	0	0	0
D_7	MEMR	1	1	0	1	0	0	0	0	1	0

Ⓝ STATUS WORD

Table 4-1. 8080 Status Bit Definitions

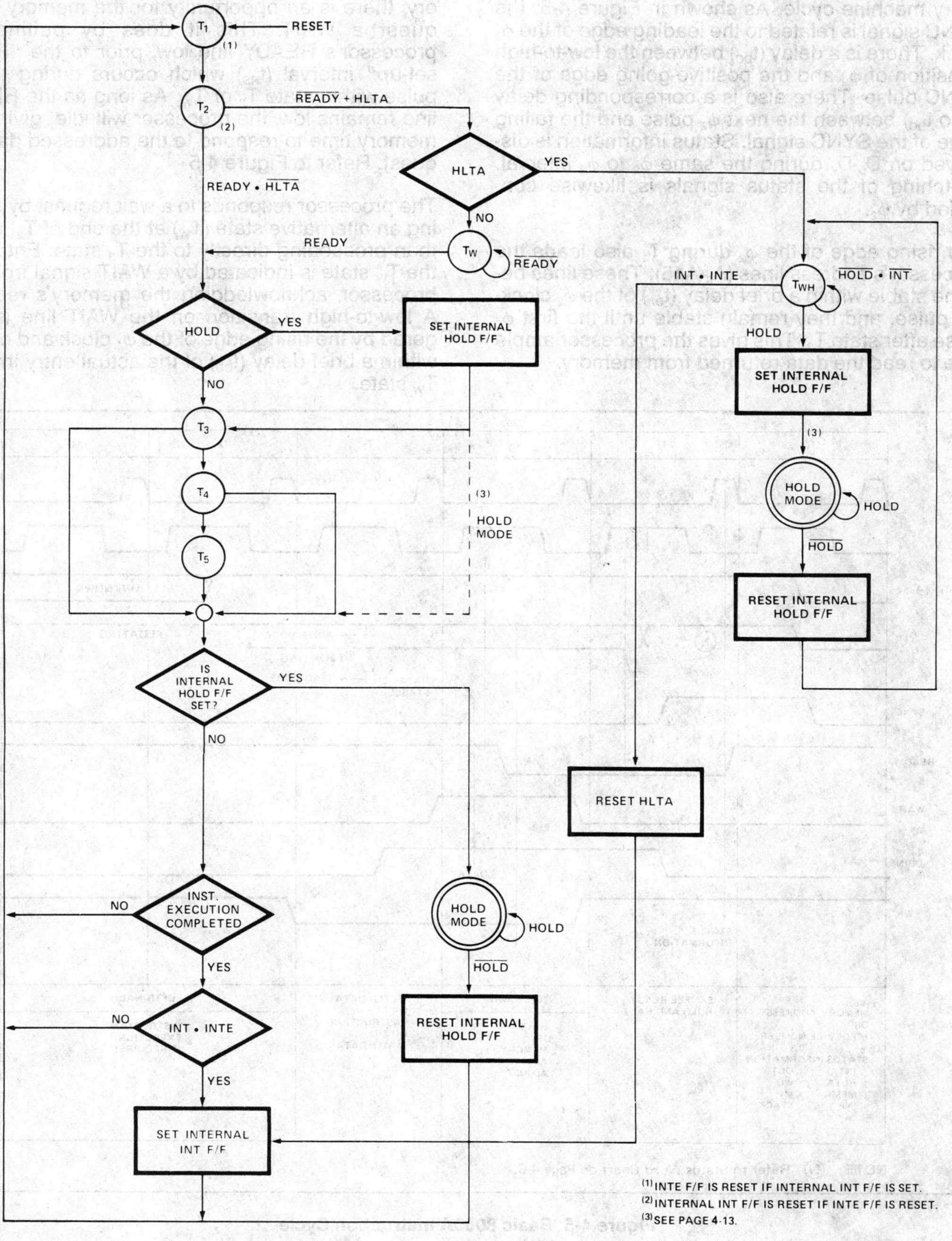

Figure 4-4. CPU State Transition Diagram

The SYNC signal identifies the first state (T_1) in every machine cycle. As shown in Figure 4-5, the SYNC signal is related to the leading edge of the ϕ_2 clock. There is a delay (t_{DC}) between the low-to-high transition of ϕ_2 and the positive-going edge of the SYNC pulse. There also is a corresponding delay (also t_{DC}) between the next ϕ_2 pulse and the falling edge of the SYNC signal. Status information is displayed on D_0-D_7 during the same ϕ_2 to ϕ_2 interval. Switching of the status signals is likewise controlled by ϕ_2.

The rising edge of the ϕ_2 during T_1 also loads the processor's address lines (A_0-A15). These lines become stable within a brief delay (t_{DA}) of the ϕ_2 clocking pulse, and they remain stable until the first ϕ_2 pulse after state T_3. This gives the processor ample time to read the data returned from memory.

Once the processor has sent an address to memory, there is an opportunity for the memory to request a WAIT. This it does by pulling the processor's READY line low, prior to the "Ready set-up" interval (t_{RS}) which occurs during the ϕ_2 pulse within state T_2 or T_W. As long as the READY line remains low, the processor will idle, giving the memory time to respond to the addressed data request. Refer to Figure 4-5

The processor responds to a wait request by entering an alternative state (T_W) at the end of T_2, rather than proceeding directly to the T_3 state. Entry into the T_W state is indicated by a WAIT signal from the processor, acknowledging the memory's request. A low-to-high transition on the WAIT line is triggered by the rising edge of the ϕ_1 clock and occurs within a brief delay (t_{DC}) of the actual entry into the T_W state.

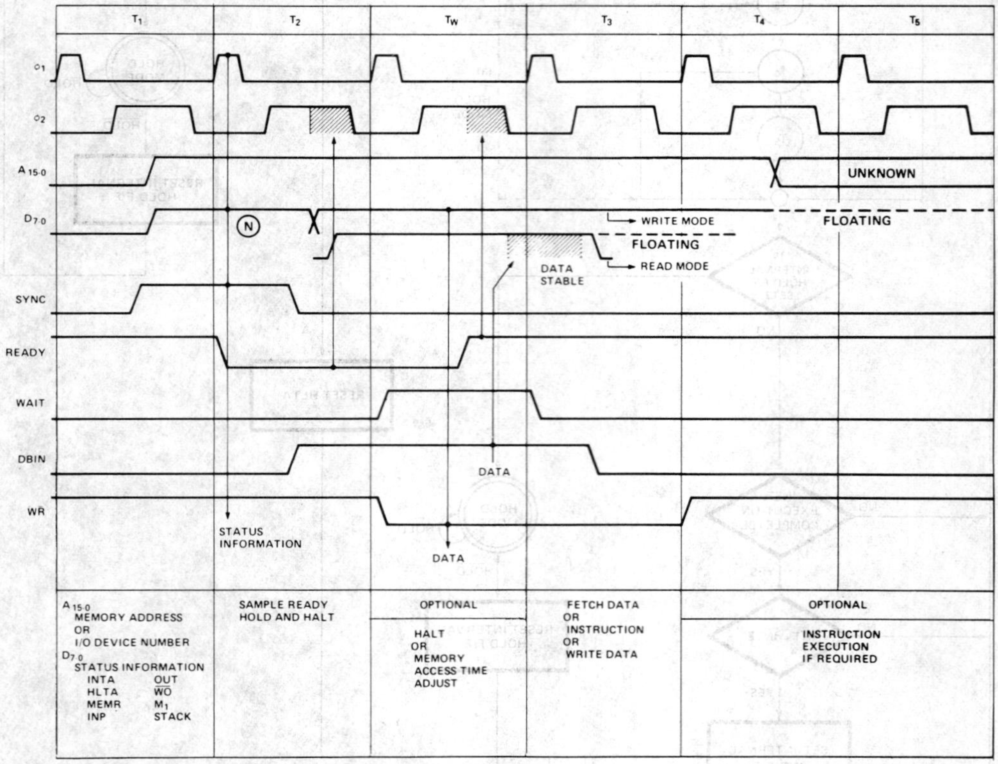

NOTE: (N) Refer to Status Word Chart on Page 4-6.

Figure 4-5 Basic 8080A Instruction Cycle

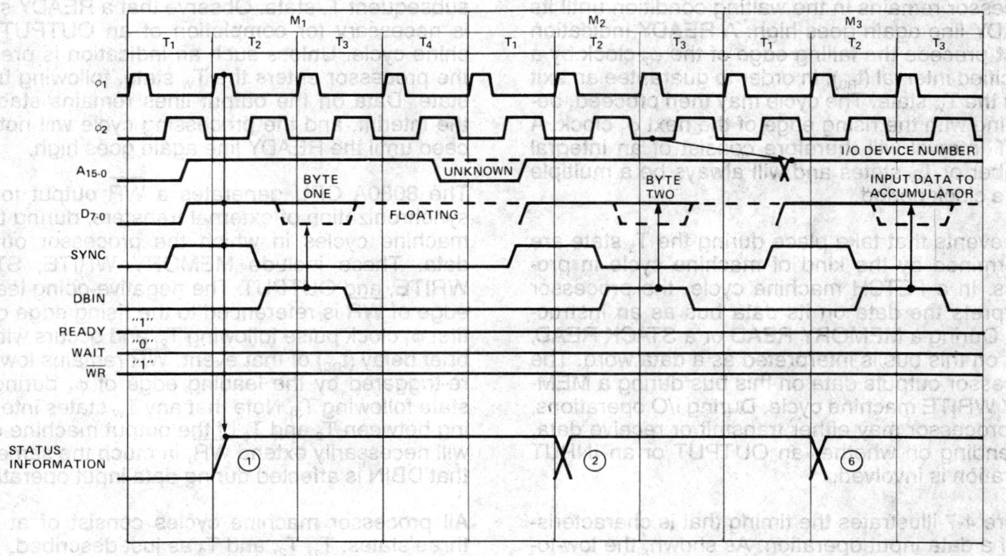

NOTE: (N) Refer to Status Word Chart on Page 4-6.

Figure 4-6. Input Instruction Cycle

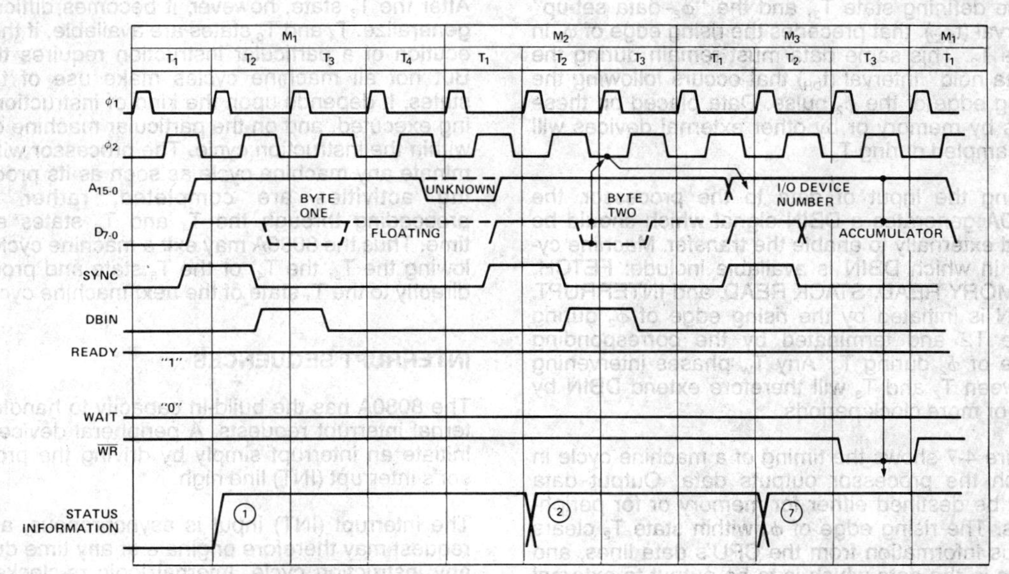

NOTE: (N) Refer to Status Word Chart on Page 4-6.

Figure 4-7. Output Instruction Cycle

A wait period may be of indefinite duration. The processor remains in the waiting condition until its READY line again goes high. A READY indication **must** precede the falling edge of the ϕ_2 clock by a specified interval (t_{RS}), in order to guarantee an exit from the T_W state. The cycle may then proceed, beginning with the rising edge of the next ϕ_1 clock. A WAIT interval will therefore consist of an integral number of T_W states and will always be a multiple of the clock period.

The events that take place during the T_3 state are determined by the kind of machine cycle in progress. In a FETCH machine cycle, the processor interprets the data on its data bus as an instruction. During a MEMORY READ or a STACK READ, data on this bus is interpreted as a data word. The processor outputs data on this bus during a MEMORY WRITE machine cycle. During I/O operations, the processor may either transmit or receive data, depending on whether an OUTPUT or an INPUT operation is involved.

Figure 4-7 illustrates the timing that is characteristic of a data input operation. As shown, the low-to-high transition of ϕ_2 during T_2 clears status information from the processor's data lines, preparing these lines for the receipt of incoming data. The data presented to the processor must have stabilized prior to both the "ϕ_1–data set-up" interval (t_{DS1}), that precedes the falling edge of the ϕ_1 pulse defining state T_3, and the "ϕ_2–data set-up" interval (t_{DS2}), that precedes the rising edge of ϕ_2 in state T_3. This same data must remain during the "data hold" interval (t_{DH}) that occurs following the rising edge of the ϕ_2 pulse. Data placed on these lines by memory or by other external devices will be sampled during T_3.

During the input of data to the processor, the 8080A generates a DBIN signal which should be used externally to enable the transfer. Machine cycles in which DBIN is available include: FETCH, MEMORY READ, STACK READ, and INTERRUPT. DBIN is initiated by the rising edge of ϕ_2 during state T2 and terminated by the corresponding edge of ϕ_2 during T_3. Any T_W phases intervening between T_2 and T_3 will therefore extend DBIN by one or more clock periods.

Figure 4-7 shows the timing of a machine cycle in which the processor outputs data. Output data may be destined either for memory or for peripherals. The rising edge of ϕ_2 within state T_2 clears status information from the CPU's data lines, and loads in the data which is to be output to external devices. This substitution takes place within the "data output delay" interval (t_{DD}) following the ϕ_2 clock's leading edge. Data on the bus remains stable throughout the remainder of the machine cycle, until replaced by updated status information in the subsequent T_1 state. Observe that a READY signal is necessary for completion of an OUTPUT machine cycle. Unless such an indication is present, the processor enters the T_W state, following the T_2 state. Data on the output lines remains stable in the interim, and the processing cycle will not proceed until the READY line again goes high.

The 8080A CPU generates a $\overline{WR}$ output for the synchronization of external transfers, during those machine cycles in which the processor outputs data. These include MEMORY WRITE, STACK WRITE, and OUTPUT. The negative-going leading edge of $\overline{WR}$ is referenced to the rising edge of the first ϕ_1 clock pulse following T_2, and occurs within a brief delay (t_{DC}) of that event. $\overline{WR}$ remains low until re-triggered by the leading edge of ϕ_1 during the state following T_3. Note that any T_W states intervening between T_2 and T_3 of the output machine cycle will necessarily extend $\overline{WR}$, in much the same way that DBIN is affected during data input operations.

All processor machine cycles consist of at least three states: T_1, T_2, and T_3 as just described. If the processor has to wait for a response from the peripheral or memory with which it is communicating, then the machine cycle may also contain one or more T_W states. During the three basic states, data is transferred to or from the processor.

After the T_3 state, however, it becomes difficult to generalize. T_4 and T_5 states are available, if the execution of a particular instruction requires them. But not all machine cycles make use of these states. It depends upon the kind of instruction being executed, and on the particular machine cycle within the instruction cycle. The processor will terminate any machine cycle as soon as its processing activities are completed, rather than proceeding through the T_4 and T_5 states every time. Thus the 8080A may exit a machine cycle following the T_3, the T_4, or the T_5 state and proceed directly to the T_1 state of the next machine cycle.

INTERRUPT SEQUENCES

The 8080A has the build-in capacity to handle external interrupt requests. A peripheral device can initiate an interrupt simply by driving the processor's interrupt (INT) line high.

The interrupt (INT) input is asynchronous, and a request may therefore originate at any time during any instruction cycle. Internal logic re-clocks the external request, so that a proper correspondence with the driving clock is established. As Figure 4-8 shows, an interrupt request (INT) arriving during the time that the interrupt enable line (INTE) is high, acts in coincidence with the ϕ_2 clock to set the internal interrupt latch. This event takes place during the last state of the instruction cycle in which the request occurs, thus ensuring that any instruction in progress is completed before the interrupt can be processed.

The INTERRUPT machine cycle which follows the arrival of an enabled interrupt request resembles an ordinary FETCH machine cycle in most respects. The M_1 status bit is transmitted as usual during the SYNC interval. It is accompanied, however, by an INTA status bit (D_0) which acknowledges the external request. The contents of the program counter are latched onto the CPU's address lines during T_1, but the counter itself is not incremented during the INTERRUPT machine cycle, as it otherwise would be. In this way, the pre-interrupt status of the program counter is preserved, so that data in the counter may be restored by the interrupted program after the interrupt request has been processed.

The interrupt cycle is otherwise indistinguishable from an ordinary FETCH machine cycle. The processor itself takes no further special action. It is the responsibility of the peripheral logic to see that an eight-bit interrupt instruction is "jammed" onto the processor's data bus during state T_3. In a typical system, this means that the data-in bus from memory must be temporarily disconnected from the processor's main data bus, so that the interrupting device can command the main bus without interference.

The 8080A's instruction set provides a special one-byte call which facilitates the processing of interrupts (the ordinary program Call takes three bytes). This is the RESTART instruction (RST). A variable three-bit field embedded in the eight-bit field of the RST enables the interrupting device to direct a Call to one of eight fixed memory locations. The decimal addresses of these dedicated locations are: 0, 8, 16, 24, 32, 40, 48, and 56. Any of these addresses may be used to store the first instruction(s) of a routine designed to service the requirements of an interrupting device. Since the (RST) is a call, completion of the instruction also stores the old program counter contents on the STACK.

HOLD SEQUENCES

The 8080A CPU contains provisions for Direct Memory Access (DMA) operations. By applying a HOLD to the appropriate control pin on the processor, an external device can cause the CPU to suspend its normal operations and relinquish control of the address and data busses. The processor

STATE	ASSOCIATED ACTIVITIES
T_1	A memory address or I/O device number is placed on the Address Bus ($A_{15\text{-}0}$); status information is placed on Data Bus ($D_{7\text{-}0}$).
T_2	The CPU samples the READY and HOLD inputs and checks for halt instruction.
TW (optional)	Processor enters wait state if READY is low or if HALT instruction has been executed.
T3	An instruction byte (FETCH machine cycle), data byte (MEMORY READ, STACK READ, INPUT) or interrupt instruction (INTERRUPT machine cycle) is input to the CPU from the Data Bus; or a data byte (MEMORY WRITE, STACK WRITE or OUTPUT machine cycle) is output onto the data bus.
T4 T5 (optional)	States T_4 and T_5 are available if the execution of a particular instruction requires them; if not, the CPU may skip one or both of them. T_4 and T_5 are only used for internal processor operations.

Table 4-2 State Definitions

responds to a request of this kind by floating its address to other devices sharing the busses. At the same time, the processor acknowledges the HOLD by placing a high on its HLDA outpin pin. During an acknowledged HOLD, the address and data busses are under control of the peripheral which originated the request, enabling it to conduct memory transfers without processor intervention.

Like the interrupt, the HOLD input is synchronized internally. A HOLD signal must be stable prior to the "Hold set-up" interval (t_{HS}), that precedes the rising edge of ϕ_2.

Figues 4-9 and 4-10 illustrate the timing involved in HOLD operations. Note the delay between the asynchronous HOLD REQUEST and the re-clocked HOLD. As shown in the diagram, a coincidence of the READY, the HOLD, and the ϕ_2 clocks sets the internal hold latch. Setting the latch enable the subsequent rising edge of the ϕ_1 clock pulse to trigger the HLDA output as described below.

Acknowledgment of the HOLD REQUEST precedes slightly the actual floating of the processor's address and data lines. The processor acknowledges a HOLD at the beginning of T_3, if a read or an input machine cycle is in progress (see Figure 4-9). Otherwise, acknowledgment is deferred until the beginning of the state following T_3 (see Figure 4-10). In both cases, however, the HLDA goes high within a specified delay (t_{DC}) of the rising edge of the selected ϕ_1 clock pulse. Address and data lines are floated within a brief delay after the rising edge of the next ϕ_2 clock pulse. This relationship is also shown in the diagrams.

To all outward appearances, the processor has suspended its operations once the address and data busses are floated. Internally, however, certain functions may continue. If a HOLD REQUEST is acknowledged at T_3, and if the processor is in the middle of a machine cycle which requires four or more states to complete, the CPU proceeds through T_4 and T_5 before coming to a rest. Not until the end of the machine cycle is reached will processing activities cease. Internal processing is thus

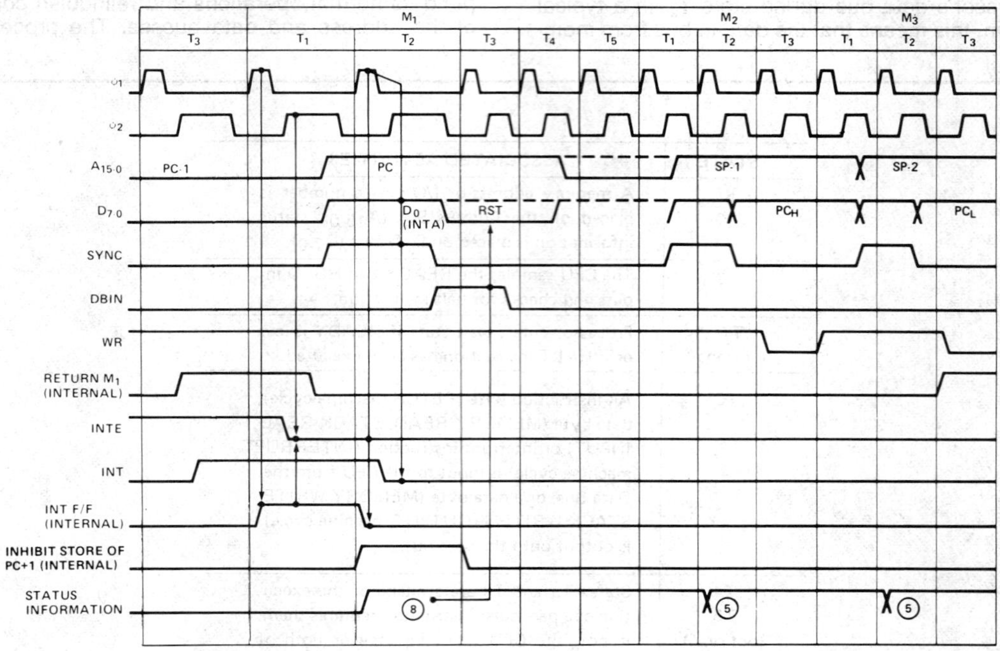

NOTE: Ⓝ Refer to Status Word Chart on Page 4-6.

Figure 4-8 Interrupt Timing

permitted to overlap the external DMA transfer, improving both the efficiency and the speed of the entire system.

The processor exists the holding state through a sequence similar to that by which it entered. A HOLD REQUEST is terminated asynchronously when the external device has completed its data transfer. The HLDA output returns to a low level following the leading edge of the next ϕ_1 clock pulse. Normal processing resumes with the machine cycle following the last cycle that was executed.

HALT SEQUENCES

When a halt instruction (HLT) is executed, the CPU enters the halt state (T_{WH}) after state T_2 of the next machine cycle, as shown in Figure 4-11. There are only three ways in which the 8080A can exit the halt state:

- A high on the RESET line will always reset the 8080A to state $T\phi_1$; RESET also clears the program counter.
- A HOLD input will cause the 8080A to enter the hold state, as previously described. When the HOLD line goes low, the 8080A re-enters the halt state on the rising edge of the next ϕ_1 clock pulse.
- An interrupt (i.e., INT goes high while INTE is enabled) will cause the 8080A to exit the Halt state and enter state T_1 on the rising edge of the next ϕ_1 clock pulse. NOTE: The interrupt enable (INTE) flag **must** be set when the halt state is entered; otherwise, the 8080A will only be able to exit via a RESET signal.

Figure 4-12 illustrates halt sequencing in flow chart form.

START-UP OF THE 8080A CPU

When power is applied initially to the 8080A, the processor begins operating immediately. The contents of its program counter, stack pointer, and the other working registers are naturally subject to random factors and cannot be specified. For this reason, it will be necessary to begin the power-up sequence with RESET.

An external RESET signal of three clock period duration (minimum) restores the processor's internal program counter to zero. Program execution thus begins with memory location zero, following a RESET. Systems which require the processor to wait for an explicit start-up signal will store a halt instruction (EI, HLT) in the first two locations. A manual or an automatic INTERRUPT will be used for starting. In other systems, the processor may begin executing its stored program immediately. Note, however, that the RESET has no effect on status flags, or on any of the processor's working registers (accumulator, registers, or stack pointer). The contents of these registers remain indeterminate, until initialized explicitly by the program.

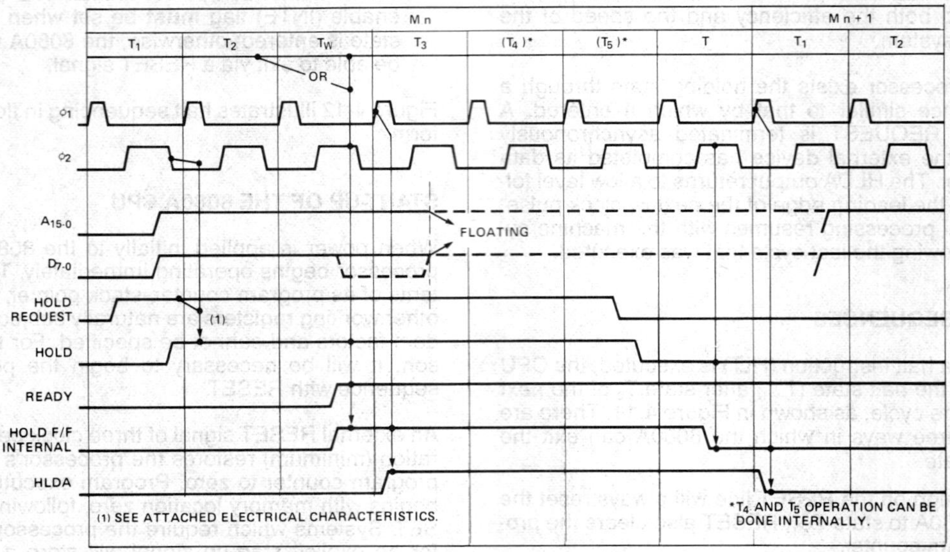

Figure 4-9. HOLD Operation (Read Mode)

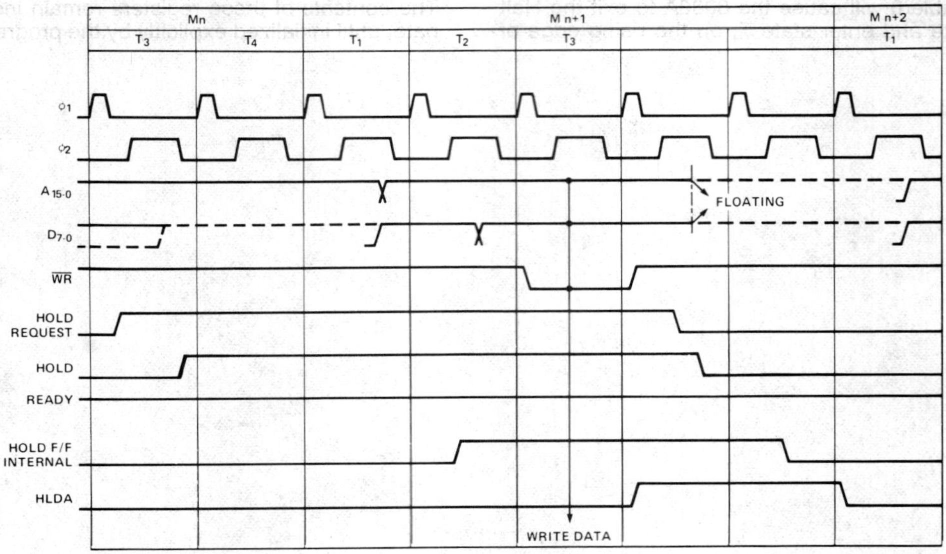

Figure 4-10. HOLD Operation (Write Mode)

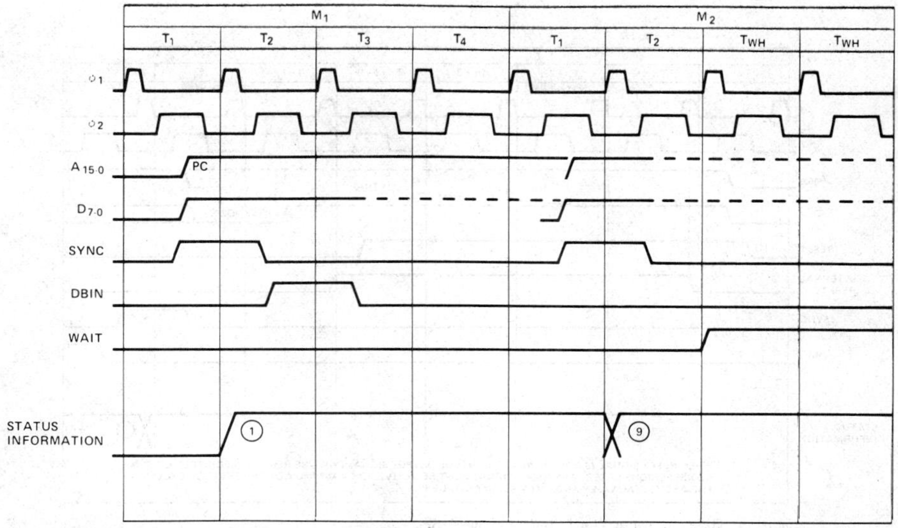

NOTE: (N) Refer to Status Word Chart on Page 4-6

Figure 4-11. HALT Timing

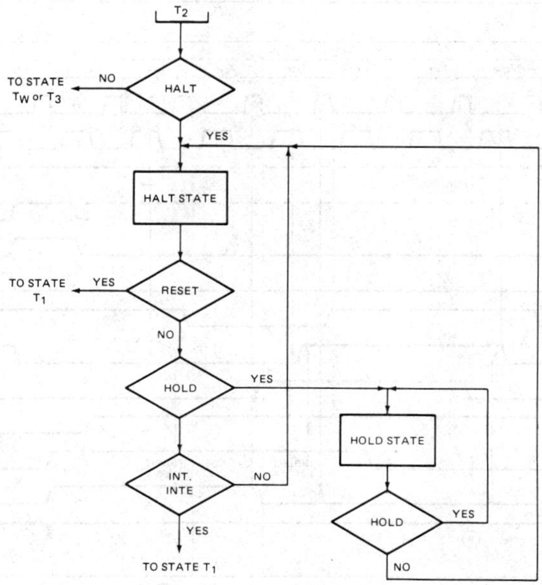

Figure 4-12. HALT Sequence Flow Chart

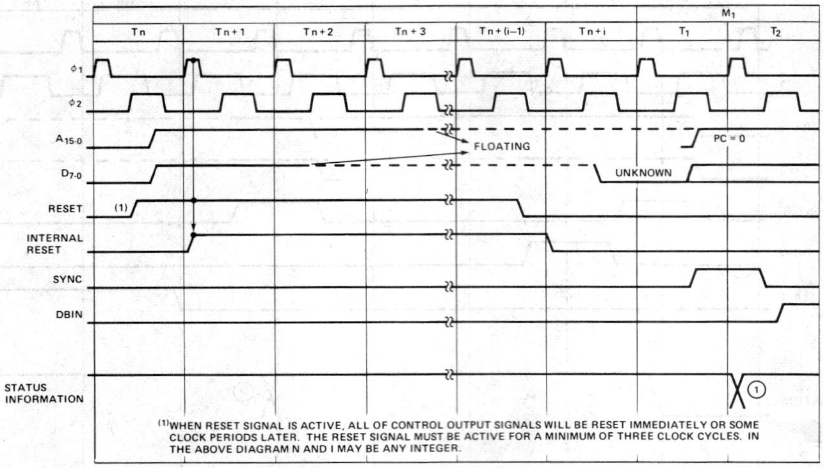

NOTE: (N) Refer to Status Word Chart on Page 4–6.

Figure 4-13. Reset

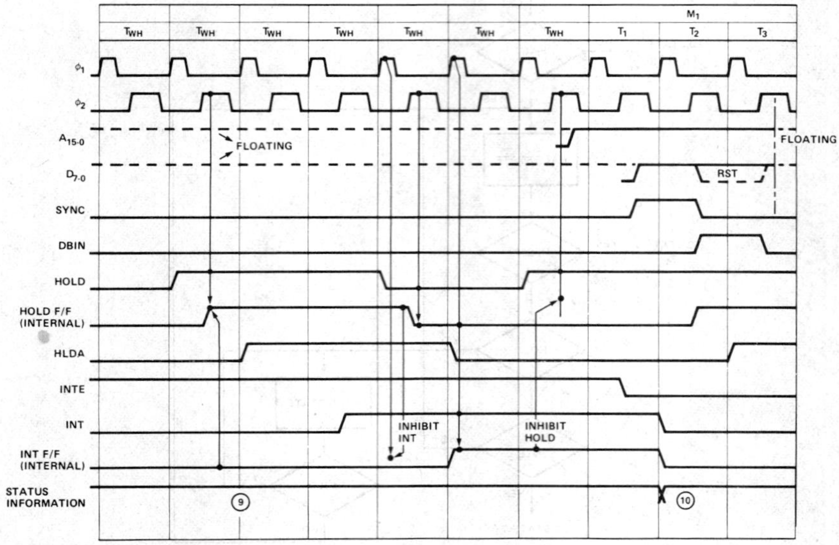

NOTE: (N) Refer to Status Word Chart on Page 4–6.

Figure 4-14. Relation between HOLD and INT in the HALT State

MNEMONIC	OP CODE		M1[1]					M2		
	$D_7 D_6 D_5 D_4$	$D_3 D_2 D_1 D_0$	T1	T2[2]	T3	T4	T5	T1	T2[2]	T3
MOV r1, r2	0 1 D D	D S S S	PC OUT STATUS	PC = PC +1	INST→TMP/IR	(SSS)→TMP	(TMP)→DDD	[5]		
MOV r, M	0 1 D D	D 1 1 0				X[3]		HL OUT STATUS[6]	DATA →	DDD
MOV M, r	0 1 1 1	0 S S S				(SSS)→TMP		HL OUT STATUS[7]	(TMP) →	DATA BUS
SPHL	1 1 1 1	1 0 0 1				(HL) →	SP			
MVI r, data	0 0 D D	D 1 1 0				X		PC OUT STATUS[6]	PC = PC + 1 B2 →	DDD
MVI M, data	0 0 1 1	0 1 1 0				X			PC = PC + 1 B2 →	TMP
LXI rp, data	0 0 R P	0 0 0 1				X			PC = PC + 1 B2 →	rl
LDA addr	0 0 1 1	1 0 1 0				X			PC = PC + 1 B2 →	Z
STA addr	0 0 1 1	0 0 1 0				X			PC = PC + 1 B2 →	Z
LHLD addr	0 0 1 0	1 0 1 0				X			PC = PC + 1 B2 →	Z
SHLD addr	0 0 1 0	0 0 1 0				X		PC OUT STATUS[6]	PC = PC + 1 B2 →	Z
LDAX rp[4]	0 0 R P	1 0 1 0				X		rp OUT STATUS[6]	DATA →	A
STAX rp[4]	0 0 R P	0 0 1 0				X		rp OUT STATUS[7]	(A) →	DATA BUS
XCHG	1 1 1 0	1 0 1 1				X		[11]	(HL)↔(DE)	
ADD r	1 0 0 0	0 S S S				(SSS)→TMP (A)→ACT		[9]	(ACT)+(TMP)→A	
ADD M	1 0 0 0	0 1 1 0				(A)→ACT		HL OUT STATUS[6]	DATA →	TMP
ADI data	1 1 0 0	0 1 1 0				(A)→ACT		PC OUT STATUS[6]	PC = PC + 1 B2 →	TMP
ADC r	1 0 0 0	1 S S S				(SSS)→TMP (A)→ACT		[9]	(ACT)+(TMP)+CY→A	
ADC M	1 0 0 0	1 1 1 0				(A)→ACT		HL OUT STATUS[6]	DATA →	TMP
ACI data	1 1 0 0	1 1 1 0				(A)→ACT		PC OUT STATUS[6]	PC = PC + 1 B2 →	TMP
SUB r	1 0 0 1	0 S S S				(SSS)→TMP (A)→ACT		[9]	(ACT)-(TMP)→A	
SUB M	1 0 0 1	0 1 1 0				(A)→ACT		HL OUT STATUS[6]	DATA →	TMP
SUI data	1 1 0 1	0 1 1 0				(A)→ACT		PC OUT STATUS[6]	PC = PC + 1 B2 →	TMP
SBB r	1 0 0 1	1 S S S				(SSS)→TMP (A)→ACT		[9]	(ACT)-(TMP)-CY→A	
SBB M	1 0 0 1	1 1 1 0				(A)→ACT		HL OUT STATUS[6]	DATA →	TMP
SBI data	1 1 0 1	1 1 1 0				(A)→ACT		PC OUT STATUS[6]	PC = PC + 1 B2 →	TMP
INR r	0 0 D D	D 1 0 0				(DDD)→TMP (TMP) + 1→ALU	ALU→DDD			
INR M	0 0 1 1	0 1 0 0				X		HL OUT STATUS[6]	DATA → (TMP)+1 →	TMP ALU
DCR r	0 0 D D	D 1 0 1				(DDD)→TMP (TMP)-1→ALU	ALU→DDD			
DCR M	0 0 1 1	0 1 0 1				X		HL OUT STATUS[6]	DATA → (TMP)-1 →	TMP ALU
INX rp	0 0 R P	0 0 1 1				(RP) + 1 →	RP			
DCX rp	0 0 R P	1 0 1 1				(RP) - 1 →	RP			
DAD rp[8]	0 0 R P	1 0 0 1				X		(rl)→ACT	(L)→TMP, (ACT)+(TMP)→ALU	ALU→L, CY
DAA	0 0 1 0	0 1 1 1				66→ACT [10] (A)→TMP		[9]	DAA→A FLAGS [10]	
ANA r	1 0 1 0	0 S S S				(SSS)→TMP (A)→ACT		[9]	(ACT)+(TMP)→A	
ANA M	1 0 1 0	0 1 1 0	PC OUT STATUS	PC = PC + 1	INST→TMP/IR	(A)→ACT		HL OUT STATUS[6]	DATA →	TMP

M3			M4			M5				
T1	T2[2]	T3	T1	T2[2]	T3	T1	T2[2]	T3	T4	T5
HL OUT STATUS[7]		(TMP) → DATA BUS								
PC OUT STATUS[6]	PC = PC + 1	B3 → rh								
↑	PC = PC + 1	B3 → W	WZ OUT STATUS[6]	DATA → A						
	PC = PC + 1	B3 → W	WZ OUT STATUS[7]	(A) → DATA BUS						
↓	PC = PC + 1	B3 → W	WZ OUT STATUS[6]	DATA → L WZ = WZ + 1		WZ OUT STATUS[6]	DATA → H			
PC OUT STATUS[6]	PC = PC + 1	B3 → W	WZ OUT STATUS[7]	(L) → DATA BUS WZ = WZ + 1		WZ OUT STATUS[7]	(H) → DATA BUS			
[9]	(ACT)+(TMP)→A									
[9]	(ACT)+(TMP)→A									
[9]	(ACT)+(TMP)+CY→A									
[9]	(ACT)+(TMP)+CY→A									
[9]	(ACT)-(TMP)→A									
[9]	(ACT)-(TMP)→A									
[9]	(ACT)-(TMP)-CY→A									
[9]	(ACT)-(TMP)-CY→A									
HL OUT STATUS[7]		ALU → DATA BUS								
HL OUT STATUS[7]		ALU → DATA BUS								
(rh)→ACT	(H)→TMP (ACT)+(TMP)+CY→ALU	ALU→H, CY								
[9]	(ACT)+(TMP)→A									

MNEMONIC	OP CODE		M1[1]					M2		
	$D_7 D_6 D_5 D_4$	$D_3 D_2 D_1 D_0$	T1	T2[2]	T3	T4	T5	T1	T2[2]	T3
ANI data	1 1 1 0	0 1 1 0	PC OUT STATUS	PC = PC + 1	INST→TMP/IR	(A)→ACT		PC OUT STATUS[6]	PC = PC + 1 B2	→TMP
XRA r	1 0 1 0	1 S S S				(A)→ACT (SSS)→TMP		[9]	(ACT)+(TPM)→A	
XRA M	1 0 1 0	1 1 1 0				(A)→ACT		HL OUT STATUS[6]	DATA	→TMP
XRI data	1 1 1 0	1 1 1 0				(A)→ACT		PC OUT STATUS[6]	PC = PC + 1 B2	→TMP
ORA r	1 0 1 1	0 S S S				(A)→ACT (SSS)→TMP		[9]	(ACT)+(TMP)→A	
ORA M	1 0 1 1	0 1 1 0				(A)→ACT		HL OUT STATUS[6]	DATA	→TMP
ORI data	1 1 1 1	0 1 1 0				(A)→ACT		PC OUT STATUS[6]	PC = PC + 1 B2	→TMP
CMP r	1 0 1 1	1 S S S				(A)→ACT (SSS)→TMP		[9]	(ACT)-(TMP), FLAGS	
CMP M	1 0 1 1	1 1 1 0				(A)→ACT		HL OUT STATUS[6]	DATA	→TMP
CPI data	1 1 1 1	1 1 1 0				(A)→ACT		PC OUT STATUS[6]	PC = PC + 1 B2	→TMP
RLC	0 0 0 0	0 1 1 1				(A)→ALU ROTATE		[9]	ALU→A, CY	
RRC	0 0 0 0	1 1 1 1				(A)→ALU ROTATE		[9]	ALU→A, CY	
RAL	0 0 0 1	0 1 1 1				(A), CY→ALU ROTATE		[9]	ALU→A, CY	
RAR	0 0 0 1	1 1 1 1				(A), CY→ALU ROTATE		[9]	ALU→A, CY	
CMA	0 0 1 0	1 1 1 1				A→ALU COMPLEMENT		[9]	ALU→A	
CMC	0 0 1 1	1 1 1 1				CY→ALU COMPLEMENT		[9]	ALU→CY	
STC	0 0 1 1	0 1 1 1				1→ALU		[9]	ALU→CY	
JMP addr	1 1 0 0	0 0 1 1				X		PC OUT STATUS[6]	PC = PC + 1 B2	→Z
J cond addr[17]	1 1 C C	C 0 1 0				JUDGE CONDITION		PC OUT STATUS[6]	PC = PC + 1 B2	→Z
CALL addr	1 1 0 0	1 1 0 1				SP = SP - 1		PC OUT STATUS[6]	PC = PC + 1 B2	→Z
C cond addr[17]	1 1 C C	C 1 0 0				JUDGE CONDITION IF TRUE, SP = SP - 1		PC OUT STATUS[6]	PC = PC + 1 B2	→Z
RET	1 1 0 0	1 0 0 1				X		SP OUT STATUS[15]	SP = SP + 1 DATA	→PCL
R cond addr[17]	1 1 C C	C 0 0 0			INST→TMP/IR	JUDGE CONDITION[14]		SP OUT STATUS[15]	SP = SP + 1 DATA	→PCL
RST n	1 1 N N	N 1 1 1			ϕ→W INST→TMP/IR	SP = SP - 1		SP OUT STATUS[16]	SP = SP - 1 (PCH)	→DATA BUS
PCHL	1 1 1 0	1 0 0 1			INST→TMP/IR	(HL) → PC				
PUSH rp	1 1 R P	0 1 0 1				SP = SP - 1		SP OUT STATUS[16]	SP = SP - 1 (rh)	→DATA BUS
PUSH PSW	1 1 1 1	0 1 0 1				SP = SP - 1		SP OUT STATUS[16]	SP = SP - 1 (A)	→DATA BUS
POP rp	1 1 R P	0 0 0 1				X		SP OUT STATUS[15]	SP = SP + 1 DATA	→rl
POP PSW	1 1 1 1	0 0 0 1				X		SP OUT STATUS[15]	SP = SP + 1 DATA	→FLAGS
XTHL	1 1 1 0	0 0 1 1				X		SP OUT STATUS[15]	SP = SP + 1 DATA	→Z
IN port	1 1 0 1	1 0 1 1				X		PC OUT STATUS[6]	PC = PC + 1 B2	→Z, W
OUT port	1 1 0 1	0 0 1 1				X		PC OUT STATUS[6]	PC = PC + 1 B2	→Z, W
EI	1 1 1 1	1 0 1 1				X		SET INTE F/F [11]		
DI	1 1 1 1	0 0 1 1				X		RESET INTE F/F [11]		
HLT	0 1 1 1	0 1 1 0				X		PC OUT STATUS	HALT MODE[19]	
NOP	0 0 0 0	0 0 0 0	PC OUT STATUS	PC = PC + 1	INST→TMP/IR	X				

M3			M4			M5						
T1	T2[2]	T3	T1	T2[2]	T3	T1	T2[2]	T3	T4	T5		
[9]	(ACT)+(TMP)→A											
[9]	(ACT)+(TMP)→A											
[9]	(ACT)+(TMP)→A											
[9]	(ACT)+(TMP)→A											
[9]	(ACT)+(TMP)→A											
[9]	(ACT)-(TMP); FLAGS											
[9]	(ACT)-(TMP); FLAGS											
PC OUT STATUS[6]	PC = PC + 1 B3 → W										WZ OUT STATUS[11]	(WZ) + 1 → PC
PC OUT STATUS[6]	PC = PC + 1 B3 → W										WZ OUT STATUS[11,12]	(WZ) + 1 → PC
PC OUT STATUS[6]	PC = PC + 1 B3 → W		SP OUT STATUS[16]	(PCH) → DATA BUS SP = SP - 1		SP OUT STATUS[16]	(PCL) → DATA BUS				WZ OUT STATUS[11]	(WZ) + 1 → PC
PC OUT STATUS[6]	PC = PC + 1 B3 → W[13]		SP OUT STATUS[16]	(PCH) → DATA BUS SP = SP - 1		SP OUT STATUS[16]	(PCL) → DATA BUS				WZ OUT STATUS[11,12]	(WZ) + 1 → PC
SP OUT STATUS[15]	SP = SP + 1 DATA → PCH											
SP OUT STATUS[15]	SP = SP + 1 DATA → PCH											
SP OUT STATUS[16]	(TMP = 00NNN000) → Z (PCL) → DATA BUS										WZ OUT STATUS[11]	(WZ) + 1 → PC
SP OUT STATUS[16]	(rl) → DATA BUS											
SP OUT STATUS[16]	FLAGS → DATA BUS											
SP OUT STATUS[15]	SP = SP + 1 DATA → rh											
SP OUT STATUS[15]	SP = SP + 1 DATA → A											
SP OUT STATUS[15]	DATA → W		SP OUT STATUS[16]	(H) → DATA BUS SP = SP − 1		SP OUT STATUS[16]	(L) → DATA BUS		(WZ) → HL			
WZ OUT STATUS[18]	DATA → A											
WZ OUT STATUS[18]	(A) → DATA BUS											

NOTES:

1. The first memory cycle (M1) is always an instruction fetch; the first (or only) byte, containing the op code, is fetched during this cycle.
2. If the READY input from memory is not high during T2 of each memory cycle, the processor will enter a wait state (TW) until READY is sampled as high.
3. States T4 and T5 are present, as required, for operations which are completely internal to the CPU. The contents of the internal bus during T4 and T5 are available at the data bus; this is designed for testing purposes only. An "X" denotes that the state is present, but is only used for such internal operations as instruction decoding.
4. Only register pairs rp = B (registers B and C) or rp = D (registers D and E) may be specified.
5. The shaded states are skipped.
6. Memory read sub-cycles; an instruction or data word will be read.
7. Memory write sub-cycle.
8. The READY signal is not required during the second and third sub-cycles (M2 and M3). The HOLD signal is accepted during M2 and M3). The HOLD signal is accepted during M2 and M3. The SYNC signal is not generated during M2 and M3. During the execution of DAD, M2 and M3 are required for an internal register-pair add; memory is not referenced.
9. The results of these arithmetic, logical or rotate instructions are not moved into the accumulator (A) until state T2 of the next instruction cycle. That is, A is loaded while the next instruction is being fetched; this overlapping of operations allows for faster processing.
10. If the value of the least significant 4-bits of the accumulator is greater than 9 _or_ if the auxiliary carry bit is set, 6 is added to the accumulator. If the value of the most significant 4-bits of the accumulator is now greater than 9, _or_ if the carry bit is set, 6 is added to the most significant 4-bits of the accumulator.
11. This represents the first sub-cycle (the instruction fetch) of the next instruction cycle.
12. If the condition was met, the contents of the register pair WZ are output on the address lines (A_{0-15}) instead of the contents of the program counter (PC).
13. If the condition was not met, sub-cycles M4 and M5 are skipped; the processor instead proceeds immediately to the instruction fetch (M1) of the next instruction cycle.
14. If the condition was not met, sub-cycles M2 and M3 are skipped; the processor instead proceeds immediately to the instruction fetch (M1) of the next instruction cycle.
15. Stack read sub-cycle.
16. Stack write sub-cycle.
17. CONDITION / CCC

CONDITION	CCC
NZ – not zero (Z = 0)	000
Z – zero (Z = 1)	001
NC – no carry (CY = 0)	010
C – carry (CY = 1)	011
PO – parity odd (P = 0)	100
PE – parity even (P = 1)	101
P – plus (S = 0)	110
M – minus (S = 1)	111

18. I/O sub-cycle: the I/O port's 8-bit select code is duplicated on address lines 0-7 (A_{0-7}) and 8-15 (A_{8-15}).
19. The processor will remain idle in the halt state until an interrupt, a reset or a hold is accepted. When a hold request is accepted, the CPU enters the hold mode; after the hold mode is terminated, the processor returns to the halt state. After a reset is accepted, the processor begins execution at memory location zero. After an interrupt is accepted, the processor executes the instruction forced onto the data bus (usually a restart instruction).

Instruction Set

5

CHAPTER 5
THE INSTRUCTION SET

5.1 WHAT THE INSTRUCTION SET IS

A computer, no matter how sophisticated, can do only what it is instructed to do. A program is a sequence of instructions, each of which is recognized by the computer and causes it to perform an operation. Once a program is placed in memory space that is accessible to your CPU, you may run that same sequence of instructions as often as you wish to solve the same problem or to do the same function. The set of instructions to which the 8085A CPU will respond is permanently fixed in the design of the chip.

Each computer instruction allows you to initiate the performance of a specific operation. The 8085A implements a group of instructions that move data between registers, between a register and memory, and between a register and an I/O port. It also has arithmetic and logic instructions, conditional and unconditional branch instructions, and machine control instructions. The CPU recognizes these instructions only when they are coded in binary form.

5.2 SYMBOLS AND ABBREVIATIONS:

The following symbols and abbreviations are used in the subsequent description of the 8085A instructions:

SYMBOLS	MEANING
accumulator	Register A
addr	16-bit address quantity
data	8-bit quantity
data 16	16-bit data quantity
byte 2	The second byte of the instruction
byte 3	The third byte of the instruction
port	8-bit address of an I/O device
r,r1,r2	One of the registers A,B,C,D,E,H,L
DDD,SSS	The bit pattern designating one of the registers A,B,C,D,E,H,L (DDD = destination, SSS = source):

DDD or SSS	REGISTER NAME
111	A
000	B
001	C
010	D
011	E
100	H
101	L

SYMBOLS	MEANING
rp	One of the register pairs: B represents the B,C pair with B as the high-order register and C as the low-order register; D represents the D,E pair with D as the high-order register and E as the low-order register; H represents the H,L pair with H as the high-order register and L as the low-order register; SP represents the 16-bit stack pointer register.
RP	The bit pattern designating one of the register pairs B,D,H,SP:

RP	REGISTER PAIR
00	B-C
01	D-E
10	H-L
11	SP

SYMBOLS	MEANING
rh	The first (high-order) register of a designated register pair.
rl	The second (low-order) register of a designated register pair.

PC	16-bit program counter register (PCH and PCL are used to refer to the high-order and low-order 8 bits respectively).
SP	16-bit stack pointer register (SPH and SPL are used to refer to the high-order and low-order 8 bits respectively).
r_m	Bit m of the register r (bits are number 7 through 0 from left to right).
LABEL	16-bit address of subroutine.
	The condition flags:
Z	Zero
S	Sign
P	Parity
CY	Carry
AC	Auxiliary Carry
( )	The contents of the memory location or registers enclosed in the parentheses.
←	"Is transferred to"
∧	Logical AND
⊻	Exclusive OR
∧	Inclusive OR
+	Addition
−	Two's complement subtraction
*	Multiplication
↔	"Is exchanged with"
‾‾	The one's complement (e.g., $\overline{(A)}$)
n	The restart number 0 through 7
NNN	The binary representation 000 through 111 for restart number 0 through 7 respectively.

The instruction set encyclopedia is a detailed description of the 8085A instruction set. Each instruction is described in the following manner:

1. The 8085 Family macro assembler format, consisting of the instruction mnemonic and operand fields, is printed in **BOLDFACE** on the first line.
2. The name of the instruction is enclosed in parentheses following the mnemonic.
3. The next lines contain a symbolic description of what the instruction does.
4. This is followed by a narrative description of the operation of the instruction.
5. The boxes describe the binary codes that comprise the machine instruction.
6. The last four lines contain information about the execution of the instruction. The number of machine cycles and states required to execute the instruction are listed first. If the instruction has two possible execution times, as in a conditional jump, both times are listed, separated by a slash. Next, data addressing modes are listed if applicable. The last line lists any of the five flags that are affected by the execution of the instruction.

5.3 INSTRUCTION AND DATA FORMATS

Memory used in the 8085 system is organized in 8-bit bytes. Each byte has a unique location in physical memory. That location is described by one of a sequence of 16-bit binary addresses. The 8085A can address up to 64K (K = 1024, or 2^{10}; hence, 64K represents the decimal number 65,536) bytes of memory, which may consist of both random-access, read-write memory (RAM) and read-only memory (ROM), which is also random-access.

Data in the 8085A is stored in the form of 8-bit binary integers:

DATA WORD

D_7	D_6	D_5	D_4	D_3	D_2	D_1	D_0

MSB LSB

When a register or data word contains a binary number, it is necessary to establish the order in which the bits of the number are written. In the Intel 8085A, BIT 0 is referred to as the **Least Significant Bit (LSB)**, and BIT 7 (of an 8-bit number) is referred to as the **Most Significant Bit (MSB)**.

An 8085A program instruction may be one, two or three bytes in length. Multiple-byte instructions must be stored in successive memory locations; the address of the first byte is always used as the address of the instruction. The exact instruction format will depend on the particular operation to be executed.

Single Byte Instructions

	D_7 … D_0	Op Code

Two-Byte Instructions

Byte One	D_7 … D_0	Op Code
Byte Two	D_7 … D_0	Data or Address

*All mnemonics copyrighted © Intel Corporation 1976.

Three-Byte Instructions

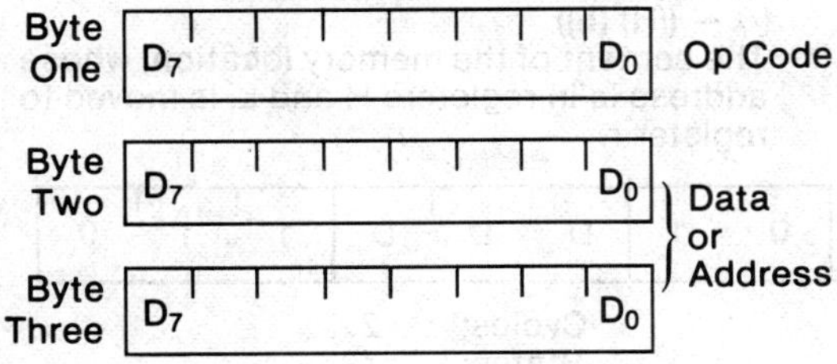

5.4 ADDRESSING MODES:

Often the data that is to be operated on is stored in memory. When multi-byte numeric data is used, the data, like instructions, is stored in successive memory locations, with the least significant byte first, followed by increasingly significant bytes. The 8085A has four different modes for addressing data stored in memory or in registers:

- Direct — Bytes 2 and 3 of the instruction contain the exact memory address of the data item (the low-order bits of the address are in byte 2, the high-order bits in byte 3).
- Register — The instruction specifies the register or register pair in which the data is located.
- Register Indirect — The instruction specifies a register pair which contains the memory address where the data is located (the high-order bits of the address are in the first register of the pair the low-order bits in the second).
- Immediate — The instruction contains the data itself. This is either an 8-bit quantity or a 16-bit quantity (least significant byte first, most significant byte second).

Unless directed by an interrupt or branch institution, the execution of instructions proceeds through consecutively increasing memory locations. A branch instruction can specify the address of the next instruction to be executed in one of two ways:

- Direct — The branch instruction contains the address of the next instruction to be executed. (Except for the 'RST' instruction, byte 2 contains the low-order address and byte 3 the high-order address.)
- Register Indirect — The branch instruction indicates a register-pair which contains the address of the next instruction to be executed. (The high-order bits of the address are in the first register of the pair, the low-order bits in the second.)

The RST instruction is a special one-byte call instruction (usually used during interrupt sequences). RST includes a three-bit field; program control is transferred to the instruction whose address is eight times the contents of this three-bit field.

5.5 CONDITION FLAGS:

There are five condition flags associated with the execution of instructions on the 8085A. They are Zero, Sign, Parity, Carry, and Auxiliary Carry. Each is represented by a 1-bit register (or flip-flop) in the CPU. A flag is set by forcing the bit to 1; it is reset by forcing the bit to 0.

Unless indicated otherwise, when an instruction affects a flag, it affects it in the following manner:

Zero: If the result of an instruction has the value 0, this flag is set; otherwise it is reset.

Sign: If the most significant bit of the result of the operation has the value 1, this flag is set; otherwise it is reset.

Parity: If the modulo 2 sum of the bits of the result of the operation is 0, (i.e., if the result has even parity), this flag is set; otherwise it is reset (i.e., if the result has odd parity).

Carry: If the instruction resulted in a carry (from addition), or a borrow (from subtraction or a comparison) out of the high-order bit, this flag is set; otherwise it is reset.

Auxiliary Carry: If the instruction caused a carry out of bit 3 and into bit 4 of the resulting value, the auxiliary carry is set; otherwise it is reset. This flag is affected by single-precision additions, subtractions, increments, decrements, comparisons, and logical operations, but is principally used with additions and increments preceding a DAA (Decimal Adjust Accumulator) instruction.

5.6 INSTRUCTION SET ENCYCLOPEDIA*

In the ensuing dozen pages, the complete 8085A instruction set is described, grouped in order under five different functional headings, as follows:

1. **Data Transfer Group** — Moves data between registers or between memory locations and registers. Includes moves, loads, stores, and exchanges. (See below.)
2. **Arithmetic Group** — Adds, subtracts, increments, or decrements data in registers or memory. (See page 5-13.)
3. **Logic Group** — ANDs, ORs, XORs, compares, rotates, or complements data in registers or between memory and a register. (See page 5-16.)
4. **Branch Group** — Initiates conditional or unconditional jumps, calls, returns, and restarts. (See page 5-20.)
5. **Stack, I/O, and Machine Control Group** — Includes instructions for maintaining the stack, reading from input ports, writing to output ports, setting and reading interrupt masks, and setting and clearing flags. (See page 5-22.)

The formats described in the encyclopedia reflect the assembly language processed by Intel-supplied assembler, used with the Intellec® development systems.

5.6.1 Data Transfer Group

This group of instructions transfers data to and from registers and memory. **Condition flags are not affected by any instruction in this group.**

MOV r1, r2 (Move Register)

(r1) ← (r2)

The content of register r2 is moved to register r1.

0	1	D	D	D	S	S	S

Cycles: 1
States: 4 (8085), 5 (8080)
Addressing: register
Flags: none

MOV r, M (Move from memory)

(r) ← ((H) (L))

The content of the memory location, whose address is in registers H and L, is moved to register r.

0	1	D	D	D	1	1	0

Cycles: 2
States: 7
Addressing: reg. indirect
Flags: none

MOV M, r (Move to memory)

((H)) (L)) ← (r)

The content of register r is moved to the memory location whose address is in registers H and L.

0	1	1	1	0	S	S	S

Cycles: 2
States: 7
Addressing: reg. indirect
Flags: none

MVI r, data (Move Immediate)

(r) ← (byte 2)

The content of byte 2 of the instruction is moved to register r.

0	0	D	D	D	1	1	0
data							

Cycles: 2
States: 7
Addressing: immediate
Flags: none

MVI M, data (Move to memory immediate)

((H) (L)) ← (byte 2)

The content of byte 2 of the instruction is moved to the memory location whose address is in registers H and L.

0	0	1	1	0	1	1	0
data							

Cycles: 3
States: 10
Addressing: immed./reg. indirect
Flags: none

LXI rp, data 16 (Load register pair immediate)
(rh) ← (byte 3),
(rl) ← (byte 2)
Byte 3 of the instruction is moved into the high-order register (rh) of the register pair rp. Byte 2 of the instruction is moved into the low-order register (rl) of the register pair rp.

0	0	R	P	0	0	0	1
low-order data							
high-order data							

Cycles: 3
States: 10
Addressing: immediate
Flags: none

LDA addr (Load Accumulator direct)
(A) ← ((byte 3)(byte 2))
The content of the memory location, whose address is specified in byte 2 and byte 3 of the instruction, is moved to register A.

0	0	1	1	1	0	1	0
low-order addr							
high-order addr							

3A

Cycles: 4
States: 13
Addressing: direct
Flags: none

STA addr (Store Accumulator direct)
((byte 3)(byte 2)) ← (A)
The content of the accumulator is moved to the memory location whose address is specified in byte 2 and byte 3 of the instruction.

0	0	1	1	0	0	1	0
low-order addr							
high-order addr							

32

Cycles: 4
States: 13
Addressing: direct
Flags: none

LHLD addr (Load H and L direct)
(L) ← ((byte 3)(byte 2))
(H) ← ((byte 3)(byte 2) + 1)
The content of the memory location, whose address is specified in byte 2 and byte 3 of the instruction, is moved to register L. The content of the memory location at the succeeding address is moved to register H.

0	0	1	0	1	0	1	0
low-order addr							
high-order addr							

Cycles: 5
States: 16
Addressing: direct
Flags: none

SHLD addr (Store H and L direct)
((byte 3)(byte 2)) ← (L)
((byte 3)(byte 2) + 1) ← (H)
The content of register L is moved to the memory location whose address is specified in byte 2 and byte 3. The content of register H is moved to the succeeding memory location.

0	0	1	0	0	0	1	0
low-order addr							
high-order addr							

Cycles: 5
States: 16
Addressing: direct
Flags: none

LDAX rp (Load accumulator indirect)
(A) ← ((rp))
The content of the memory location, whose address is in the register pair rp, is moved to register A. Note: only register pairs rp = B (registers B and C) or rp = D (registers D and E) may be specified.

0	0	R	P	1	0	1	0

Cycles: 2
States: 7
Addressing: reg. indirect
Flags: none

STAX rp (Store accumulator indirect)
((rp)) ← (A)
The content of register A is moved to the memory location whose address is in the register pair rp. Note: only register pairs rp = B (registers B and C) or rp = D (registers D and E) may be specified.

0	0	R	P	0	0	1	0

Cycles: 2
States: 7
Addressing: reg. indirect
Flags: none

XCHG (Exchange H and L with D and E)
(H) ↔ (D)
(L) ↔ (E)
The contents of registers H and L are exchanged with the contents of registers D and E.

1	1	1	0	1	0	1	1

Cycles: 1
States: 4
Addressing: register
Flags: none

5.6.2 Arithmetic Group

This group of instructions performs arithmetic operations on data in registers and memory.

Unless indicated otherwise, all instructions in this group affect the Zero, Sign, Parity, Carry, and Auxiliary Carry flags according to the standard rules.

All subtraction operations are performed via two's complement arithmetic and set the carry flag to one to indicate a borrow and clear it to indicate no borrow.

ADD r (Add Register)
(A) ← (A) + (r)
The content of register r is added to the content of the accumulator. The result is placed in the accumulator.

1	0	0	0	0	S	S	S

Cycles: 1
States: 4
Addressing: register
Flags: Z,S,P,CY,AC

ADD M (Add memory)
(A) ← (A) + ((H) (L))
The content of the memory location whose address is contained in the H and L registers is added to the content of the accumulator. The result is placed in the accumulator.

1	0	0	0	0	1	1	0

86

Cycles: 2
States: 7
Addressing: reg. indirect
Flags: Z,S,P,CY,AC

ADI data (Add immediate)
(A) ← (A) + (byte 2)
The content of the second byte of the instruction is added to the content of the accumulator. The result is placed in the accumulator.

1	1	0	0	0	1	1	0
data							

Cycles: 2
States: 7
Addressing: immediate
Flags: Z,S,P,CY,AC

ADC r (Add Register with carry)
(A) ← (A) + (r) + (CY)
The content of register r and the content of the carry bit are added to the content of the accumulator. The result is placed in the accumulator.

1	0	0	0	1	S	S	S

Cycles: 1
States: 4
Addressing: register
Flags: Z,S,P,CY,AC

ADC M (Add memory with carry)

(A) ← (A) + ((H) (L)) + (CY)

The content of the memory location whose address is contained in the H and L registers and the content of the CY flag are added to the accumulator. The result is placed in the accumulator.

1	0	0	0	1	1	1	0

Cycles: 2
States: 7
Addressing: reg. indirect
Flags: Z,S,P,CY,AC

ACI data (Add immediate with carry)

(A) ← (A) + (byte 2) + (CY)

The content of the second byte of the instruction and the content of the CY flag are added to the contents of the accumulator. The result is placed in the accumulator.

1	1	0	0	1	1	1	0
data							

Cycles: 2
States: 7
Addressing: immediate
Flags: Z,S,P,CY,AC

SUB r (Subtract Register)

(A) ← (A) − (r)

The content of register r is subtracted from the content of the accumulator. The result is placed in the accumulator.

1	0	0	1	0	S	S	S

Cycles: 1
States: 4
Addressing: register
Flags: Z,S,P,CY,AC

SUB M (Subtract memory)

(A) ← (A) − ((H) (L))

The content of the memory location whose address is contained in the H and L registers is subtracted from the content of the accumulator. The result is placed in the accumulator.

1	0	0	1	0	1	1	0

Cycles: 2
States: 7
Addressing: reg. indirect
Flags: Z,S,P,CY,AC

SUI data (Subtract immediate)

(A) ← (A) − (byte 2)

The content of the second byte of the instruction is subtracted from the content of the accumulator. The result is placed in the accumulator.

1	1	0	1	0	1	1	0
data							

Cycles: 2
States: 7
Addressing: immediate
Flags: Z,S,P,CY,AC

SBB r (Subtract Register with borrow)

(A) ← (A) − (r) − (CY)

The content of register r and the content of the CY flag are both subtracted from the accumulator. The result is placed in the accumulator.

1	0	0	1	1	S	S	S

Cycles: 1
States: 4
Addressing: register
Flags: Z,S,P,CY,AC

SBB M (Subtract memory with borrow)
(A) ← (A) − ((H) (L)) − (CY)
The content of the memory location whose address is contained in the H and L registers and the content of the CY flag are both subtracted from the accumulator. The result is placed in the accumulator.

1	0	0	1	1	1	1	0

Cycles:	2
States:	7
Addressing:	reg. indirect
Flags:	Z,S,P,CY,AC

SBI data (Subtract immediate with borrow)
(A) ← (A) − (byte 2) − (CY)
The contents of the second byte of the instruction and the contents of the CY flag are both subtracted from the accumulator. The result is placed in the accumulator.

1	1	0	1	1	1	1	0
data							

Cycles:	2
States:	7
Addressing:	immediate
Flags:	Z,S,P,CY,AC

INR r (Increment Register)
(r) ← (r) + 1
The content of register r is incremented by one. Note: All condition flags **except CY** are affected.

0	0	D	D	D	1	0	0

Cycles:	1
States:	4 (8085), 5 (8080)
Addressing:	register
Flags:	Z,S,P,AC

INR M (Increment memory)
((H) (L)) ← ((H) (L)) + 1
The content of the memory location whose address is contained in the H and L registers is incremented by one. Note: All condition flags **except CY** are affected.

0	0	1	1	0	1	0	0

Cycles:	3
States:	10
Addressing:	reg. indirect
Flags:	Z,S,P,AC

DCR r (Decrement Register)
(r) ← (r) − 1
The content of register r is decremented by one. Note: All condition flags **except CY** are affected.

0	0	D	D	D	1	0	1

Cycles:	1
States:	4 (8085), 5 (8080)
Addressing:	register
Flags:	Z,S,P,AC

DCR M (Decrement memory)
((H) (L)) ← ((H) (L)) − 1
The content of the memory location whose address is contained in the H and L registers is decremented by one. Note: All condition flags **except CY** are affected.

0	0	1	1	0	1	0	1

Cycles:	3
States:	10
Addressing:	reg. indirect
Flags:	Z,S,P,AC

INX rp (Increment register pair)
(rh) (rl) ← (rh) (rl) + 1
The content of the register pair rp is incremented by one. Note: **No condition flags are affected.**

0	0	R	P	0	0	1	1

Cycles: 1
States: 6 (8085), 5 (8080)
Addressing: register
Flags: none

DCX rp (Decrement register pair)
(rh) (rl) ← (rh) (rl) − 1
The content of the register pair rp is decremented by one. Note: **No condition flags are affected.**

0	0	R	P	1	0	1	1

Cycles: 1
States: 6 (8085), 5 (8080)
Addressing: register
Flags: none

DAD rp (Add register pair to H and L)
(H) (L) ← (H) (L) + (rh) (rl)
The content of the register pair rp is added to the content of the register pair H and L. The result is placed in the register pair H and L. Note: **Only the CY flag is affected.** It is set if there is a carry out of the double precision add; otherwise it is reset.

0	0	R	P	1	0	0	1

Cycles: 3
States: 10
Addressing: register
Flags: CY

DAA (Decimal Adjust Accumulator)
The eight-bit number in the accumulator is adjusted to form two four-bit Binary-Coded-Decimal digits by the following process:

1. If the value of the lease significant 4 bits of the accumulator is greater than 9 **or** if the AC flag is set, 6 is added to the accumulator.
2. If the value of the most significant 4 bits of the accumulator is now greater than 9, **or** if the CY flag is set, 6 is added to the most significant 4 bits of the accumulator.

NOTE: All flags are affected.

0	0	1	0	0	1	1	1

Cycles: 1
States: 4
Flags: Z,S,P,CY,AC

5.6.3 Logical Group

This group of instructions performs logical (Boolean) operations on data in registers and memory and on condition flags.

Unless indicated otherwise, all instructions in this group affect the Zero, Sign, Parity, Auxiliary Carry, and Carry flags according to the standard rules.

ANA r (AND Register)
(A) ← (A) ∧ (r)
The content of register r is logically ANDed with the content of the accumulator. The result is placed in the accumulator. **The CY flag is cleared and AC is set (8085). The CY flag is cleared and AC is set to the OR'ing of bits 3 of the operands (8080).**

1	0	1	0	0	S	S	S

Cycles: 1
States: 4
Addressing: register
Flags: Z,S,P,CY,AC

ANA M (AND memory)

(A) ← (A) ∧ ((H) (L))

The contents of the memory location whose address is contained in the H and L registers is logically ANDed with the content of the accumulator. The result is placed in the accumulator. **The CY flag is cleared and AC is set (8085). The CY flag is cleared and AC is set to the OR'ing of bits 3 of the operands (8080).**

1	0	1	0	0	1	1	0

Cycles: 2
States: 7
Addressing: reg. indirect
Flags: Z,S,P,CY,AC

ANI data (AND immediate)

(A) ← (A) ∧ (byte 2)

The content of the second byte of the instruction is logically ANDed with the contents of the accumulator. The result is placed in the accumulator. **The CY flag is cleared and AC is set (8085). The CY flag is cleared and AC is set to the OR'ing of bits 3 of the operands (8080).**

1	1	1	0	0	1	1	0
data							

Cycles: 2
States: 7
Addressing: immediate
Flags: Z,S,P,CY,AC

XRA r (Exclusive OR Register)

(A) ← (A) ∀ (r)

The content of register r is exclusive-OR'd with the content of the accumulator. The result is placed in the accumulator. **The CY and AC flags are cleared.**

1	0	1	0	1	S	S	S

Cycles: 1
States: 4
Addressing: register
Flags: Z,S,P,CY,AC

XRA M (Exclusive OR Memory)

(A) ← (A) ∀ ((H) (L))

The content of the memory location whose address is contained in the H and L registers is exclusive-OR'd with the content of the accumulator. The result is placed in the accumulator. **The CY and AC flags are cleared.**

1	0	1	0	1	1	1	0

Cycles: 2
States: 7
Addressing: reg. indirect
Flags: Z,S,P,CY,AC

XRI data (Exclusive OR immediate)

(A) ← (A) ∀ (byte 2)

The content of the second byte of the instruction is exclusive-OR'd with the content of the accumulator. The result is placed in the accumulator. **The CY and AC flags are cleared.**

1	1	1	0	1	1	1	0
data							

Cycles: 2
States: 7
Addressing: immediate
Flags: Z,S,P,CY,AC

ORA r (OR Register)

(A) ← (A) V (r)

The content of register r is inclusive-OR'd with the content of the accumulator. The result is placed in the accumulator. **The CY and AC flags are cleared.**

1	0	1	1	0	S	S	S

Cycles: 1
States: 4
Addressing: register
Flags: Z,S,P,CY,AC

ORA M (OR memory)

(A) ← (A) V ((H) (L))

The content of the memory location whose address is contained in the H and L registers is inclusive-OR'd with the content of the accumulator. The result is placed in the accumulator. **The CY and AC flags are cleared.**

1	0	1	1	0	1	1	0

Cycles: 2
States: 7
Addressing: reg. indirect
Flags: Z,S,P,CY,AC

ORI data (OR Immediate)

(A) ← (A) V (byte 2)

The content of the second byte of the instruction is inclusive-OR'd with the content of the accumulator. The result is placed in the accumulator. **The CY and AC flags are cleared..**

1	1	1	1	0	1	1	0
data							

Cycles: 2
States: 7
Addressing: immediate
Flags: Z,S,P,CY,AC

CMP r (Compare Register)

(A) − (r)

The content of register r is subtracted from the accumulator. The accumulator remains unchanged. The condition flags are set as a result of the subtraction. **The Z flag is set to 1 if (A) = (r). The CY flag is set to 1 if (A) < (r).**

1	0	1	1	1	S	S	S

Cycles: 1
States: 4
Addressing: register
Flags: Z,S,P,CY,AC

CMP M (Compare memory)

(A) − ((H) (L))

The content of the memory location whose address is contained in the H and L registers is subtracted from the accumulator. The accumulator remains unchanged. The condition flags are set as a result of the subtraction. **The Z flag is set to 1 if (A) = ((H) (L)). The CY flag is set to 1 if (A) < ((H) (L)).**

1	0	1	1	1	1	1	0

Cycles: 2
States: 7
Addressing: reg. indirect
Flags: Z,S,P,CY,AC

CPI data (Compare immediate)

(A) − (byte 2)

The content of the second byte of the instruction is subtracted from the accumulator. The condition flags are set by the result of the subtraction. **The Z flag is set to 1 if (A) = (byte 2). The CY flag is set to 1 if (A) < (byte 2).**

1	1	1	1	1	1	1	0
data							

Cycles: 2
States: 7
Addressing: immediate
Flags: Z,S,P,CY,AC

RLC (Rotate left)

$(A_{n+1}) \leftarrow (A_n)$; $(A_0) \leftarrow (A_7)$

$(CY) \leftarrow (A_7)$

The content of the accumulator is rotated left one position. The low order bit and the CY flag are both set to the value shifted out of the high order bit position. **Only the CY flag is affected.**

0	0	0	0	0	1	1	1

Cycles: 1
States: 4
Flags: CY

RRC (Rotate right)

$(A_n) \leftarrow (A_{n+1})$; $(A_7) \leftarrow (A_0)$
$(CY) \leftarrow (A_0)$

The content of the accumulator is rotated right one position. The high order bit and the CY flag are both set to the value shifted out of the low order bit position. **Only the CY flag is affected.**

0	0	0	0	1	1	1	1

Cycles: 1
States: 4
Flags: CY

RAL (Rotate left through carry)

$(A_{n+1}) \leftarrow (A_n)$; $(CY) \leftarrow (A_7)$
$(A_0) \leftarrow (CY)$

The content of the accumulator is rotated left one position through the CY flag. The low order bit is set equal to the CY flag and the CY flag is set to the value shifted out of the high order bit. **Only the CY flag is affected.**

0	0	0	1	0	1	1	1

Cycles: 1
States: 4
Flags: CY

RAR (Rotate right through carry)

$(A_n) \leftarrow (A_{n+1})$; $(CY) \leftarrow (A_0)$
$(A_7) \leftarrow (CY)$

The content of the accumulator is rotated right one position through the CY flag. The high order bit is set to the CY flag and the CY flag is set to the value shifted out of the low order bit. **Only the CY flag is affected.**

0	0	0	1	1	1	1	1

Cycles: 1
States: 4
Flags: CY

CMA (Complement accumulator)

$(A) \leftarrow (\overline{A})$

The contents of the accumulator are complemented (zero bits become 1, one bits become 0). **No flags are affected.**

0	0	1	0	1	1	1	1

Cycles: 1
States: 4
Flags: none

CMC (Complement carry)

$(CY) \leftarrow (\overline{CY})$

The CY flag is complemented. **No other flags are affected.**

0	0	1	1	1	1	1	1

Cycles: 1
States: 4
Flags: CY

STC (Set carry)

$(CY) \leftarrow 1$

The CY flag is set to 1. **No other flags are affected.**

0	0	1	1	0	1	1	1

Cycles: 1
States: 4
Flags: CY

5.6.4 Branch Group

This group of instructions alter normal sequential program flow.

Condition flags are not affected by any instruction in this group.

The two types of branch instructions are unconditional and conditional. Unconditional transfers simply perform the specified operation on register PC (the program counter). Conditional transfers examine the status of one of the four processor flags to determine if the specified branch is to be executed. The conditions that may be specified are as follows:

CONDITION		**CCC**
NZ —	not zero (Z = 0)	000
Z —	zero (Z = 1)	001
NC —	no carry (CY = 0)	010
C —	carry (CY = 1)	011
PO —	parity odd (P = 0)	100
PE —	parity even (P = 1)	101
P —	plus (S = 0)	110
M —	minus (S = 1)	111

JMP addr (Jump)

(PC) ← (byte 3) (byte 2)

Control is transferred to the instruction whose address is specified in byte 3 and byte 2 of the current instruction.

1	1	0	0	0	0	1	1
low-order addr							
high-order addr							

Cycles: 3
States: 10
Addressing: immediate
Flags: none

Jcondition addr (Conditional jump)

If (CCC),

(PC) ← (byte 3) (byte 2)

If the specified condition is true, control is transferred to the instruction whose address is specified in byte 3 and byte 2 of the current instruciton; otherwise, control continues sequentially.

1	1	C	C	C	0	1	0
low-order addr							
high-order addr							

Cycles: 2/3 (8085), 3 (8080)
States: 7/10 (8085), 10 (8080)
Addressing: immediate
Flags: none

CALL addr (Call)

((SP) − 1) ← (PCH)

((SP) − 2) ← (PCL)

(SP) ← (SP) − 2

(PC) ← (byte 3) (byte 2)

The high-order eight bits of the next instruction address are moved to the memory location whose address is one less than the content of register SP. The low-order eight bits of the next instruction address are moved to the memory location whose address is two less than the content of register SP. The content of register SP is decremented by 2. Control is transferred to the instruction whose address is specified in byte 3 and byte 2 of the current instruction.

1	1	0	0	1	1	0	1
low-order addr							
high-order addr							

Cycles: 5
States: 18 (8085), 17 (8080)
Addressing: immediate/ reg. indirect
Flags: none

Ccondition addr (Condition call)
If (CCC),
((SP) − 1) ← (PCH)
((SP) − 2) ← (PCL)
(SP) ← (SP) − 2
(PC) ← (byte 3) (byte 2)
If the specified condition is true, the actions specified in the CALL instruction (see above) are performed; otherwise, control continues sequentially.

1	1	C	C	C	1	0	0
low-order addr							
high-order addr							

Cycles: 2/5 (8085), 3/5 (8080)
States: 9/18 (8085), 11/17 (8080)
Addressing: immediate/ reg. indirect
Flags: none

RET (Return)
(PCL) ← ((SP));
(PCH) ← ((SP) + 1);
(SP) ← (SP) + 2;
The content of the memory location whose address is specified in register SP is moved to the low-order eight bits of register PC. The content of the memory location whose address is one more than the content of register SP is moved to the high-order eight bits of register PC. The content of register SP is incremented by 2.

1	1	0	0	1	0	0	1

Cycles: 3
States: 10
Addressing: reg. indirect
Flags: none

Rcondition (Conditional return)
If (CCC),
(PCL) ← ((SP))
(PCH) ← ((SP) + 1)
(SP) ← (SP) + 2
If the specified condition is true, the actions specified in the RET instruction (see above) are performed; otherwise, control continues sequentially.

1	1	C	C	C	0	0	0

Cycles: 1/3
States: 6/12 (8085), 5/11 (8080)
Addressing: reg. indirect
Flags: none

RST n (Restart)
((SP) − 1) ← (PCH)
((SP) − 2) ← (PCL)
(SP) ← (SP) − 2
(PC) ← 8 * (NNN)
The high-order eight bits of the next instruction address are moved to the memory location whose address is one less than the content of register SP. The low-order eight bits of the next instruction address are moved to the memory location whose address is two less than the content of register SP. The content of register SP is decremented by two. Control is transferred to the instruction whose address is eight times the content of NNN.

1	1	N	N	N	1	1	1

Cycles: 3
States: 12 (8085), 11 (8080)
Addressing: reg. indirect
Flags: none

15	14	13	12	11	10	9	8	7	6	5	4	3	2	1	0
0	0	0	0	0	0	0	0	0	0	N	N	N	0	0	0

Program Counter After Restart

PCHL (Jump H and L indirect — move H and L to PC)

(PCH) ← (H)
(PCL) ← (L)

The content of register H is moved to the high-order eight bits of register PC. The content of register L is moved to the low-order eight bits of register PC.

1	1	1	0	1	0	0	1

Cycles: 1
States: 6 (8085), 5 (8080)
Addressing: register
Flags: none

5.6.5 Stack, I/O, and Machine Control Group

This group of instructions performs I/O, manipulates the Stack, and alters internal control flags.

Unless otherwise specified, **condition flags are not affected by any instructions in this group.**

PUSH rp (Push)

((SP) − 1) ← (rh)
((SP) − 2) ← (rl)
((SP) ← (SP) − 2

The content of the high-order register of register pair rp is moved to the memory location whose address is one less than the content of register SP. The content of the low-order register of register pair rp is moved to the memory location whose address is two less than the content of register SP. The content of register SP is decremented by 2. **Note: Register pair rp = SP may not be specified.**

1	1	R	P	0	1	0	1

Cycles: 3
States: 12 (8085), 11 (8080)
Addressing: reg. indirect
Flags: none

PUSH PSW (Push processor status word)

((SP) − 1) ← (A)
$((SP) - 2)_0$ ← (CY) , $((SP) - 2)_1$ ← X
$((SP) - 2)_2$ ← (P) , $((SP) - 2)_3$ ← X
$((SP) - 2)_4$ ← (AC) , $((SP) - 2)_5$ ← X
$((SP) - 2)_6$ ← (Z) , $((SP) - 2)_7$ ← (S)
(SP) ← (SP) − 2 X: Undefined.

The content of register A is moved to the memory location whose address is one less than register SP. The contents of the condition flags are assembled into a processor status word and the word is moved to the memory location whose address is two less than the content of register SP. The content of register SP is decremented by two.

1	1	1	1	0	1	0	1

Cycles: 3
States: 12 (8085), 11 (8080)
Addressing: reg. indirect
Flags: none

FLAG WORD

D_7	D_6	D_5	D_4	D_3	D_2	D_1	D_0
S	Z	X	AC	X	P	X	CY

X: undefined

POP rp (Pop)

(rl) ← ((SP))
(rh) ← ((SP) + 1)
(SP) ← (SP) + 2

The content of the memory location, whose address is specified by the content of register SP, is moved to the low-order register of register pair rp. The content of the memory location, whose address is one more than the content of register SP, is moved to the high-order register of register rp. The content of register SP is incremented by 2. **Note: Register pair rp = SP may not be specified.**

1	1	R	P	0	0	0	1

Cycles: 3
States: 10
Addressing: reg.indirect
Flags: none

POP PSW (Pop processor status word)

(CY) ← $((SP))_0$
(P) ← $((SP))_2$
(AC) ← $((SP))_4$
(Z) ← $((SP))_6$
(S) ← $((SP))_7$
(A) ← ((SP) + 1)
(SP) ← (SP) + 2

The content of the memory location whose address is specified by the content of register SP is used to restore the condition flags. The content of the memory location whose address is one more than the content of register SP is moved to register A. The content of register SP is incremented by 2.

1	1	1	1	0	0	0	1

Cycles: 3
States: 10
Addressing: reg. indirect
Flags: Z,S,P,CY,AC

XTHL (Exchange stack top with H and L)

(L) ↔ ((SP))
(H) ↔ ((SP) + 1)

The content of the L register is exchanged with the content of the memory location whose address is specified by the content of register SP. The content of the H register is exchanged with the content of the memory location whose address is one more than the content of register SP.

1	1	1	0	0	0	1	1

Cycles: 5
States: 16 (8085), 18 (8080)
Addressing: reg. indirect
Flags: none

SPHL (Move HL to SP)

(SP) ← (H) (L)

The contents of registers H and L (16 bits) are moved to register SP.

1	1	1	1	1	0	0	1

Cycles: 1
States: 6 (8085), 5 (8080)
Addressing: register
Flags: none

IN port (Input)

(A) ← (data)

The data placed on the eight bit bi-directional data bus by the specified port is moved to register A.

1	1	0	1	1	0	1	1
port							

Cycles: 3
States: 10
Addressing: direct
Flags: none

OUT port (Output)

(data) ← (A)

The content of register A is placed on the eight bit bi-directional data bus for transmission to the specified port.

1	1	0	1	0	0	1	1
port							

Cycles: 3
States: 10
Addressing: direct
Flags: none

EI (Enable interrupts)

The interrupt system is enabled **following the execution of the next instruction. Interrupts are not recognized during the EI instruction.**

1	1	1	1	1	0	1	1

Cycles: 1
States: 4
Flags: none

NOTE: Placing an EI instruction on the bus in response to $\overline{\text{INTA}}$ during an INA cycle is prohibited. (8085)

DI (Disable interrupts)

The interrupt system is disabled **immediately following the execution of the DI instruction. Interrupts are not recognized during the DI instruction.**

1	1	1	1	0	0	1	1

Cycles: 1
States: 4
Flags: none

NOTE: Placing a DI instruction on the bus in response to $\overline{\text{INTA}}$ during an INA cycle is prohibited. (8085)

HLT (Halt)

The processor is stopped. The registers and flags are unaffected. (8080) A second ALE is generated during the execution of HLT to strobe out the Halt cycle status information. (8085)

0	1	1	1	0	1	1	0

Cycles: 1+ (8085), 1 (8080)
States: 5 (8085), 7 (8080)
Flags: none

NOP (No op)

No operation is performed. The registers and flags are unaffected.

0	0	0	0	0	0	0	0

Cycles: 1
States: 4
Flags: none

RIM (Read Interrupt Masks) (8085 only)

The RIM instruction loads data into the accumulator relating to interrupts and the serial input. This data contains the following information:

- Current interrupt mask status for the RST 5.5, 6.5, and 7.5 hardware interrupts (1 = mask disabled)
- Current interrupt enable flag status (1 = interrupts enabled) except immediately following a TRAP interrupt. (See below.)
- Hardware interrupts pending (i.e., signal received but not yet serviced), on the RST 5.5, 6.5, and 7.5 lines.
- Serial input data.

Immediately following a TRAP interrupt, the RIM instruction must be executed as a part of the service routine if you need to retrieve current interrupt status later. Bit 3 of the accumulator is (in this special case only) loaded with the interrupt enable (IE) flag status that existed prior to the TRAP interrupt. Following an RST 5.5, 6.5, 7.5, or INTR interrupt, the interrupt flag flip-flop reflects the current interrupt enable status. Bit 6 of the accumulator (I7.5) is loaded with the status of the RST 7.5 flip-flop, which is always set (edge-triggered) by an input on the RST 7.5 input line, even when that interrupt has been previously masked. (See SIM Instruction.)

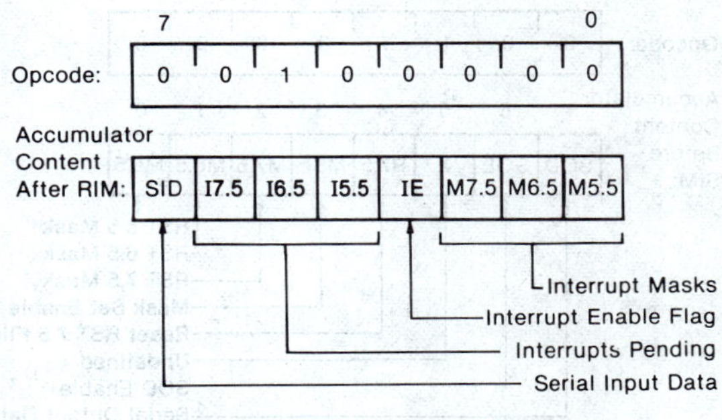

Cycles: 1
States: 4
Flags: none

SIM (Set Interrupt Masks) (8085 only)

The execution of the SIM instruction uses the contents of the accumulator (which must be previously loaded) to perform the following functions:

- Program the interrupt mask for the RST 5.5, 6.5, and 7.5 hardware interrupts.
- Reset the edge-triggered RST 7.5 input latch.
- Load the SOD output latch.

To program the interrupt masks, first set accumulator bit 3 to 1 and set to 1 any bits 0, 1, and 2, which disable interrupts RST 5.5, 6.5, and 7.5, respectively. Then do a SIM instruction. If accumulator bit 3 is 0 when the SIM instruction is executed, the interrupt mask register will not change. If accumulator bit 4 is 1 when the SIM instruction is executed, the RST 7.5 latch is then reset. RST 7.5 is distinguished by the fact that its latch is always set by a rising edge on the RST 7.5 input pin, even if the jump to service routine is inhibited by masking. This latch remains high until cleared by a $\overline{\text{RESET IN}}$, by a SIM Instruction with accumulator bit 4 high, or by an internal processor acknowledge to an RST 7.5 interrupt subsequent to the removal of the mask (by a SIM instruction). The $\overline{\text{RESET IN}}$ signal always sets all three RST mask bits.

If accumulator bit 6 is at the 1 level when the SIM instruction is executed, the state of accumulator bit 7 is loaded into the SOD latch and thus becomes available for interface to an external device. The SOD latch is unaffected by the SIM instruction if bit 6 is 0. SOD is always reset by the $\overline{\text{RESET IN}}$ signal.

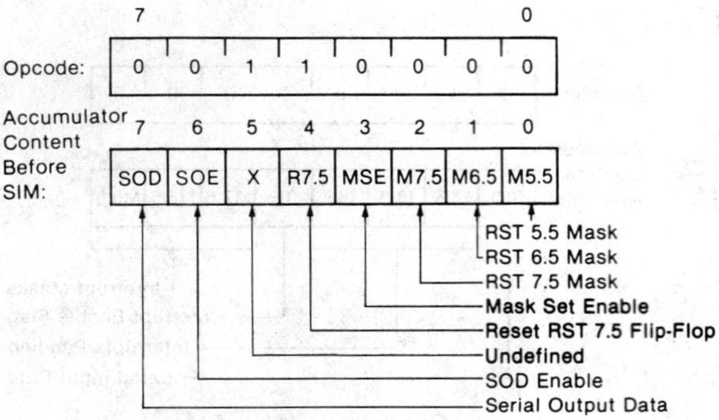

Cycles: 1
States: 4
Flags: none

8080A/8085A INSTRUCTION SET INDEX
Table 5-1

Instruction		Code	Bytes	T States		Machine Cycles
				8085A	8080A	
ACI	DATA	CE data	2	7	7	F R
ADC	REG	1000 1SSS	1	4	4	F
ADC	M	8E	1	7	7	F R
ADD	REG	1000 0SSS	1	4	4	F
ADD	M	86	1	7	7	F R
ADI	DATA	C6 data	2	7	7	F R
ANA	REG	1010 0SSS	1	4	4	F
ANA	M	A6	1	7	7	F R
ANI	DATA	E6 data	2	7	7	F R
CALL	LABEL	CD addr	3	18	17	S R R W W*
CC	LABEL	DC addr	3	9/18	11/17	S R•/S R R W W*
CM	LABEL	FC addr	3	9/18	11/17	S R•/S R R W W*
CMA		2F	1	4	4	F
CMC		3F	1	4	4	F
CMP	REG	1011 1SSS	1	4	4	F
CMP	M	BE	1	7	7	F R
CNC	LABEL	D4 addr	3	9/18	11/17	S R•/S R R W W*
CNZ	LABEL	C4 addr	3	9/18	11/17	S R•/S R R W W*
CP	LABEL	F4 addr	3	9/18	11/17	S R•/S R R W W*
CPE	LABEL	EC addr	3	9/18	11/17	S R•/S R R W W*
CPI	DATA	FE data	2	7	7	F R
CPO	LABEL	E4 addr	3	9/18	11/17	S R•/S R R W W*
CZ	LABEL	CC addr	3	9/18	11/17	S R•/S R R W W*
DAA		27	1	4	4	F
DAD	RP	00RP 1001	1	10	10	F B B
DCR	REG	00SS S101	1	4	5	F*
DCR	M	35	1	10	10	F R W
DCX	RP	00RP 1011	1	6	5	S*
DI		F3	1	4	4	F
EI		FB	1	4	4	F
HLT		76	1	5	7	F B
IN	PORT	DB data	2	10	10	F R I
INR	REG	00SS S100	1	4	5	F*
INR	M	34	1	10	10	F R W
INX	RP	00RP 0011	1	6	5	S*
JC	LABEL	DA addr	3	7/10	10	F R/F R R†
JM	LABEL	FA addr	3	7/10	10	F R/F R R†
JMP	LABEL	C3 addr	3	10	10	F R R
JNC	LABEL	D2 addr	3	7/10	10	F R/F R R†
JNZ	LABEL	C2 addr	3	7/10	10	F R/F R R†
JP	LABEL	F2 addr	3	7/10	10	F R/F R R†
JPE	LABEL	EA addr	3	7/10	10	F R/F R R†
JPO	LABEL	E2 addr	3	7/10	10	F R/F R R†
JZ	LABEL	CA addr	3	7/10	10	F R/F R R†
LDA	ADDR	3A addr	3	13	13	F R R R
LDAX	RP	000X 1010	1	7	7	F R
LHLD	ADDR	2A addr	3	16	16	F R R R R
LXI	RP,DATA16	00RP 0001 data16	3	10	10	F R R
MOV	REG,REG	01DD DSSS	1	4	5	F*
MOV	M,REG	0111 0SSS	1	7	7	F W
MOV	REG,M	01DD D110	1	7	7	F R
MVI	REG,DATA	00DD D110 data	2	7	7	F R
MVI	M,DATA	36 data	2	10	10	F R W
NOP		00	1	4	4	F
ORA	REG	1011 0SSS	1	4	4	F
ORA	M	B6	1	7	7	F R
ORI	DATA	F6 data	2	7	7	F R
OUT	PORT	D3 data	2	10	10	F R O
PCHL		E9	1	6	5	S*
POP	RP	11RP 0001	1	10	10	F R R
PUSH	RP	11RP 0101	1	12	11	S W W*
RAL		17	1	4	4	F
RAR		1F	1	4	4	F
RC		D8	1	6/12	5/11	S/S R R*
RET		C9	1	10	10	F R R
RIM (8085A only)		20	1	4	–	F
RLC		07	1	4	4	F
RM		F8	1	6/12	5/11	S/S R R*
RNC		D0	1	6/12	5/11	S/S R R*
RNZ		C0	1	6/12	5/11	S/S R R*
RP		F0	1	6/12	5/11	S/S R R*
RPE		E8	1	6/12	5/11	S/S R R*
RPO		E0	1	6/12	5/11	S/S R R*
RRC		0F	1	4	4	F
RST	N	11XX X111	1	12	11	S W W*
RZ		C8	1	6/12	5/11	S/S R R*
SBB	REG	1001 1SSS	1	4	4	F
SBB	M	9E	1	7	7	F R
SBI	DATA	DE data	2	7	7	F R
SHLD	ADDR	22 addr	3	16	16	F R R W W
SIM (8085A only)		30	1	4	–	F
SPHL		F9	1	6	5	S*
STA	ADDR	32 addr	3	13	13	F R R W
STAX	RP	000X 0010	1	7	7	F W
STC		37	1	4	4	F
SUB	REG	1001 0SSS	1	4	4	F
SUB	M	96	1	7	7	F R
SUI	DATA	D6 data	2	7	7	F R
XCHG		EB	1	4	4	F
XRA	REG	1010 1SSS	1	4	4	F
XRA	M	AE	1	7	7	F R
XRI	DATA	EE data	2	7	7	F R
XTHL		E3	1	16	18	F R R W W

Machine cycle types:

F	Four clock period instr fetch	
S	Six clock period instr fetch	
R	Memory read	
I	I/O read	
W	Memory write	
O	I/O write	
B	Bus idle	
X	Variable or optional binary digit	
DDD	Binary digits identifying a destination register	B = 000, C = 001, D = 010 Memory = 110
SSS	Binary digits identifying a source register	E = 011, H = 100, L = 101 A = 111
RP	Register Pair	BC = 00, HL = 10 DE = 01, SP = 11

*Five clock period instruction fetch with 8080A.

†The longer machine cycle sequence applies regardless of condition evaluation with 8080A.

•An extra READ cycle (R) will occur for this condition with 8080A.

8085A CPU INSTRUCTIONS IN OPERATION CODE SEQUENCE
Table 5-2

OP CODE	MNEMONIC	OP CODE	MNEMONIC	OP CODE	MNEMONIC	OP CODE	MNEMONIC	OP CODE	MNEMONIC	OP CODE	MNEMONIC
00	NOP	2B	DCX H	56	MOV D,M	81	ADD C	AC	XRA H	D7	RST 2
01	LXI B,D16	2C	INR L	57	MOV D,A	82	ADD D	AD	XRA L	D8	RC
02	STAX B	2D	DCR L	58	MOV E,B	83	ADD E	AE	XRA M	D9	—
03	INX B	2E	MVI L,D8	59	MOV E,C	84	ADD H	AF	XRA A	DA	JC Adr
04	INR B	2F	CMA	5A	MOV E,D	85	ADD L	B0	ORA B	DB	IN D8
05	DCR B	30	SIM	5B	MOV E,E	86	ADD M	B1	ORA C	DC	CC Adr
06	MVI B,D8	31	LXI SP,D16	5C	MOV E,H	87	ADD A	B2	ORA D	DD	—
07	RLC	32	STA Adr	5D	MOV E,L	88	ADC B	B3	ORA E	DE	SBI D8
08	—	33	INX SP	5E	MOV E,M	89	ADC C	B4	ORA H	DF	RST 3
09	DAD B	34	INR M	5F	MOV E,A	8A	ADC D	B5	ORA L	E0	RPO
0A	LDAX B	35	DCR M	60	MOV H,B	8B	ADC E	B6	ORA M	E1	POP H
0B	DCX B	36	MVI M,D8	61	MOV H,C	8C	ADC H	B7	ORA A	E2	JPO Adr
0C	INR C	37	STC	62	MOV H,D	8D	ADC L	B8	CMP B	E3	XTHL
0D	DCR C	38	—	63	MOV H,E	8E	ADC M	B9	CMP C	E4	CPO Adr
0E	MVI C,D8	39	DAD SP	64	MOV H,H	8F	ADC A	BA	CMP D	E5	PUSH H
0F	RRC	3A	LDA Adr	65	MOV H,L	90	SUB B	BB	CMP E	E6	ANI D8
10	—	3B	DCX SP	66	MOV H,M	91	SUB C	BC	CMP H	E7	RST 4
11	LXI D,D16	3C	INR A	67	MOV H,A	92	SUB D	BD	CMP L	E8	RPE
12	STAX D	3D	DCR A	68	MOV L,B	93	SUB E	BE	CMP M	E9	PCHL
13	INX D	3E	MVI A,D8	69	MOV L,C	94	SUB H	BF	CMP A	EA	JPE Adr
14	INR D	3F	CMC	6A	MOV L,D	95	SUB L	C0	RNZ	EB	XCHG
15	DCR D	40	MOV B,B	6B	MOV L,E	96	SUB M	C1	POP B	EC	CPE Adr
16	MVI D,D8	41	MOV B,C	6C	MOV L,H	97	SUB A	C2	JNZ Adr	ED	—
17	RAL	42	MOV B,D	6D	MOV L,L	98	SBB B	C3	JMP Adr	EE	XRI D8
18	—	43	MOV B,E	6E	MOV L,M	99	SBB C	C4	CNZ Adr	EF	RST 5
19	DAD D	44	MOV B,H	6F	MOV L,A	9A	SBB D	C5	PUSH B	F0	RP
1A	LDAX D	45	MOV B,L	70	MOV M,B	9B	SBB E	C6	ADI D8	F1	POP PSW
1B	DCX D	46	MOV B,M	71	MOV M,C	9C	SBB H	C7	RST 0	F2	JP Adr
1C	INR E	47	MOV B,A	72	MOV M,D	9D	SBB L	C8	RZ	F3	DI
1D	DCR E	48	MOV C,B	73	MOV M,E	9E	SBB M	C9	RET Adr	F4	CP Adr
1E	MVI E,D8	49	MOV C,C	74	MOV M,H	9F	SBB A	CA	JZ	F5	PUSH PSW
1F	RAR	4A	MOV C,D	75	MOV M,L	A0	ANA B	CB	—	F6	ORI D8
20	RIM	4B	MOV C,E	76	HLT	A1	ANA C	CC	CZ Adr	F7	RST 6
21	LXI H,D16	4C	MOV C,H	77	MOV M,A	A2	ANA D	CD	CALL Adr	F8	RM
22	SHLD Adr	4D	MOV C,L	78	MOV A,B	A3	ANA E	CE	ACI D8	F9	SPHL
23	INX H	4E	MOV C,M	79	MOV A,C	A4	ANA H	CF	RST 1	FA	JM Adr
24	INR H	4F	MOV C,A	7A	MOV A,D	A5	ANA L	D0	RNC	FB	EI
25	DCR H	50	MOV D,B	7B	MOV A,E	A6	ANA M	D1	POP D	FC	CM Adr
26	MVI H,D8	51	MOV D,C	7C	MOV A,H	A7	ANA A	D2	JNC Adr	FD	—
27	DAA	52	MOV D,D	7D	MOV A,L	A8	XRA B	D3	OUT D8	FE	CPI D8
28	—	53	MOV D,E	7E	MOV A,M	A9	XRA C	D4	CNC Adr	FF	RST 7
29	DAD H	54	MOV D,H	7F	MOV A,A	AA	XRA D	D5	PUSH D		
2A	LHLD Adr	55	MOV D,L	80	ADD B	AB	XRA E	D6	SUI D8		

D8 = constant, or logical/arithmetic expression that evaluates to an 8-bit data quantity

Adr = 16-bit address.

D16 = constant, or logical/arithmetic expression that evaluates to a 16-bit data quantity.

8085A INSTRUCTION SET SUMMARY BY FUNCTIONAL GROUPING
Table 5-3

Mnemonic	Description	Instruction Code (1) D_7	D_6	D_5	D_4	D_3	D_2	D_1	D_0	Page
MOVE, LOAD, AND STORE										
MOVr1 r2	Move register to register	0	1	D	D	D	S	S	S	5-4
MOV M.r	Move register to memory	0	1	1	1	0	S	S	S	5-4
MOV r.M	Move memory to register	0	1	D	D	D	1	1	0	5-4
MVI r	Move immediate register	0	0	D	D	D	1	1	0	5-4
MVI M	Move immediate memory	0	0	1	1	0	1	1	0	5-4
LXI B	Load immediate register Pair B & C	0	0	0	0	0	0	0	1	5-5
LXI D	Load immediate register Pair D & E	0	0	0	1	0	0	0	1	5-5
LXI H	Load immediate register Pair H & L	0	0	1	0	0	0	0	1	5-5
STAX B	Store A indirect	0	0	0	0	0	0	1	0	5-6
STAX D	Store A indirect	0	0	0	1	0	0	1	0	5-6
LDAX B	Load A indirect	0	0	0	0	1	0	1	0	5-5
LDAX D	Load A indirect	0	0	0	1	1	0	1	0	5-5
STA	Store A direct	0	0	1	1	0	0	1	0	5-5
LDA	Load A direct	0	0	1	1	1	0	1	0	5-5
SHLD	Store H & L direct	0	0	1	0	0	0	1	0	5-5
LHLD	Load H & L direct	0	0	1	0	1	0	1	0	5-5
XCHG	Exchange D & E. H & L Registers	1	1	1	0	1	0	1	1	5-6
STACK OPS										
PUSH B	Push register Pair B & C on stack	1	1	0	0	0	1	0	1	5-15
PUSH D	Push register Pair D & E on stack	1	1	0	1	0	1	0	1	5-15
PUSH H	Push register Pair H & L on stack	1	1	1	0	0	1	0	1	5-15
PUSH PSW	Push A and Flags on stack	1	1	1	1	0	1	0	1	5-15
POP B	Pop register Pair B & C off stack	1	1	0	0	0	0	0	1	5-15
POP D	Pop register Pair D & E off stack	1	1	0	1	0	0	0	1	5-15
POP H	Pop register Pair H & L off stack	1	1	1	0	0	0	0	1	5-15
POP PSW	Pop A and Flags off stack	1	1	1	1	0	0	0	1	5-15
XTHL	Exchange top of stack. H & L	1	1	1	0	0	0	1	1	5-16
SPHL	H & L to stack pointer	1	1	1	1	1	0	0	1	5-16
LXI SP	Load immediate stack pointer	0	0	1	1	0	0	0	1	5-5
INX SP	Increment stack pointer	0	0	1	1	0	0	1	1	5-9
DCX SP	Decrement stack pointer	0	0	1	1	1	0	1	1	5-9
JUMP										
JMP	Jump unconditional	1	1	0	0	0	0	1	1	5-13
JC	Jump on carry	1	1	0	1	1	0	1	0	5-13
JNC	Jump on no carry	1	1	0	1	0	0	1	0	5-13
JZ	Jump on zero	1	1	0	0	1	0	1	0	5-13
JNZ	Jump on no zero	1	1	0	0	0	0	1	0	5-13
JP	Jump on positive	1	1	1	1	0	0	1	0	5-13
JM	Jump on minus	1	1	1	1	1	0	1	0	5-13
JPE	Jump on parity even	1	1	1	0	1	0	1	0	5-13
JPO	Jump on parity odd	1	1	1	0	0	0	1	0	5-13
PCHL	H & L to program counter	1	1	1	0	1	0	0	1	5-15
CALL										
CALL	Call unconditional	1	1	0	0	1	1	0	1	5-13
CC	Call on carry	1	1	0	1	1	1	0	0	5-14
CNC	Call on no carry	1	1	0	1	0	1	0	0	5-14
CZ	Call on zero	1	1	0	0	1	1	0	0	5-14
CNZ	Call on no zero	1	1	0	0	0	1	0	0	5-14
CP	Call on positive	1	1	1	1	0	1	0	0	5-14
CM	Call on minus	1	1	1	1	1	1	0	0	5-14
CPE	Call on parity even	1	1	1	0	1	1	0	0	5-14
CPO	Call on parity odd	1	1	1	0	0	1	0	0	5-14
RETURN										
RET	Return	1	1	0	0	1	0	0	1	5-14
RC	Return on carry	1	1	0	1	1	0	0	0	5-14
RNC	Return on no carry	1	1	0	1	0	0	0	0	5-14
RZ	Return on zero	1	1	0	0	1	0	0	0	5-14
RNZ	Return on no zero	1	1	0	0	0	0	0	0	5-14
RP	Return on positive	1	1	1	1	0	0	0	0	5-14
RM	Return on minus	1	1	1	1	1	0	0	0	5-14
RPE	Return on parity even	1	1	1	0	1	0	0	0	5-14
RPO	Return on parity odd	1	1	1	0	0	0	0	0	5-14
RESTART										
RST	Restart	1	1	A	A	A	1	1	1	5-14
INPUT/OUTPUT										
IN	Input	1	1	0	1	1	0	1	1	5-16
OUT	Output	1	1	0	1	0	0	1	1	5-16
INCREMENT AND DECREMENT										
INR r	Increment register	0	0	D	D	D	1	0	0	5-8
DCR r	Decrement register	0	0	D	D	D	1	0	1	5-8
INR M	Increment memory	0	0	1	1	0	1	0	0	5-8
DCR M	Decrement memory	0	0	1	1	0	1	0	1	5-8
INX B	Increment B & C registers	0	0	0	0	0	0	1	1	5-9
INX D	Increment D & E registers	0	0	0	1	0	0	1	1	5-9
INX H	Increment H & L registers	0	0	1	0	0	0	1	1	5-9
DCX B	Decrement B & C	0	0	0	0	1	0	1	1	5-9
DCX D	Decrement D & E	0	0	0	1	1	0	1	1	5-9
DCX H	Decrement H & L	0	0	1	0	1	0	1	1	5-9
ADD										
ADD r	Add register to A	1	0	0	0	0	S	S	S	5-6
ADC r	Add register to A with carry	1	0	0	0	1	S	S	S	5-6
ADD M	Add memory to A	1	0	C	0	0	1	1	0	5-6
ADC M	Add memory to A with carry	1	0	0	0	1	1	1	0	5-7
ADI	Add immediate to A	1	1	0	0	0	1	1	0	5-6
ACI	Add immediate to A with carry	1	1	0	0	1	1	1	0	5-7
DAD B	Add B & C to H & L	0	0	0	0	1	0	0	1	5-9
DAD D	Add D & E to H & L	0	0	0	1	1	0	0	1	5-9
DAD H	Add H & L to H & L	0	0	1	0	1	0	0	1	5-9
DAD SP	Add stack pointer to H & L	0	0	1	1	1	0	0	1	5-9
SUBTRACT										
SUB r	Subtract register from A	1	0	0	1	0	S	S	S	5-7
SBB r	Subtract register from A with borrow	1	0	0	1	1	S	S	S	5-7
SUB M	Subtract memory from A	1	0	0	1	0	1	1	0	5-7
SBB M	Subtract memory from A with borrow	1	0	0	1	1	1	1	0	5-8
SUI	Subtract immediate from A	1	1	0	1	0	1	1	0	5-7

8085A INSTRUCTION SET SUMMARY (Cont'd)
Table 5-3

Mnemonic	Description	Instruction Code (1) D_7	D_6	D_5	D_4	D_3	D_2	D_1	D_0	Page
SBI	Subtract immediate from A with borrow	1	1	0	1	1	1	1	0	5-8
LOGICAL										
ANA r	And register with A	1	0	1	0	0	S	S	S	5-9
XRA r	Exclusive OR register with A	1	0	1	0	1	S	S	S	5-10
ORA r	OR register with A	1	0	1	1	0	S	S	S	5-10
CMP r	Compare register with A	1	0	1	1	1	S	S	S	5-11
ANA M	And memory with A	1	0	1	0	0	1	1	0	5-10
XRA M	Exclusive OR memory with A	1	0	1	0	1	1	1	0	5-10
ORA M	OR memory with A	1	0	1	1	0	1	1	0	5-11
CMP M	Compare memory with A	1	0	1	1	1	1	1	0	5-11
ANI	And immediate with A	1	1	1	0	0	1	1	0	5-10
XRI	Exclusive OR immediate with A	1	1	1	0	1	1	1	0	5-10
ORI	OR immediate with A	1	1	1	1	0	1	1	0	5-11
CPI	Compare immediate with A	1	1	1	1	1	1	1	0	5-11
ROTATE										
RLC	Rotate A left	0	0	0	0	0	1	1	1	5-11
RRC	Rotate A right	0	0	0	0	1	1	1	1	5-12
RAL	Rotate A left through carry	0	0	0	1	0	1	1	1	5-12
RAR	Rotate A right through carry	0	0	0	1	1	1	1	1	5-12
SPECIALS										
CMA	Complement A	0	0	1	0	1	1	1	1	5-12
STC	Set carry	0	0	1	1	0	1	1	1	5-12
CMC	Complement carry	0	0	1	1	1	1	1	1	5-12
DAA	Decimal adjust A	0	0	1	0	0	1	1	1	5-9
CONTROL										
EI	Enable Interrupts	1	1	1	1	1	0	1	1	5-17
DI	Disable Interrupt	1	1	1	1	0	0	1	1	5-17
NOP	No-operation	0	0	0	0	0	0	0	0	5-17
HLT	Halt	0	1	1	1	0	1	1	0	5-17
NEW 8085A INSTRUCTIONS										
RIM	Read Interrupt Mask	0	0	1	0	0	0	0	0	5-17
SIM	Set Interrupt Mask	0	0	1	1	0	0	0	0	5-18

NOTES: 1. DDS or SSS: B 000, C 001, D 010, E011, H 100, L 101, Memory 110, A 111.
2. Two possible cycle times. (6/12) indicate instruction cycles dependent on condition flags.

Device Specifications 6

8080A/808A-1/8080A-2
8-BIT N-CHANNEL MICROPROCESSOR

- **TTL Drive Capability**
- **2 μs (—1:1.3 μs, —2:1.5 μs) Instruction Cycle**
- **Powerful Problem Solving Instruction Set**
- **6 General Purpose Registers and an Accumulator**
- **16-Bit Program Counter for Directly Addressing up to 64K Bytes of Memory**
- **16-Bit Stack Pointer and Stack Manipulation Instructions for Rapid Switching of the Program Environment**
- **Decimal, Binary, and Double Precision Arithmetic**
- **Ability to Provide Priority Vectored Interrupts**
- **512 Directly Addressed I/O Ports**
- **Available in EXPRESS — Standard Temperature Range**
- **Available in 40-Lead Cerdip and Plastic Packages**
(See Packaging Spec, Order #231369)

The Intel® 8080A is a complete 8-bit parallel central processing unit (CPU). It is fabricated on a single LSI chip using Intel's n-channel silicon gate MOS process. This offers the user a high performance solution to control and processing applications.

The 8080A contains 6 8-bit general purpose working registers and an accumulator. The 6 general purpose registers may be addressed individually or in pairs providing both single and double precision operators. Arithmetic and logical instructions set or reset 4 testable flags. A fifth flag provides decimal arithmetic operation.

The 8080A has an external stack feature wherein any portion of memory may be used as a last in/first out stack to store/retrieve the contents of the accumulator, flags, program counter, and all of the 6 general purpose registers. The 16-bit stack pointer controls the addressing of this external stack. This stack gives the 8080A the ability to easily handle multiple level priority interrupts by rapidly storing and restoring processor status. It also provides almost unlimited subroutine nesting.

This microprocessor has been designed to simplify systems design. Separate 16-line address and 8-line bidirectional data busses are used to facilitate easy interface to memory and I/O. Signals to control the interface to memory and I/O are provided directly by the 8080A. Ultimate control of the address and data busses resides with the HOLD signal. It provides the ability to suspend processor operation and force the address and data busses into a high impedance state. This permits OR-tying these busses with other controlling devices for (DMA) direct memory access or multi-processor operation.

NOTE:
The 8080A is functionally and electrically compatible with the Intel® 8080.

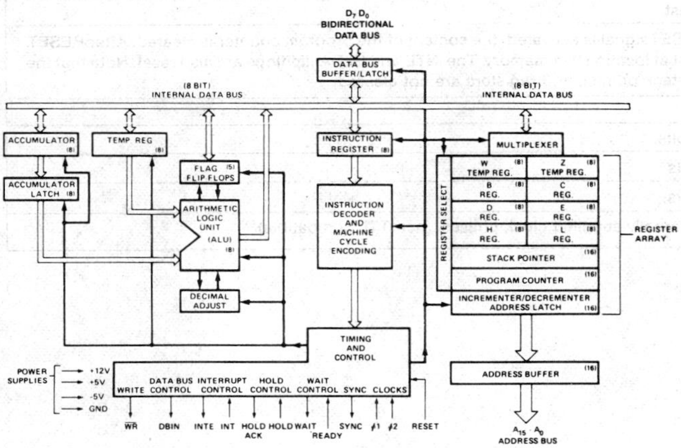

Figure 1. Block Diagram

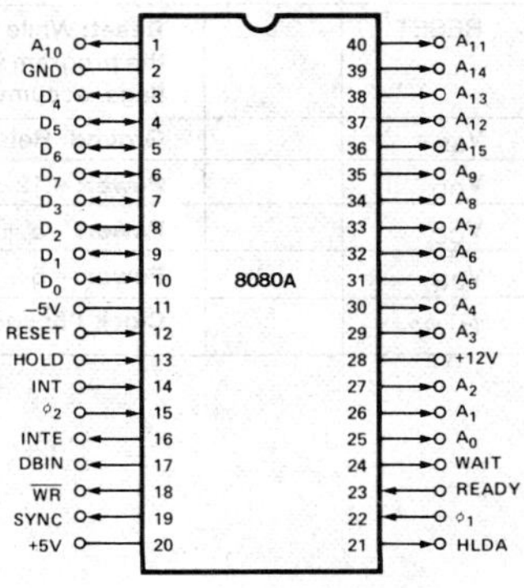

Figure 2. Pin Configuration

Table 1. Pin Description

Symbol	Type	Name and Function
A_{15}-A_0	O	**Address Bus:** The address bus provides the address to memory (up to 64K 8-bit words) or denotes the I/O device number for up to 256 input and 256 output devices. A_0 is the least significant address bit.
D_7-D_0	I/O	**Data Bus:** The data bus provides bi-directional communication betweeen the CPU, memory, and I/O devices for instructions and data transfers. Also, during the first clock cycle of each machine cycle, the 8080A outputs a status word on the data bus that describes the current machine cycle. D_0 is the least significant bit.
SYNC	O	**Synchronizing Signal:** The SYNC pin provides a signal to indicate the beginning of each machine cycle.
DBIN	O	**Data Bus In:** The DBIN signal indicates to external circuits that the data bus is in the input mode. This signal should be used to enable the gating of data onto the 8080A data bus from memory or I/O.
READY	I	**Ready:** The READY signal indicates to the 8080A that valid memory or input data is available on the 8080A data bus. This signal is used to synchronize the CPU with slower memory or I/O devices. If after sending an address out the 8080A does not receive a READY input, the 8080A will enter a WAIT state for as long as the READY line is low. READY can also be used to single step the CPU.
WAIT	O	**Wait:** The WAIT signal acknowledges that the CPU is in a WAIT state.
$\overline{WR}$	O	**Write:** The $\overline{WR}$ signal is used for memory WRITE or I/O output control. The data on the data bus is stable while the $\overline{WR}$ signal is active low ($\overline{WR}$ = 0).
HOLD	I	**Hold:** The HOLD signal requests the CPU to enter the HOLD state. The HOLD state allows an external device to gain control of the 8080A address and data bus as soon as the 8080A has completed its use of these busses for the current machine cycle. It is recognized under the following conditions: • the CPU is in the HALT state. • the CPU is in the T2 or TW state and the READY signal is active. As a result of entering the HOLD state the CPU ADDRESS BUS (A_{15}-A_0) and DATA BUS (D_7-D_0) will be in their high impedance state. The CPU acknowledges its state with the HOLD ACKNOWLEDGE (HLDA) pin.
HLDA	O	**Hold Acknowledge:** The HLDA signal appears in response to the HOLD signal and indicates that the data and address bus will go to the high impedance state. The HLDA signal begins at: • T3 for READ memory or input. • The Clock Period following T3 for WRITE memory or OUTPUT operation. In either case, the HLDA signal appears after the rising edge of ϕ_2.
INTE	O	**Interrupt Enable:** Indicates the content of the internal interrupt enable flip/flop. This flip/flop may be set or reset by the Enable and Disable Interrupt instructions and inhibits interrupts from being accepted by the CPU when it is reset. It is automatically reset (disabling further interrupts) at time T1 of the instruction fetch cycle (M1) when an interrupt is accepted and is also reset by the RESET signal.
INT	I	**Interrupt Request:** The CPU recognizes an interrupt request on this line at the end of the current instruction or while halted. If the CPU is in the HOLD state or if the Interrupt Enable flip/flop is reset it will not honor the request.
RESET[1]	I	**Reset:** While the RESET signal is activated, the content of the program counter is cleared. After RESET, the program will start at location 0 in memory. The INTE and HLDA flip/flops are also reset. Note that the flags, accumulator, stack pointer, and registers are not cleared.
V_{SS}		**Ground:** Reference.
V_{DD}		**Power:** +12 ±5% Volts.
V_{CC}		**Power:** +5 ±5% Volts.
V_{BB}		**Power:** −5 ±5% Volts.
ϕ_1, ϕ_2		**Clock Phases:** 2 externally supplied clock phases. (non TTL compatible)

ABSOLUTE MAXIMUM RATINGS*

Temperature Under Bias . . . . 0°C to +70° C
Storage Temperature . . . . -65°C to +150°C
All Input or Output Voltages
With Respect to V_{BB} . . . . -0.3V to +20V
V_{CC}, V_{DD} and V_{SS} With Respect to V_{BB} -0.3V to +20V
Power Dissipation 1.5W

**NOTICE: Stresses above those listed under "Absolute Maximum Ratings" may cause permanent damage to the device. This is a stress rating only and functional operation of the device at these or any other conditions above those indicated in the operational sections of this specification is not implied. Exposure to absolute maximum rating conditions for extended periods may affect device reliability.*

D.C. CHARACTERISTICS (T_A = 0°C to 70°C, V_{DD} = +12V ±5%, V_{CC} = +5V ±5%, V_{BB} = −5V ±5%, V_{SS} =0V; unless otherwise noted)

Symbol	Parameter	Min.	Typ.	Max.	Unit	Test Condition
V_{ILC}	Clock Input Low Voltage	$V_{SS}-1$		$V_{SS}+0.8$	V	
V_{IHC}	Clock Input High Voltage	9.0		$V_{DD}+1$	V	
V_{IL}	Input Low Voltage	$V_{SS}-1$		$V_{SS}+0.8$	V	
V_{IH}	Input High Voltage	3.3		$V_{CC}+1$	V	
V_{OL}	Output Low Voltage			0.45	V	I_{OL} = 1.9mA on all outputs,
V_{OH}	Output High Voltage	3.7			V	I_{OH} = −150μA.
$I_{DD\,(AV)}$	Avg. Power Supply Current (V_{DD})		40	70	mA	Operation
$I_{CC\,(AV)}$	Avg. Power Supply Current (V_{CC})		60	80	mA	T_{CY} = .48 μsec
$I_{BB\,(AV)}$	Avg. Power Supply Current (V_{BB})		.01	1	mA	
I_{IL}	Input Leakage			±10	μA	$V_{SS} \leq V_{IN} \leq V_{CC}$
I_{CL}	Clock Leakage			±10	μA	$V_{SS} \leq V_{CLOCK} \leq V_{DD}$
I_{DL}	Data Bus Leakage in Input Mode			-100 -2.0	μA mA	$V_{SS} \leq V_{IN} \leq V_{SS}+0.8V$ $V_{SS}+0.8V \leq V_{IN} \leq V_{CC}$
I_{FL}	Address and Data Bus Leakage During HOLD			+10 -100	μA	$V_{ADDR/DATA} = V_{CC}$ $V_{ADDR/DATA} = V_{SS} + 0.45V$

CAPACITANCE (T_A = 25°C, V_{CC} = V_{DD} = V_{SS} = 0V, V_{BB} = −5V)

Symbol	Parameter	Typ.	Max.	Unit	Test Condition
C_ϕ	Clock Capacitance	17	25	pf	f_c = 1 MHz
C_{IN}	Input Capacitance	6	10	pf	Unmeasured Pins
C_{OUT}	Output Capacitance	10	20	pf	Returned to V_{SS}

NOTES:

1. The RESET signal must be active for a minimum of 3 clock cycles.
2. ΔI supply / ΔT_A = -0.45%/°C.

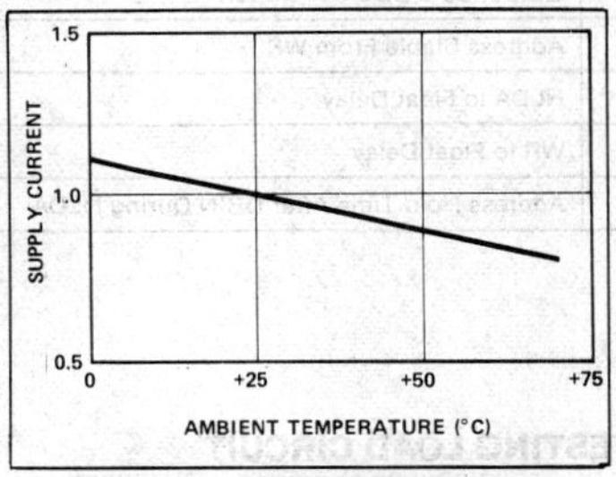

Typical Supply Current vs. Temperature, Normalized[2]

A.C. CHARACTERISTICS (8080A)

(T_A = 0°C to 70°C, V_{DD} = +12V ±5%, V_{CC} = +5V ±5%, V_{BB} = −5V ±5%, V_{SS} = 0V; unless otherwise noted)

Symbol	Parameter	Min.	Max.	-1 Min.	-1 Max.	-2 Min.	-2 Max.	Unit	Test Condition
t_{CY}[3]	Clock Period	0.48	2.0	0.32	2.0	0.38	2.0	μsec	
t_r, t_f	Clock Rise and Fall Time	0	50	0	25	0	50	nsec	
$t_{\phi 1}$	ϕ_1 Pulse Width	60		50		60		nsec	
$t_{\phi 2}$	ϕ_2 Pulse Width	220		145		175		nsec	
t_{D1}	Delay ϕ_1 to ϕ_2	0		0		0		nsec	
t_{D2}	Delay ϕ_2 to ϕ_1	70		60		70		nsec	
t_{D3}	Delay ϕ_1 to ϕ_2 Leading Edges	80		60		70	nsec		
t_{DA}	Address Output Delay From ϕ_2		200		150		175	nsec	C_L = 100 pF
t_{DD}	Data Output Delay From ϕ_2		200		180		200	nsec	
t_{DC}	Signal Output Delay From ϕ_1 or ϕ_2 (SYNC, WR, WAIT, HLDA)		120		110		120	nsec	C_L = 50 pF
t_{DF}	DBIN Delay From ϕ_2	25	140	25	130	25	140	nsec	
t_{DI}[1]	Delay for Input Bus to Enter Input Mode		t_{DF}		t_{DF}		t_{DF}	nsec	
t_{DS1}	Data Setup Time During ϕ_1 and DBIN	30		10		20		nsec	
t_{DS2}	Data Setup Time to ϕ_2 During DBIN	150		120		130		nsec	
t_{DH}[1]	Data Holt time From ϕ_2 and DBIN	[1]		[1]		[1]		nsec	
t_{IE}	INTE Output Delay From ϕ_2		200		200		200	nsec	C_L = 50 pF
t_{RS}	READY Setup Time During ϕ_2	120		90		90		nsec	
t_{HS}	HOLD Setup Time During ϕ_2	140		120		120		nsec	
t_{IS}	INT Setup Time During ϕ_2	120		100		100		nsec	
t_H	Hold Time From ϕ_2 (READY, INT, HOLD)	0		0		0		nsec	
t_{FD}	Delay to Float During Hold (Address and Data Bus)		120		120		120	nsec	
t_{AW}	Address Stable Prior to WR	[5]		[5]		[5]		nsec	
t_{DW}	Output Data Stable Prior to WR	[6]		[6]		[6]		nsec	
t_{WD}	Output Data Stable From WR	[7]		[7]		[7]		nsec	
t_{WA}	Address Stable From WR	[7]		[7]		[7]		nsec	
t_{HF}	HLDA to Float Delay	[8]		[8]		[8]		nsec	
t_{WF}	WR to Float Delay	[9]		[9]		[9]		nsec	
t_{AH}	Address Hold Time After DBIN During HLDA	-20		-20		-20		nsec	

A.C. TESTING LOAD CIRCUIT

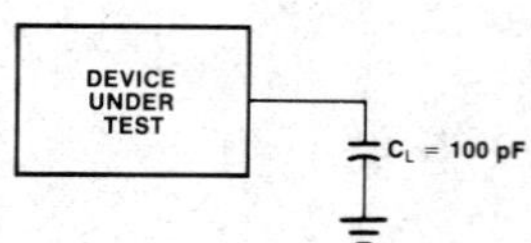

C_L = 100 pF
C_L INCLUDES JIG CAPACITANCE

WAVEFORMS

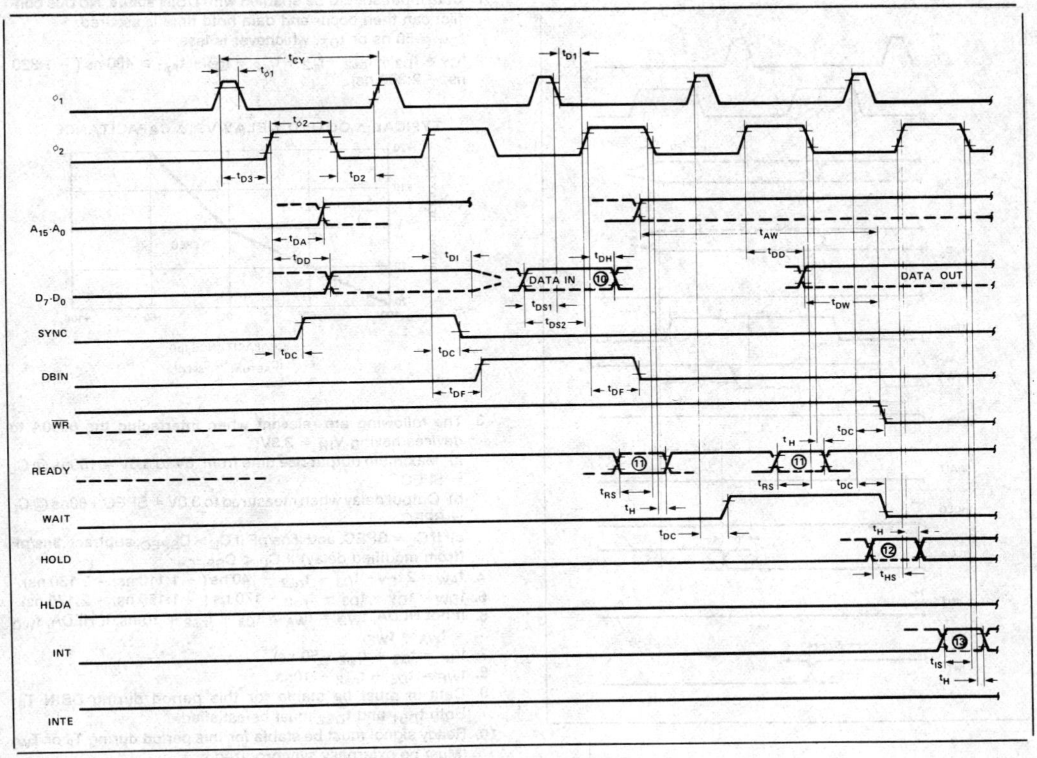

NOTE:
Timing measurements are made at the following reference voltages: CLOCK "1" = 8.0V, "0" = 1.0V; INPUTS "1" = 3.3V, "0" = 0.8V; OUTPUTS "1" = 2.0V, "0" = 0.8V.

WAVEFORMS (Continued)

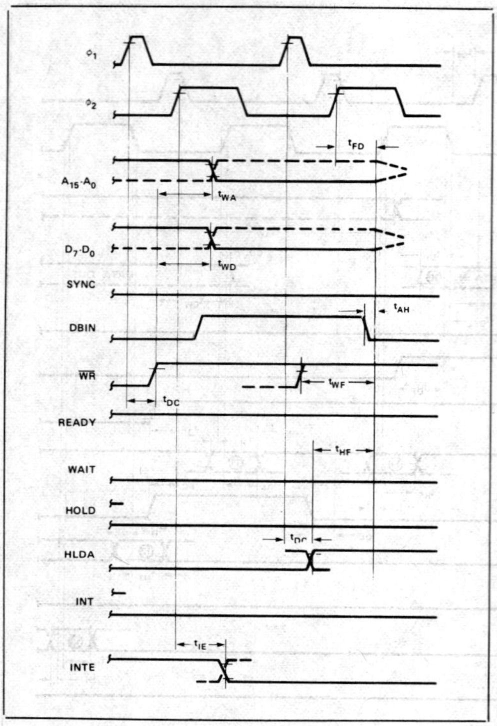

NOTES: (Parenthesis gives -1, -2 specifications, respectively)

1. Data input should be enabled with DBIN status. No bus conflict can then occur and data hold time is assured. $t_{DH} = 50$ ns or t_{DF}, whichever is less.
2. $t_{CY} = t_{D3} + t_{r\phi2} + t_{\phi2} + t_{f\phi2} + t_{D2} + t_{r\phi1} \geq 480$ ns (− 1:320 ns, − 2:380 ns).

TYPICAL Δ OUTPUT DELAY VS. Δ CAPACITANCE

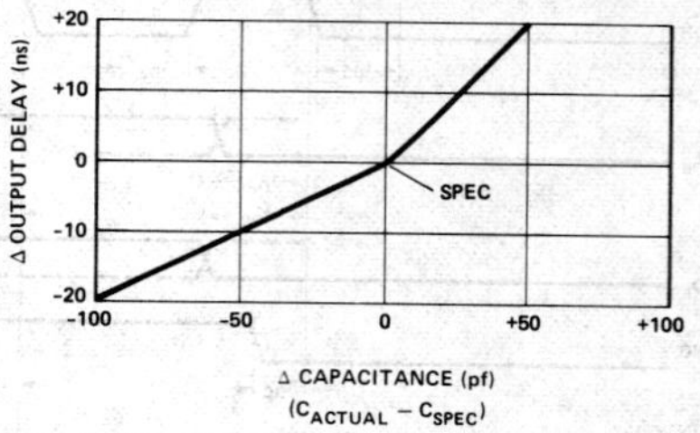

3. The following are relevant when interfacing the 8080A to devices having $V_{IH} = 3.3V$:
   a) Maximum output rise time from .8V to 3.3V = 100ns @ C_L = SPEC.
   b) Output delay when measured to 3.0V = SPEC +60ns @ C_L = SPEC.
   c) If C_L = SPEC, add .6ns/pF if $C_L > C_{SPEC}$, subtract .3ns/pF (from modified delay) if $C_L < C_{SPEC}$.
4. $t_{AW} = 2\,t_{CY} - t_{D3} - t_{r\phi2} - 140$ ns (− 1:110 ns, − 2:130 ns).
5. $t_{DW} = t_{CY} - t_{D3} - t_{r\phi2} - 170$ ns (− 1:150 ns, − 2:170 ns).
6. If not HLDA, $t_{WD} = t_{WA} = t_{D3} + t_{r\phi2} + 10$ ns. If HLDA, $t_{WD} = t_{WA} = t_{WF}$.
7. $t_{HF} = t_{D3} + t_{r\phi2} - 50$ ns).
8. $t_{WF} = t_{D3} + t_{r\phi2} - 10$ns.
9. Data in must be stable for this period during DBIN T_3. Both t_{DS1} and t_{DS2} must be satisfied.
10. Ready signal must be stable for this period during T_2 or T_W. (Must be externally synchronized.)
11. Hold signal must be stable for this period during T_2 or T_W when entering hold mode, and during T_3, T_4, T_5 and T_{WH} when in hold mode. (External synchronization is not required.)
12. Interrupt signal must be stable during this period of the last clock cycle of any instruction in order to be recognized on the following instruction. (External synchronization is not required.)
13. This timing diagram shows timing relationships only; it does not represent any specific machine cycle.

INSTRUCTION SET

The accumulator group instructions include arithmetic and logical operators with direct, indirect, and immediate addressing modes.

Move, load, and store instruction groups provide the ability to move either 8 or 16 bits of data between memory, the six working registers and the accumulator using direct, indirect, and immediate addressing modes.

The ability to branch to different portions of the program is provided with jump, jump conditional, and computed jumps. Also the ability to call to and return from subroutines is provided both conditionally and unconditionally. The RESTART (or single byte call instruction) is useful for interrupt vector operation.

Double precision operators such as stack manipulation and double add instructions extend both the arithmetic and interrupt handling capability of the 8080A. The ability to increment and decrement memory, the six general registers and the accumulator is provided as well as extended increment and decrement instructions to operate on the register pairs and stack pointer. Further capability is provided by the ability to rotate the accumulator left or right through or around the carry bit.

Input and output may be accomplished using memory addresses as I/O ports or the directly addressed I/O provided for in the 8080A instruction set.

The following special instruction group completes the 8080A instruction set: the NOP instruction, HALT to stop processor execution and the DAA instructions provide decimal arithmetic capability. STC allows the carry flag to be directly set, and the CMC instruction allows it to be complemented. CMA complements the contents of the accumulator and XCHG exchanges the contents of two 16-bit register pairs directly.

Data and Instruction Formats

Data in the 8080A is stored in the form of 8-bit binary integers. All data transfers to the system data bus will be in the same format.

D_7 D_6 D_5 D_4 D_3 D_2 D_1 D_0

DATA WORD

The program instructions may be one, two, or three bytes in length. Multiple byte instructions must be stored in successive words in program memory. The instruction formats then depend on the particular operation executed.

		TYPICAL INSTRUCTIONS
One Byte Instructions		
D_7 D_6 D_5 D_4 D_3 D_2 D_1 D_0	OP CODE	Register to register, memory reference, arithmetic or logical, rotate, return, push, pop, enable or disable Interrupt instructions
Two Byte Instructions		
D_7 D_6 D_5 D_4 D_3 D_2 D_1 D_0	OP CODE	
D_7 D_6 D_5 D_4 D_3 D_2 D_1 D_0	OPERAND	Immediate mode or I/O instructions
Three Byte Instructions		
D_7 D_6 D_5 D_4 D_3 D_2 D_1 D_0	OP CODE	Jump, call or direct load and store instructions
D_7 D_6 D_5 D_4 D_3 D_2 D_1 D_0	LOW ADDRESS OR OPERAND 1	
D_7 D_6 D_5 D_4 D_3 D_2 D_1 D_0	HIGH ADDRESS OR OPERAND 2	

For the 8080A a logic "1" is defined as a high level and a logic "0" is defined as a low level.

Table 2. Instruction Set Summary

Mnemonic	Instruction Code [1] D7	D6	D5	D4	D3	D2	D1	D0	Operations Description	Clock Cycles [2]
MOVE, LOAD, AND STORE										
MOVr1,r2	0	1	D	D	D	S	S	S	Move register to register	5
MOV M,r	0	1	1	1	0	S	S	S	Move register to memory	7
MOV r,M	0	1	D	D	D	1	1	0	Move memory to register	7
MVI r	0	0	D	D	D	1	1	0	Move immediate register	7
MVI M	0	0	1	1	0	1	1	0	Move immediate memory	10
LXI B	0	0	0	0	0	0	0	1	Load immediate register Pair B & C	10
LXI D	0	0	0	1	0	0	0	1	Load immediate register Pair D & E	10
LXI H	0	0	1	0	0	0	0	1	Load immediate register Pair H & L	10
STAX B	0	0	0	0	0	0	1	0	Store A indirect	7
STAX D	0	0	0	1	0	0	1	0	Store A indirect	7
LDAX B	0	0	0	0	1	0	1	0	Load A indirect	7
LDAX D	0	0	0	1	1	0	1	0	Load A indirect	7
STA	0	0	1	1	0	0	1	0	Store A direct	13
LDA	0	0	1	1	1	0	1	0	Load A direct	13
SHLD	0	0	1	0	0	0	1	0	Store H & L direct	16
LHLD	0	0	1	0	1	0	1	0	Load H & L direct	16
XCHG	1	1	1	0	1	0	1	1	Exchange D & E, H & L Registers	4
STACK OPS										
PUSH B	1	1	0	0	0	1	0	1	Push register Pair B & C on stack	11
PUSH D	1	1	0	1	0	1	0	1	Push register Pair D & E on stack	11
PUSH H	1	1	1	0	0	1	0	1	Push register Pair H & L on stack	11
PUSH PSW	1	1	1	1	0	1	0	1	Push A and Flags on stack	11
POP B	1	1	0	0	0	0	0	1	Pop register Pair B & C off stack	10
POP D	1	1	0	1	0	0	0	1	Pop register Pair D & E off stack	10
POP H	1	1	1	0	0	0	0	1	Pop register Pair H & L off stack	10
POP PSW	1	1	1	1	0	0	0	1	Pop A and Flags off stack	10
XTHL	1	1	1	0	0	0	1	1	Exchange top of stack, H & L	18
SPHL	1	1	1	1	1	0	0	1	H & L to stack pointer	5
LXI SP	0	0	1	1	0	0	0	1	Load immediate stack pointer	10
INX SP	0	0	1	1	0	0	1	1	Increment stack pointer	5
DCX SP	0	0	1	1	1	0	1	1	Decrement stack pointer	5
JUMP										
JMP	1	1	0	0	0	0	1	1	Jump unconditional	10
JC	1	1	0	1	1	0	1	0	Jump on carry	10
JNC	1	1	0	1	0	0	1	0	Jump on no carry	10
JZ	1	1	0	0	1	0	1	0	Jump on zero	10
JNZ	1	1	0	0	0	0	1	0	Jump on no zero	10
JP	1	1	1	1	0	0	1	0	Jump on positive	10
JM	1	1	1	1	1	0	1	0	Jump on minus	10
JPE	1	1	1	0	1	0	1	0	Jump on parity even	10
JPO	1	1	1	0	0	0	1	0	Jump on parity odd	10
PCHL	1	1	1	0	1	0	0	1	H & L to program counter	5
CALL										
CALL	1	1	0	0	1	1	0	1	Call unconditional	17
CC	1	1	0	1	1	1	0	0	Call on carry	11/17
CNC	1	1	0	1	0	1	0	0	Call on no carry	11/17
CZ	1	1	0	0	1	1	0	0	Call on zero	11/17
CNZ	1	1	0	0	0	1	0	0	Call on no zero	11/17
CP	1	1	1	1	0	1	0	0	Call on positive	11/17
CM	1	1	1	1	1	1	0	0	Call on minus	11/17
CPE	1	1	1	0	1	1	0	0	Call on parity even	11/17
CPO	1	1	1	0	0	1	0	0	Call on parity odd	11/17
RETURN										
RET	1	1	0	0	1	0	0	1	Return	10
RC	1	1	0	1	1	0	0	0	Return on carry	5/11
RNC	1	1	0	1	0	0	0	0	Return on no carry	5/11
RZ	1	1	0	0	1	0	0	0	Return on zero	5/11
RNZ	1	1	0	0	0	0	0	0	Return on no zero	5/11
RP	1	1	1	1	0	0	0	0	Return on positive	5/11
RM	1	1	1	1	1	0	0	0	Return on minus	5/11
RPE	1	1	1	0	1	0	0	0	Return on parity even	5/11
RPO	1	1	1	0	0	0	0	0	Return on parity odd	5/11
RESTART										
RST	1	1	A	A	A	1	1	1	Restart	11
INCREMENT AND DECREMENT										
INR r	0	0	D	D	D	1	0	0	Increment register	5
DCR r	0	0	D	D	D	1	0	1	Decrement register	5
INR M	0	0	1	1	0	1	0	0	Increment memory	10
DCR M	0	0	1	1	0	1	0	1	Decrement memory	10
INX B	0	0	0	0	0	0	1	1	Increment B & C registers	5
INX D	0	0	0	1	0	0	1	1	Increment D & E registers	5
INX H	0	0	1	0	0	0	1	1	Increment H & L registers	5
DCX B	0	0	0	0	1	0	1	1	Decrement B & C	5
DCX D	0	0	0	1	1	0	1	1	Decrement D & E	5
DCX H	0	0	1	0	1	0	1	1	Decrement H & L	5
ADD										
ADD r	1	0	0	0	0	S	S	S	Add register to A	4
ADC r	1	0	0	0	1	S	S	S	Add register to A with carry	4
ADD M	1	0	0	0	0	1	1	0	Add memory to A	7
ADC M	1	0	0	0	1	1	1	0	Add memory to A with carry	7
ADI	1	1	0	0	0	1	1	0	Add immediate to A	7
ACI	1	1	0	0	1	1	1	0	Add immediate to A with carry	7
DAD B	0	0	0	0	1	0	0	1	Add B & C to H & L	10
DAD D	0	0	0	1	1	0	0	1	Add D & E to H & L	10
DAD H	0	0	1	0	1	0	0	1	Add H & L to H & L	10
DAD SP	0	0	1	1	1	0	0	1	Add stack pointer to H & L	10

Summary of Processor Instructions (Cont.)

Mnemonic	Instruction Code [1] D_7	D_6	D_5	D_4	D_3	D_2	D_1	D_0	Operations Description	Clock Cycles [2]
SUBTRACT										
SUB r	1	0	0	1	0	S	S	S	Subtract register from A	4
SBB r	1	0	0	1	1	S	S	S	Subtract register from A with borrow	4
SUB M	1	0	0	1	0	1	1	0	Subtract memory from A	7
SBB M	1	0	0	1	1	1	1	0	Subtract memory from A with borrow	7
SUI	1	1	0	1	0	1	1	0	Subtract immediate from A	7
SBI	1	1	0	1	1	1	1	0	Subtract immediate from A with borrow	7
LOGICAL										
ANA r	1	0	1	0	0	S	S	S	And register with A	4
XRA r	1	0	1	0	1	S	S	S	Exclusive Or register with A	4
ORA r	1	0	1	1	0	S	S	S	Or register with A	4
CMP r	1	0	1	1	1	S	S	S	Compare register with A	4
ANA M	1	0	1	0	0	1	1	0	And memory with A	7
XRA M	1	0	1	0	1	1	1	0	Exclusive Or memory with A	7
ORA M	1	0	1	1	0	1	1	0	Or memory with A	7
CMP M	1	0	1	1	1	1	1	0	Compare memory with A	7
ANI	1	1	1	0	0	1	1	0	And immediate with A	7
XRI	1	1	1	0	1	1	1	0	Exclusive Or immediate with A	7
ORI	1	1	1	1	0	1	1	0	Or immediate with A	7
CPI	1	1	1	1	1	1	1	0	Compare immediate with A	7

Mnemonic	Instruction Code [1] D_7	D_6	D_5	D_4	D_3	D_2	D_1	D_0	Operations Description	Clock Cycles [2]
ROTATE										
RLC	0	0	0	0	0	1	1	1	Rotate A left	4
RRC	0	0	0	0	1	1	1	1	Rotate A right	4
RAL	0	0	0	1	0	1	1	1	Rotate A left through carry	4
RAR	0	0	0	1	1	1	1	1	Rotate A right through carry	4
SPECIALS										
CMA	0	0	1	0	1	1	1	1	Complement A	4
STC	0	0	1	1	0	1	1	1	Set carry	4
CMC	0	0	1	1	1	1	1	1	Complement carry	4
DAA	0	0	1	0	0	1	1	1	Decimal adjust A	4
INPUT/OUTPUT										
IN	1	1	0	1	1	0	1	1	Input	10
OUT	1	1	0	1	0	0	1	1	Output	10
CONTROL										
EI	1	1	1	1	1	0	1	1	Enable Interrupts	4
DI	1	1	1	1	0	0	1	1	Disable Interrupt	4
NOP	0	0	0	0	0	0	0	0	No-operation	4
HLT	0	1	1	1	0	1	1	0	Halt	7

NOTES:

1. DDD or SSS: B=000, C=001, D=010, E=011, H=100, L=101, Memory=110, A=111.
2. Two possible cycle times (6/12) indicate instruction cycles dependent on condition flags.

8085AH/8085AH-2/8085AH-1
8-BIT HMOS MICROPROCESSORS

- **Single +5V Power Supply with 10% Voltage Margins**
- **3 MHz, 5 MHz and 6 MHz Selections Available**
- **20% Lower Power Consumption than 8085A for 3 MHz and 5 MHz**
- **1.3 μs Instruction Cycle (8085AH); 0.8 μs (8085AH-2); 0.67 μs (8085AH-1)**
- **100% Software Compatible with 8080A**
- **On-Chip Clock Generator (with External Crystal, LC or RC Network)**
- **On-Chip System Controller; Advanced Cycle Status Information Available for Large System Control**
- **Four Vectored Interrupt Inputs (One is Non-Maskable) Plus an 8080A-Compatible Interrupt**
- **Serial In/Serial Out Port**
- **Decimal, Binary and Double Precision Arithmetic**
- **Direct Addressing Capability to 64K Bytes of Memory**
- **Available in 40-Lead Cerdip and Plastic Packages**
  (See Packaging Spec, Order #231369)

The Intel® 8085AH is a complete 8 bit parallel Central Processing Unit (CPU) implemented in N-channel, depletion load, silicon gate technology (HMOS). Its instruction set is 100% software compatible with the 8080A microprocessor, and it is designed to improve the present 8080A's performance by higher system speed. Its high level of system integration allows a minimum system of three IC's [8085AH (CPU), 8156H (RAM/IO) and 8755A (EPROM/IO)] while maintaining total system expandability. The 8085AH-2 and 8085AH-1 are faster versions of the 8085 AH.

The 8085AH incorporates all of the features that the 8224 (clock generator) and 8228 (system controller) provided for the 8080A, thereby offering a higher level of system integration.

The 8085AH uses a multiplexed data bus. The address is split between the 8 bit address bus and the 8 bit data bus. The on-chip address latches of 8155H/8156H/8755A memory products allow a direct interface with the 8085AH.

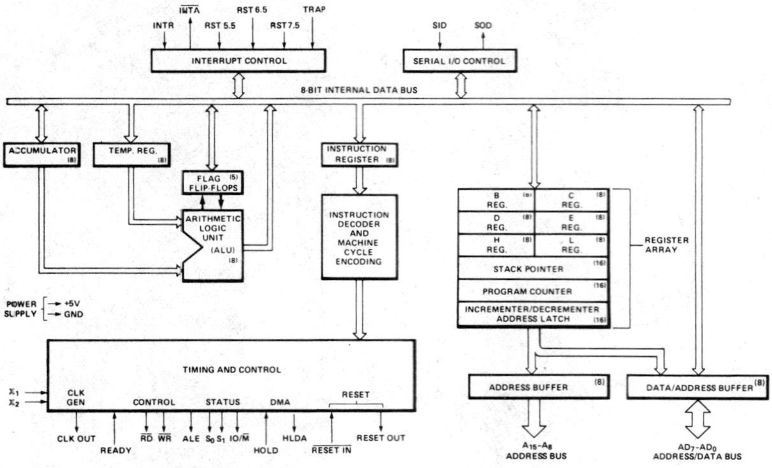

Figure 1. 8085AH CPU Functional Block Diagram

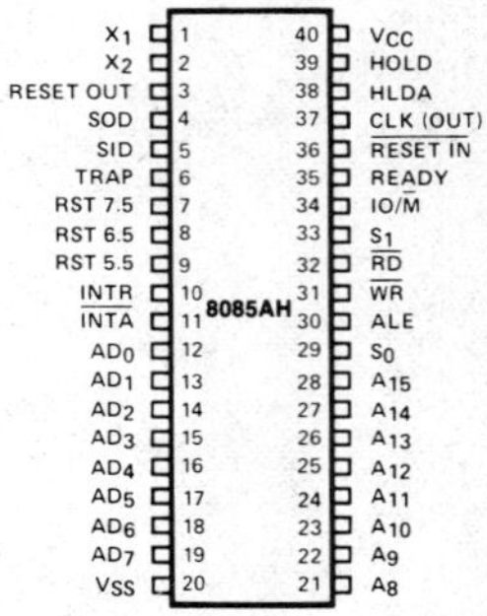

Figure 2. 8085AH Pin Configuration

Table 1. Pin Description

Symbol	Type	Name and Function
A_8–A_{15}	O	**Address Bus:** The most significant 8 bits of the memory address or the 8 bits of the I/O address, 3-stated during Hold and Halt modes and during RESET.
AD_{0-7}	I/O	**Multiplexed Address/Data Bus:** Lower 8 bits of the memory address (or I/O address) appear on the bus during the first clock cycle (T state) of a machine cycle. It then becomes the data bus during the second and third clock cycles.
ALE	O	**Address Latch Enable:** It occurs during the first clock state of a machine cycle and enables the address to get latched into the on-chip latch of peripherals. The falling edge of ALE is set to guarantee setup and hold times for the address information. The falling edge of ALE can also be used to strobe the status information. ALE is never 3-stated.
S_0, S_1, and IO/$\overline{M}$	O	**Machine Cycle Status:** IO/$\overline{M}$ S_1 S_0 Status 0 0 1 Memory write 0 1 0 Memory read 1 0 1 I/O write 1 1 0 I/O read 0 1 1 Opcode fetch 1 1 1 Interrupt Acknowledge * 0 0 Halt * X X Hold * X X Reset * = 3-state (high impedance) X = unspecified S_1 can be used as an advanced R/$\overline{W}$ status. IO/$\overline{M}$, S_0 and S_1 become valid at the beginning of a machine cycle and remain stable throughout the cycle. The falling edge of ALE may be used to latch the state of these lines.
$\overline{RD}$	O	**Read Control:** A low level on $\overline{RD}$ indicates the selected memory or I/O device is to be read and that the Data Bus is available for the data transfer, 3-stated during Hold and Halt modes and during RESET.
$\overline{WR}$	O	**Write Control:** A low level on $\overline{WR}$ indicates the data on the Data Bus is to be written into the selected memory or I/O location. Data is set up at the trailing edge of $\overline{WR}$. 3-stated during Hold and Halt modes and during RESET.
READY	I	**Ready:** If READY is high during a read or write cycle, it indicates that the memory or peripheral is ready to send or receive data. If READY is low, the cpu will wait an integral number of clock cycles for READY to go high before completing the read or write cycle. READY must conform to specified setup and hold times.
HOLD	I	**Hold:** Indicates that another master is requesting the use of the address and data buses. The cpu, upon receiving the hold request, will relinquish the use of the bus as soon as the completion of the current bus transfer. Internal processing can continue. The processor can regain the bus only after the HOLD is removed. When the HOLD is acknowledged, the Address, Data $\overline{RD}$, $\overline{WR}$, and IO/$\overline{M}$ lines are 3-stated.
HLDA	O	**Hold Acknowledge:** Indicates that the cpu has received the HOLD request and that it will relinquish the bus in the next clock cycle. HLDA goes low after the Hold request is removed. The cpu takes the bus one half clock cycle after HLDA goes low.
INTR	I	**Interrupt Request:** Is used as a general purpose interrupt. It is sampled only during the next to the last clock cycle of an instruction and during Hold and Halt states. If it is active, the Program Counter (PC) will be inhibited from incrementing and an $\overline{INTA}$ will be issued. During this cycle a RESTART or CALL instruction can be inserted to jump to the interrupt service routine. The INTR is enabled and disabled by software. It is disabled by Reset and immediately after an interrupt is accepted.
$\overline{INTA}$	O	**Interrupt Acknowledge:** Is used instead of (and has the same timing as) $\overline{RD}$ during the Instruction cycle after an INTR is accepted. It can be used to activate an 8259A Interrupt chip or some other interrupt port.
RST 5.5 RST 6.5 RST 7.5	I	**Restart Interrupts:** These three inputs have the same timing as INTR except they cause an internal RESTART to be automatically inserted. The priority of these interrupts is ordered as shown in Table 2. These interrupts have a higher priority than INTR. In addition, they may be individually masked out using the SIM instruction.

Table 1. Pin Description (Continued)

Symbol	Type	Name and Function
TRAP	I	**Trap:** Trap interrupt is a non-maskable RESTART interrupt. It is recognized at the same time as INTR or RST 5.5-7.5. It is unaffected by any mask or Interrupt Enable. It has the highest priority of any interrupt. (See Table 2.)
$\overline{\text{RESET IN}}$	I	**Reset In:** Sets the Program Counter to zero and resets the Interrupt Enable and HLDA flip-flops. The data and address buses and the control lines are 3-stated during RESET and because of the asynchronous nature of RESET, the processor's internal registers and flags may be altered by RESET with unpredictable results. $\overline{\text{RESET IN}}$ is a Schmitt-triggered input, allowing connection to an R-C network for power-on RESET delay (see Figure 3). Upon power-up, $\overline{\text{RESET IN}}$ must remain low for at least 10 ms after minimum V_{CC} has been reached. For proper reset operation after the power-up duration, $\overline{\text{RESET IN}}$ should be kept low a minimum of three clock periods. The CPU is held in the reset condition as long as $\overline{\text{RESET IN}}$ is applied.
RESET OUT	O	**Reset Out:** Reset Out indicates cpu is being reset. Can be used as a system reset. The signal is synchronized to the processor clock and lasts an integral number of clock periods.
X_1, X_2	I	**X_1 and X_2:** Are connected to a crystal, LC, or RC network to drive the internal clock generator. X_1 can also be an external clock input from a logic gate. The input frequency is divided by 2 to give the processor's internal operating frequency.
CLK	O	**Clock:** Clock output for use as a system clock. The period of CLK is twice the X_1, X_2 input period.
SID	I	**Serial Input Data Line:** The data on this line is loaded into accumulator bit 7 whenever a RIM instruction is executed.
SOD	O	**Serial Output Data Line:** The output SOD is set or reset as specified by the SIM instruction.
V_{CC}		**Power:** +5 volt supply.
V_{SS}		**Ground:** Reference.

Table 2. Interrupt Priority, Restart Address, and Sensitivity

Name	Priority	Address Branched To (1) When Interrupt Occurs	Type Trigger
TRAP	1	24H	Rising edge AND high level until sampled.
RST 7.5	2	3CH	Rising edge (latched).
RST 6.5	3	34H	High level until sampled.
RST 5.5	4	2CH	High level until sampled.
INTR	5	See Note (2).	High level until sampled.

NOTES:

1. The processor pushes the PC on the stack before branching to the indicated address.
2. The address branched to depends on the instruction provided to the cpu when the interrupt is acknowledged.

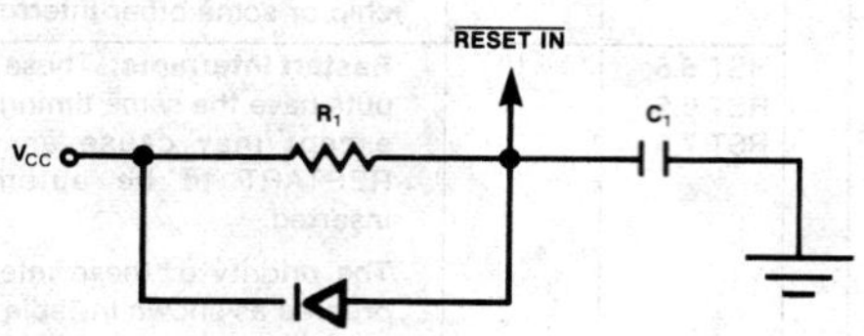

Figure 3. Power-On Reset Circuit

FUNCTIONAL DESCRIPTION

The 8085AH is a complete 8-bit parallel central processor. It is designed with N-channel, depletion load, silicon gate technology (HMOS), and requires a single +5 volt supply. Its basic clock speed is 3 MHz (8085AH), 5 MHz (8085AH-2), or 6 MHz (8085AH-1), thus improving on the present 8080A's performance with higher system speed. Also it is designed to fit into a minimum system of three IC's: The CPU (8085AH), a RAM/IO (8156H), and an EPROM/IO chip (8755A).

The 8085AH has twelve addressable 8-bit registers. Four of them can function only as two 16-bit register pairs. Six others can be used interchangeably as 8-bit registers or as 16-bit register pairs. The 8085AH register set is as follows:

Mnemonic	Register	Contents
ACC or A	Accumulator	8 bits
PC	Program Counter	16-bit address
BC,DE,HL	General-Purpose Registers; data pointer (HL)	8 bits x 6 or 16 bits x 3
SP	Stack Pointer	16-bit address
Flags or F	Flag Register	5 flags (8-bit space)

The 8085AH uses a multiplexed Data Bus. The address is split between the higher 8-bit Address Bus and the lower 8-bit Address/Data Bus. During the first T state (clock cycle) of a machine cycle the low order address is sent out on the Address/Data bus. These lower 8 bits may be latched externally by the Address Latch Enable signal (ALE). During the rest of the machine cycle the data bus is used for memory or I/O data.

The 8085AH provides $\overline{RD}$, $\overline{WR}$, S_0, S_1, and $IO/\overline{M}$ signals for bus control. An Interrupt Acknowledge signal ($\overline{INTA}$) is also provided. HOLD and all Interrupts are synchronized with the processor's internal clock. The 8085AH also provides Serial Input Data (SID) and Serial Output Data (SOD) lines for simple serial interface.

In addition to these features, the 8085AH has three maskable, vector interrupt pins, one nonmaskable TRAP interrupt, and a bus vectored interrupt, INTR.

INTERRUPT AND SERIAL I/O

The 8085AH has 5 interrupt inputs: INTR, RST 5.5, RST 6.5, RST 7.5, and TRAP. INTR is identical in function to the 8080A INT. Each of the three RESTART inputs, 5.5, 6.5, and 7.5, has a programmable mask. TRAP is also a RESTART interrupt but it is nonmaskable.

The three maskable interrupts cause the internal execution of RESTART (saving the program counter in the stack and branching to the RESTART address) if the interrupts are enabled and if the interrupt mask is not set. The nonmaskable TRAP causes the internal execution of a RESTART vector independent of the state of the interrupt enable or masks. (See Table 2.)

There are two different types of inputs in the restart interrupts. RST 5.5 and RST 6.5 are *high level-sensitive* like INTR (and INT on the 8080) and are recognized with the same timing as INTR. RST 7.5 is *rising edge-sensitive.*

For RST 7.5, only a pulse is required to set an internal flip-flop which generates the internal interrupt request (a normally high level signal with a low going pulse is recommended for highest system noise immunity). The RST 7.5 request flip-flop remains set until the request is serviced. Then it is reset automatically. This flip-flop may also be reset by using the SIM instruction or by issuing a $\overline{\text{RESET IN}}$ to the 8085AH. The RST 7.5 internal flip-flop will be set by a pulse on the RST 7.5 pin even when the RST 7.5 interrupt is masked out.

The status of the three RST interrupt masks can only be affected by the SIM instruction and $\overline{\text{RESET IN}}$. (See SIM, Chapter 5 of the 8080/8085 User's Manual.)

The interrupts are arranged in a fixed priority that determines which interrupt is to be recognized if more than one is pending as follows: TRAP—highest priority, RST 7.5, RST 6.5, RST 5.5, INTR—lowest priority. This priority scheme does not take into account the priority of a routine that was started by a higher priority interrupt. RST 5.5 can interrupt an RST 7.5 routine if the interrupts are re-enabled before the end of the RST 7.5 routine.

The TRAP interrupt is useful for catastrophic events such as power failure or bus error. The TRAP input is recognized just as any other interrupt but has the highest priority. It is not affected by any flag or mask. The TRAP input is both *edge and level sensitive*. The TRAP input must go high and remain high until it is acknowledged. It will not be recognized again until it goes low, then high again. This avoids any false triggering due to noise or logic glitches. Figure 4 illustrates the TRAP interrupt request circuitry within the 8085AH. Note that the servicing of any interrupt (TRAP, RST 7.5, RST 6.5, RST 5.5, INTR) disables all future interrupts (except TRAPs) until an EI instruction is executed.

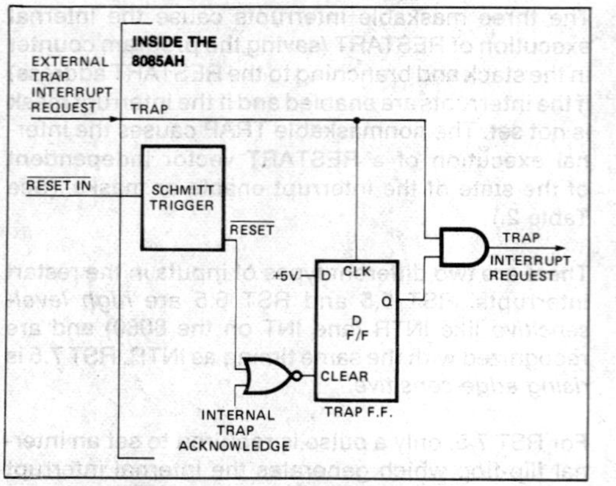

Figure 4. TRAP and RESET IN Circuit

The TRAP interrupt is special in that it disables interrupts, but preserves the previous interrupt enable status. Performing the first RIM instruction following a TRAP interrupt allows you to determine whether interrupts were enabled or disabled prior to the TRAP. All subsequent RIM instructions provide current interrupt enable status. Performing a RIM instruction following INTR, or RST 5.5-7.5 will provide current Interrupt Enable status, revealing that interrupts are disabled. See the description of the RIM instruction in the 8080/8085 Family User's Manual.

The serial I/O system is also controlled by the RIM and SIM instructions. SID is read by RIM, and SIM sets the SOD data.

DRIVING THE X_1 AND X_2 INPUTS

You may drive the clock inputs of the 8085AH, 8085AH-2, or 8085AH-1 with a crystal, an LC tuned circuit, an RC network, or an external clock source. The crystal frequency must be at least 1 MHz, and must be twice the desired internal clock frequency; hence, the 8085AH is operated with a 6 MHz crystal (for 3 MHz clock), the 8085AH-2 operated with a 10 MHz crystal (for 5 MHz clock), and the 8085AH-1 can be operated with a 12 MHz crystal (for 6 MHz clock). If a crystal is used, it must have the following characteristics:

Parallel resonance at twice the clock frequency desired
C_L (load capacitance) $\leq$ 30 pF
C_S (shunt capacitance) $\leq$ 7 pF
R_S (equivalent shunt resistance) $\leq$ 75 Ohms
Drive level: 10 mW
Frequency tolerance: $\pm$.005% (suggested)

Note the use of the 20 pF capacitor between X_2 and ground. This capacitor is required with crystal frequencies below 4 MHz to assure oscillator startup at the correct frequency. A parallel-resonant LC circuit may be used as the frequency-determining network for the 8085AH, providing that its frequency tolerance of approximately $\pm$10% is acceptable. The components are chosen from the formula:

$$f = \frac{1}{2\pi\sqrt{L(C_{ext} + C_{int})}}$$

To minimize variations in frequency, it is recommended that you choose a value for C_{ext} that is at least twice that of C_{int}, or 30 pF. The use of an LC circuit is not recommended for frequencies higher than approximately 5 MHz.

An RC circuit may be used as the frequency-determining network for the 8085AH if maintaining a precise clock frequency is of no importance. Variations in the on-chip timing generation can cause a wide variation in frequency when using the RC mode. Its advantage is its low component cost. The driving frequency generated by the circuit shown is approximately 3 MHz. It is not recommended that frequencies greatly higher or lower than this be attempted.

Figure 5 shows the recommended clock driver circuits. Note in D and E that pullup resistors are required to assure that the high level voltage of the input is at least 4V and maximum low level voltage of 0.8V.

For driving frequencies up to and including 6 MHz you may supply the driving signal to X_1 and leave X_2 open-circuited (Figure 5D). If the driving frequency is from 6 MHz to 12 MHz, stability of the clock generator will be improved by driving both X_1 and X_2 with a push-pull source (Figure 5E). To prevent self-oscillation of the 8085AH, be sure that X_2 is not coupled back to X_1 through the driving circuit.

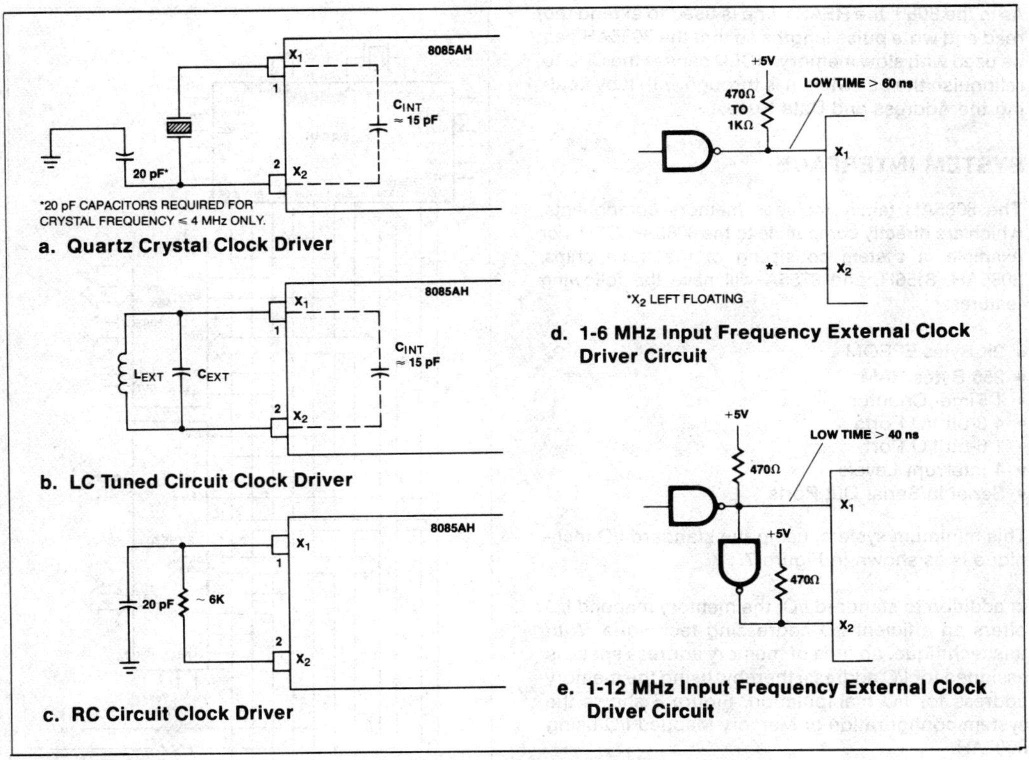

Figure 5. Clock Driver Circuits

GENERATING AN 8085AH WAIT STATE

If your system requirements are such that slow memories or peripheral devices are being used, the circuit shown in Figure 6 may be used to insert one WAIT state in each 8085AH machine cycle.

The D flip-flops should be chosen so that

- CLK is rising edge-triggered
- CLEAR is low-level active.

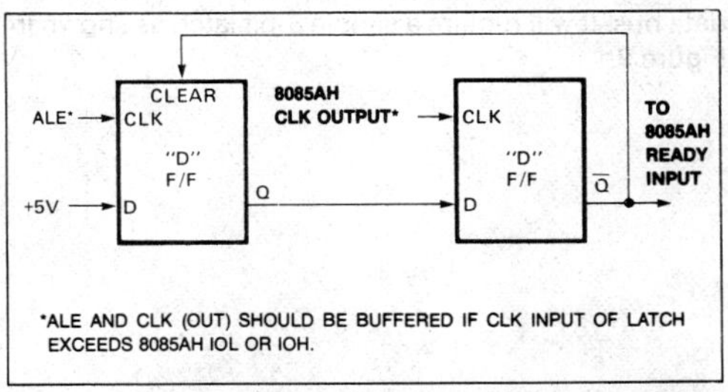

Figure 6. Generation of a Wait State for 8085AH CPU

As in the 8080, the READY line is used to extend the read and write pulse lengths so that the 8085AH can be used with slow memory. HOLD causes the CPU to relinquish the bus when it is through with it by floating the Address and Data Buses.

SYSTEM INTERFACE

The 8085AH family includes memory components, which are directly compatible to the 8085AH CPU. For example, a system consisting of the three chips, 8085AH, 8156H, and 8755A will have the following features:

- 2K Bytes EPROM
- 256 Bytes RAM
- 1 Timer/Counter
- 4 8-bit I/O Ports
- 1 6-bit I/O Port
- 4 Interrupt Levels
- Serial In/Serial Out Ports

This minimum system, using the standard I/O technique is as shown in Figure 7.

In addition to standard I/O, the memory mapped I/O offers an efficient I/O addressing technique. With this technique, an area of memory address space is assigned for I/O address, thereby, using the memory address for I/O manipulation. Figure 8 shows the system configuration of Memory Mapped I/O using 8085AH.

The 8085AH CPU can also interface with the standard memory that does *not* have the multiplexed address/data bus. It will require a simple 8-bit latch as shown in Figure 9.

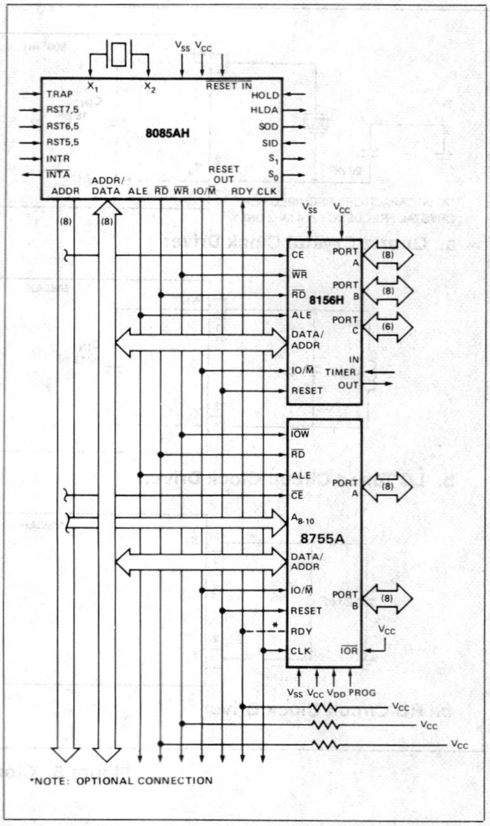

Figure 7. 8085AH Minimum System (Standard I/O Technique)

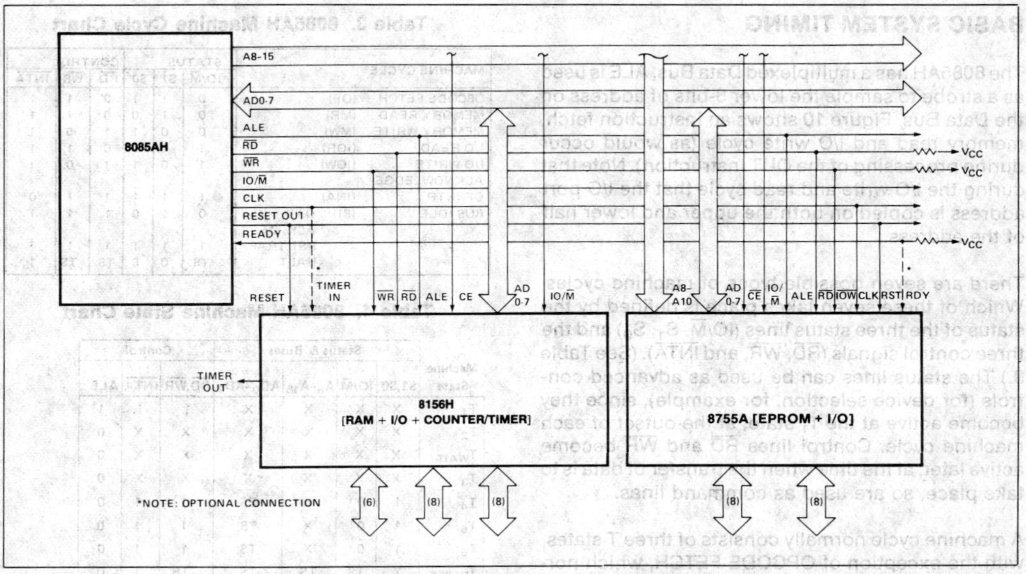

Figure 8. 8085 Minimum System (Memory Mapped I/O)

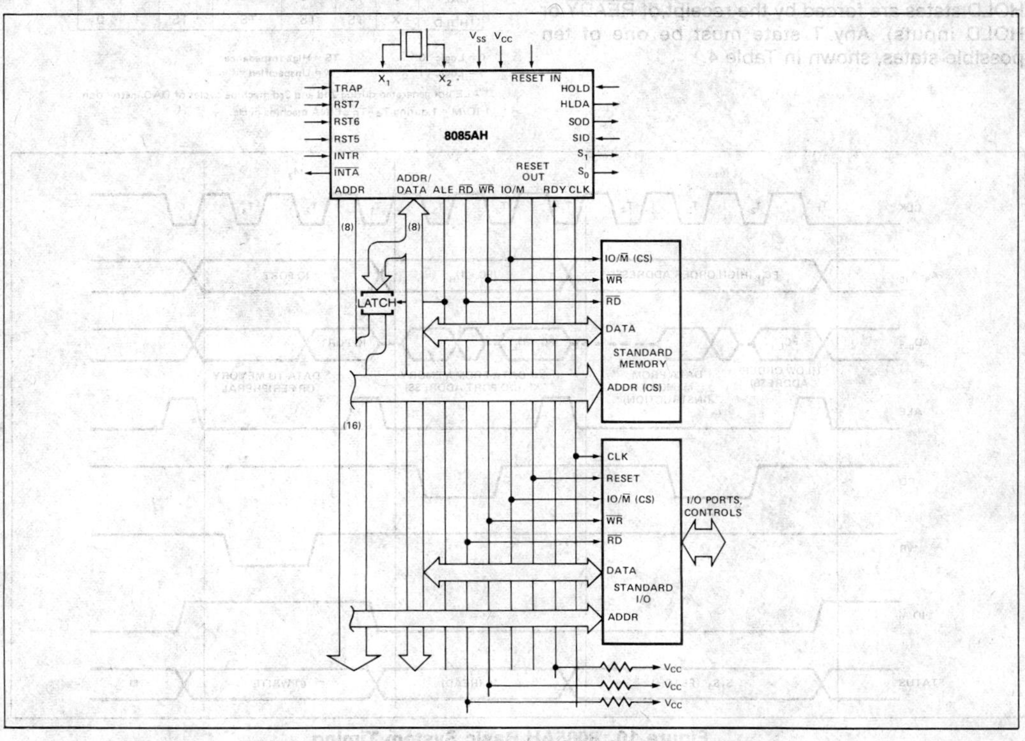

Figure 9. 8085 System (Using Standard Memories)

BASIC SYSTEM TIMING

The 8085AH has a multiplexed Data Bus. ALE is used as a strobe to sample the lower 8-bits of address on the Data Bus. Figure 10 shows an instruction fetch, memory read and I/O write cycle (as would occur during processing of the OUT instruction). Note that during the I/O write and read cycle that the I/O port address is copied on both the upper and lower half of the address.

There are seven possible types of machine cycles. Which of these seven takes place is defined by the status of the three status lines ($IO/\overline{M}$, S_1, S_0) and the three control signals ($\overline{RD}$, $\overline{WR}$, and $\overline{INTA}$). (See Table 3.) The status lines can be used as advanced controls (for device selection, for example), since they become active at the T_1 state, at the outset of each machine cycle. Control lines $\overline{RD}$ and $\overline{WR}$ become active later, at the time when the transfer of data is to take place, so are used as command lines.

A machine cycle normally consists of three T states, with the exception of OPCODE FETCH, which normally has either four or six T states (unless WAIT or HOLD states are forced by the receipt of $\overline{READY}$ or HOLD inputs). Any T state must be one of ten possible states, shown in Table 4.

Table 3. 8085AH Machine Cycle Chart

MACHINE CYCLE		STATUS			CONTROL		
		$IO/\overline{M}$	S1	S0	$\overline{RD}$	$\overline{WR}$	$\overline{INTA}$
OPCODE FETCH	(OF)	0	1	1	0	1	1
MEMORY READ	(MR)	0	1	0	0	1	1
MEMORY WRITE	(MW)	0	0	1	1	0	1
I/O READ	(IOR)	1	1	0	0	1	1
I/O WRITE	(IOW)	1	0	1	1	0	1
ACKNOWLEDGE OF INTR	(INA)	1	1	1	1	1	0
BUS IDLE	(BI): DAD	0	1	0	1	1	1
	ACK. OF RST,TRAP	1	1	1	1	1	1
	HALT	TS	0	0	TS	TS	1

Table 4. 8085AH Machine State Chart

Machine State	Status & Buses				Control		
	S1,S0	$IO/\overline{M}$	A_8-A_{15}	AD_0-AD_7	$\overline{RD}$,$\overline{WR}$	$\overline{INTA}$	ALE
T_1	X	X	X	X	1	1	1*
T_2	X	X	X	X	X	X	0
T_{WAIT}	X	X	X	X	X	X	0
T_3	X	X	X	X	X	X	0
T_4	1	0†	X	TS	1	1	0
T_5	1	0†	X	TS	1	1	0
T_6	1	0†	X	TS	1	1	0
T_{RESET}	X	TS	TS	TS	TS	1	0
T_{HALT}	0	TS	TS	TS	TS	1	0
T_{HOLD}	X	TS	TS	TS	TS	1	0

0 = Logic "0" TS = High Impedance
1 = Logic "1" X = Unspecified

* ALE not generated during 2nd and 3rd machine cycles of DAD instruction.
† IO/M = 1 during T_4-T_6 of INA machine cycle.

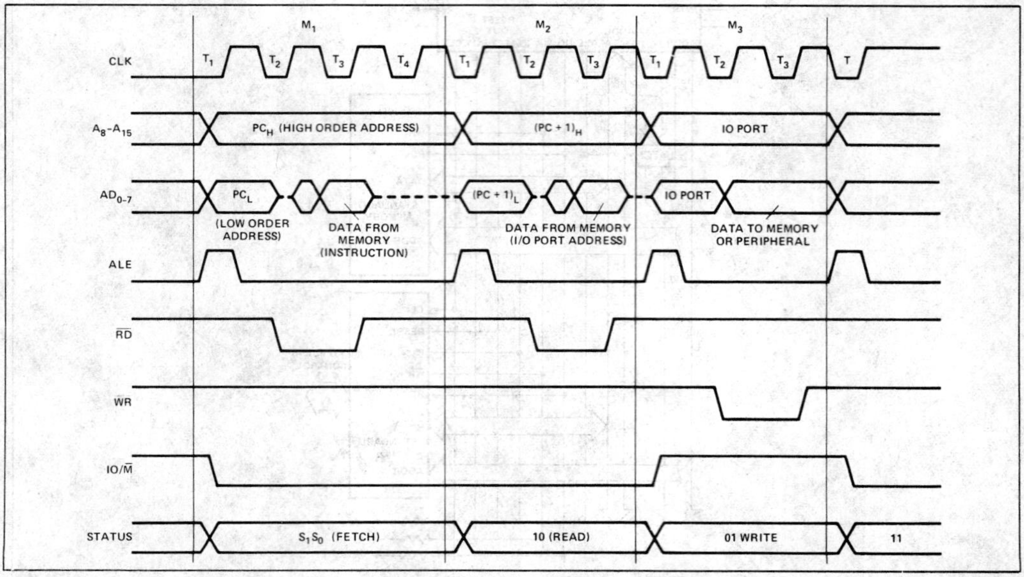

Figure 10. 8085AH Basic System Timing

ABSOLUTE MAXIMUM RATINGS*

Ambient Temperature Under Bias ....0°C to 70°C
Storage Temperature .... −65°C to +150°C
Voltage on Any Pin
With Respect to Ground .... −0.5V to +7V
Power Dissipation .... 1.5 Watt

**NOTICE: Stresses above those listed under "Absolute Maximum Ratings" may cause permanent damage to the device. This is a stress rating only and functional operation of the device at these or any other conditions above those indicated in the operational sections of this specification is not implied. Exposure to absolute maximum rating conditions for extended periods may affect device reliability.*

D.C. CHARACTERISTICS

8085AH, 8085AH-2: (T_A = 0°C to 70°C, V_{CC} = 5V ±10%, V_{SS} = 0V; unless otherwise specified)*
8085AH-1: (T_A = 0°C to 70°C, V_{CC} = 5V ±5%, V_{SS} = 0V; unless otherwise specified)

Symbol	Parameter	Min.	Max.	Units	Test Conditions
V_{IL}	Input Low Voltage	−0.5	+0.8	V	
V_{IH}	Input High Voltage	2.0	V_{CC} +0.5	V	
V_{OL}	Output Low Voltage		0.45	V	I_{OL} = 2mA
V_{OH}	Output High Voltage	2.4		V	I_{OH} = −400μA
I_{CC}	Power Supply Current		135	mA	8085AH, 8085AH-2
			200	mA	8085AH-1
I_{IL}	Input Leakage		±10	μA	0 ≤ V_{IN} ≤ V_{CC}
I_{LO}	Output Leakage		±10	μA	0.45V ≤ V_{OUT} ≤ V_{CC}
V_{ILR}	Input Low Level, RESET	−0.5	+0.8	V	
V_{IHR}	Input High Level, RESET	2.4	V_{CC} +0.5	V	
V_{HY}	Hysteresis, RESET	0.15		V	

A.C. CHARACTERISTICS

8085AH, 8085AH-2: (T_A = 0°C to 70°C, V_{CC} = 5V ±10%, V_{SS} = OV)*
8085AH-1: (T_A = 0°C to 70°C, V_{CC} = 5V ±5%, V_{SS} = 0V)

Symbol	Parameter	8085AH[2]		8085AH-2[2]		8085AH-1[2]		Units
		Min.	Max.	Min.	Max.	Min.	Max.	
t_{CYC}	CLK Cycle Period	320	2000	200	2000	167	2000	ns
t_1	CLK Low Time (Standard CLK Loading)	80		40		20		ns
t_2	CLK High Time (Standard CLK Loading)	120		70		50		ns
t_r, t_f	CLK Rise and Fall Time		30		30		30	ns
t_{XKR}	X_1 Rising to CLK Rising	20	120	20	100	20	100	ns
t_{XKF}	X_1 Rising to CLK Falling	20	150	20	110	20	110	ns
t_{AC}	A_{8-15} Valid to Leading Edge of Control[1]	270		115		70		ns
t_{ACL}	A_{0-7} Valid to Leading Edge of Control	240		115		60		ns
t_{AD}	A_{0-15} Valid to Valid Data In		575		350		225	ns
t_{AFR}	Address Float After Leading Edge of $\overline{READ}$ ($\overline{INTA}$)		0		0		0	ns
t_{AL}	A_{8-15} Valid Before Trailing Edge of ALE[1]	115		50		25		ns

***Note:** For Extended Temperature EXPRESS use M8085AH Electricals Parameters.

A.C. CHARACTERISTICS (Continued)

Symbol	Parameter	8085AH[2]		8085AH-2[2]		8085AH-1[2]		Units
		Min.	Max.	Min.	Max.	Min.	Max.	
t_{ALL}	A_{0-7} Valid Before Trailing Edge of ALE	90		50		25		ns
t_{ARY}	READY Valid from Address Valid		220		100		40	ns
t_{CA}	Address (A_{8-15}) Valid After Control	120		60		30		ns
t_{CC}	Width of Control Low ($\overline{RD}$, $\overline{WR}$, INTA) Edge of ALE	400		230		150		ns
t_{CL}	Trailing Edge of Control to Leading Edge of ALE	50		25		0		ns
t_{DW}	Data Valid to Trailing Edge of $\overline{WRITE}$	420		230		140		ns
t_{HABE}	HLDA to Bus Enable		210		150		150	ns
t_{HABF}	Bus Float After HLDA		210		150		150	ns
t_{HACK}	HLDA Valid to Trailing Edge of CLK	110		40		0		ns
t_{HDH}	HOLD Hold Time	0		0		0		ns
t_{HDS}	HOLD Setup Time to Trailing Edge of CLK	170		120		120		ns
t_{INH}	INTR Hold Time	0		0		0		ns
t_{INS}	INTR, RST, and TRAP Setup Time to Falling Edge of CLK	160		150		150		ns
t_{LA}	Address Hold Time After ALE	100		50		20		ns
t_{LC}	Trailing Edge of ALE to Leading Edge of Control	130		60		25		ns
t_{LCK}	ALE Low During CLK High	100		50		15		ns
t_{LDR}	ALE to Valid Data During Read		460		270		175	ns
t_{LDW}	ALE to Valid Data During Write		200		140		110	ns
t_{LL}	ALE Width	140		80		50		ns
t_{LRY}	ALE to READY Stable		110		30		10	ns
t_{RAE}	Trailing Edge of $\overline{READ}$ to Re-Enabling of Address	150		90		50		ns
t_{RD}	$\overline{READ}$ (or $\overline{INTA}$) to Valid Data		300		150		75	ns
t_{RV}	Control Trailing Edge to Leading Edge of Next Control	400		220		160		ns
t_{RDH}	Data Hold Time After $\overline{READ}$ $\overline{INTA}$	0		0		0		ns
t_{RYH}	READY Hold Time	0		0		5		ns
t_{RYS}	READY Setup Time to Leading Edge of CLK	110		100		100		ns
t_{WD}	Data Valid After Trailing Edge of $\overline{WRITE}$	100		60		30		ns
t_{WDL}	LEADING Edge of $\overline{WRITE}$ to Data Valid		40		20		30	ns

NOTES:

1. A_8–A_{15} address Specs apply IO/$\overline{M}$, S_0, and S_1 except A_8–A_{15} are undefined during T_4–T_6 of OF cycle whereas IO/$\overline{M}$, S_0, and S_1 are stable.
2. *Test Conditions:* t_{CYC} = 320 ns (8085AH)/200 ns (8085AH-2);/ 167 ns (8085AH-1); C_L = 150 pF.
3. For all output timing where $C_L \neq$ 150 pF use the following correction factors:
   25 pF $\leq C_L <$ 150 pF: −0.10 ns/pF
   150 pF $< C_L \leq$ 300 pF: +0.30 ns/pF
4. Output timings are measured with purely capacitive load.
5. To calculate timing specifications at other values of t_{CYC} use Table 5.

A.C. TESTING INPUT, OUTPUT WAVEFORM

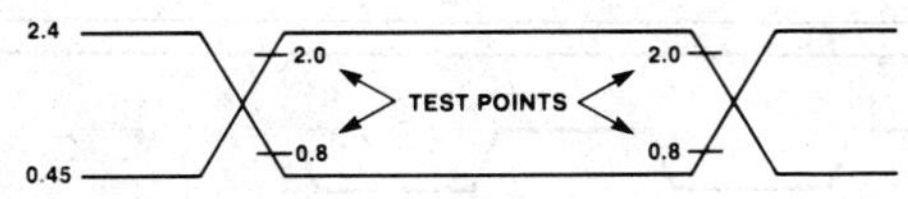

A.C. TESTING: INPUTS ARE DRIVEN AT 2.4V FOR A LOGIC "1" AND 0.45V FOR A LOGIC "0." TIMING MEASUREMENTS ARE MADE AT 2.0V FOR A LOGIC "1" AND 0.8V FOR A LOGIC "0."

A.C. TESTING LOAD CIRCUIT

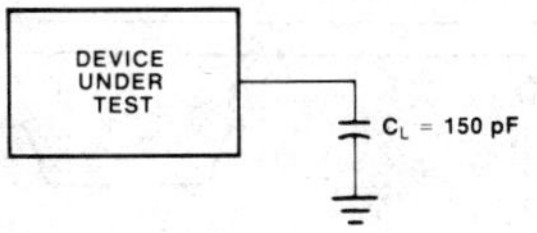

C_L = 150 pF
C_L INCLUDES JIG CAPACITANCE

Table 5. Bus Timing Specification as a T_{CYC} Dependent

Symbol	8085AH	8085AH-2	8085AH-1	
t_{AL}	(1/2) T − 45	(1/2) T − 50	(1/2) T − 58	Minimum
t_{LA}	(1/2) T − 60	(1/2) T − 50	(1/2) T − 63	Minimum
t_{LL}	(1/2) T − 20	(1/2) T − 20	(1/2) T − 33	Minimum
t_{LCK}	(1/2) T − 60	(1/2) T − 50	(1/2) T − 68	Minimum
t_{LC}	(1/2) T − 30	(1/2) T − 40	(1/2) T − 58	Minimum
t_{AD}	(5/2 + N) T − 225	(5/2 + N) T − 150	(5/2 + N) T − 192	Maximum
t_{RD}	(3/2 + N) T − 180	(3/2 + N) T − 150	(3/2 + N) T − 175	Maximum
t_{RAE}	(1/2) T − 10	(1/2) T − 10	(1/2) T − 33	Minimum
t_{CA}	(1/2) T − 40	(1/2) T − 40	(1/2) T − 53	Minimum
t_{DW}	(3/2 + N) T − 60	(3/2 + N) T − 70	(3/2 + N) T − 110	Minimum
t_{WD}	(1/2) T − 60	(1/2) T − 40	(1/2) T − 53	Minimum
t_{CC}	(3/2 + N) T − 80	(3/2 + N) T − 70	(3/2 + N) T − 100	Minimum
t_{CL}	(1/2) T − 110	(1/2) T − 75	(1/2) T − 83	Minimum
t_{ARY}	(3/2) T − 260	(3/2) T − 200	(3/2) T − 210	Maximum
t_{HACK}	(1/2) T − 50	(1/2) T − 60	(1/2) T − 83	Minimum
t_{HABF}	(1/2) T + 50	(1/2) T + 50	(1/2) T + 67	Maximum
t_{HABE}	(1/2) T + 50	(1/2) T + 50	(1/2) T + 67	Maximum
t_{AC}	(2/2) T − 50	(2/2) T − 85	(2/2) T − 97	Minimum
t_1	(1/2) T − 80	(1/2) T − 60	(1/2) T − 63	Minimum
t_2	(1/2) T − 40	(1/2) T − 30	(1/2) T − 33	Minimum
t_{RV}	(3/2) T − 80	(3/2) T− 80	(3/2) T − 90	Minimum
t_{LDR}	(4/2) T − 180	(4/2) T − 130	(4/2) T − 159	Maximum

NOTE: N is equal to the total WAIT states. T = t_{CYC}.

WAVEFORMS

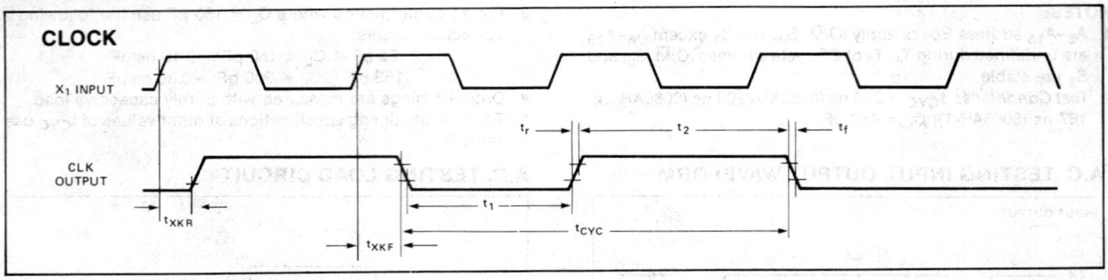
CLOCK
X1 INPUT
CLK OUTPUT
tr
t2
tf
t1
tXKR
tCYC
tXKF

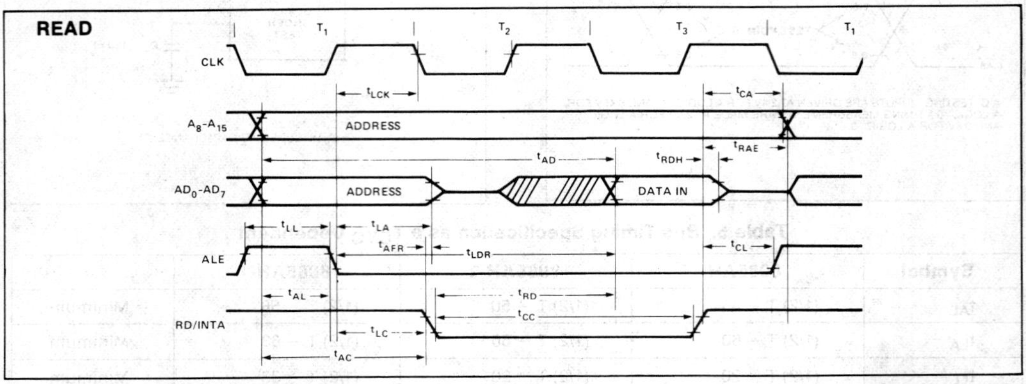
READ
T1
T2
T3
T1
CLK
tLCK
tCA
A8-A15
ADDRESS
tAD
tRDH
tRAE
AD0-AD7
ADDRESS
DATA IN
tLL
tLA
tAFR
tLDR
tCL
ALE
tAL
tRD
tCC
RD/INTA
tLC
tAC

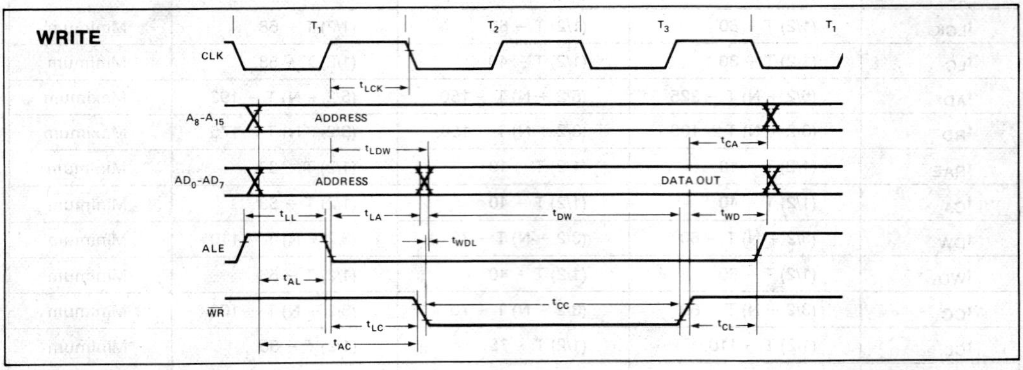
WRITE
T1
T2
T3
T1
CLK
tLCK
A8-A15
ADDRESS
tCA
tLDW
AD0-AD7
ADDRESS
DATA OUT
tLL
tLA
tDW
tWD
ALE
tWDL
tAL
tCC
WR
tLC
tCL
tAC

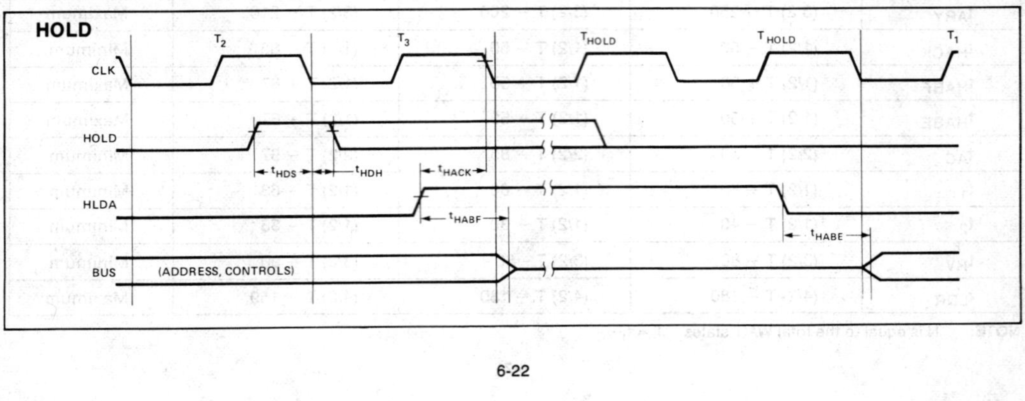
HOLD
T2
T3
THOLD
THOLD
T1
CLK
HOLD
tHDS
tHDH
tHACK
HLDA
tHABF
tHABE
BUS
(ADDRESS, CONTROLS)

WAVEFORMS (Continued)

READ OPERATION WITH WAIT CYCLE (TYPICAL) — SAME READY TIMING APPLIES TO WRITE

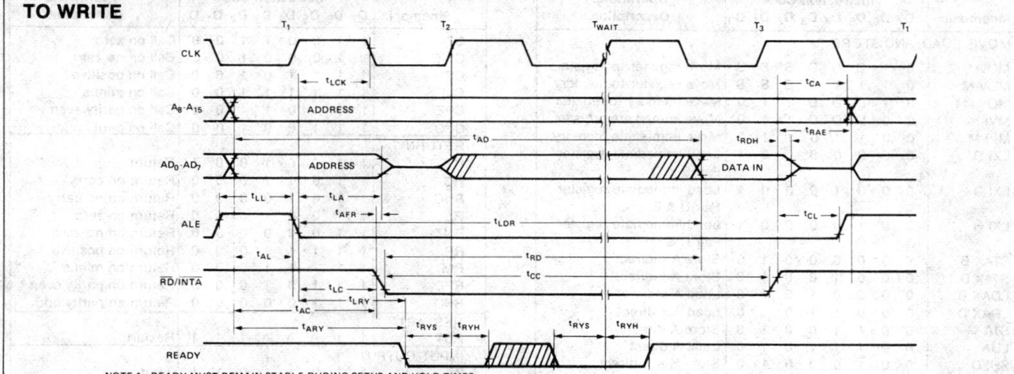

NOTE 1: READY MUST REMAIN STABLE DURING SETUP AND HOLD TIMES.

INTERRUPT AND HOLD

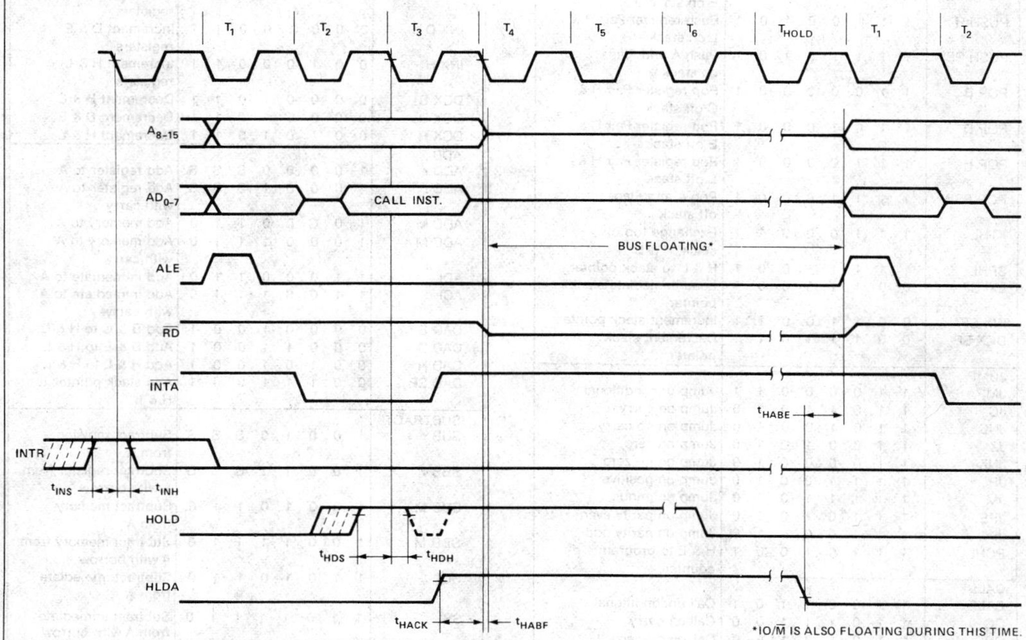

Table 6. Instruction Set Summary

Mnemonic	D_7	D_6	D_5	D_4	D_3	D_2	D_1	D_0	Operations Description
MOVE, LOAD, AND STORE									
MOVr1 r2	0	1	D	D	D	S	S	S	Move register to register
MOV M.r	0	1	1	1	0	S	S	S	Move register to memory
MOV r.M	0	1	D	D	D	1	1	0	Move memory to register
MVI r	0	0	D	D	D	1	1	0	Move immediate register
MVI M	0	0	1	1	0	1	1	0	Move immediate memory
LXI B	0	0	0	0	0	0	0	1	Load immediate register Pair B & C
LXI D	0	0	0	1	0	0	0	1	Load immediate register Pair D & E
LXI H	0	0	1	0	0	0	0	1	Load immediate register Pair H & L
STAX B	0	0	0	0	0	0	1	0	Store A indirect
STAX D	0	0	0	1	0	0	1	0	Store A indirect
LDAX B	0	0	0	0	1	0	1	0	Load A indirect
LDAX D	0	0	0	1	1	0	1	0	Load A indirect
STA	0	0	1	1	0	0	1	0	Store A direct
LDA	0	0	1	1	1	0	1	0	Load A direct
SHLD	0	0	1	0	0	0	1	0	Store H & L direct
LHLD	0	0	1	0	1	0	1	0	Load H & L direct
XCHG	1	1	1	0	1	0	1	1	Exchange D & E, H & L Registers
STACK OPS									
PUSH B	1	1	0	0	0	1	0	1	Push register Pair B & C on stack
PUSH D	1	1	0	1	0	1	0	1	Push register Pair D & E on stack
PUSH H	1	1	1	0	0	1	0	1	Push register Pair H & L on stack
PUSH PSW	1	1	1	1	0	1	0	1	Push A and Flags on stack
POP B	1	1	0	0	0	0	0	1	Pop register Pair B & C off stack
POP D	1	1	0	1	0	0	0	1	Pop register Pair D & E off stack
POP H	1	1	1	0	0	0	0	1	Pop register Pair H & L off stack
POP PSW	1	1	1	1	0	0	0	1	Pop A and Flags off stack
XTHL	1	1	1	0	0	0	1	1	Exchange top of stack, H & L
SPHL	1	1	1	1	1	0	0	1	H & L to stack pointer
LXI SP	0	0	1	1	0	0	0	1	Load immediate stack pointer
INX SP	0	0	1	1	0	0	1	1	Increment stack pointer
DCX SP	0	0	1	1	1	0	1	1	Decrement stack pointer
JUMP									
JMP	1	1	0	0	0	0	1	1	Jump unconditional
JC	1	1	0	1	1	0	1	0	Jump on carry
JNC	1	1	0	1	0	0	1	0	Jump on no carry
JZ	1	1	0	0	1	0	1	0	Jump on zero
JNZ	1	1	0	0	0	0	1	0	Jump on no zero
JP	1	1	1	1	0	0	1	0	Jump on positive
JM	1	1	1	1	1	0	1	0	Jump on minus
JPE	1	1	1	0	1	0	1	0	Jump on parity even
JPO	1	1	1	0	0	0	1	0	Jump on parity odd
PCHL	1	1	1	0	1	0	0	1	H & L to program counter
CALL									
CALL	1	1	0	0	1	1	0	1	Call unconditional
CC	1	1	0	1	1	1	0	0	Call on carry
CNC	1	1	0	1	0	1	0	0	Call on no carry
CZ	1	1	0	0	1	1	0	0	Call on zero
CNZ	1	1	0	0	0	1	0	0	Call on no zero
CP	1	1	1	1	0	1	0	0	Call on positive
CM	1	1	1	1	1	1	0	0	Call on minus
CPE	1	1	1	0	1	1	0	0	Call on parity even
CPO	1	1	1	0	0	1	0	0	Call on parity odd
RETURN									
RET	1	1	0	0	1	0	0	1	Return
RC	1	1	0	1	1	0	0	0	Return on carry
RNC	1	1	0	1	0	0	0	0	Return on no carry
RZ	1	1	0	0	1	0	0	0	Return on zero
RNZ	1	1	0	0	0	0	0	0	Return on no zero
RP	1	1	1	1	0	0	0	0	Return on positive
RM	1	1	1	1	1	0	0	0	Return on minus
RPE	1	1	1	0	1	0	0	0	Return on parity even
RPO	1	1	1	0	0	0	0	0	Return on parity odd
RESTART									
RST	1	1	A	A	A	1	1	1	Restart
INPUT/OUTPUT									
IN	1	1	0	1	1	0	1	1	Input
OUT	1	1	0	1	0	0	1	1	Output
INCREMENT AND DECREMENT									
INR r	0	0	D	D	D	1	0	0	Increment register
DCR r	0	0	D	D	D	1	0	1	Decrement register
INR M	0	0	1	1	0	1	0	0	Increment memory
DCR M	0	0	1	1	0	1	0	1	Decrement memory
INX B	0	0	0	0	0	0	1	1	Increment B & C registers
INX D	0	0	0	1	0	0	1	1	Increment D & E registers
INX H	0	0	1	0	0	0	1	1	Increment H & L registers
DCX B	0	0	0	0	1	0	1	1	Decrement B & C
DCX D	0	0	0	1	1	0	1	1	Decrement D & E
DCX H	0	0	1	0	1	0	1	1	Decrement H & L
ADD									
ADD r	1	0	0	0	0	S	S	S	Add register to A
ADC r	1	0	0	0	1	S	S	S	Add register to A with carry
ADD M	1	0	C	0	0	1	1	0	Add memory to A
ADC M	1	0	0	0	1	1	1	0	Add memory to A with carry
ADI	1	1	0	0	0	1	1	0	Add immediate to A
ACI	1	1	0	0	1	1	1	0	Add immediate to A with carry
DAD B	0	0	0	0	1	0	0	1	Add B & C to H & L
DAD D	0	0	0	1	1	0	0	1	Add D & E to H & L
DAD H	0	0	1	0	1	0	0	1	Add H & L to H & L
DAD SP	0	0	1	1	1	0	0	1	Add stack pointer to H & L
SUBTRACT									
SUB r	1	0	0	1	0	S	S	S	Subtract register from A
SBB r	1	0	0	1	1	S	S	S	Subtract register from A with borrow
SUB M	1	0	0	1	0	1	1	0	Subtract memory from A
SBB M	1	0	0	1	1	1	1	0	Subtract memory from A with borrow
SUI	1	1	0	1	0	1	1	0	Subtract immediate from A
SBI	1	1	0	1	1	1	1	0	Subtract immediate from A with borrow

Table 6. Instruction Set Summary (Continued)

Mnemonic	D_7	D_6	D_5	D_4	D_3	D_2	D_1	D_0	Operations Description
LOGICAL									
ANA r	1	0	1	0	0	S	S	S	And register with A
XRA r	1	0	1	0	1	S	S	S	Exclusive OR register with A
ORA r	1	0	1	1	0	S	S	S	OR register with A
CMP r	1	0	1	1	1	S	S	S	Compare register with A
ANA M	1	0	1	0	0	1	1	0	And memory with A
XRA M	1	0	1	0	1	1	1	0	Exclusive OR memory with A
ORA M	1	0	1	1	0	1	1	0	OR memory with A
CMP M	1	0	1	1	1	1	1	0	Compare memory with A
ANI	1	1	1	0	0	1	1	0	And immediate with A
XRI	1	1	1	0	1	1	1	0	Exclusive OR immediate with A
ORI	1	1	1	1	0	1	1	0	OR immediate with A
CPI	1	1	1	1	1	1	1	0	Compare immediate with A
ROTATE									
RLC	0	0	0	0	0	1	1	1	Rotate A left
RRC	0	0	0	0	1	1	1	1	Rotate A right
RAL	0	0	0	1	0	1	1	1	Rotate A left through carry
RAR	0	0	0	1	1	1	1	1	Rotate A right through carry

Mnemonic	D_7	D_6	D_5	D_4	D_3	D_2	D_1	D_0	Operations Description
SPECIALS									
CMA	0	0	1	0	1	1	1	1	Complement A
STC	0	0	1	1	0	1	1	1	Set carry
CMC	0	0	1	1	1	1	1	1	Complement carry
DAA	0	0	1	0	0	1	1	1	Decimal adjust A
CONTROL									
EI	1	1	1	1	1	0	1	1	Enable Interrupts
DI	1	1	1	1	0	0	1	1	Disable Interrupt
NOP	0	0	0	0	0	0	0	0	No-operation
HLT	0	1	1	1	0	1	1	0	Halt
NEW 8085AH INSTRUCTIONS									
RIM	0	0	1	0	0	0	0	0	Read Interrupt Mask
SIM	0	0	1	1	0	0	0	0	Set Interrupt Mask

NOTES:

1. DDS or SSS: B 000, C 001, D 010, E011, H 100, L 101, Memory 110, A 111.
2. Two possible cycle times (6/12) indicate instruction cycles dependent on condition flags.

8155H/8156H/8155H-2/8156H-2
2048-BIT STATIC HMOS RAM WITH I/O PORTS AND TIMER

- **Single +5V Power Supply with 10% Voltage Margins**
- **30% Lower Power Consumption than the 8155 and 8156**
- **256 Word x 8 Bits**
- **Completely Static Operation**
- **Internal Address Latch**
- **2 Programmable 8-Bit I/O Ports**
- **1 Programmable 6-Bit I/O Port**
- **Programmable 14-Bit Binary Counter/ Timer**
- **Compatible with 8085AH and 8088 CPU**
- **Multiplexed Address and Data Bus**
- **Available in EXPRESS**
  - **Standard Temperature Range**
  - **Extended Temperature Range**

The Intel® 8155H and 8156H are RAM and I/O chips implemented in N-Channel, depletion load, silicon gate technology (HMOS), to be used in the 8085AH and 8088 microprocessor systems. The RAM portion is designed with 2048 static cells organized as 256 x 8. They have a maximum access time of 400 ns to permit use with no wait states in 8085AH CPU. The 8155H-2 and 8156H-2 have maximum access times of 330 ns for use with the 8085AH-2 and the 5 MHz 8088 CPU.

The I/O portion consists of three general purpose I/O ports. One of the three ports can be programmed to be status pins, thus allowing the other two ports to operate in handshake mode.

A 14-bit programmable counter/timer is also included on chip to provide either a square wave or terminal count pulse for the CPU system depending on timer mode.

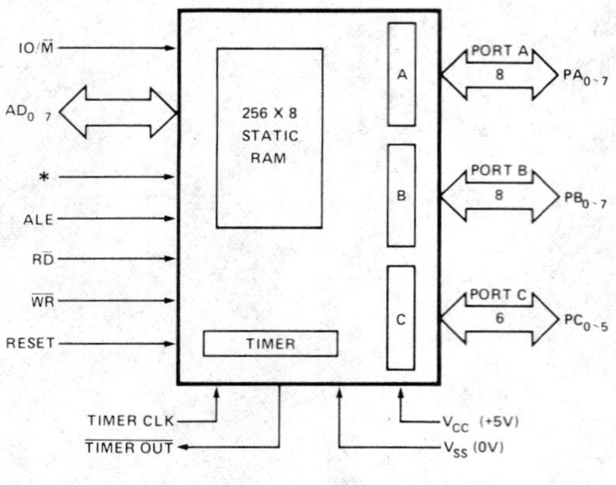

*8155H/8155H-2 = C̄Ē, 8156H/8156H-2 = CE

Figure 1. Block Diagram

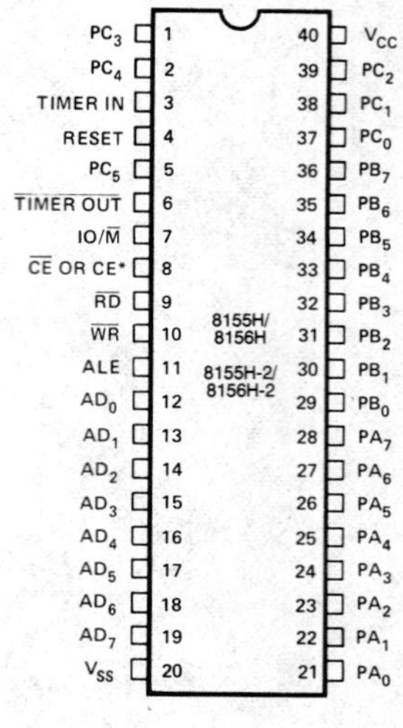

Figure 2. Pin Configuration

Table 1. Pin Description

Symbol	Type	Name and Function
RESET	I	**Reset:** Pulse provided by the 8085AH to initialize the system (connect to 8085AH RESET OUT). Input high on this line resets the chip and initializes the three I/O ports to input mode. The width of RESET pulse should typically be two 8085AH clock cycle times.
AD_{0-7}	I/O	**Address/Data:** 3-state Address/Data lines that interface with the CPU lower 8-bit Address/Data Bus. The 8-bit address is latched into the address latch inside the 8155H/56H on the falling edge of ALE. The address can be either for the memory section or the I/O section depending on the $IO/\overline{M}$ input. The 8-bit data is either written into the chip or read from the chip, depending on the $\overline{WR}$ or $\overline{RD}$ input signal.
CE or $\overline{CE}$	I	**Chip Enable:** On the 8155H, this pin is $\overline{CE}$ and is ACTIVE LOW. On the 8156H, this pin is CE and is ACTIVE HIGH.
$\overline{RD}$	I	**Read Control:** Input low on this line with the Chip Enable active enables and AD_{0-7} buffers. If $IO/\overline{M}$ pin is low, the RAM content will be read out to the AD bus. Otherwise the content of the selected I/O port or command/status registers will be read to the AD bus.
$\overline{WR}$	I	**Write Control:** Input low on this line with the Chip Enable active causes the data on the Address/Data bus to be written to the RAM or I/O ports and command/status register, depending on $IO/\overline{M}$.
ALE	I	**Address Latch Enable:** This control signal latches both the address on the AD_{0-7} lines and the state of the Chip Enable and $IO/\overline{M}$ into the chip at the falling edge of ALE.
$IO/\overline{M}$	I	**I/O Memory:** Selects memory if low and I/O and command/status registers if high.
PA_{0-7}(8)	I/O	**Port A:** These 8 pins are general purpose I/O pins. The in/out direction is selected by programming the command register.
PB_{0-7}(8)	I/O	**Port B:** These 8 pins are general purpose I/O pins. The in/out direction is selected by programming the command register.
PC_{0-5}(6)	I/O	**Port C:** These 6 pins can function as either input port, output port, or as control signals for PA and PB. Programming is done through the command register. When PC_{0-5} are used as control signals, they will provide the following: PC_0 — A INTR (Port A Interrupt) PC_1 — ABF (Port A Buffer Full) PC_2 — $\overline{A\ STB}$ (Port A Strobe) PC_3 — B INTR (Port B Interrupt) PC_4 — B BF (Port B Buffer Full) PC_5 — $\overline{B\ STB}$ (Port B Strobe)
TIMER IN	I	**Timer Input:** Input to the counter-timer.
$\overline{TIMER\ OUT}$	O	**Timer Output:** This output can be either a square wave or a pulse, depending on the timer mode.
V_{CC}		**Voltage:** +5 volt supply.
V_{SS}		**Ground:** Ground reference.

FUNCTIONAL DESCRIPTION

The 8155H/8156H contains the following:

- 2k Bit Static RAM organized as 256 x 8
- Two 8-bit I/O ports (PA & PB) and one 6-bit I/O port (PC)
- 14-bit timer-counter

The $IO/\overline{M}$ (IO/Memory Select) pin selects either the five registers (Command, Status, PA_{0-7}, PB_{0-7}, PC_{0-5}) or the memory (RAM) portion.

The 8-bit address on the Address/Data lines, Chip Enable input CE or $\overline{CE}$, and $IO/\overline{M}$ are all latched on-chip at the falling edge of ALE.

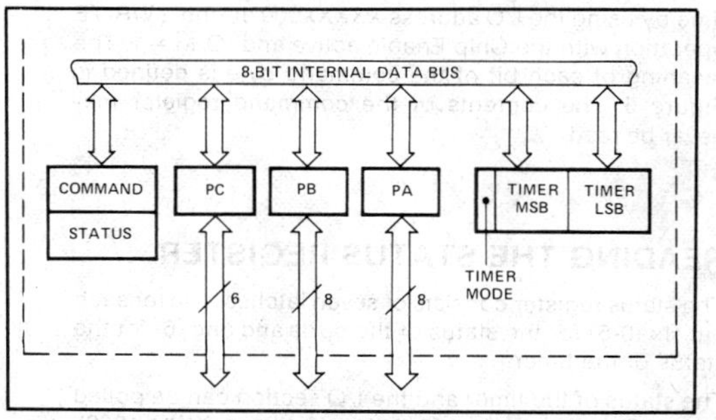

Figure 3. 8155H/8156H Internal Registers

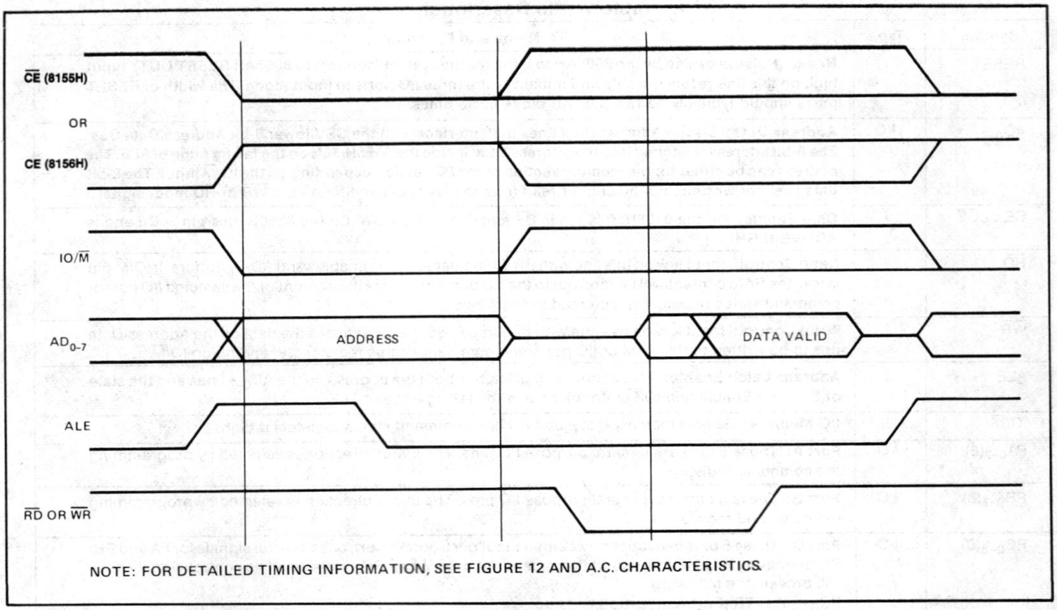

Figure 4. 8155H/8156H On-Board Memory Read/Write Cycle

PROGRAMMING OF THE COMMAND REGISTER

The command register consists of eight latches. Four bits (0-3) define the mode of the ports, two bits (4-5) enable or disable the interrupt from port C when it acts as control port, and the last two bits (6-7) are for the timer.

The command register contents can be altered at any time by using the I/O address XXXXX000 during a WRITE operation with the Chip Enable active and IO/$\overline{M}$ = 1. The meaning of each bit of the command byte is defined in Figure 5. The contents of the command register may never be read.

READING THE STATUS REGISTER

The status register consists of seven latches, one for each bit; six (0-5) for the status of the ports and one (6) for the status of the timer.

The status of the timer and the I/O section can be polled by reading the Status Register (Address XXXXX000). Status word format is shown in Figure 6. Note that you may never write to the status register since the command register shares the same I/O address and the command register is selected when a write to that address is issued.

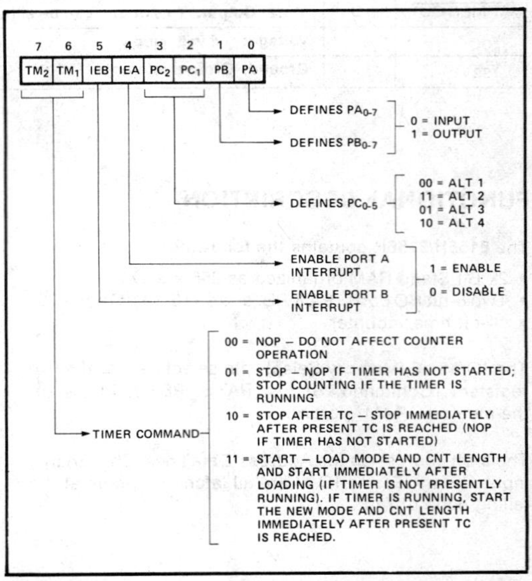

Figure 5. Command Register Bit Assignment

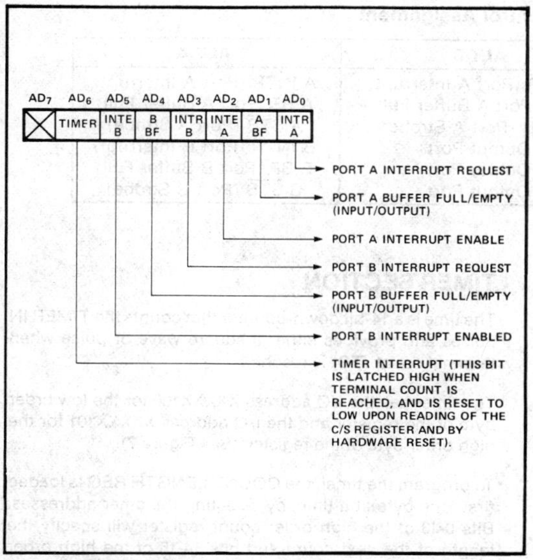

Figure 6. Status Register Bit Assignment

INPUT/OUTPUT SECTION

The I/O section of the 8155H/8156H consists of five registers: (See Figure 7.)

- **Command/Status Register (C/S)** — Both registers are assigned the address XXXXX000. The C/S address serves the dual purpose.

  When the C/S registers are selected during WRITE operation, a command is written into the command register. The contents of this register are *not* accessible through the pins.

  When the C/S (XXXXX000) is selected during a READ operation, the status information of the I/O ports and the timer becomes available on the AD_{0-7} lines.

- **PA Register** — This register can be programmed to be either input or output ports depending on the status of the contents of the C/S Register. Also depending on the command, this port can operate in either the basic mode or the strobed mode (See timing diagram). The I/O pins assigned in relation to this register are PA_{0-7}. The address of this register is XXXXX001.

- **PB Register** — This register functions the same as PA Register. The I/O pins assigned are PB_{0-7}. The address of this register is XXXXX010.

- **PC Register** — This register has the address XXXXX011 and contains only 6 bits. The 6 bits can be programmed to be either input ports, output ports or as control signals for PA and PB by properly programming the AD_2 and AD_3 bits of the C/S register.

  When PC_{0-5} is used as a control port, 3 bits are assigned for Port A and 3 for Port B. The first bit is an interrupt that the 8155H sends out. The second is an output signal indicating whether the buffer is full or empty, and the third is an input pin to accept a strobe for the strobed input mode. (See Table 2.)

When the 'C' port is programmed to either ALT3 or ALT4, the control signals for PA and PB are initialized as follows:

CONTROL	INPUT MODE	OUTPUT MODE
BF	Low	Low
INTR	Low	High
STB	Input Control	Input Control

I/O ADDRESS†								SELECTION
A7	A6	A5	A4	A3	A2	A1	A0	
X	X	X	X	X	0	0	0	Interval Command/Status Register
X	X	X	X	X	0	0	1	General Purpose I/O Port A
X	X	X	X	X	0	1	0	General Purpose I/O Port B
X	X	X	X	X	0	1	1	Port C — General Purpose I/O or Control
X	X	X	X	X	1	0	0	Low-Order 8 bits of Timer Count
X	X	X	X	X	1	0	1	High 6 bits of Timer Count and 2 bits of Timer Mode

X: Don't Care.

†: I/O Address must be qualified by CE = 1 (8156H) or $\overline{CE}$ = 0 (8155H) and IO/$\overline{M}$ = 1 in order to select the appropriate register.

Figure 7. I/O Port and Timer Addressing Scheme

Figure 8 shows how I/O PORTS A and B are structured within the 8155H and 8156H:

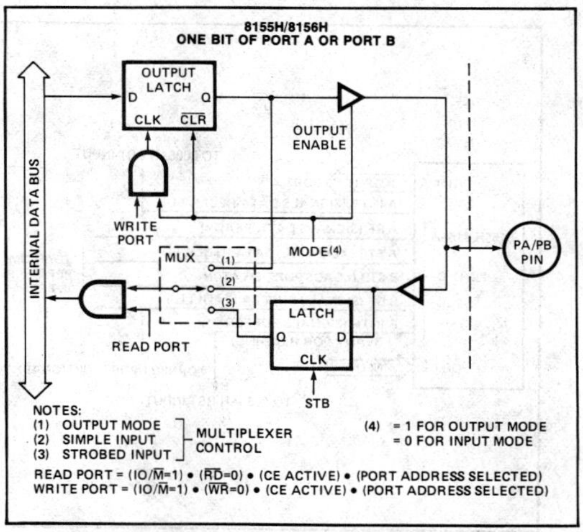

Figure 8. 8155H/8156H Port Functions

Table 2. Port Control Assignment

Pin	ALT 1	ALT 2	ALT 3	ALT 4
PC0	Input Port	Output Port	A INTR (Port A Interrupt)	A INTR (Port A Interrupt)
PC1	Input Port	Output Port	A BF (Port A Buffer Full)	A BF (Port A Buffer Full)
PC2	Input Port	Output Port	A $\overline{STB}$ (Port A Strobe)	A $\overline{STB}$ (Port A Strobe)
PC3	Input Port	Output Port	Output Port	B INTR (Port B Interrupt)
PC4	Input Port	Output Port	Output Port	B BF (Port B Buffer Full)
PC5	Input Port	Output Port	Output Port	B $\overline{STB}$ (Port B Strobe)

Note in the diagram that when the I/O ports are programmed to be output ports, the contents of the output ports can still be read by a READ operation when appropriately addressed.

The outputs of the 8155H/8156H are "glitch-free" meaning that you can write a "1" to a bit position that was previsouly "1" and the level at the output pin will not change.

Note also that the output latch is cleared when the port enters the input mode. The output latch cannot be loaded by writing to the port if the port is in the input mode. The result is that each time a port mode is changed from input to output, the output pins witll go low. When the 8155H/56H is RESET, the output latches are all cleared and all 3 ports enter the input mode.

When inthe ALT 1 or ALT 2 modes, the bits of PORT C are structured like the diagram above in the simple input or output mode, respectively.

Reading from an input port with nothing connected to the pins will provide unpredictable results.

Figure 9 shows how the 8155H/8156H I/O ports might be configured in a typical MCS-85 system.

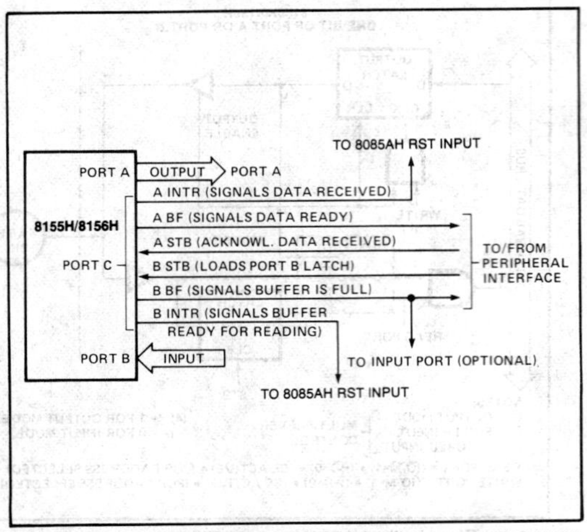

Figure 9. Example: Command Register = 00111001

TIMER SECTION

The time is a 14-bit down-counter that counts the TIMER IN pulses and provides either a square wave or pulse when terminal count (TC) is reached.

The timer has the I/O address XXXXX100 for the low order byte of the register and the I/O address XXXXX101 for the high order byte of the register. (See Figure 7).

To program the timer, the COUNT LENGTH REG is loaded first, one byte at a time, by selecting the timer addresses. Bits 0-13 of the high order count register will specify the length of the next count and bits 14-15 of the high order register will specify the timer output mode (see Figure 10). The value loaded into the count length register can have any value from 2H through 3FFFH in Bits 0-13.

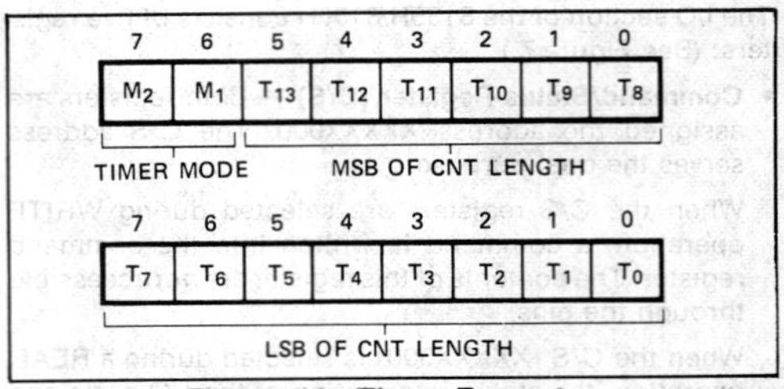

Figure 10. Timer Format

There are four modes to choose from: M2 and M1 define the timer mode, as shown in Figure 11.

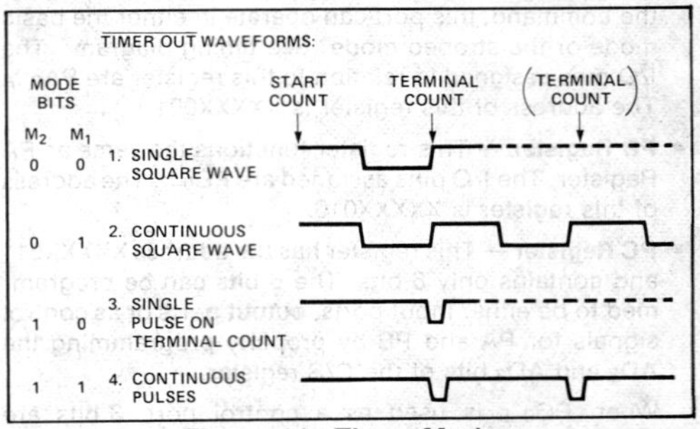

Figure 11. Timer Modes

Bits 6-7 (TM_2 and TM_1) of command register contents are used to start and stop the counter. There are four commands to choose from:

TM_2	TM_1	
0	0	NOP — Do not affect counter operation.
0	1	STOP — NOP if timer has not started; stop counting if the timer is running.
1	0	STOP AFTER TC — Stop immediately after present TC is reached (NOP if timer has not started)
1	1	START — Load mode and CNT length and start immediately after loading (if timer is not presently running). If timer is running, start the new mode and CNT length immediately after present TC is reached.

Note that while the counter is counting, you may load a new count and mode into the count length registers. Before the new count and mode will be used by the counter, you must issue a START command to the counter. This applies even though you may only want to change the count and use the previous mode.

In case of an odd-numbered count, the first half-cycle of the squarewave output, which is high, is one count longer than the second (low) half-cycle, as shown in Figure 12.

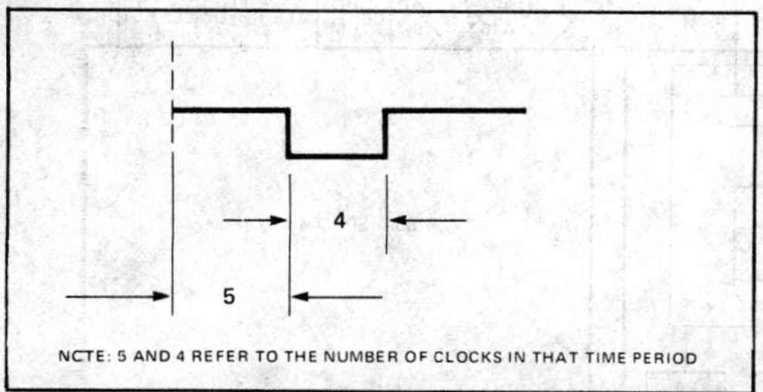

Figure 12. Asymmetrical Square-Wave Output Resulting from Count of 9

The counter in the 8155H is not initialized to any particular mode or count when hardware RESET occurs, but RESET does *stop* the counting. Therefore, counting cannot begin following RESET until a START command is issued via the C/S register.

Please note that the timer circuit on the 8155H/8156H chip is designed to be a square-wave timer, not an event counter. To achieve this, it counts down by twos twice in completing one cycle. Thus, its registers do not contain values directly representing the number of TIMER IN pulses received. You cannot load an initial value of 1 into the count register and cause the timer to operate, as its terminal count value is 10 (binary) or 2 (decimal). (For the detection of single pulses, it is suggested that one of the hardware interrupt pins on the 8085AH be used.) After the timer has started counting down, the values residing in the count registers can be used to calculate the actual number of TIMER IN pulses required to complete the timer cycle if desired. To obtain the remaining count, perform the following operations in order:

1. Stop the count
2. Read in the 16-bit value from the count length registers
3. Reset the upper two mode bits
4. Reset the carry and rotate right one position all 16 bits through carry
5. If carry is set, add 1/2 of the full original count (1/2 full count — 1 if full count is odd).

Note: If you started with an odd count and you read the count length register before the third count pulse occurs, you will not be able to discern whether one or two counts has occurred. Regardless of this, the 8155H/56H always counts out the right number of pulses in generating the TIMER OUT waveforms.

8085A MINIMUM SYSTEM CONFIGURATION

Figure 13a shows a minimum system using three chips, containing:

- 256 Bytes RAM
- 2K Bytes EPROM
- 38 I/O Pins
- 1 Interval Timer
- 4 Interrupt Levels

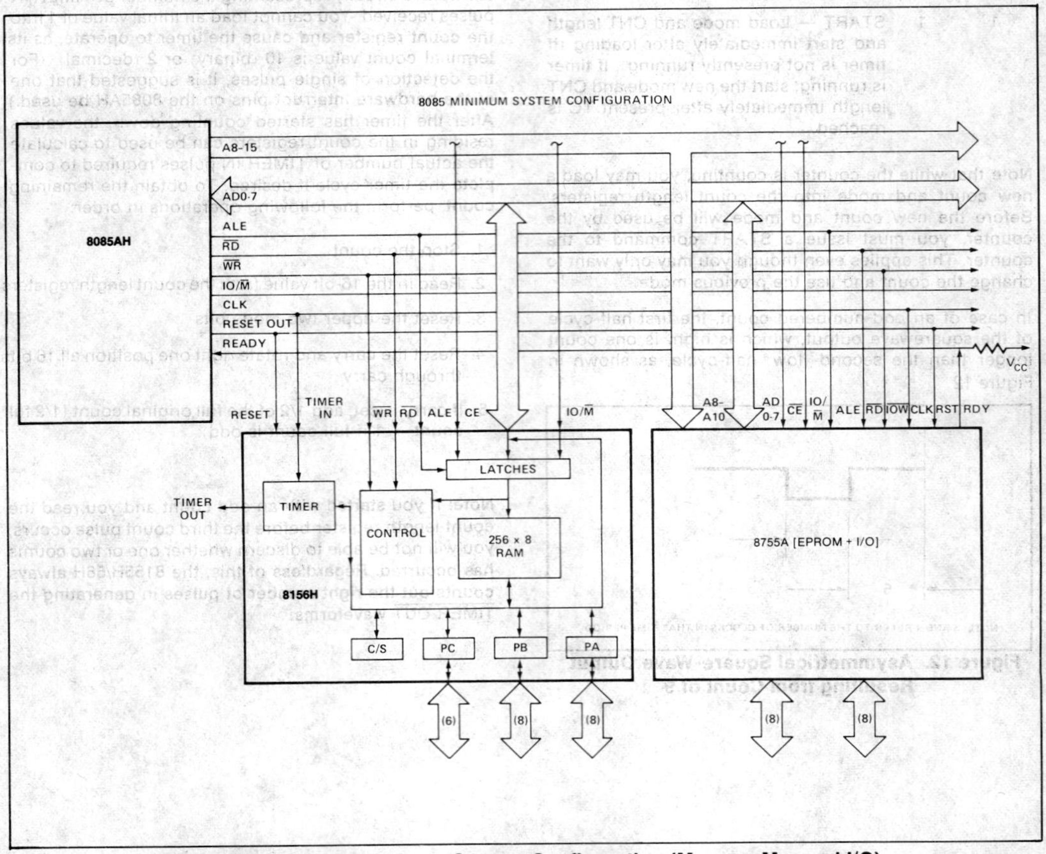

Figure 13a. 8085AH Minimum System Configuration (Memory Mapped I/O)

8088 FIVE CHIP SYSTEM

Figure 13b shows a five chip system containing:

- 1.25K Bytes RAM
- 2K Bytes EPROM
- 38 I/O Pins
- 1 Interval Timer
- 2 Interrupt Levels

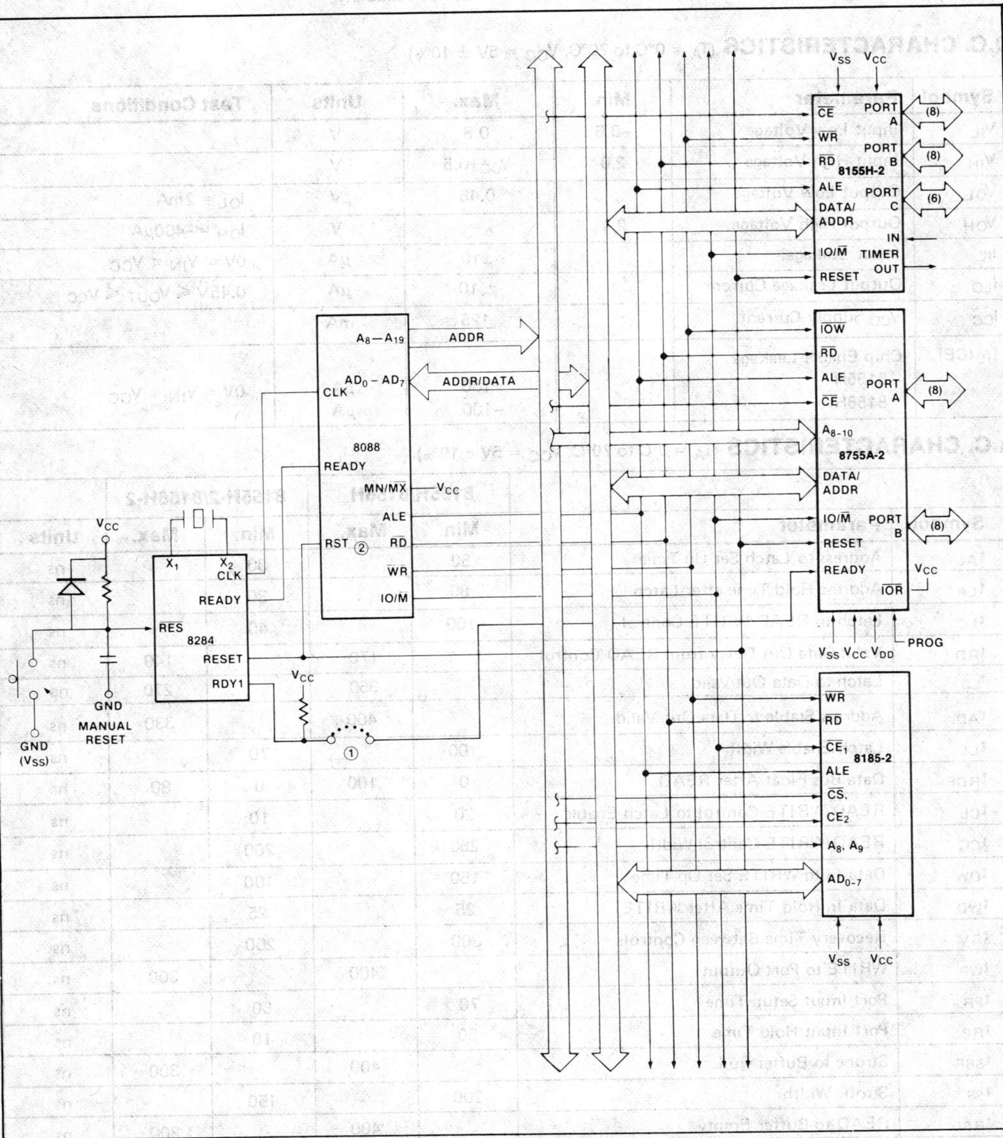

Figure 13b. 8088 Five Chip System Configuration

ABSOLUTE MAXIMUM RATINGS*

Temperature Under Bias .... 0°C to +70°C
Storage Temperature .... -65°C to +150°C
Voltage on Any Pin
With Respect to Ground .... -0.5V to +7V
Power Dissipation 1.5W

**NOTICE: Stresses above those listed under "Absolute Maximum Ratings" may cause permanent damage to the device. This is a stress rating only and functional operation of the device at these or any other conditions above those indicated in the operational sections of this specification is not implied. Exposure to absolute maximum rating conditions for extended periods may affect device reliability.*

D.C. CHARACTERISTICS (T_A = 0°C to 70°C, V_{CC} = 5V ± 10%)

Symbol	Parameter	Min.	Max.	Units	Test Conditions
V_{IL}	Input Low Voltage	-0.5	0.8	V	
V_{IH}	Input High Voltage	2.0	V_{CC}+0.5	V	
V_{OL}	Output Low Voltage		0.45	V	I_{OL} = 2mA
V_{OH}	Output High Voltage	2.4		V	I_{OH} = -400μA
I_{IL}	Input Leakage		±10	μA	0V ≤ V_{IN} ≤ V_{CC}
I_{LO}	Output Leakage Current		± 10	μA	0.45V ≤ V_{OUT} ≤ V_{CC}
I_{CC}	V_{CC} Supply Current		125	mA	
I_{IL}(CE)	Chip Enable Leakage 8155H 8156H		 +100 −100	 μA μA	0V ≤ V_{IN} ≤ V_{CC}

A.C. CHARACTERISTICS (T_A = 0°C to 70°C, V_{CC} = 5V ±10%)

		8155H/8156H		8155H-2/8156H-2		
Symbol	Parameter	Min.	Max.	Min.	Max.	Units
t_{AL}	Address to Latch Set Up Time	50		30		ns
t_{LA}	Address Hold Time after Latch	80		30		ns
t_{LC}	Latch to READ/WRITE Control	100		40		ns
t_{RD}	Valid Data Out Delay from READ Control		170		140	ns
t_{LD}	Latch to Data Out Valid		350		270	ns
t_{AD}	Address Stable to Data Out Valid		400		330	ns
t_{LL}	Latch Enable Width	100		70		ns
t_{RDF}	Data Bus Float After READ	0	100	0	80	ns
t_{CL}	READ/WRITE Control to Latch Enable	20		10		ns
t_{CC}	READ/WRITE Control Width	250		200		ns
t_{DW}	Data In to WRITE Set Up Time	150		100		ns
t_{WD}	Data In Hold Time After WRITE	25		25		ns
t_{RV}	Recovery Time Between Controls	300		200		ns
t_{WP}	WRITE to Port Output		400		300	ns
t_{PR}	Port Input Setup Time	70		50		ns
t_{RP}	Port Input Hold Time	50		10		ns
t_{SBF}	Strobe to Buffer Full		400		300	ns
t_{SS}	Strobe Width	200		150		ns
t_{RBE}	READ to Buffer Empty		400		300	ns
t_{SI}	Strobe to INTR On		400		300	ns

A.C. CHARACTERISTICS (Continued) (T_A = 0°C to 70°C, V_{CC} = 5V ±10%)

		8155H/8156H		8155H-2/8156H-2		
Symbol	**Parameter**	**Min.**	**Max.**	**Min.**	**Max.**	**Units**
t_{RDI}	READ to INTR Off		400		300	ns
t_{PSS}	Port Setup Time to Strobe Strobe	50		0		ns
t_{PHS}	Port Hold Time After Strobe	120		100		ns
t_{SBE}	Strobe to Buffer Empty		400		300	ns
t_{WBF}	WRITE to Buffer Full		400		300	ns
t_{WI}	WRITE to INTR Off		400		300	ns
t_{TL}	TIMER-IN to $\overline{\text{TIMER-OUT}}$ Low		400		300	ns
t_{TH}	TIMER-IN to $\overline{\text{TIMER-OUT}}$ High		400		300	ns
t_{RDE}	Data Bus Enable from READ Control	10		10		ns
t_1	TIMER-IN Low Time	80		40		ns
t_2	TIMER-IN High Time	120		70		ns
t_{WT}	WRITE to TIMER-IN (for writes which start counting)	360		200		ns

A.C. TESTING INPUT, OUTPUT WAVEFORM

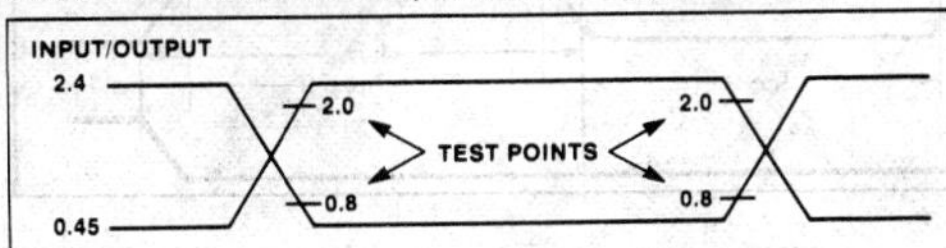

A.C. TESTING: INPUTS ARE DRIVEN AT 2.4V FOR A LOGIC "1" AND 0.45V FOR A LOGIC "0." TIMING MEASUREMENTS ARE MADE AT 2.0V FOR A LOGIC "1" AND 0.8V FOR A LOGIC "0."

A.C. TESTING LOAD CIRCUIT

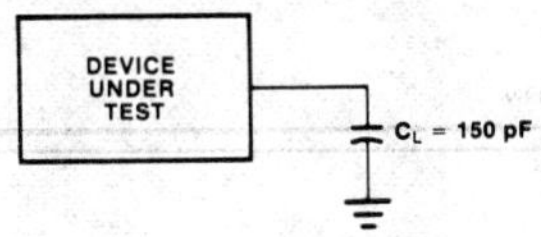

C_L = 150 pF
C_L INCLUDES JIG CAPACITANCE

WAVEFORMS

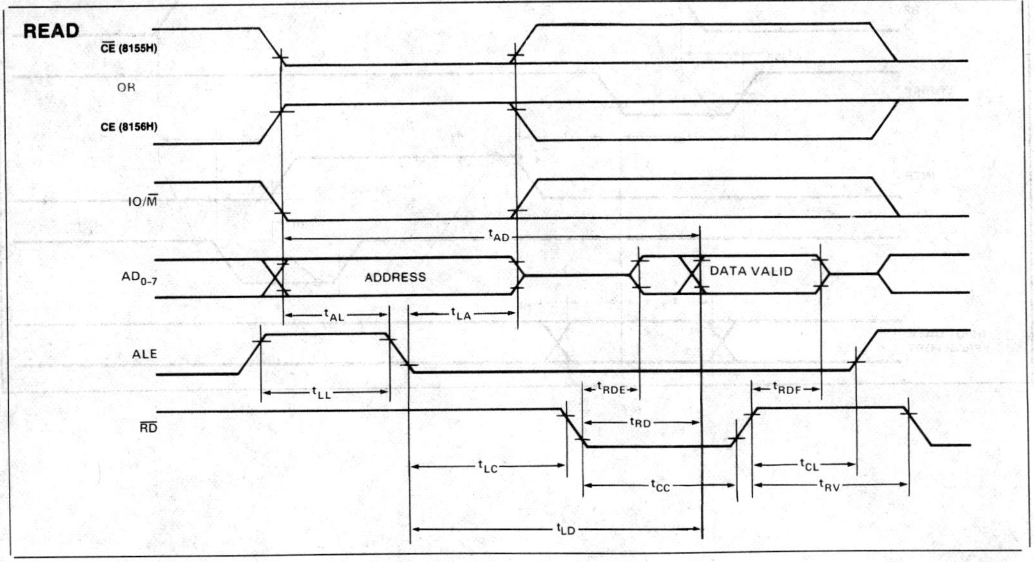

WAVEFORMS (Continued)

WRITE

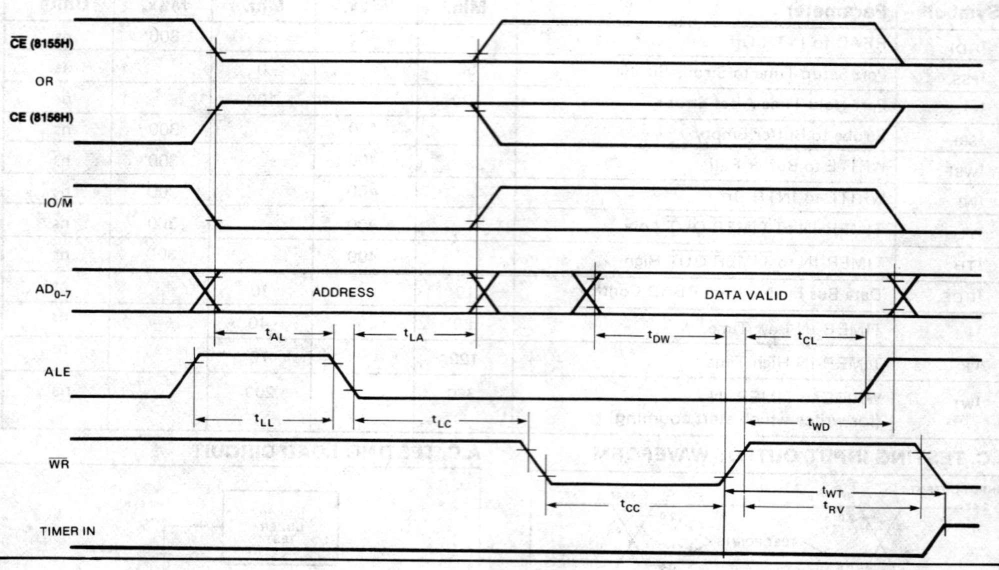

STROBED INPUT

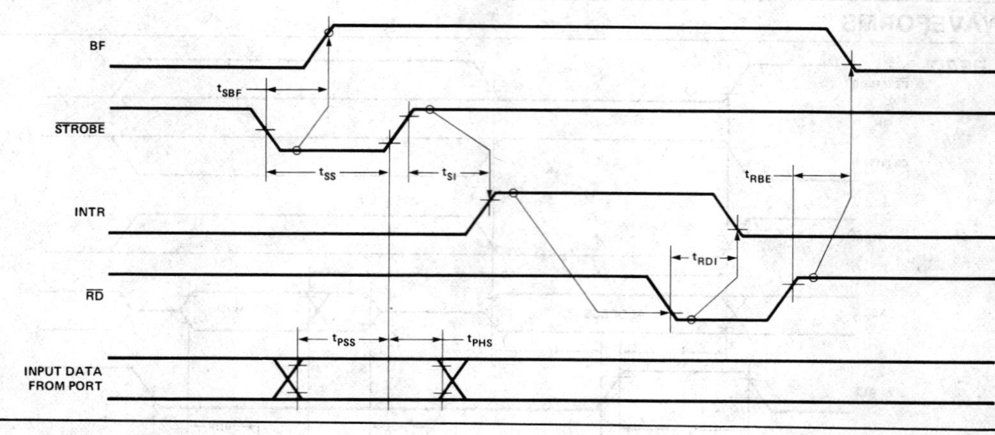

WAVEFORMS (Continued)

STROBED OUTPUT

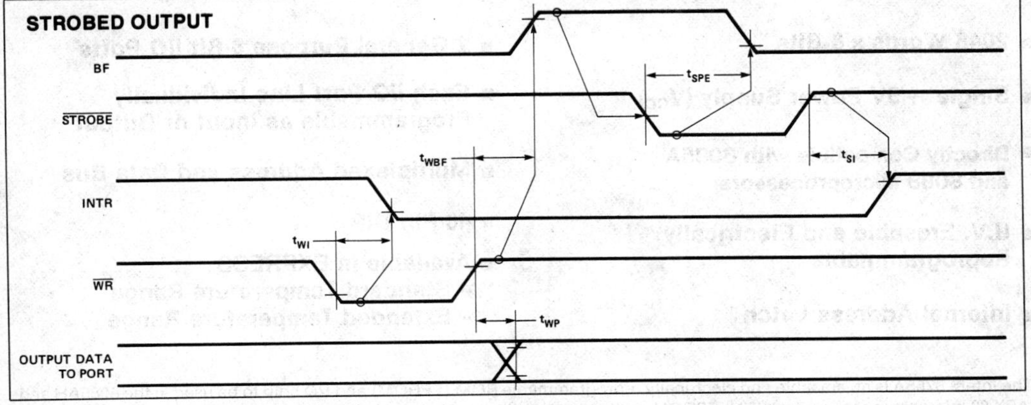

BASIC INPUT

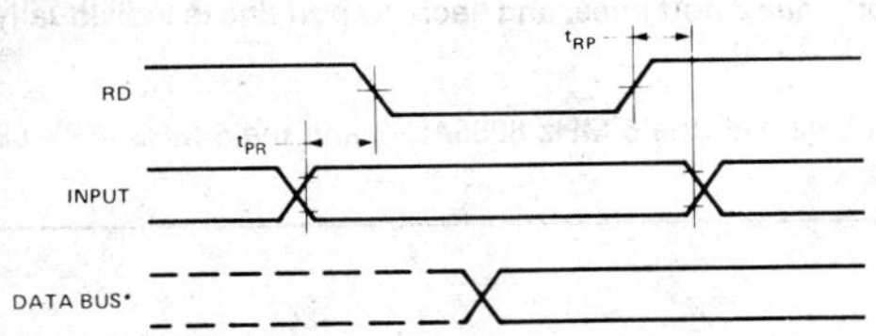

BASIC OUTPUT

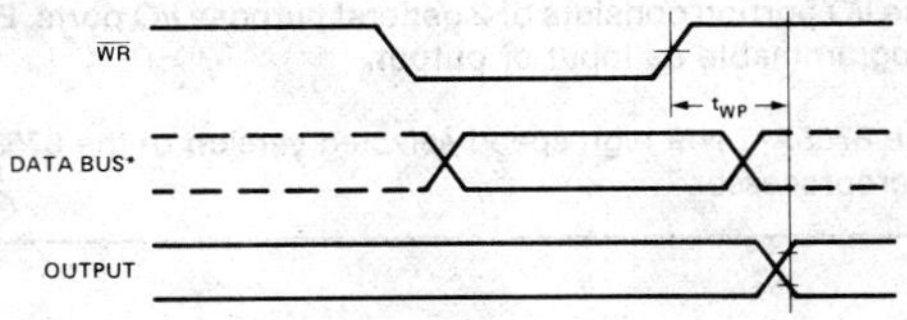

*DATA BUS TIMING IS SHOWN IN FIGURE 7.

TIMER OUTPUT COUNTDOWN FROM 5 TO 1

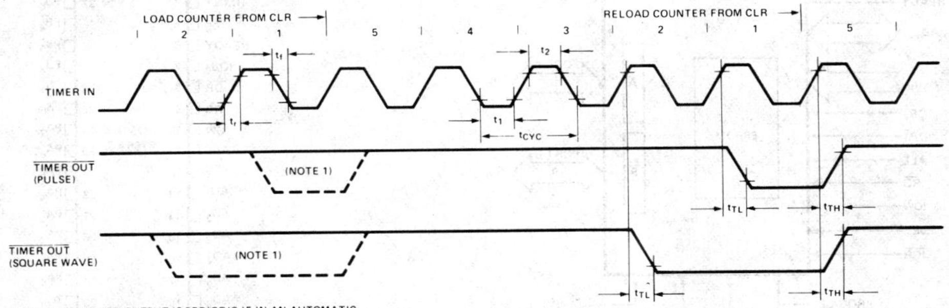

NOTE 1: THE TIMER OUTPUT IS PERIODIC IF IN AN AUTOMATIC RELOAD MODE (M_1 MODE BIT = 1)

8755A/8755A-2
16,384-BIT EPROM WITH I/O

- **2048 Words × 8 Bits**
- **Single +5V Power Supply (V_{CC})**
- **Directly Compatible with 8085A and 8088 Microprocessors**
- **U.V. Erasable and Electrically Reprogrammable**
- **Internal Address Latch**
- **2 General Purpose 8-Bit I/O Ports**
- **Each I/O Port Line Individually Programmable as Input or Output**
- **Multiplexed Address and Data Bus**
- **40-Pin DIP**
- **Available in EXPRESS**
  - **Standard Temperature Range**
  - **Extended Temperature Range**

The Intel® 8755A is an erasable and electrically reprogrammable ROM (EPROM) and I/O chip to be used in the 8085AH and iAPX 88 microprocessor systems. The EPROM portion is organized as 2048 words by 8 bits. It has a maximum access time of 450 ns to permit use with no wait states in an 8085AH CPU.

The I/O portion consists of 2 general purpose I/O ports. Each I/O port has 8 port lines, and each I/O port line is individually programmable as input or output.

The 8755A-2 is a high speed selected version of the 8755A compatible with the 5 MHz 8085AH-2 and the 5 MHz iAPX 88 microprocessor.

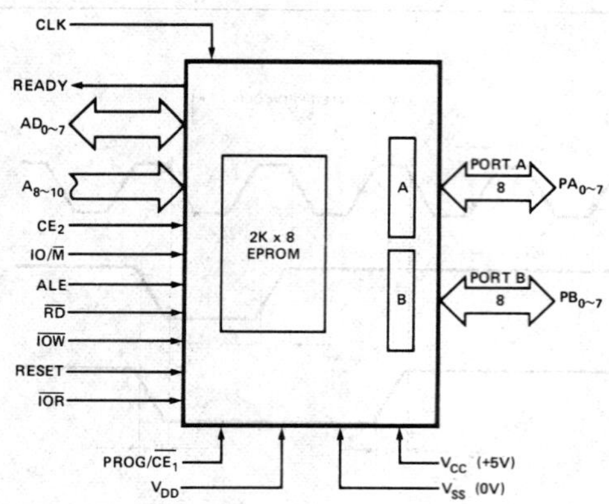

Figure 1. Block Diagram

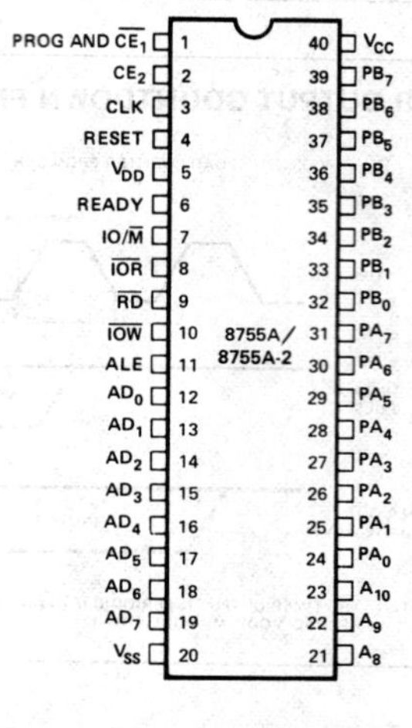

Figure 2. Pin Configuration

Table 1. Pin Description

Symbol	Type	Name and Function
ALE	I	**Address Latch Enable:** When Address Latch Enable goes *high*, AD_{0-7}, $IO/\overline{M}$, A_{8-10}, CE_2, and $\overline{CE_1}$ enter the address latches. The signals (AD, $IO/\overline{M}$ AD_{8-10}, CE_2, $\overline{CE_1}$) are latched in at the trailing edge of ALE.
AD_{0-7}	I	**Bidirectional Address/Data Bus:** The lower 8-bits of the PROM or I/O address are applied to the bus lines when ALE is high. During an I/O cycle, Port A or B is selected based on the latched value of AD_0. If $\overline{RD}$ or $\overline{IOR}$ is low when the latched Chip Enables are active, the output buffers present data on the bus.
A_{8-10}	I	**Address Bus:** These are the high order bits of the PROM address. They do not affect I/O operations.
PROG/$\overline{CE_1}$ CE_2	I	**Chip Enable Inputs:** $\overline{CE_1}$ is active low and CE_2 is active high. The 8755A can be accessed only when *both* Chip Enables are active at the time the ALE signal latches them up. If either Chip Enable input is not active, the AD_{0-7} and READY outputs will be in a high impedance state. $\overline{CE_1}$ is also used as a programming pin. (See section on programming.)
$IO/\overline{M}$	I	**I/O Memory:** If the latched $IO/\overline{M}$ is high when $\overline{RD}$ is low, the output data comes from an I/O port. If it is low the output data comes from the PROM.
$\overline{RD}$	I	**Read:** If the latched Chip Enables are active when $\overline{RD}$ goes low, the AD_{0-7} output buffers are enabled and output either the selected PROM location or I/O port. When both $\overline{RD}$ and $\overline{IOR}$ are high, the AD_{0-7} output buffers are 3-stated.
$\overline{IOW}$	I	**I/O Write:** If the latched Chip Enables are active, a low on $\overline{IOW}$ causes the output port pointed to by the latched value of AD_0 to be written with the data on AD_{0-7}. The state of $IO/\overline{M}$ is ignored.
CLK	I	**Clock:** The CLK is used to force the READY into its high impedance state after it has been forced low by $\overline{CE_1}$ low, CE_2 high, and ALE high.
READY	O	**Ready** is a 3-state output controlled by $\overline{CE_1}$, CE_2, ALE and CLK. READY is forced low when the Chip Enables are active during the time ALE is high, and remains low until the rising edge of the next CLK. (See Figure 6c.)
PA_{0-7}	I/O	**Port A:** These are general purpose I/O pins. Their input/output direction is determined by the contents of Data Direction Register (DDR). Port A is selected for write operations when the Chip Enables are active and $\overline{IOW}$ is low and a 0 was previously latched from AD_0, AD_1. Read Operation is selected by either $\overline{IOR}$ low and active Chip Enables and AD_0 and AD_1 low, *or* $IO/\overline{M}$ high, $\overline{RD}$ low, active Chip Enables, and AD_0 and AD_1 low.
PB_{0-7}	I/O	**Port B:** This general purpose I/O port is identical to Port A except that it is selected by a 1 latched from AD_0 and a 0 from AD_1.
RESET	I	**Reset:** In normal operation, an input high on RESET causes all pins in Ports A and B to assume input mode (clear DDR register).
$\overline{IOR}$	I	**I/O Read:** When the Chip Enables are active, a low on $\overline{IOR}$ will output the selected I/O port onto the AD bus. $\overline{IOR}$ low performs the same function as the combination of $IO/\overline{M}$ high and $\overline{RD}$ low. When $\overline{IOR}$ is not used in a system, $\overline{IOR}$ should be tied to V_{CC} ("1").
V_{CC}		**Power:** +5 volt supply.
V_{SS}		**Ground:** Reference.
V_{DD}		**Power Supply:** V_{DD} is a programming voltage, and must be tied to V_{CC} when the 8755A is being read. For programming, a high voltage is supplied with V_{DD} = 25V, typical. (See section on programming.)

FUNCTIONAL DESCRIPTION

PROM Section

The 8755A contains an 8-bit address latch which allows it to interface directly to MCS-48, MCS-85 and iAPX 88/10 Microcomputers without additional hardware.

The PROM section of the chip is addressed by the 11-bit address and the Chip Enables. The address, $\overline{CE_1}$ and CE_2 are latched into the address latches on the falling edge of ALE. If the latched Chip Enables are active and IO/$\overline{M}$ is low when $\overline{RD}$ goes low, the contents of the PROM location addressed by the latched address are put out on the AD_{0-7} lines (provided that V_{DD} is tied to V_{CC}.)

I/O Section

The I/O section of the chip is addressed by the latched value of AD_{0-1}. Two 8-bit Data Direction Registers (DDR) in 8755A determine the input/output status of each pin in the corresponding ports. A "0" in a particular bit position of a DDR signifies that the corresponding I/O port bit is in the input mode. A "1" in a particular bit position signifies that the corresponding I/O port bit is in the output mode. In this manner the I/O ports of the 8755A are bit-by-bit programmable as inputs or outputs. The table summarizes port and DDR designation. DDR's cannot be read.

AD_1	AD_0	Selection
0	0	Port A
0	1	Port B
1	0	Port A Data Direction Register (DDR A)
1	1	Port B Data Direction Register (DDR B)

When $\overline{IOW}$ goes low and the Chip Enables are active, the data on the AD_{0-7} is written into I/O port selected by the latched value of AD_{0-1}. During this operation all I/O bits of the selected port are affected, regardless of their I/O mode and the state of IO/$\overline{M}$. The actual output level does not change until $\overline{IOW}$ returns high. (glitch free output)

A port can be read out when the latched Chip Enables are active and either $\overline{RD}$ goes low with IO/$\overline{M}$ high, or $\overline{IOR}$ goes low. Both input and output mode bits of a selected port will appear on lines AD_{0-7}.

To clarify the function of the I/O Ports and Data Direction Registers, the following diagram shows the configuration of one bit of PORT A and DDR A. The same logic applies to PORT B and DDR B.

8755A
ONE BIT OF PORT A AND DDR A:

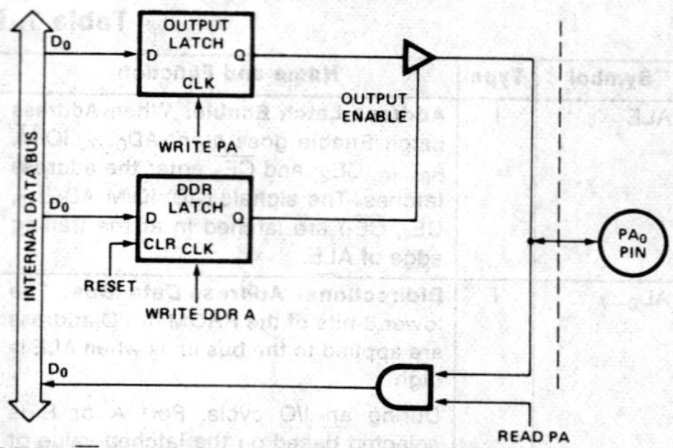

WRITE PA = ($\overline{IOW}$=0) • (CHIP ENABLES ACTIVE) • (PORT A ADDRESS SELECTED)
WRITE DDR A = ($\overline{IOW}$=0) • (CHIP ENABLES ACTIVE) • (DDR A ADDRESS SELECTED)
READ PA = {[(IO/$\overline{M}$=1) • ($\overline{RD}$=0)] + ($\overline{IOR}$=0)} • (CHIP ENABLES ACTIVE) • (PORT A ADDRESS SELECTED)

NOTE: WRITE PA IS NOT QUALIFIED BY IO/$\overline{M}$.

Note that hardware RESET or writing a zero to the DDR latch will cause the output latch's output buffer to be disabled, preventing the data in the Output Latch from being passed through to the pin. This is equivalent to putting the port in the input mode. Note also that the data can be written to the Output Latch even though the Output Buffer has been disabled. This enables a port to be initialized with a value prior to enabling the output.

The diagram also shows that the contents of PORT A and PORT B can be read even when the ports are configured as outputs.

TABLE 1. 8755A PROGRAMMING MODULE CROSS REFERENCE

MODULE NAME	USE WITH
UPP 955	UPP(4)
UPP UP2(2)	UPP 855
PROMPT 975	PROMPT 80/85(3)
PROMPT 475	PROMPT 48(1)

NOTES:
1. Described on p. 13-34 of 1978 Data Catalog.
2. Special adaptor socket.
3. Described on p. 13-39 of 1978 Data Catalog.
4. Described on p. 13-71 of 1978 Data Catalog.

ERASURE CHARACTERISTICS

The erasure characteristics of the 8755A are such that erasure begins to occur when exposed to light with wavelengths shorter than approximately 4000 Angstroms (Å). It should be noted that sunlight and certain types of fluorescent lamps have wavelengths in the 3000-4000Å range Data show that constant exposure to room level fluorescent lighting could erase the typical 8755A in approximately 3 years while it would take approximately 1 week to cause erasure when exposed to direct sunlight. If the 8755A is to be exposed to these types of lighting conditions for extended periods of time, opaque labels are available from Intel which should be placed over the 8755 window to prevent unintentional erasure.

The recommended erasure procedure for the 8755A is exposure to shortwave ultraviolet light which has a wavelength of 2537 Angstroms (Å). The integrated dose (i.e., UV intensity X exposure time) for erasure should be a minimum of 15W-sec/cm². The erasure time with this dosage is approximately 15 to 20 minutes using an ultraviolet lamp with a 12000μW/cm² power rating. The 8755A should be placed within one inch from the lamp tubes during erasure. Some lamps have a filter on their tubes and this filter should be removed before erasure.

PROGRAMMING

Initially, and after each erasure, all bits of the EPROM portions of the 8755A are in the "1" state. Information is introduced by selectively programming "0" into the desired bit locations. A programmed "0" can only be changed to a "1" by UV erasure.

The 8755A can be programmed on the Intel® Universal PROM Programmer (UPP), and the PROMPT™ 80/85 and PROMPT-48™ design aids. The appropriate programming modules and adapters for use in programming both 8755A's and 8755's are shown in Table 1.

The program mode itself consists of programming a single address at a time, giving a single 50 msec pulse for every address. Generally, it is desirable to have a verify cycle after a program cycle for the same address as shown in the attached timing diagram. In the verify cycle (i.e., normal memory read cycle) 'V_{DD}' should be at +5V.

Preliminary timing diagrams and parameter values pertaining to the 8755A programming operation are contained in Figure 7.

SYSTEM APPLICATIONS

System Interface with 8085AH and iAPX 88

A system using the 8755A can use either one of the two I/O Interface techniques:

- Standard I/O
- Memory Mapped I/O

If a standard I/O technique is used, the system can use the feature of both CE_2 and $\overline{CE_1}$. By using a combination of unused address lines A_{11-15} and the Chip Enable inputs, the 8085AH system can use up to 5 each 8755A's without requiring a CE decoder. See Figure 4a and 4b.

If a memory mapped I/O approach is used the 8755A will be selected by the combination of both the Chip Enables and IO/$\overline{M}$ using AD_{8-15} address lines. See Figure 3.

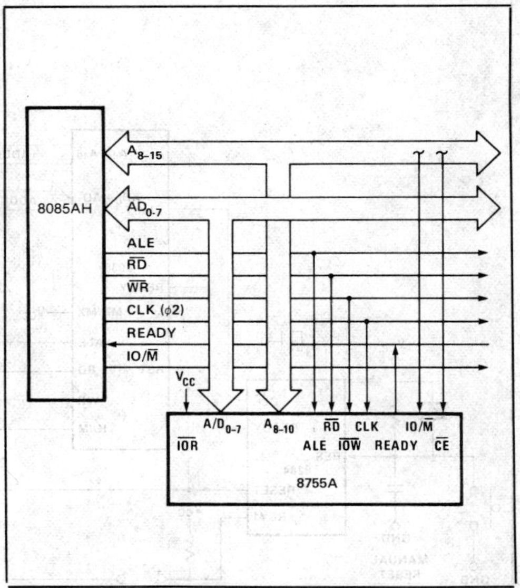

Figure 3. 8755A in 8085AH System (Memory-Mapped I/O)

iAPX 88 FIVE CHIP SYSTEM

Figure 4 shows a five chip system containing:

- 1.25K Bytes RAM
- 2K Bytes EPROM
- 38 I/O Pins
- 1 Interval Timer
- 2 Interrupt Levels

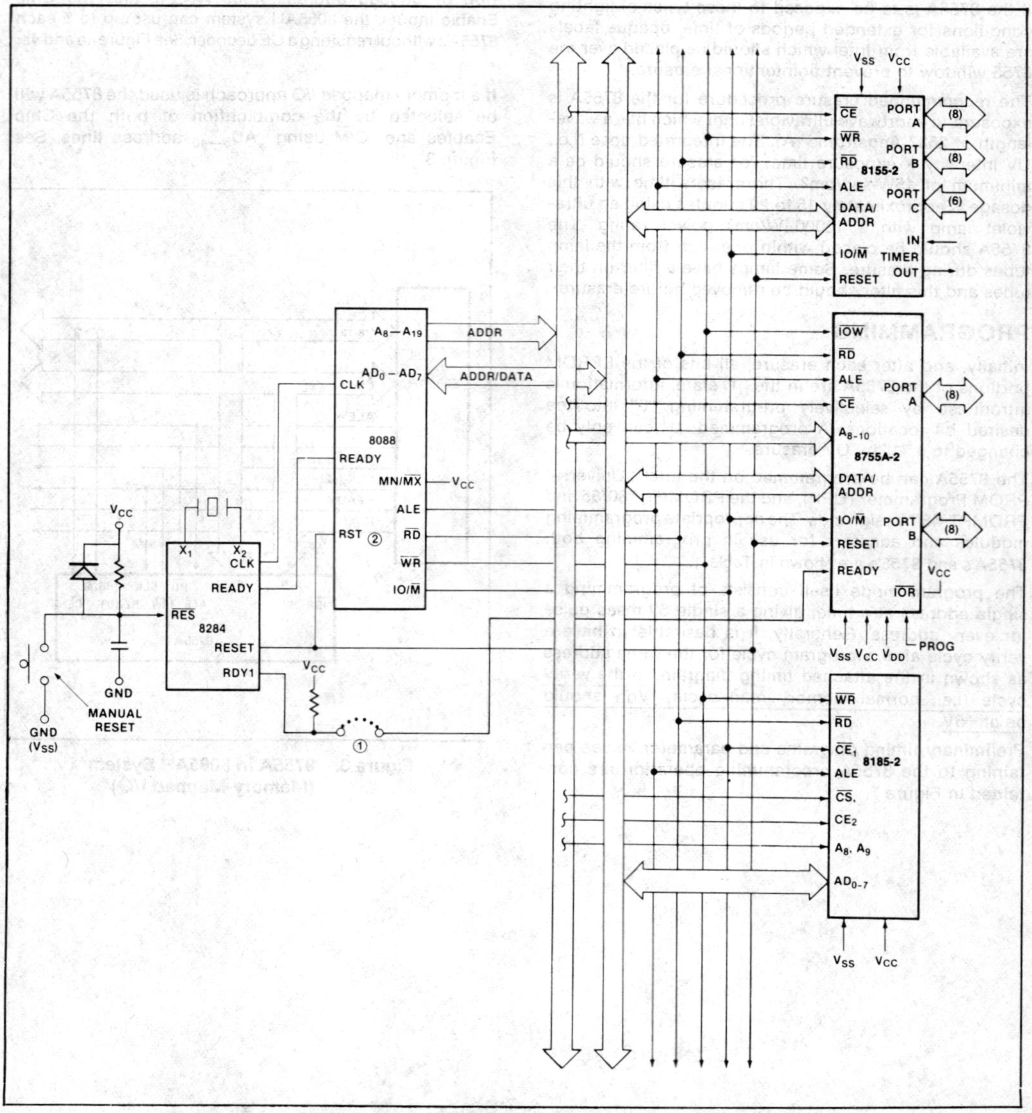

Figure 4a. iAPX 88 Five Chip System Configuration

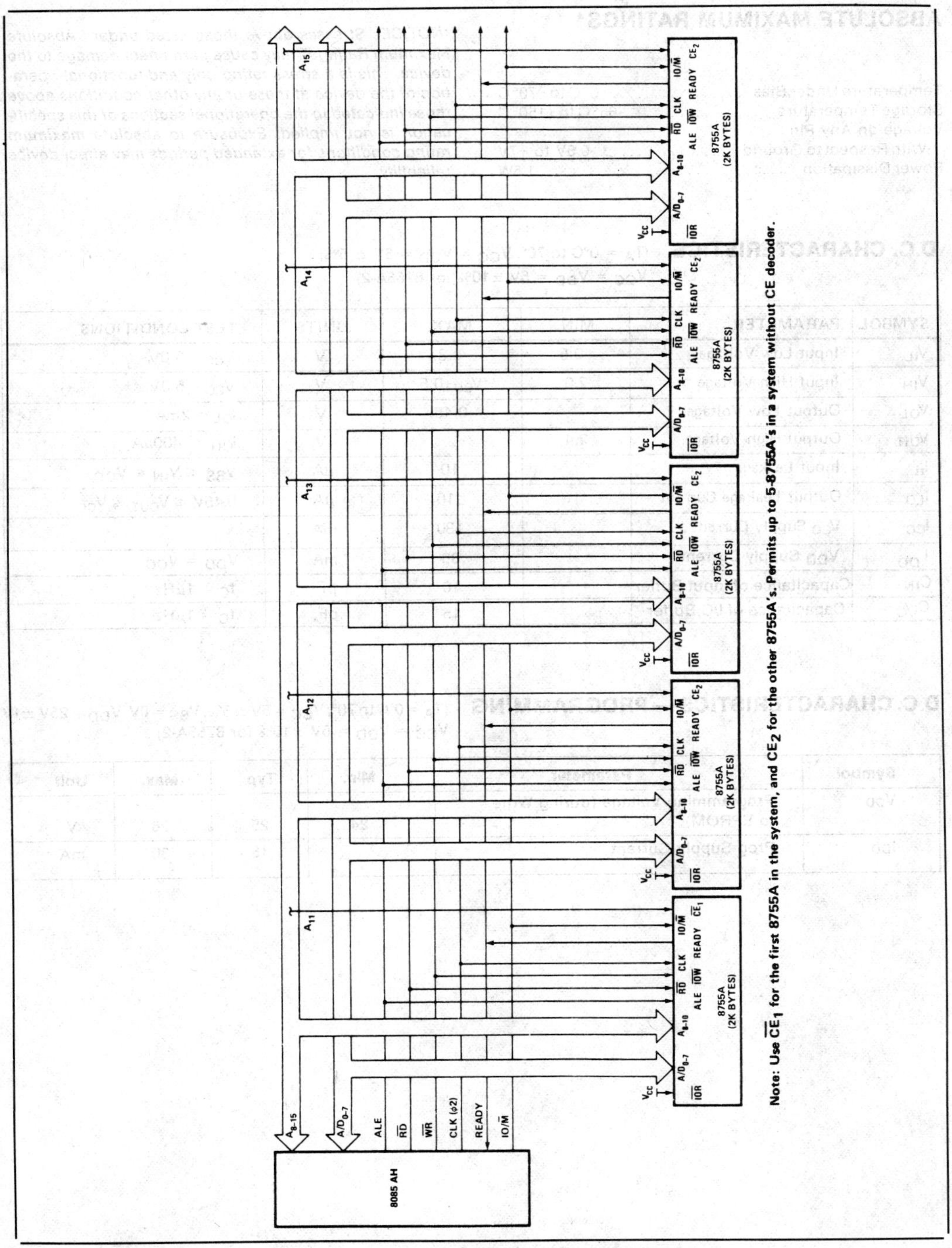

Figure 4b. 8755A in 8085A System (Standard I/O)

ABSOLUTE MAXIMUM RATINGS*

Temperature Under Bias .... 0°C to +70°C
Storage Temperature .... -65°C to +150°C
Voltage on Any Pin
With Respect to Ground .... -0.5V to +7V
Power Dissipation 1.5W

**NOTICE: Stresses above those listed under "Absolute Maximum Ratings" may cause permanent damage to the device. This is a stress rating only and functional operation of the device at these or any other conditions above those indicated in the operational sections of this specification is not implied. Exposure to absolute maximum rating conditions for extended periods may affect device reliability.*

D.C. CHARACTERISTICS

(T_A = 0°C to 70°, V_{CC} = V_{DD} = 5V ± 5%; V_{CC} = V_{DD} = 5V ±10% for 8755A-2)

SYMBOL	PARAMETER	MIN.	MAX.	UNITS	TEST CONDITIONS
V_{IL}	Input Low Voltage	-0.5	0.8	V	V_{CC} = 5.0V
V_{IH}	Input High Voltage	2.0	V_{CC}+0.5	V	V_{CC} = 5.0V
V_{OL}	Output Low Voltage		0.45	V	I_{OL} = 2mA
V_{OH}	Output High Voltage	2.4		V	I_{OH} = -400μA
I_{IL}	Input Leakage		10	μA	$V_{SS} \leq V_{IN} \leq V_{CC}$
I_{LO}	Output Leakage Current		±10	μA	$0.45V \leq V_{OUT} \leq V_{CC}$
I_{CC}	V_{CC} Supply Current		180	mA	
I_{DD}	V_{DD} Supply Current		30	mA	V_{DD} = V_{CC}
C_{IN}	Capacitance of Input Buffer		10	pF	f_C = 1μHz
$C_{I/O}$	Capacitance of I/O Buffer		15	pF	f_C = 1μHz

D.C. CHARACTERISTICS — PROGRAMMING

(T_A = 0°C to 70°, V_{CC} = 5V ± 5%, V_{SS} = 0V, V_{DD} = 25V ±1V; V_{CC} = V_{DD} = 5V ±10% for 8755A-2)

Symbol	Parameter	Min.	Typ.	Max.	Unit
V_{DD}	Programming Voltage (during Write to EPROM)	24	25	26	V
I_{DD}	Prog Supply Current		15	30	mA

A.C. CHARACTERISTICS

(T_A = 0°C to 70°, V_{CC} = 5V ± 5%; V_{CC} = V_{DD} = 5V ±10% for 8755A-2)

Symbol	Parameter	8755A		8755A-2 (Preliminary)		Units
		Min.	Max.	Min.	Max.	
t_{CYC}	Clock Cycle Time	320		200		ns
T_1	CLK Pulse Width	80		40		ns
T_2	CLK Pulse Width	120		70		ns
t_f, t_r	CLK Rise and Fall Time		30		30	ns
t_{AL}	Address to Latch Set Up Time	50		30		ns
t_{LA}	Address Hold Time after Latch	80		45		ns
t_{LC}	Latch to READ/WRITE Control	100		40		ns
t_{RD}	Valid Data Out Delay from READ Control*		170		140	ns
t_{AD}	Address Stable to Data Out Valid**		450		300	ns
t_{LL}	Latch Enable Width	100		70		ns
t_{RDF}	Data Bus Float after READ	0	100	0	85	ns
t_{CL}	READ/WRITE Control to Latch Enable	20		10		ns
t_{CC}	READ/WRITE Control Width	250		200		ns
t_{DW}	Data In to Write Set Up Time	150		150		ns
t_{WD}	Data In Hold Time After WRITE	30		10		ns
t_{WP}	WRITE to Port Output		400		300	ns
t_{PR}	Port Input Set Up Time	50		50		ns
t_{RP}	Port Input Hold Time to Control	50		50		ns
t_{RYH}	READY HOLD Time to Control	0	160	0	160	ns
t_{ARY}	ADDRESS (CE) to READY		160		160	ns
t_{RV}	Recovery Time Between Controls	300		200		ns
t_{RDE}	READ Control to Data Bus Enable	10		10		ns

NOTE:

C_{LOAD} = 150pF.

*Or T_{AD} − (T_{AL} + T_{LC}), whichever is greater.

**Defines ALE to Data Out Valid in conjunction with T_{AL}.

A.C. CHARACTERISTICS — PROGRAMMING

(T_A = 0°C to 70°, V_{CC} = 5V ± 5%, V_{SS} = 0V, V_{DD} = 25V ±1V; V_{CC} = V_{DD} = 5V ±10% for 8755A-2)

Symbol	Parameter	Min.	Typ.	Max.	Unit
t_{PS}	Data Setup Time	10			ns
t_{PD}	Data Hold Time	0			ns
t_S	Prog Pulse Setup Time	2			μs
t_H	Prog Pulse Hold Time	2			μs
t_{PR}	Prog Pulse Rise Time	0.01	2		μs
t_{PF}	Prog Pulse Fall Time	0.01	2		μs
t_{PRG}	Prog Pulse Width	45	50		msec

A.C. TESTING INPUT, OUTPUT WAVEFORM

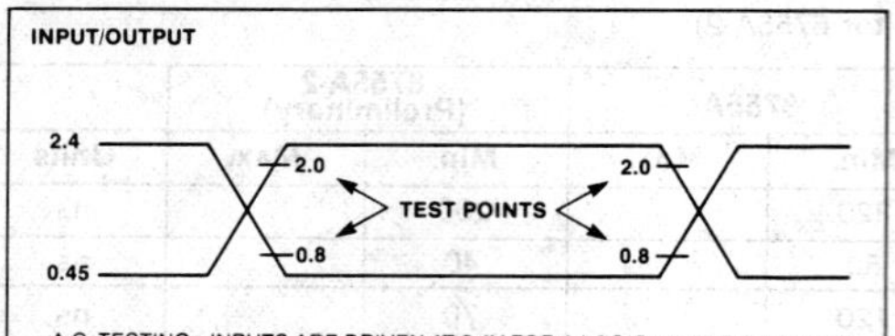

A.C. TESTING: INPUTS ARE DRIVEN AT 2.4V FOR A LOGIC "1" AND 0.45V FOR A LOGIC "0." TIMING MEASUREMENTS ARE MADE AT 2.0V FOR A LOGIC "1" AND 0.8V FOR A LOGIC "0."

A.C. TESTING LOAD CIRCUIT

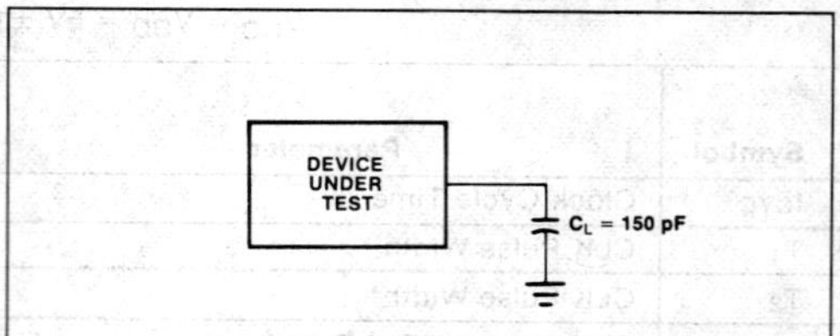

C_L = 150 pF
C_L INCLUDES JIG CAPACITANCE

WAVEFORMS

CLOCK SPECIFICATION FOR 8755A

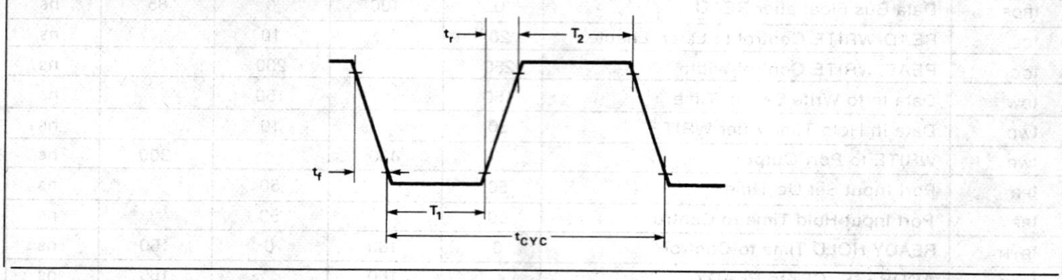

PROM READ, I/O READ AND WRITE

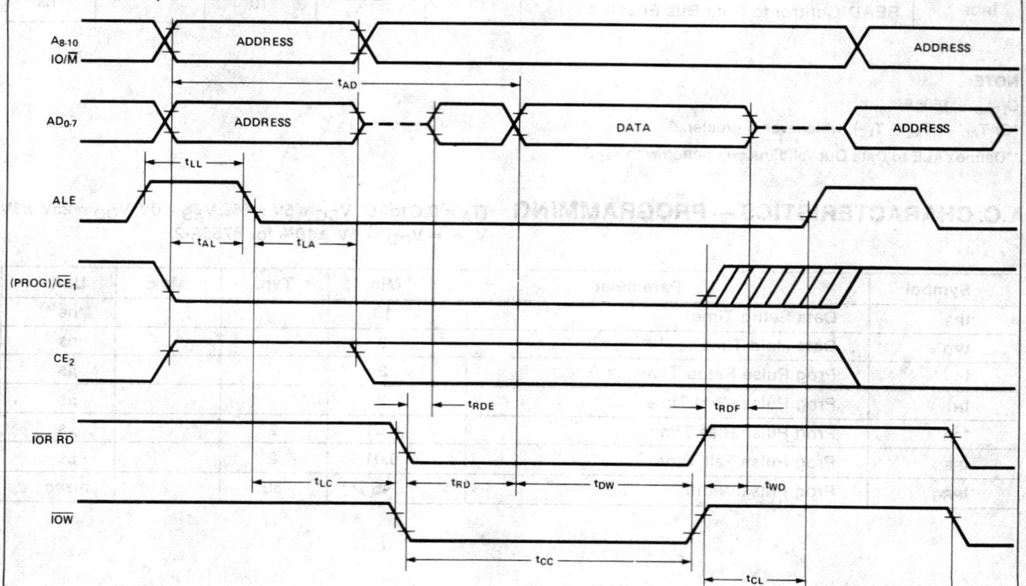

Please note that $\overline{CE}_1$ must remain low for the entire cycle.

WAVEFORMS (Continued)

I/O PORT

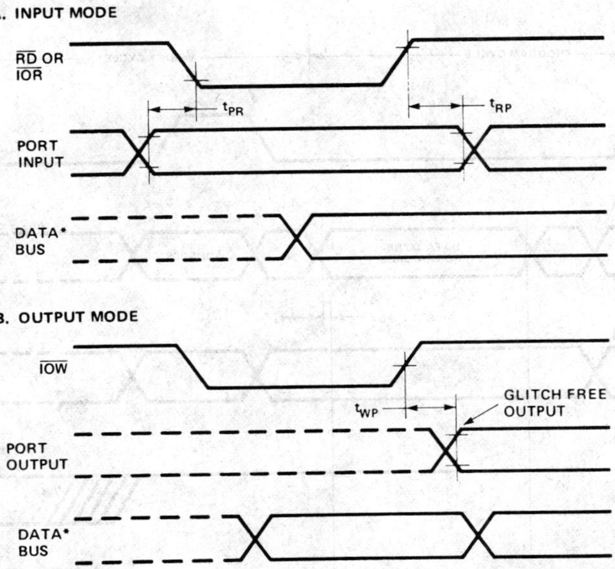

WAIT STATE (READY = 0)

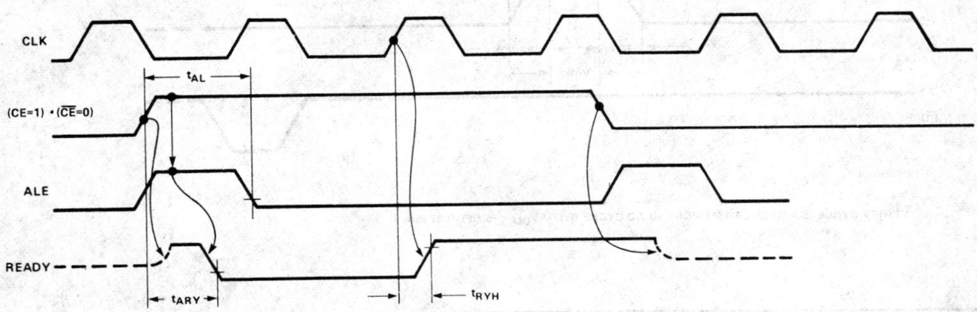

WAVEFORMS (Continued)

8755A PROGRAM MODE

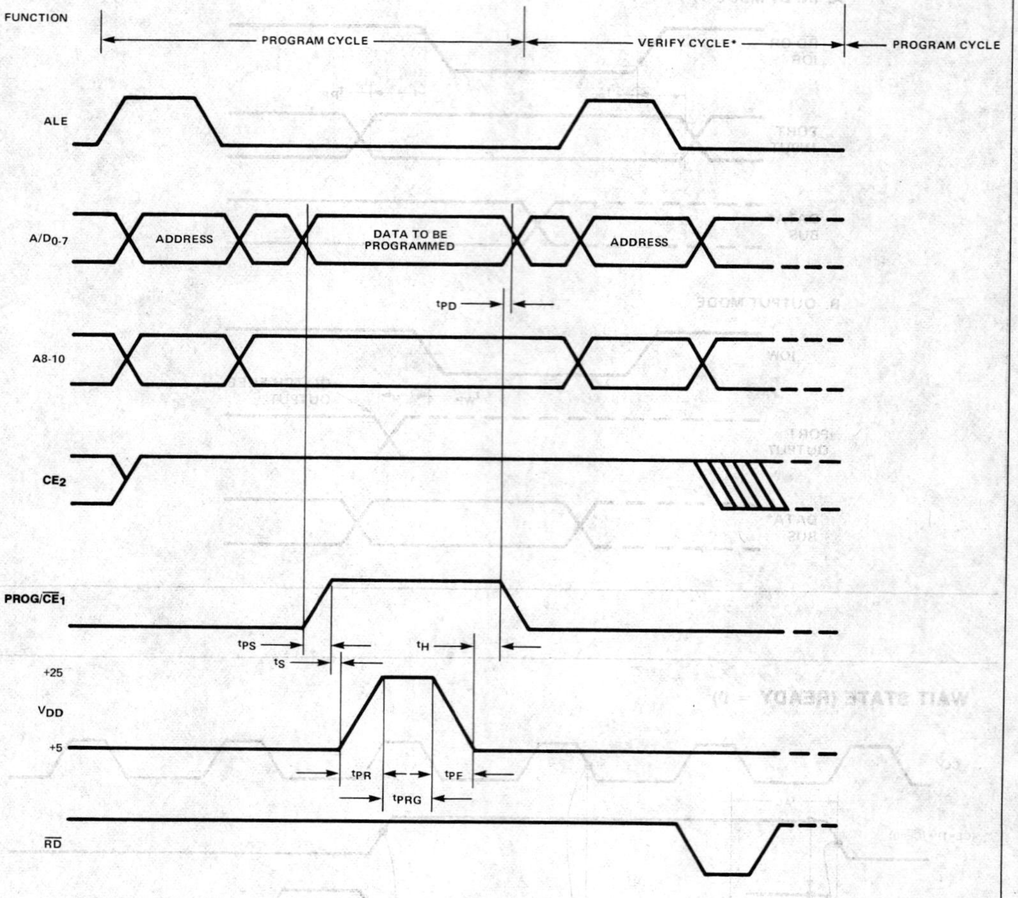

*VERIFY CYCLE IS A REGULAR MEMORY READ CYCLE (WITH V_{DD} = +5V FOR 8755A)

intel®

8251A
PROGRAMMABLE COMMUNICATION INTERFACE

- **Synchronous and Asynchronous Operation**
- **Synchronous 5–8 Bit Characters; Internal or External Character Synchronization; Automatic Sync Insertion**
- **Asynchronous 5–8 Bit Characters; Clock Rate—1, 16 or 64 Times Baud Rate; Break Character Generation; 1, 1½, or 2 Stop Bits; False Start Bit Detection; Automatic Break Detect and Handling**
- **Synchronous Baud Rate—DC to 64K Baud**
- **Asynchronous Baud Rate—DC to 19.2K Baud**
- **Full-Duplex, Double-Buffered Transmitter and Receiver**
- **Error Detection—Parity, Overrun and Framing**
- **Compatible with an Extended Range of Intel Microprocessors**
- **28-Pin DIP Package**
- **All Inputs and Outputs are TTL Compatible**
- **Available in EXPRESS**
  - **—Standard Temperature Range**
  - **—Extended Temperature Range**

The Intel® 8251A is the enhanced version of the industry standard, Intel 8251 Universal Synchronous/Asynchronous Receiver/Transmitter (USART), designed for data communications with Intel's microprocessor families such as MCS-48, 80, 85, and iAPX-86, 88. The 8251A is used as a peripheral device and is programmed by the CPU to operate using virtually any serial data transmission technique presently in use (including IBM "bi-sync"). The USART accepts data characters from the CPU in parallel format and then converts them into a continuous serial data stream for transmission. Simultaneously, it can receive serial data streams and convert them into parallel data characters for the CPU. The USART will signal the CPU whenever it can accept a new character for transmission or whenever it has received a character for the CPU. The CPU can read the complete status of the USART at any time. These include data transmission errors and control signals such as SYNDET, TxEMPTY. The chip is fabricated using N-channel silicon gate technology.

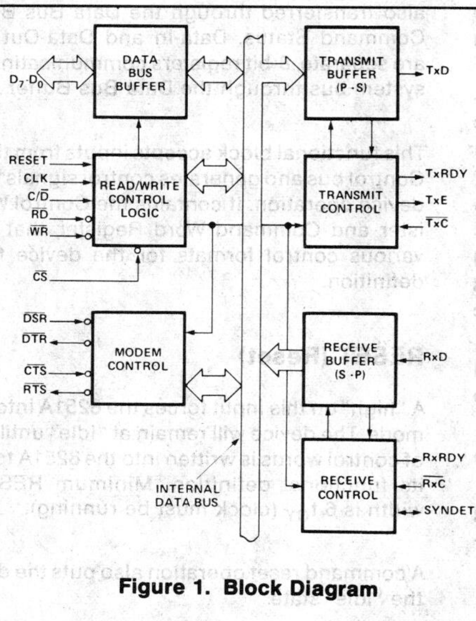

Figure 1. Block Diagram

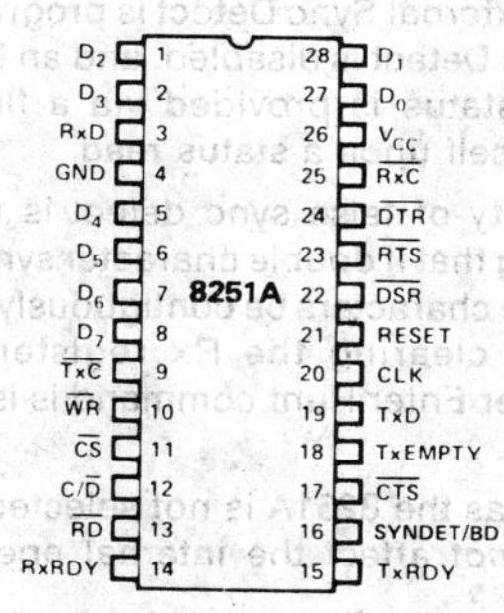

Figure 2. Pin Configuration

September 1984
207780-001

FEATURES AND ENHANCEMENTS

The 8251A is an advanced design of the industry standard USART, the Intel® 8251. The 8251A operates with an extended range of Intel microprocessors and maintains compatibility with the 8251. Familiarization time is minimal because of compatibility and involves only knowing the additional features and enhancements, and reviewing the AC and DC specifications of the 8251A.

The 8251A incorporates all the key features of the 8251 and has the following additional features and enhancements:

- 8251A has double-buffered data paths with separate I/O registers for control, status, Data In, and Data Out, which considerably simplifies control programming and minimizes CPU overhead.
- In asynchronous operations, the Receiver detects and handles "break" automatically, relieving the CPU of this task.
- A refined Rx initialization prevents the Receiver from starting when in "break" state, preventing unwanted interrupts from a disconnected USART.
- At the conclusion of a transmission, TxD line will always return to the marking state unless SBRK is programmed.
- Tx Enable logic enhancement prevents a Tx Disable command from halting transmission until all data previously written has been transmitted. The logic also prevents the transmitter from turning off in the middle of a word.
- When External Sync Detect is programmed, Internal Sync Detect is disabled, and an External Sync Detect status is provided via a flip-flop which clears itself upon a status read.
- Possibility of false sync detect is minimized by ensuring that if double character sync is programmed, the characters be contiguously detected and also by clearing the Rx register to all ones whenever Enter Hunt command is issued in Sync mode.
- As long as the 8251A is not selected, the $\overline{RD}$ and $\overline{WR}$ do not affect the internal operation of the device.
- The 8251A Status can be read at any time but the status update will be inhibited during status read.
- The 8251A is free from extraneous glitches and has enhanced AC and DC characteristics, providing higher speed and better operating margins.
- Synchronous Baud rate from DC to 64K.

FUNCTIONAL DESCRIPTION

General

The 8251A is a Universal Synchronous/Asynchronous Receiver/Transmitter designed for a wide range of Intel microcomputers such as 8048, 8080, 8085, 8086 and 8088. Like other I/O devices in a microcomputer system, its functional configuration is programmed by the system's software for maximum flexibility. The 8251A can support most serial data techniques in use, including IBM "bi-sync."

In a communication environment an interface device must convert parallel format system data into serial format for transmission and convert incoming serial format data into parallel system data for reception. The interface device must also delete or insert bits or characters that are functionally unique to the communication technique. In essence, the interface should appear "transparent" to the CPU, a simple input or output of byte-oriented system data.

Data Bus Buffer

This 3-state, bidirectional, 8-bit buffer is used to interface the 8251A to the system Data Bus. Data is transmitted or received by the buffer upon execution of INput or OUTput instructions of the CPU. Control words, Command words and Status information are also transferred through the Data Bus Buffer. The Command Status, Data-In and Data-Out registers are separate, 8-bit registers communicating with the system bus through the Data Bus Buffer.

This functional block accepts inputs from the system Control bus and generates control signals for overall device operation. It contains the Control Word Register and Command Word Register that store the various control formats for the device functional definition.

RESET (Reset)

A "high" on this input forces the 8251A into an "Idle" mode. The device will remain at "Idle" until a new set of control words is written into the 8251A to program its functional definition. Minimum RESET pulse width is 6 t_{CY} (clock must be running).

A command reset operation also puts the device into the "Idle" state.

CLK (Clock)

The CLK input is used to generate internal device timing and is normally connected to the Phase 2 (TTL) output of the Clock Generator. No external inputs or outputs are referenced to CLK but the frequency of CLK must be greater than 30 times the Receiver or Transmitter data bit rates.

$\overline{\text{WR}}$ (Write)

A "low" on this input informs the 8251A that the CPU is writing data or control words to the 8251A.

$\overline{\text{RD}}$ (Read)

A "low" on this input informs the 8251A that the CPU is reading data or status information from the 8251A.

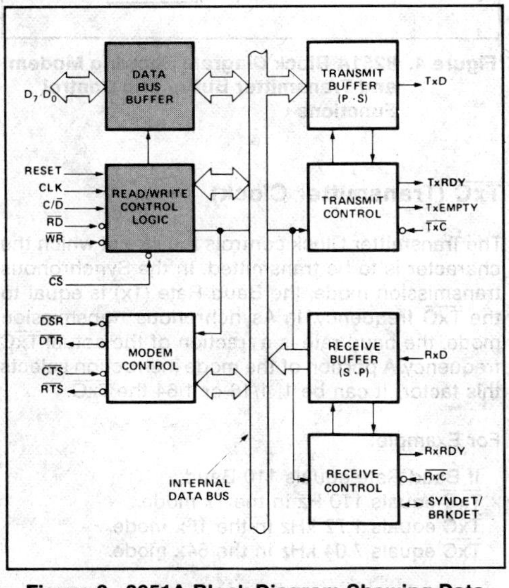

Figure 3. 8251A Block Diagram Showing Data Bus Buffer and Read/Write Logic Functions

C/$\overline{\text{D}}$	$\overline{\text{RD}}$	$\overline{\text{WR}}$	$\overline{\text{CS}}$	
0	0	1	0	8251A DATA ⇒ DATA BUS
0	1	0	0	DATA BUS ⇒ 8251A DATA
1	0	1	0	STATUS ⇒ DATA BUS
1	1	0	0	DATA BUS ⇒ CONTROL
X	1	1	0	DATA BUS ⇒ 3-STATE
X	X	X	1	DATA BUS ⇒ 3-STATE

C/$\overline{\text{D}}$ (Control/Data)

This input, in conjunction with the $\overline{\text{WR}}$ and $\overline{\text{RD}}$ inputs, informs the 8251A that the word on the Data Bus is either a data character, control word or status information.

1 = CONTROL/STATUS; 0 = DATA.

$\overline{\text{CS}}$ (Chip Select)

A "low" on this input selects the 8251A. No reading or writing will occur unless the device is selected. When $\overline{\text{CS}}$ is high, the Data Bus is in the float state and $\overline{\text{RD}}$ and $\overline{\text{WR}}$ have no effect on the chip.

Modem Control

The 8251A has a set of control inputs and outputs that can be used to simplify the interface to almost any modem. The modem control signals are general purpose in nature and can be used for functions other than modem control, if necessary.

$\overline{\text{DSR}}$ (Data Set Ready)

The $\overline{\text{DSR}}$ input signal is a general-purpose, 1-bit inverting input port. Its condition can be tested by the CPU using a Status Read operation. The $\overline{\text{DSR}}$ input is normally used to test modem conditions such as Data Set Ready.

$\overline{\text{DTR}}$ (Data Terminal Ready)

The $\overline{\text{DTR}}$ output signal is a general-purpose, 1-bit inverting output port. It can be set "low" by programming the appropriate bit in the Command Instruction word. The $\overline{\text{DTR}}$ output signal is normally used for modem control such as Data Terminal Ready.

$\overline{\text{RTS}}$ (Request to Send)

The $\overline{\text{RTS}}$ output signal is a general-purpose, 1-bit inverting output port. It can be set "low" by programming the appropriate bit in the Command Instruction word. The $\overline{\text{RTS}}$ output signal is normally used for modem control such as Request to Send.

$\overline{\text{CTS}}$ (Clear to Send)

A "low" on this input enables the 8251A to transmit serial data if the Tx Enable bit in the Command byte is set to a "one." If either a Tx Enable off or $\overline{\text{CTS}}$ off condition occurs while the Tx is in operation, the Tx will transmit all the data in the USART, written prior to Tx Disable command before shutting down.

Transmitter Buffer

The Transmitter Buffer accepts parallel data from the Data Bus Buffer, converts it to a serial bit stream, inserts the appropriate characters or bits (based on the communication technique) and outputs a composite serial stream of data on the TxD output pin on the falling edge of $\overline{TxC}$. The transmitter will begin transmission upon being enabled if $\overline{CTS} = 0$. The TxD line will be held in the marking state immediately upon a master Reset or when Tx Enable or $\overline{CTS}$ is off or the transmitter is empty.

Transmitter Control

The Transmitter Control manages all activities associated with the transmission of serial data. It accepts and issues signals both externally and internally to accomplish this function.

TxRDY (Transmitter Ready)

This output signals the CPU that the transmitter is ready to accept a data character. The TxRDY output pin can be used as an interrupt to the system, since it is masked by TxEnable; or, for Polled operation, the CPU can check TxRDY using a Status Read operation. TxRDY is automatically reset by the leading edge of $\overline{WR}$ when a data character is loaded from the CPU.

Note that when using the Polled operation, the TxRDY status bit is *not* masked by TxEnable, but will only indicate the Empty/Full Status of the Tx Data Input Register.

TxE (Transmitter Empty)

When the 8251A has no characters to send, the TxEMPTY output will go "high." It resets upon receiving a character from CPU if the transmitter is enabled. TxEMPTY remains high when the transmitter is disabled. TxEMPTY can be used to indicate the end of a transmission mode, so that the CPU "knows" when to "turn the line around" in the half-duplex operational mode.

In the Synchronous mode, a "high" on this output indicates that a character has not been loaded and the SYNC character or characters are about to be or are being transmitted automatically as "fillers." TxEMPTY does not go low when the SYNC characters are being shifted out.

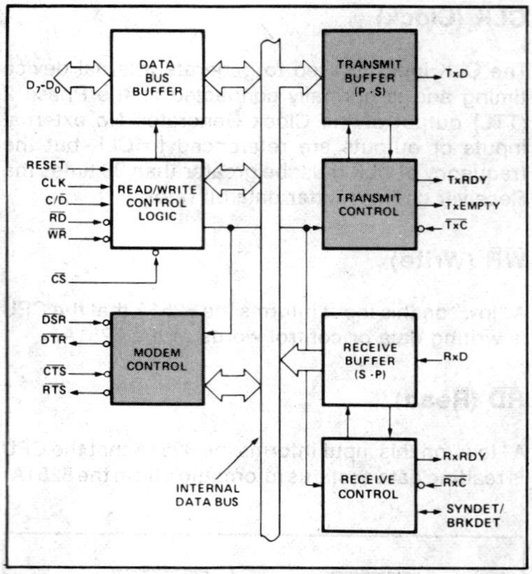

Figure 4. 8251A Block Diagram Showing Modem and Transmitter Buffer and Control Functions

$\overline{TxC}$ (Transmitter Clock)

The Transmitter Clock controls the rate at which the character is to be transmitted. In the Synchronous transmission mode, the Baud Rate (1x) is equal to the $\overline{TxC}$ frequency. In Asynchronous transmission mode, the baud rate is a fraction of the actual $\overline{TxC}$ frequency. A portion of the mode instruction selects this factor; it can be 1, 1/16 or 1/64 the $\overline{TxC}$.

For Example:

If Baud Rate equals 110 Baud,
$\overline{TxC}$ equals 110 Hz in the 1x mode.
$\overline{TxC}$ equals 1.72 kHz in the 16x mode.
$\overline{TxC}$ equals 7.04 kHz in the 64x mode.

The falling edge of $\overline{TxC}$ shifts the serial data out of the 8251A.

Receiver Buffer

The Receiver accepts serial data, converts this serial input to parallel format, checks for bits or characters that are unique to the communication technique and sends an "assembled" character to the CPU. Serial data is input to RxD pin, and is clocked in on the rising edge of $\overline{RxC}$.

Receiver Control

This functional block manages all receiver-related activities which consists of the following features.

The RxD initialization circuit prevents the 8251A from mistaking an unused input line for an active low data line in the "break condition." Before starting to receive serial characters on the RxD line, a valid "1" must first be detected after a chip master Reset. Once this has been determined, a search for a valid low (Start bit) is enabled. This feature is only active in the asynchronous mode, and is only done once for each master Reset.

The False Start bit detection circuit prevents false starts due to a transient noise spike by first detecting the falling edge and then strobing the nominal center of the Start bit (RxD = low).

Parity error detection sets the corresponding status bit.

The Framing Error status bit is set if the Stop bit is absent at the end of the data byte (asynchronous mode).

RxRDY (Receiver Ready)

This output indicates that the 8251A contains a character that is ready to be input to the CPU. RxRDY can be connected to the interrupt structure of the CPU or, for polled operation, the CPU can check the condition of RxRDY using a Status Read operation.

RxEnable, when off, holds RxRDY in the Reset Condition. For Asynchronous mode, to set RxRDY, the Receiver must be enabled to sense a Start Bit and a complete character must be assembled and transferred to the Data Output Register. For Synchronous mode, to set RxRDY, the Receiver must be enabled and a character must finish assembly and be transferred to the Data Output Register.

Failure to read the received character from the Rx Data Output Register prior to the assembly of the next Rx Data character will set overrun condition error and the previous character will be written over and lost. If the Rx Data is being read by the CPU when the internal transfer is occurring, overrun error will be set and the old character will be lost.

$\overline{\text{RxC}}$ (Receiver Clock)

The Receiver Clock controls the rate at which the character is to be received. In Synchronous Mode, the Baud Rate (1x) is equal to the actual frequency of $\overline{\text{RxC}}$. In Asynchronous Mode, the Baud Rate is a fraction of the actual $\overline{\text{RxC}}$ frequency. A portion of the mode instruction selects this factor: 1, 1/16 or 1/64 the $\overline{\text{RxC}}$.

For example:

Baud Rate equals 300 Baud, if
$\overline{\text{RxC}}$ equals 300 Hz in the 1x mode;
$\overline{\text{RxC}}$ equals 4800 Hz in the 16x mode;
$\overline{\text{RxC}}$ equals 19.2 kHz in the 64x mode.

Baud Rate equals 2400 Baud, if
$\overline{\text{RxC}}$ equals 2400 Hz in the 1x mode;
$\overline{\text{RxC}}$ equals 38.4 kHz in the 16x mode;
$\overline{\text{RxC}}$ equals 153.6 kHz in the 64x mode.

Data is sampled into the 8251A on the rising edge of $\overline{\text{RxC}}$.

NOTE: In most communications systems, the 8251A will be handling both the transmission and reception operations of a single link. Consequently, the Receive and Transmit Baud Rates will be the same. Both $\overline{\text{TxC}}$ and $\overline{\text{RxC}}$ will require identical frequencies for this operation and can be tied together and connected to a single frequency source (Baud Rate Generator) to simplify the interface.

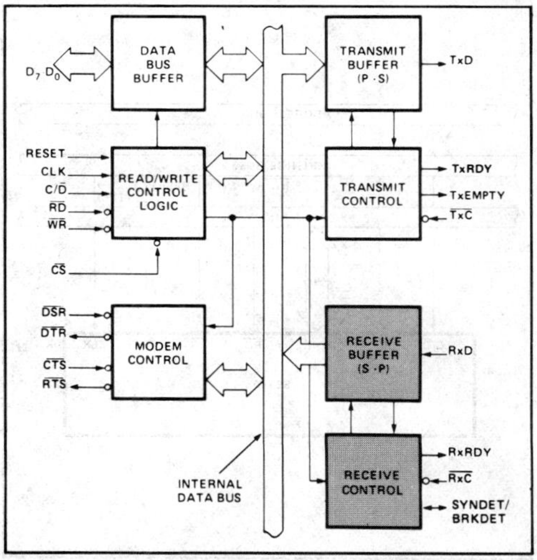

Figure 5. 8251A Block Diagram Showing Receiver Buffer and Control Functions

SYNDET (SYNC Detect/ BRKDET Break Detect)

This pin is used in Synchronous Mode for SYNDET and may be used as either input or output, programmable through the Control Word. It is reset to output mode low upon RESET. When used as an output (internal Sync mode), the SYNDET pin will go "high" to indicate that the 8251A has located the SYNC character in the Receive mode. If the 8251A is programmed to use double Sync characters (bi-sync), then SYNDET will go "high" in the middle of the last bit of the second Sync character. SYNDET is automatically reset upon a Status Read operation.

When used as an input (external SYNC detect mode), a positive going signal will cause the 8251A to start assembling data characters on the rising edge of the next $\overline{RxC}$. Once in SYNC, the "high" input signal can be removed. When External SYNC Detect is programmed, Internal SYNC Detect is disabled.

BREAK (Async Mode Only)

This output will go high whenever the receiver remains low through two consecutive stop bit sequences (including the start bits, data bits, and parity bits). Break Detect may also be read as a Status bit. It is reset only upon a master chip Reset or Rx Data returning to a "one" state.

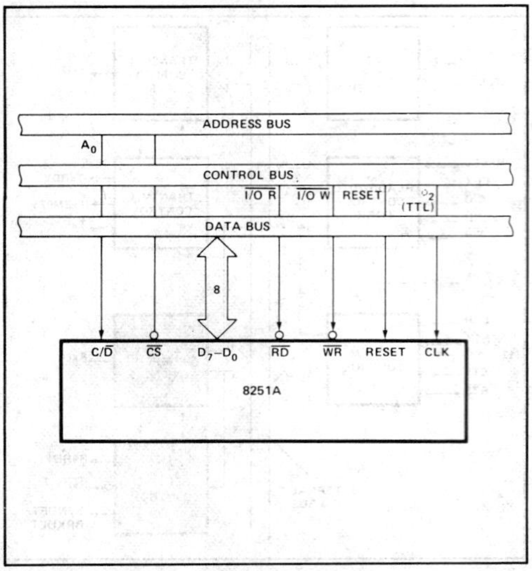

Figure 6. 8251A Interface to 8080 Standard System Bus

DETAILED OPERATION DESCRIPTION

General

The complete functional definition of the 8251A is programmed by the system's software. A set of control words must be sent out by the CPU to initialize the 8251A to support the desired communications format. These control words will program the: BAUD RATE, CHARACTER LENGTH, NUMBER OF STOP BITS, SYNCHRONOUS or ASYNCHRONOUS OPERATION, EVEN/ODD/OFF PARITY, etc. In the Synchronous Mode, options are also provided to select either internal or external character synchronization.

Once programmed, the 8251A is ready to perform its communication functions. The TxRDY output is raised "high" to signal the CPU that the 8251A is ready to receive a data character from the CPU. This output (TxRDY) is reset automatically when the CPU writes a character into the 8251A. On the other hand, the 8251A receives serial data from the MODEM or I/O device. Upon receiving an entire character, the RxRDY output is raised "high" to signal the CPU that the 8251A has a complete character ready for the CPU to fetch. RxRDY is reset automatically upon the CPU data read operation.

The 8251A cannot begin transmission until the Tx Enable (Transmitter Enable) bit is set in the Command Instruction and it has received a Clear To Send ($\overline{CTS}$) input. The TxD output will be held in the marking state upon Reset.

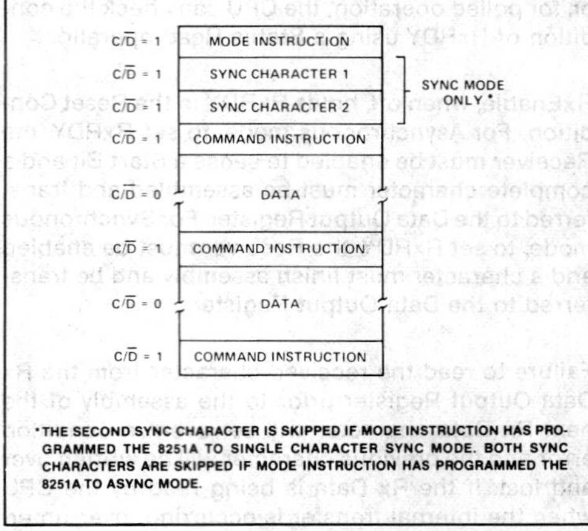

*THE SECOND SYNC CHARACTER IS SKIPPED IF MODE INSTRUCTION HAS PROGRAMMED THE 8251A TO SINGLE CHARACTER SYNC MODE. BOTH SYNC CHARACTERS ARE SKIPPED IF MODE INSTRUCTION HAS PROGRAMMED THE 8251A TO ASYNC MODE.

Figure 7. Typical Data Block

Programming the 8251A

Prior to starting data transmission or reception, the 8251A must be loaded with a set of control words generated by the CPU. These control signals define the complete functional definition of the 8251A and must immediately follow a Reset operation (internal or external).

The control words are split into two formats:

1. Mode Instruction
2. Command Instruction

Mode Instruction

This instruction defines the general operational characteristics of the 8251A. It must follow a Reset operation (internal or external). Once the Mode Instruction has been written into the 8251A by the CPU, SYNC characters or Command Instructions may be written.

Command Instruction

This instruction defines a word that is used to control the actual operation of the 8251A.

Both the Mode and Command Instructions must conform to a specified sequence for proper device operation (see Figure 7). The Mode Instruction must be written immediately following a Reset operation, prior to using the 8251A for data communication.

All control words written into the 8251A after the Mode Instruction will load the Command Instruction. Command Instructions can be written into the 8251A at any time in the data block during the operation of the 8251A. To return to the Mode Instruction format, the master Reset bit in the Command Instruction word can be set to initiate an internal Reset operation which automatically places the 8251A back into the Mode Instruction format. Command Instructions must follow the Mode Instructions or Sync characters.

Mode Instruction Definition

The 8251A can be used for either Asynchronous or Synchronous data communication. To understand how the Mode Instruction defines the functional operation of the 8251A, the designer can best view the device as two separate components, one Asynchronous and the other Synchronous, sharing the same package. The format definition can be changed only after a master chip Reset. For explanation purposes the two formats will be isolated.

NOTE: When parity is enabled it is not considered as one of the data bits for the purpose of programming the word length. The actual parity bit received on the Rx Data line cannot be read on the Data Bus. In the case of a programmed character length of less than 8 bits, the least significant Data Bus bits will hold the data; unused bits are "don't care" when writing data to the 8251A, and will be "zeros" when reading the data from the 8251A.

Asynchronous Mode (Transmission)

Whenever a data character is sent by the CPU the 8251A automatically adds a Start bit (low level) followed by the data bits (least significant bit first), and the programmed number of Stop bits to each character. Also, an even or odd Parity bit is inserted prior to the Stop bit(s), as defined by the Mode Instruction. The character is then transmitted as a serial data stream on the TxD output. The serial data is shifted out on the falling edge of $\overline{TxC}$ at a rate equal to 1, 1/16, or 1/64 that of the $\overline{TxC}$, as defined by the Mode Instruction. BREAK characters can be continuously sent to the TxD if commanded to do so.

When no data characters have been loaded into the 8251A the TxD output reamins "high" (marking) unless a Break (continuously low) has been programmed.

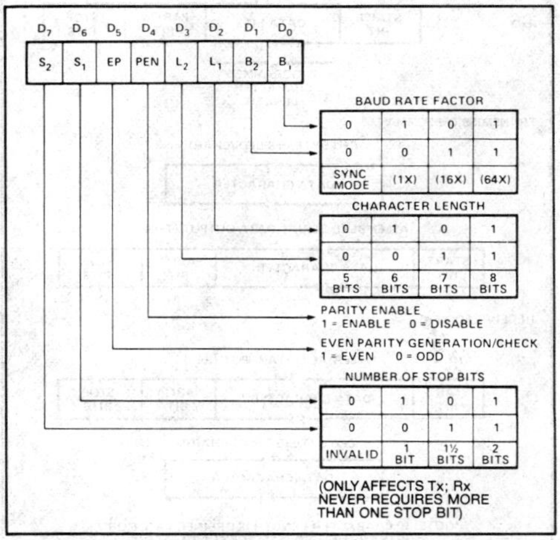

Figure 8. Mode Instruction Format, Asynchronous Mode

Asynchronous Mode (Receive)

The RxD line is normally high. A falling edge on this line triggers the beginning of a START bit. The validity of this START bit is checked by again strobing this bit at its nominal center (16X or 64X mode only). If a low is detected again, it is a valid START bit, and the bit counter will start counting. The bit counter thus locates the center of the data bits, the parity bit (if it exists) and the stop bits. If parity error occurs, the parity error flag is set. Data and parity bits are sampled on the RxD pin with the rising edge of $\overline{RxC}$. If a low level is detected as the STOP bit, the Framing Error flag will be set. The STOP bit signals the end of a character. Note that the *receiver* requires only *one* stop bit, regardless of the number of stop bits programmed. This character is then loaded into the parallel I/O buffer of the 8251A. The RxRDY pin is raised to signal the CPU that a character is ready to be fetched. If a previous character has not been fetched by the CPU, the present character replaces it in the I/O buffer, and the OVERRUN Error flag is raised (thus the previous character is lost). All of the error flags can be reset by an Error Reset Instruction. The occurrence of any of these errors will not affect the operation of the 8251A.

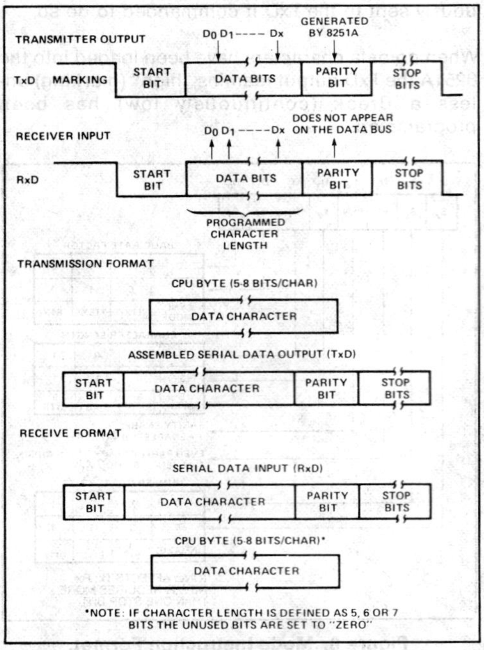

Figure 9. Asynchronous Mode

Synchronous Mode (Transmission)

The TxD output is continuously high until the CPU sends its first character to the 8251A which usually is a SYNC character. When the $\overline{CTS}$ line goes low, the first character is serially transmitted out. All characters are shifted out on the falling edge of $\overline{TxC}$. Data is shifted out at the same rate as the $\overline{TxC}$.

Once transmission has started, the data stream at the TxD output must continue at the $\overline{TxC}$ rate. If the CPU does not provide the 8251A with a data character before the 8251A Transmitter Buffers become empty, the SYNC characters (or character if in single SYNC character mode) will be automatically inserted in the TxD data stream. In this case, the TxEMPTY pin is raised high to signal that the 8251A is empty and SYNC characters are being sent out. TxEMPTY does not go low when the SYNC is being shifted out (see figure below). The TxEMPTY pin is internally reset by a data character being written into the 8251A.

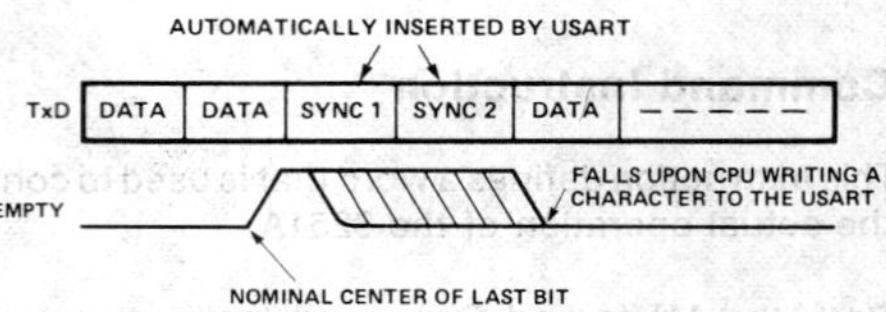

Synchronous Mode (Receive)

In this mode, character synchronization can be internally or externally achieved. If the SYNC mode has been programmed, ENTER HUNT command should be included in the first command instruction word written. Data on the RxD pin is then sampled on the rising edge of $\overline{RxC}$. The content of the Rx buffer is compared at every bit boundary with the first SYNC character until a match occurs. If the 8251A has been programmed for two SYNC characters, the subsequent received character is also compared; when both SYNC characters have been detected, the USART ends the HUNT mode and is in character synchronization. The SYNDET pin is then set high, and is reset automatically by a STATUS READ. If parity is programmed, SYNDET will not be set until the middle of the parity bit instead of the middle of the last data bit.

In the external SYNC mode, synchronization is achieved by applying a high level on the SYNDET pin, thus forcing the 8251A out of the HUNT mode. The high level can be removed after one $\overline{RxC}$ cycle. An ENTER HUNT command has no effect in the asynchronous mode of operation.

Parity error and overrun error are both checked in the same way as in the Asynchronous Rx mode. Parity is checked when not in Hunt, regardless of whether the Receiver is enabled or not.

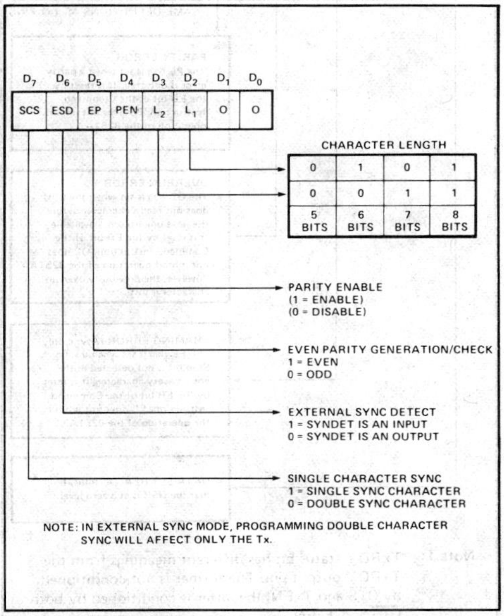

Figure 10. Mode Instruction Format, Synchronous Mode

The CPU can command the receiver to enter the HUNT mode if synchronization is lost. This will also set all the used character bits in the buffer to a "one," thus preventing a possible false SYNDET caused by data that happens to be in the Rx Buffer at ENTER HUNT time. Note that the SYNDET F/F is reset at each Status Read, regardless of whether internal or external SYNC has been programmed. This does not cause the 8251A to return to the HUNT mode. When in SYNC mode, but not in HUNT, Sync Detection is still functional, but only occurs at the "known" word boundaries. Thus, if one Status Read indicates SYNDET and a second Status Read also indicates SYNDET, then the programmed SYNDET characters have been received since the previous Status Read. (If double character sync has been programmed, then both sync characters have been contiguously received to gate a SYNDET indication.) When external SYNDET mode is selected, internal Sync Detect is disabled, and the SYNDET F/F may be set at any bit boundary.

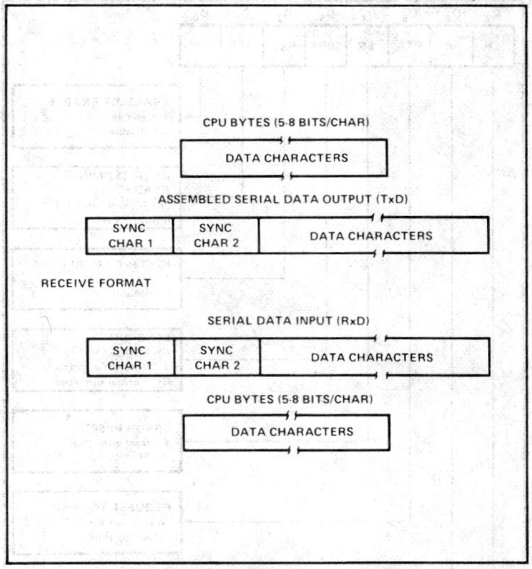

Figure 11. Data Format, Synchronous Mode

COMMAND INSTRUCTION DEFINITION

Once the functional definition of the 8251A has been programmed by the Mode Instruction and the sync characters are loaded (if in Sync Mode) then the device is ready to be used for data communication. The Command Instruction controls the actual operation of the selected format. Functions such as: Enable Transmit/Receive, Error Reset and Modem Controls are provided by the Command Instruction.

Once the Mode Instruction has been written into the 8251A and Sync characters inserted, if necessary, then all further "control writes" (C/D = 1) will load a Command Instruction. A Reset Operation (internal or external) will return the 8251A to the Mode Instruction format.

Note: Internal Reset on Power-up

When power is first applied, the 8251A may come up in the Mode, Sync character or Command format. To guarantee that the device is in the Command Instruction format before the Reset command is issued, it is safest to execute the worst-case initialization sequence (sync mode with two sync characters). Loading three 00Hs consecutively into the device with C/$\overline{D}$ = 1 configures sync operation and writes two dummy 00H sync characters. An Internal Reset command (40H) may then be issued to return the device to the "Idle" state.

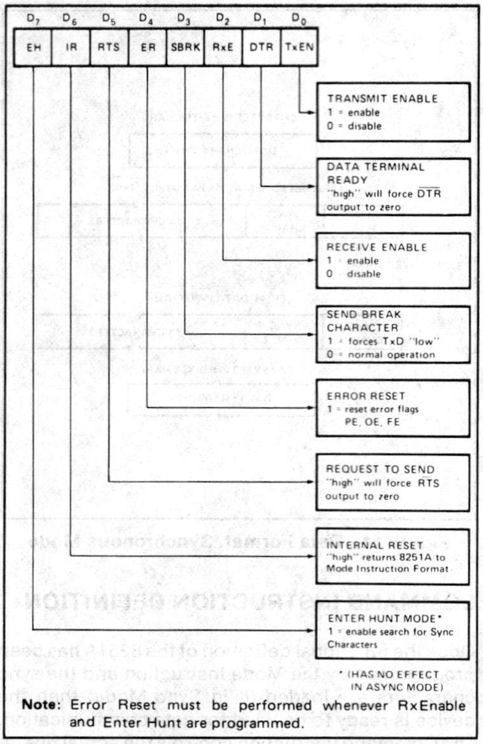

Figure 12. Command Instruction Format

STATUS READ DEFINITION

In data communication systems it is often necessary to examine the "status" of the active device to ascertain if errors have occurred or other conditions that require the processor's attention. The 8251A has facilities that allow the programmer to "read" the status of the device at any time during the functional operation. (Status update is inhibited during status read.)

A normal "read" command is issued by the CPU with $C/\overline{D} = 1$ to accomplish this function.

Some of the bits in the Status Read Format have identical meanings to external output pins so that the 8251A can be used in a completely polled or interrupt-driven environment. TxRDY is an exception.

Note that status update can have a maximum delay of 28 clock periods from the actual event affecting the status.

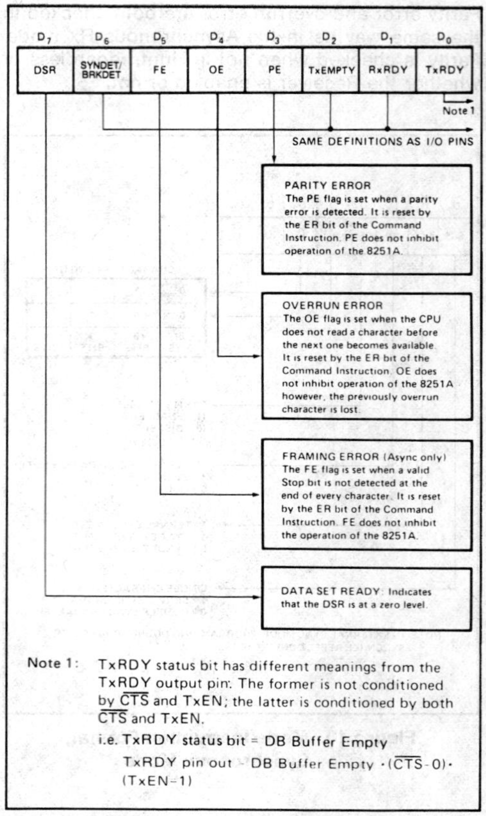

Figure 13. Status Read Format

APPLICATIONS OF THE 8251A

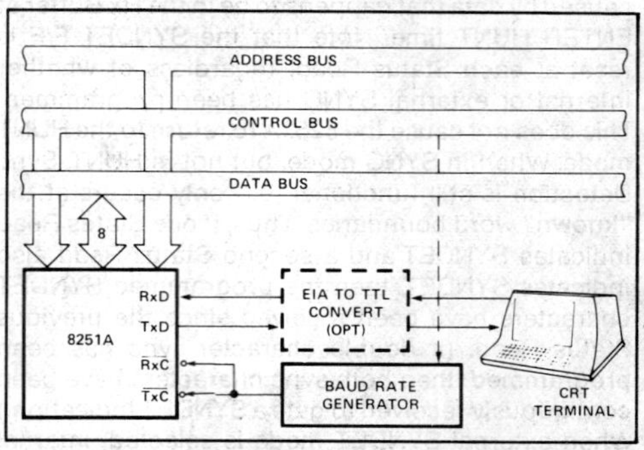

Figure 14. Asynchronous Serial Interface to CRT Terminal, DC—9600 Baud

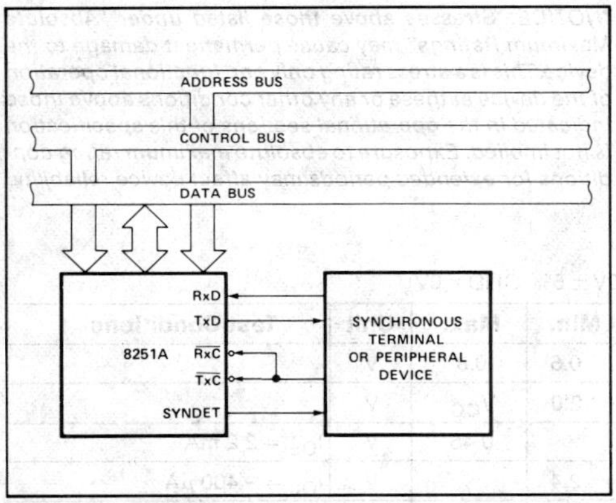

Figure 15. Synchronous Interface to Terminal or Peripheral Device

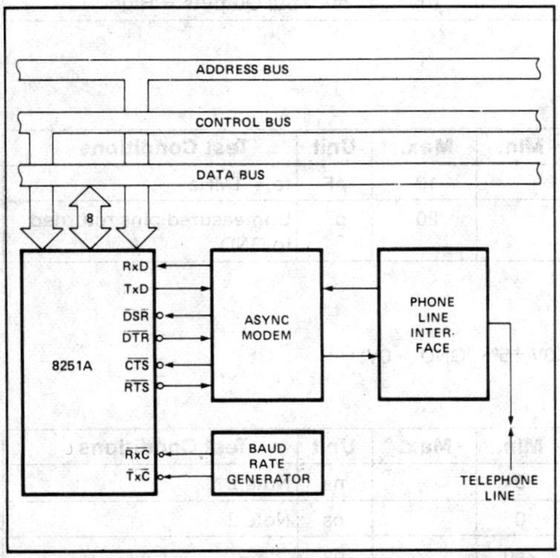

Figure 16. Asynchronous Interface to Telephone Lines

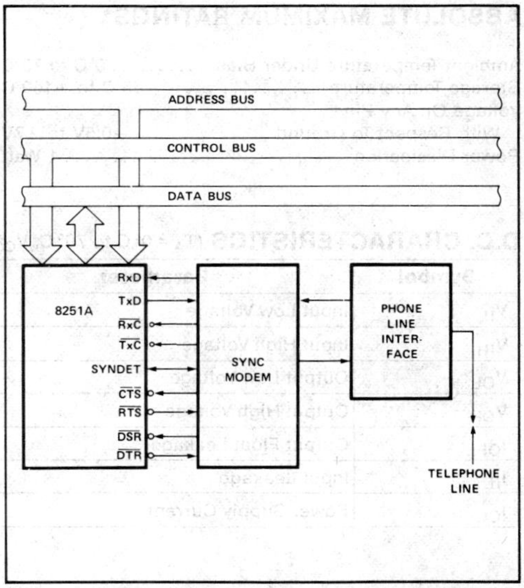

Figure 17. Synchronous Interface to Telephone Lines

ABSOLUTE MAXIMUM RATINGS*

Ambient Temperature Under Bias .... 0°C to 70°C
Storage Temperature .... −65°C to +150°C
Voltage On Any Pin
With Respect To Ground .... −0.5V to +7V
Power Dissipation .... 1 Watt

NOTICE: Stresses above those listed under "Absolute Maximum Ratings" may cause permanent damage to the device. This is a stress rating only and functional operation of the device at these or any other conditions above those indicated in the operational sections of this specification is not implied. Exposure to absolute maximum rating conditions for extended periods may affect device reliability.

D.C. CHARACTERISTICS (T_A = 0°C to 70°C, V_{CC} = 5.0V ± 5%, GND = 0V)*

Symbol	Parameter	Min.	Max.	Unit	Test Conditions
V_{IL}	Input Low Voltage	−0.5	0.8	V	
V_{IH}	Input High Voltage	2.0	V_{CC}	V	
V_{OL}	Output Low Voltage		0.45	V	I_{OL} = 2.2 mA
V_{OH}	Output High Voltage	2.4		V	I_{OL} = −400 μA
I_{OFL}	Output Float Leakage		±10	μA	V_{OUT} = V_{CC} TO 0.45V
I_{IL}	Input Leakage		±10	μA	V_{IN} = V_{CC} TO 0.45V
I_{CC}	Power Supply Current		100	mA	All Outputs = High

CAPACITANCE (T_A = 25°C, V_{CC} = GND = 0V)

Symbol	Parameter	Min.	Max.	Unit	Test Conditions
C_{IN}	Input Capacitance		10	pF	fc = 1MHz
$C_{I/O}$	I/O Capacitance		20	pF	Unmeasured pins returned to GND

A.C. CHARACTERISTICS (T_A = 0°C to 70°C, V_{CC} = 5.0V ±5%, GND = 0V)*

Bus Parameters (Note 1)

READ CYCLE

Symbol	Parameter	Min.	Max.	Unit	Test Conditions
t_{AR}	Address Stable Before $\overline{READ}$ ($\overline{CS}$, C/$\overline{D}$)	0		ns	Note 2
t_{RA}	Address Hold Time for $\overline{READ}$ ($\overline{CS}$, C/$\overline{D}$)	0		ns	Note 2
t_{RR}	$\overline{READ}$ Pulse Width	250		ns	
t_{RD}	Data Delay from $\overline{READ}$		200	ns	3, C_L = 150 pF
t_{DF}	$\overline{READ}$ to Data Floating	10	100	ns	

WRITE CYCLE

Symbol	Parameter	Min.	Max.	Unit	Test Condtions
t_{AW}	Address Stable Before $\overline{WRITE}$	0		ns	
t_{WA}	Address Hold Time for $\overline{WRITE}$	0		ns	
t_{WW}	$\overline{WRITE}$ Pulse Width	250		ns	
t_{DW}	Data Set-Up Time for $\overline{WRITE}$	150		ns	
t_{WD}	Data Hold Time for $\overline{WRITE}$	20		ns	
t_{RV}	Recovery Time Between WRITES	6		t_{CY}	Note 4

A.C. CHARACTERISTICS (Continued)

OTHER TIMINGS

Symbol	Parameter	Min.	Max.	Unit	Test Conditions
t_{CY}	Clock Period	320	1350	ns	Notes 5, 6
t_{ϕ}	Clock High Pulse Width	120	t_{CY}−90	ns	
$t_{\bar{\phi}}$	Clock Low Pulse Width	90		ns	
t_R, t_F	Clock Rise and Fall Time		20	ns	
t_{DTx}	TxD Delay from Falling Edge of $\overline{TxC}$		1	μs	
f_{Tx}	Transmitter Input Clock Frequency 1x Baud Rate 16x Baud Rate 64x Baud Rate	 DC DC DC	 64 310 615	 kHz kHz kHz	
t_{TPW}	Transmitter Input Clock Pulse Width 1x Baud Rate 16x and 64x Baud Rate	 12 1		 t_{CY} t_{CY}	
t_{TPD}	Transmitter Input Clock Pulse Delay 1x Baud Rate 16x and 64x Baud Rate	 15 3		 t_{CY} t_{CY}	
f_{Rx}	Receiver Input Clock Frequency 1x Baud Rate 16x Baud Rate 64x Baud Rate	 DC DC DC	 64 310 615	 kHz kHz kHz	
t_{RPW}	Receiver Input Clock Pulse Width 1x Baud Rate 16x and 64x Baud Rate	 12 1		 t_{CY} t_{CY}	
t_{RPD}	Receiver Input Clock Pulse Delay 1x Baud Rate 16x and 64x Baud Rate	 15 3		 t_{CY} t_{CY}	
t_{TxRDY}	TxRDY Pin Delay from Center of Last Bit		14	t_{CY}	Note 7
$t_{TxRDY\ CLEAR}$	TxRDY ↓ from Leading Edge of $\overline{WR}$		400	ns	Note 7
t_{RxRDY}	RxRDY Pin Delay from Center of Last Bit		26	t_{CY}	Note 7
$t_{RxRDY\ CLEAR}$	RxRDY ↓ from Leading Edge of $\overline{RD}$		400	ns	Note 7
t_{IS}	Internal SYNDET Delay from Rising Edge of $\overline{RxC}$		26	t_{CY}	Note 7
t_{ES}	External SYNDET Set-Up Time After Rising Edge of $\overline{RxC}$	16t_{CY}	t_{RPD}-t_{CY}	ns	Note 7
$t_{TxEMPTY}$	TxEMPTY Delay from Center of Last Bit		20	t_{CY}	Note 7
t_{WC}	Control Delay from Rising Edge of WRITE (TxEn, $\overline{DTR}$, $\overline{RTS}$)		8	t_{CY}	Note 7
t_{CR}	Control to READ Set-Up Time ($\overline{DSR}$, $\overline{CTS}$)	20		t_{CY}	Note 7

***NOTE:**
1. For Extended Temperature EXPRESS, use MIL 8251A electrical parameters.

A.C. CHARACTERISTICS (Continued)

NOTES:

1. AC timings measured $V_{OH} = 2.0$ $V_{OL} = 2.0$, $V_{OL} = 0.8$, and with load circuit of Figure 1.
2. Chip Select (CS) and Command/Data (C/D) are considered as Addresses.
3. Assumes that Address is valid before $R_D\downarrow$.
4. This recovery time is for Mode Initialization only. Write Data is allowed only when TxRDY = 1. Recovery Time between Writes for Asynchronous Mode is 8 t_{CY} and for Synchronous Mode is 16 t_{CY}.
5. The TxC and RxC frequencies have the following limitations with respect to CLK: For 1x Baud Rate, f_{Tx} or $f_{Rx} \leq 1/(30\ t_{CY})$:
   For 16x and 64x Baud Rate, f_{Tx} or $f_{Rx} \leq 1/(4.5\ t_{CY})$.
6. Reset Pulse Width = 6 t_{CY} minimum; System Clock must be running during Reset.
7. Status update can have a maximum delay of 28 clock periods from the event affecting the status.
8. In external sync mode the tes spec. requires the ratio of the system clock (clock) to receive or transmit bit ratios to be greater than 34.

TYPICAL Δ OUTPUT DELAY VS. Δ CAPACITANCE (pF)

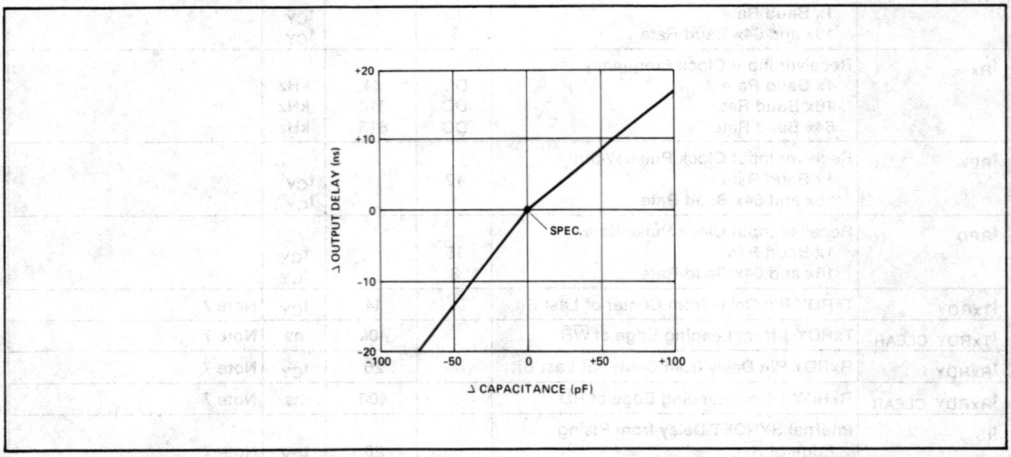

A.C. TESTING INPUT, OUTPUT WAVEFORM

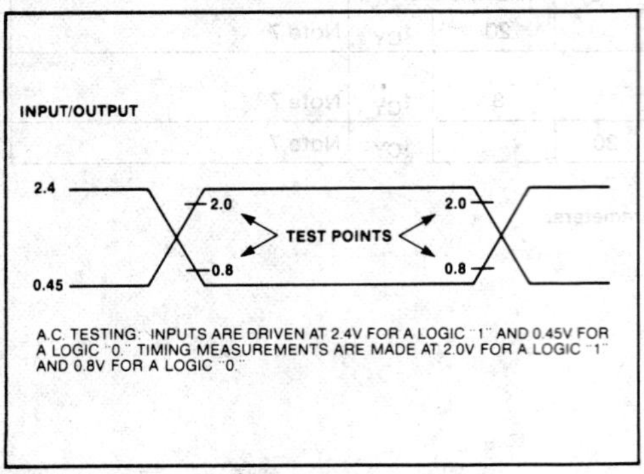

A.C. TESTING LOAD CIRCUIT

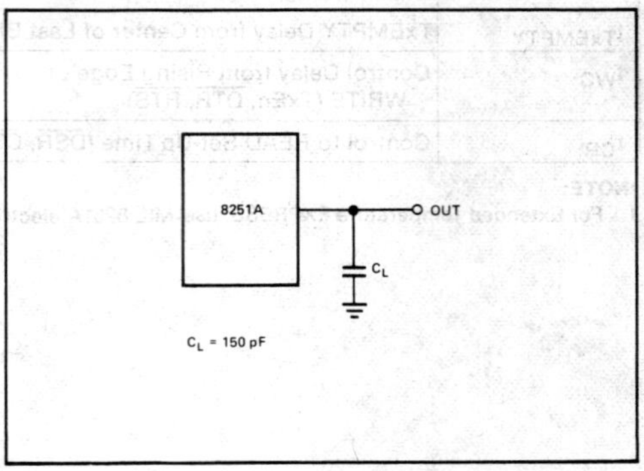

WAVEFORMS

SYSTEM CLOCK INPUT

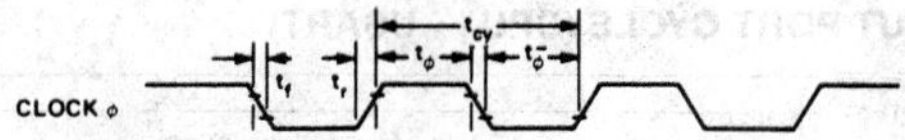

TRANSMITTER CLOCK AND DATA

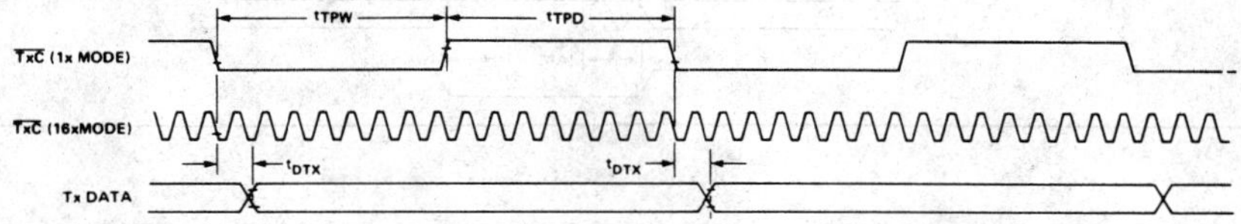

RECEIVER CLOCK AND DATA

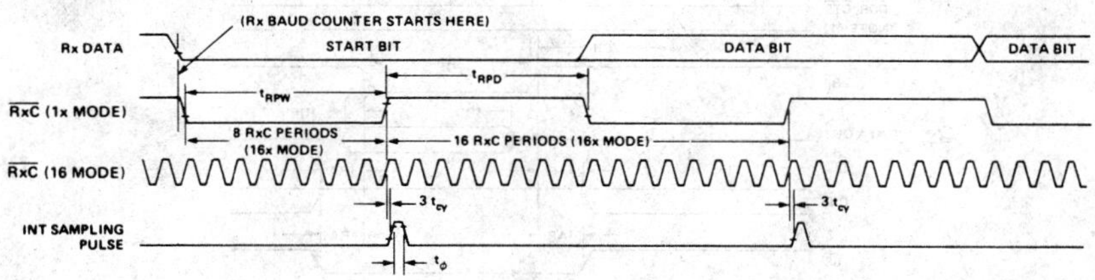

WRITE DATA CYCLE (CPU → USART)

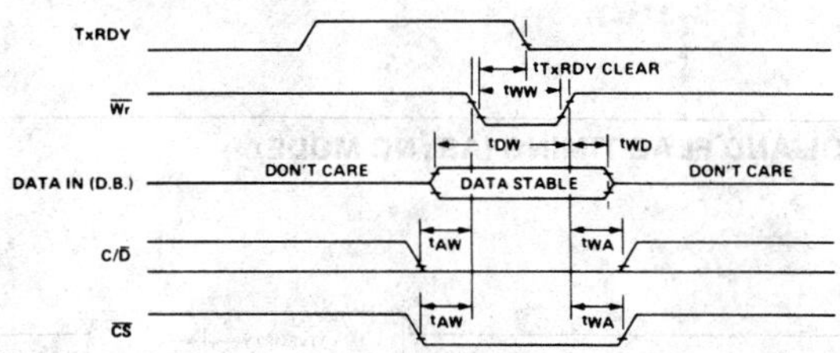

READ DATA CYCLE (CPU ← USART)

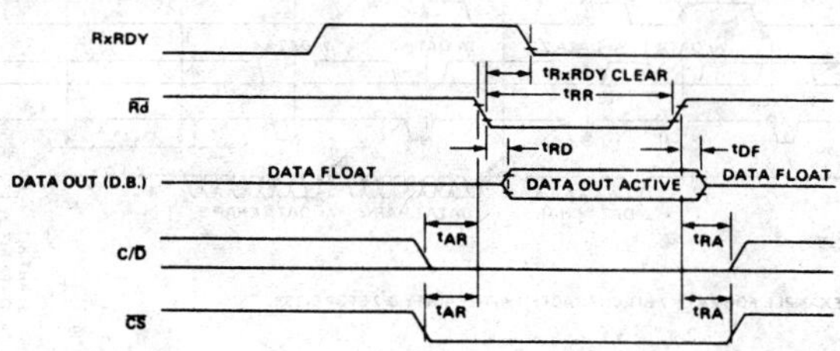

WAVEFORMS (Continued)

WRITE CONTROL OR OUTPUT PORT CYCLE (CPU → USART)

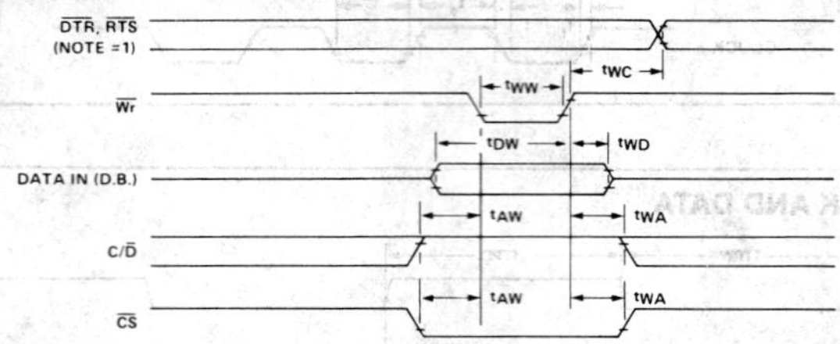

READ CONTROL OR INPUT PORT (CPU ← USART)

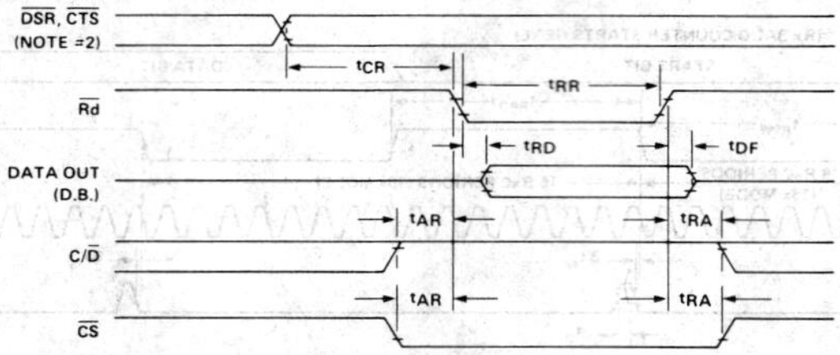

NOTE #1: T_{WC} INCLUDES THE RESPONSE TIMING OF A CONTROL BYTE.
NOTE #2: T_{CR} INCLUDES THE EFFECT OF CTS ON THE TxENBL CIRCUITRY.

TRANSMITTER CONTROL AND FLAG TIMING (ASYNC MODE)

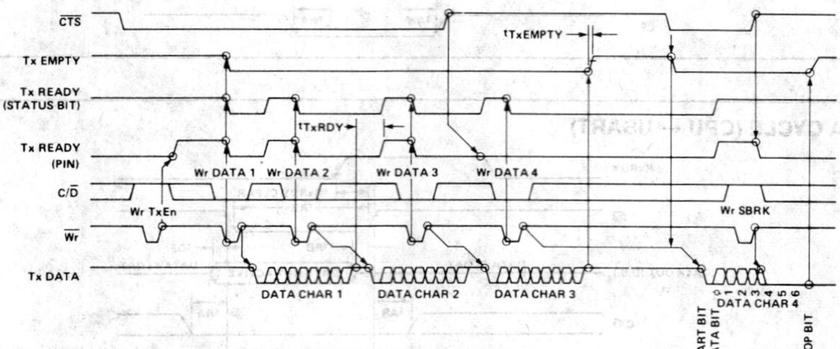

EXAMPLE FORMAT = 7 BIT CHARACTER WITH PARITY & 2 STOP BITS.

WAVEFORMS (Continued)

RECEIVER CONTROL AND FLAG TIMING (ASYNC MODE)

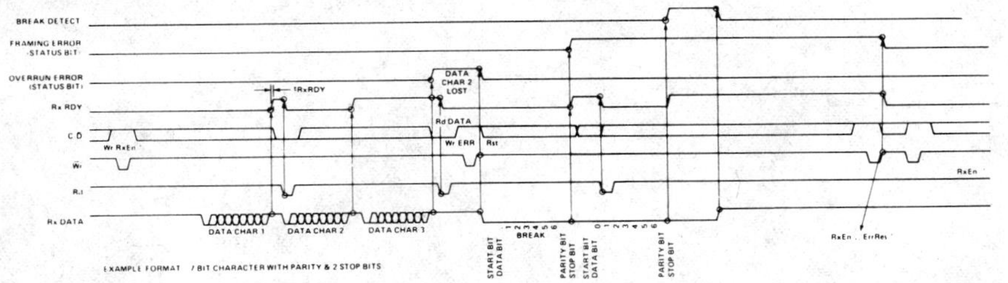

TRANSMITTER CONTROL AND FLAG TIMING (SYNC MODE)

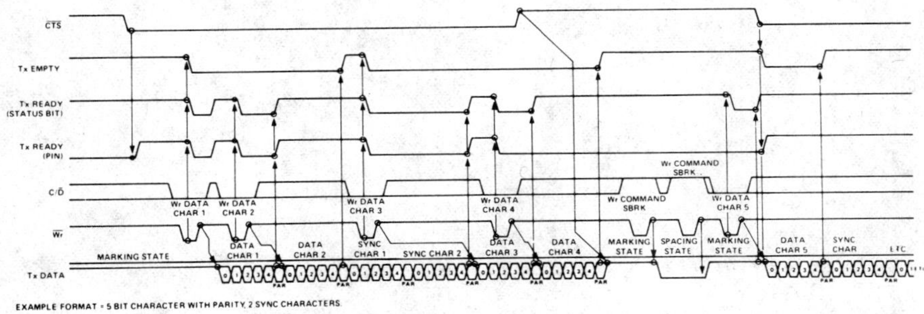

RECEIVER CONTROL AND FLAG TIMING (SYNC MODE)

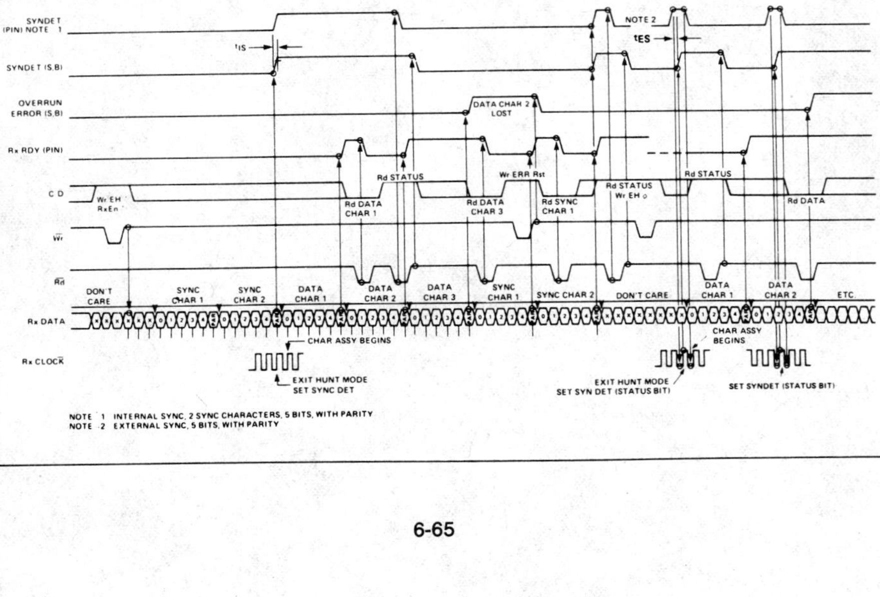

Appendix
Applications of the 8085 Family

APPENDIX 1
APPLICATIONS OF THE 8085 FAMILY

SECTION 1
INTRODUCTION

When the first microprocessor was introduced in 1971, it was largely ignored by the electronics industry. However, since that inasupicious beginning, this new device has become the hottest topic in current technology. As more and more product designers become familiar with the capabilities of microcomputers, the number of new applications increases geometrically. In most of these applications, the new technology has been used to replace designs which were formerly implemented with TTL logic and under-utilized minicomputers. However, an increasing number of products are surfacing which would have been impractical prior to the microcomputer era.

Microcomputers are being applied to a wide range of data communications tasks. The field of telephone equipment is being invaded by systems which control and monitor calls. Point of sale terminals are increasing daily with the addition of interface to coin changers, electronic scales and remote computers. Small stand-alone computers are relying heavily upon microcomputers in teleprocessing, time-sharing, data base management and similar interactive applications. An increasing number of microcomputer-based data terminals are providing local interactive intelligence with programmable character sets, vector generation and the pre-processing of data.

Instrumentation is widely utilizing the microprocessor for a variety of control and arithmetic processing functions. Microcomputers are controlling laboratory equipment such as oscilloscopes, DVM's, network analyzers and frequency synthesizers. Medical electronics are crediting microcomputers with tasks such as patient monitoring, blood analysis and X-ray scanning. Travel is becoming microcomputerized by automotive control, air and ocean navigation equipment and rapid transit systems.

8085 SYSTEM

Many possible microcomputer applications have been overlooked because of the design tasks required to build the microcomputer. These tasks include the system clock, read/write memory, I/O ports, serial communications interface and bus control logic. The 8085 system will enable the design engineer to concentrate on the application of the microcomputer, rather than on the implementation details.

The 8085 Family is yet another family of components which has the potential to provide a solution to the three problems which will always plague designers: cost, size and power. The reduced component count of an 8085 microcomputer, coupled with the increased integration of functions reduces both cost and size while increasing power.

Sample Applications

Calculating Oscilloscope
Blood Analyzer
Programmable Video Game
Process Control System
Line Printer
Intelligent Terminal
N.C. Machine
Digital Multimeter
Graphic Terminal
Automotive Control
Navigation Equipment
Vending Machine
Spectrum Analyzer
Front End Processor
Credit Verifier
Disk Controller
Patient Monitor
Network Analyzer
Frequency Synthesizer

APPLICATION	PERIPHERAL DEVICES ENCOUNTERED	8085 FAMILY COMPONENTS	
Intelligent Terminals	Cathode Ray Tube Display Printing Units Synchronous and Asynchronous data lines Cassette Tape Unit Keyboards	8275 8155 8251 8279	8085A
Gaming Machines	Keyboards, pushbuttons and switches Various display devices Coin acceptors Coin dispensers	8279 8155	8085A
Cash Registers	Keyboard or Input Switch Array Change Dispenser Digital Display Ticket Printer Magnetic Card reader Communication interface	8279 8155 8273	8085A
Accounting and Billing Machines	Keyboard Printer Unit Cassette or other magnetic tape unit "Floppy" disks	8279 8155 8257 8271	8085A
Telephone Switching Control	Telephone Line Scanner Analog Switching Network Dial Registers Class of Service Parcel	8253 8155	8085A
Numerically Controlled Machines	Magnetic or Paper Tape Reader Stepper Motors Optical Shaft Encoders	8155	8085A 8355
Process Control	Analog-to-Digital Converters Digital-to-Analog Converters Control Switches Displays	8155 8279	8085A

Baud Rate Generator

Shown in Figure 2 is a minimum system configuration with the 8156 timer output connected to an 8085 interrupt input.

This configuration allows convenient use of the timer as a baud rate generator. A 6.144 MHz crystal is used as the frequency control element of the 8085A, providing integral divisors for the standard baud rates (300, 600, 1200, 2400, 4800, 9600 baud). The timer is programmed with the appropriate divisor (Figure 1) for the selected baud rate resulting in one pulse on the timer output for each bit cell time. The clock output (CLK) of the 8085A is used to clock the timer (TIMERIN). The frequency of this clock is one-half the crystal frequency or in this example 3.072 MHz. $\overline{\text{TIMEROUT}}$ now provides a crystal controlled pulse train at the baud rate selected.

Serial Communications

By feeding the $\overline{\text{TIMEROUT}}$ signal of the 8156 back to the edge triggered RST 7.5 input of the 8085A, the processor can be interrupt driven at the required baud rate. As shown in Figure 1, the minimum system supports serial communications with only the addition of the send and receive interface circuits.

The SID (SERIAL INPUT DATA) line and the SOD (SERIAL OUTPUT DATA) line are connected directly to a TTY or RS232 interface circuit. Assuming inverted data at the SID input, a direct connection is made to the RST6.5 input for detection of the start bit.

Additional insight into using the 8085's serial I/O lines in communications application can be found in Section 2 of this Appendix.

BAUD RATE	COUNT (DECIMAL)
300	10,240
600	5,120
1200	2,560
2400	1,280
4800	640
9600	320

FIGURE 1. BAUD RATES

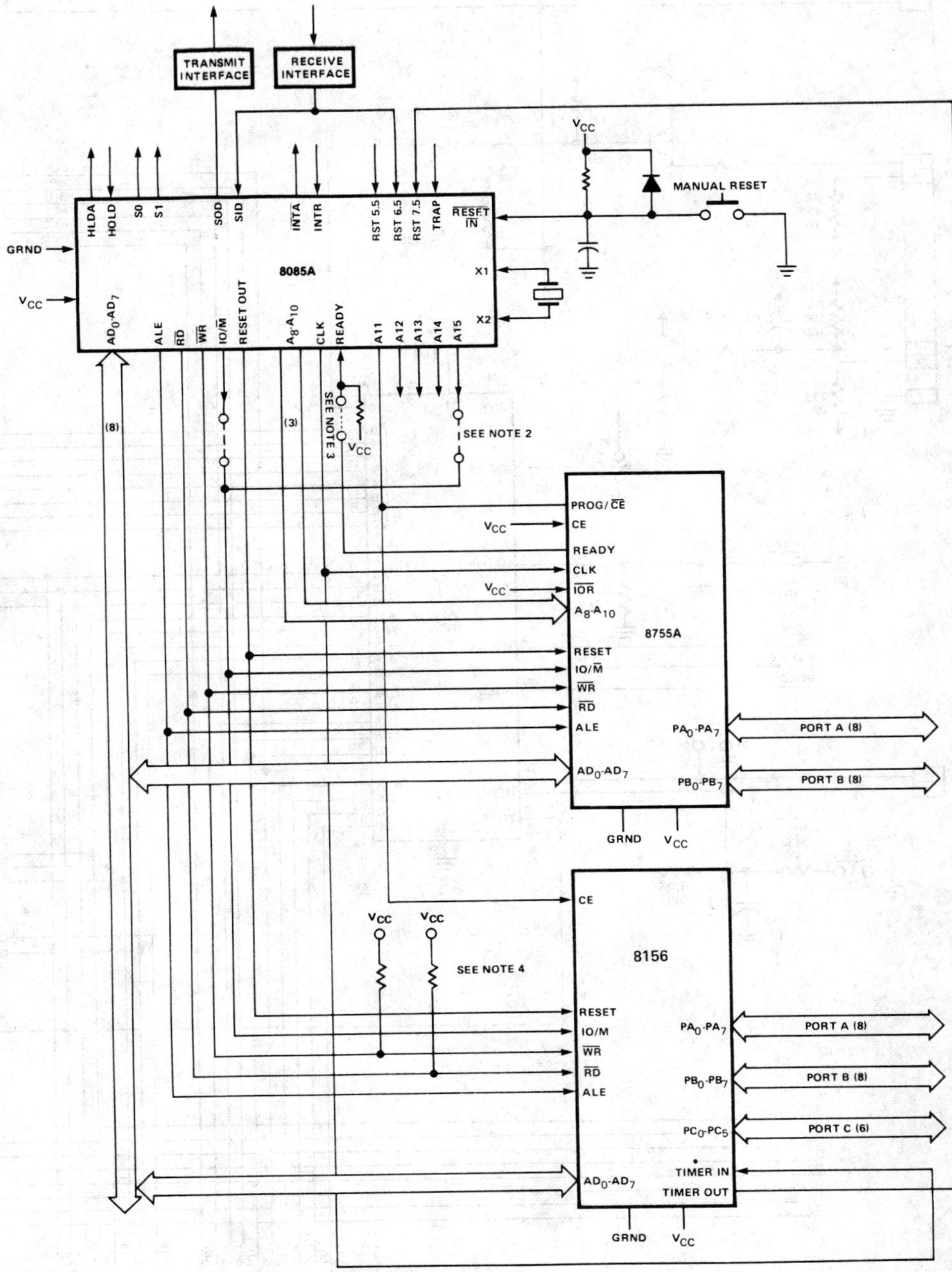

NOTE 1: TRAP, INTR, AND HOLD MUST BE GROUNDED IF THEY AREN'T USED.
NOTE 2: USE IO/M FOR STANDARD I/O MAPPING. USE A15 FOR MEMORY MAPPED I/O.
NOTE 3. CONNECTION IS NECESSARY ONLY IF ONE T_{WAIT} STATE IS DESIRED.
NOTE 4: PULL-UP RESISTORS RECOMMENDED TO AVOID SPURIOUS SELECTION WHEN $\overline{RD}$ AND $\overline{WR}$ ARE 3-STATED.

FIGURE 2. MINIMUM SYSTEM CONFIGURATION

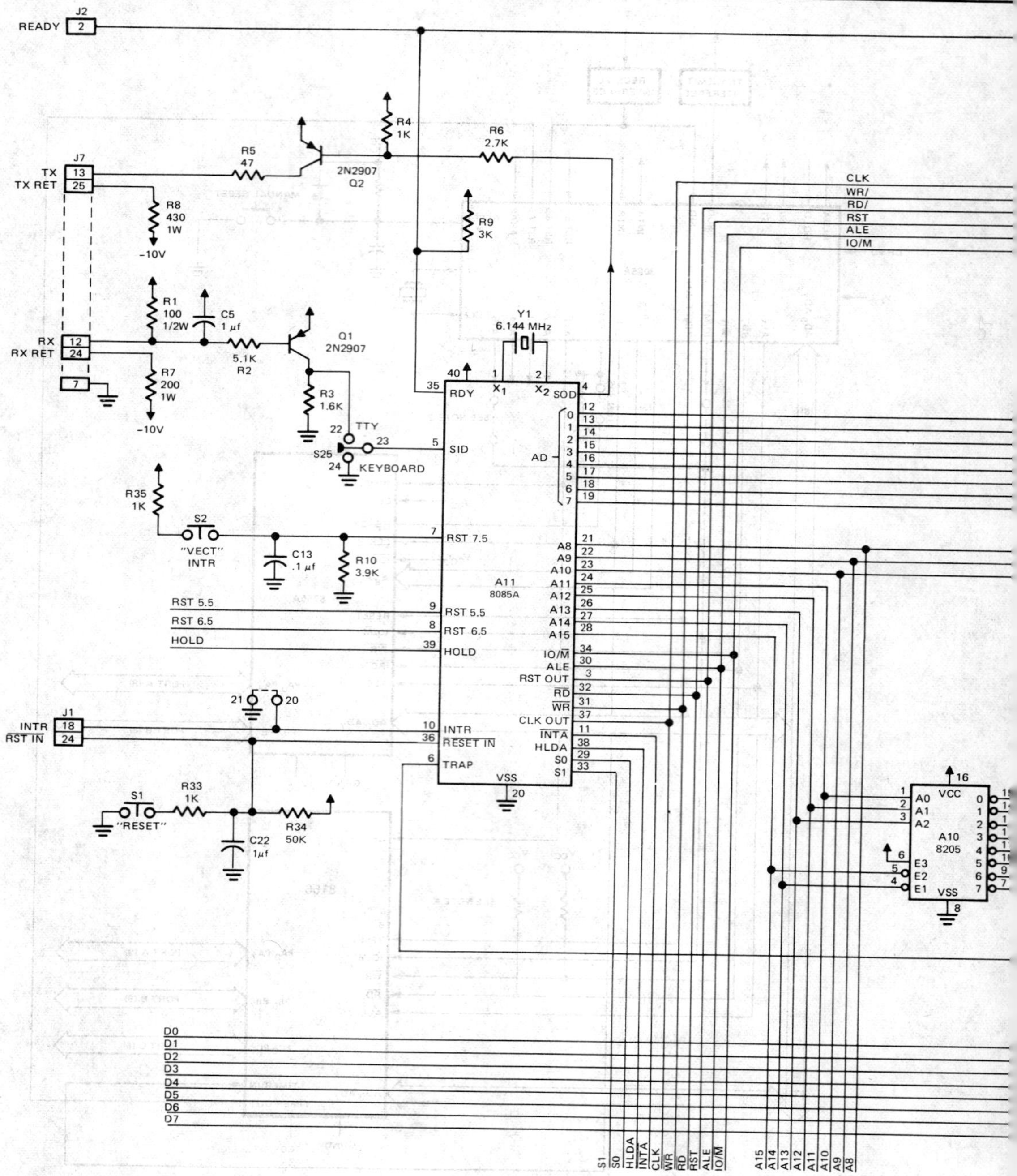

FIGURE 3. SMALL SYSTEM SCHEMATIC (similar to the schematic of Intel's SDK-85)

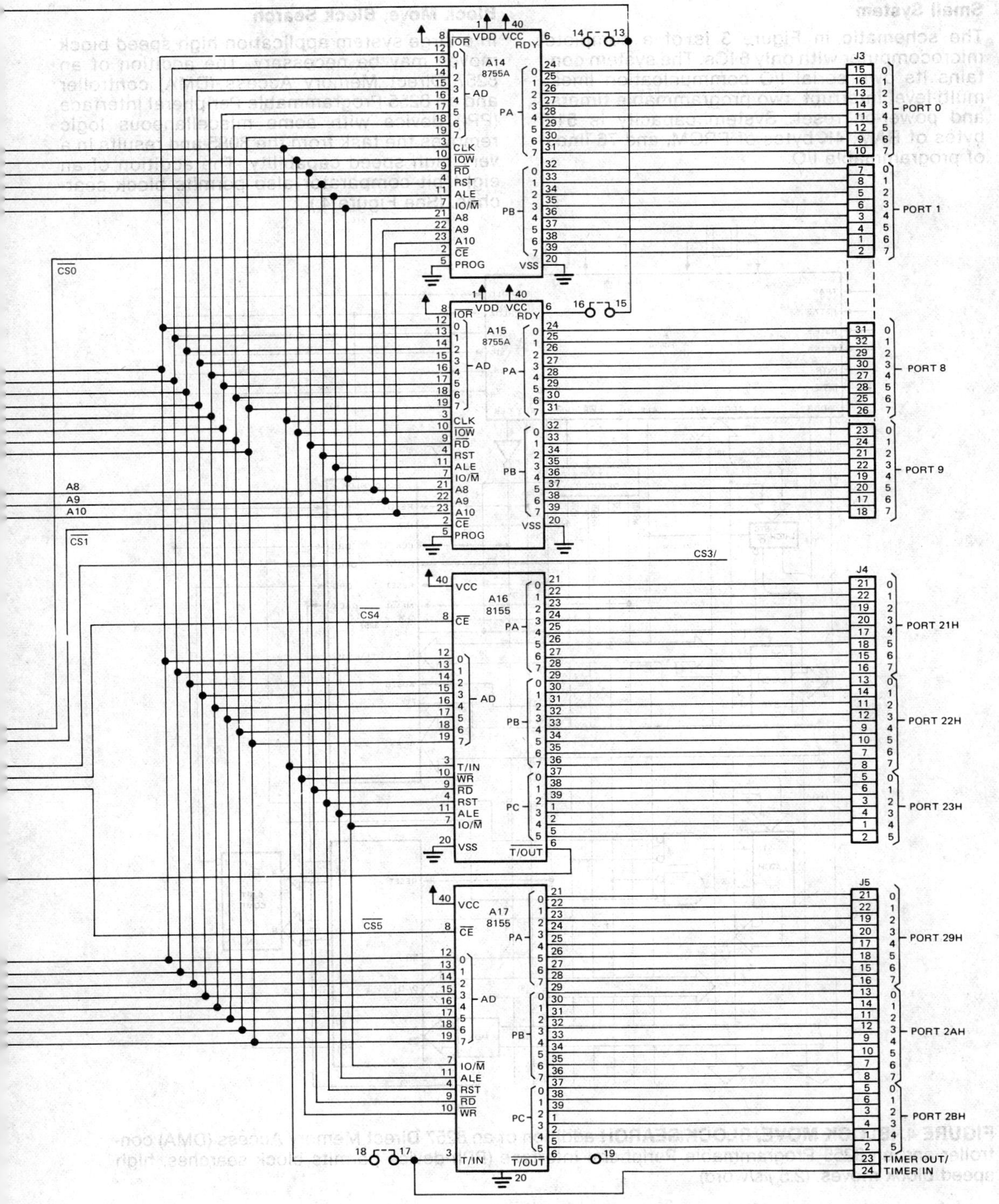

A14
8755A
A15
8755A
A16
8155
A17
8155
VDD
VCC
RDY
IOR
IOW
RD
WR
RST
ALE
IO/M
CLK
T/IN
T/OUT
CE
PROG
VSS
AD
PA
PB
PC
A8
A9
A10
CS0
CS1
CS3/
CS4
CS5
J3
J4
J5
PORT 0
PORT 1
PORT 8
PORT 9
PORT 21H
PORT 22H
PORT 23H
PORT 29H
PORT 2AH
PORT 2BH
TIMER OUT/
TIMER IN

Small System

The schematic in Figure 3 is of a complete microcomputer with only 6 ICs. The system contains its own serial I/O communication lines, multi-level interrupt, two programmable timers, and power-on reset. System capacity is 512 bytes of RAM, 4K bytes of PROM, and 76 lines of programmable I/O.

Block Move, Block Search

In a large system application high speed block moves may be necessary. The addition of an 8257 Direct Memory Access (DMA) controller and an 8255 Programmable Peripheral Interface (PPI) device with some miscellaneous logic removes the task from the 8085 and results in a very high speed capability. The addition of an eight bit comparator also permits block searches. (See Figure 4.)

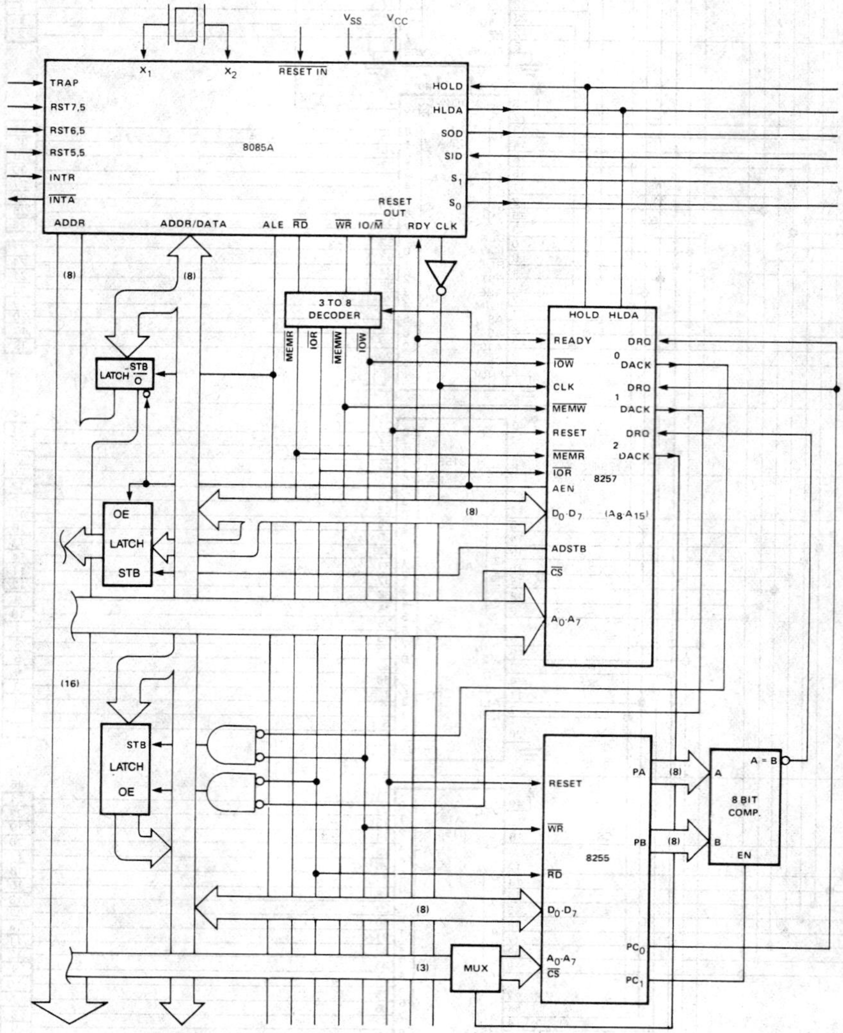

FIGURE 4. BLOCK MOVE, BLOCK SEARCH addition of an 8257 Direct Memory Access (DMA) controller and an 8255 Programmable Peripheral Interface (PPI) device permits block searches, high speed block moves. (2.5 μs/word).

Basic operation, for a block move, is that the CPU loads the 8257 with the starting address of the source block and the length* of the block into Channel 0. Channel 1 is programmed with the starting location of the destination block and the length. A bit in Port C of the 8255 is set by the CPU which initiates a DMA request on Channels 0 and 1. Because the 8257 is initialized to the rotating priority mode, the first DMA cycle is from Channel 0 which latches the data from the first location of the source block into the 8212. The second cycle will be from Channel 1 which will store the latched data into the first location of the destination block. The next cycle will return to Channel 0 and the sequence will start over again until the length (terminal count) is reached. Programming the 8257 stop bit insures that each channel will be disabled when its respective terminal count is reached.

This configuration also supports a block fill. DMA Channel 0 points to a location containing the fill value and has a length of one. Channel 1 points to the starting location of the destination block and contains the length. When the sequence is initiated the value will be loaded into the latch by Channel 0. Channel 0 reaches TC and is disabled. Priority rotates to Channel 1 which will repeatedly write into the destination block the value stored in the latch until TC is reached.

Block search operations use the 8-bit comparator and Ports A & B of the 8255 and Channel 2 of the 8257. The CPU loads Port B with the search value and the DMA channel with the search area (starting address and length). A Port C bit initiates the DMA READ request. Channel 2 DMA Acknowledge sets Port A of the 8255 up as the receiver for the DMA READ cycle by multiplexing A_0, A_1, and CS. Each cycle of the DMA then loads Port A with the value of the pointed-to location in the block. When Port A equals Port B, the output of the comparator will gate off the DMA request. The requesting program can now read the Channel 2 address which is pointing to the search value plus one. However, if the status register of the 8257 indicates that TC of Channel 2 has been reached, then no match was found.

*(The value loaded into the low-order 14-bits of the terminal count register specifies the number of DMA cycles minus one before the Terminal Count (TC) output is activated. For instance, a terminal count of 0 would cause the TC output to be active in the first DMA cycle for that channel. In general, if Length = the number of desired DMA cycles, load the value Length-1 into the low-order 14-bits of the terminal count register.)

RST 7

On the 8080A/8228 system if one tied $\overline{\text{INTA}}$ out of the 8228 to +12 volts through a 1KΩ resistor, the 8228 would generate a RST 7 instruction to the 8080A upon interrupt. This was a very inexpensive mechanism.

The 8085A has expanded this facility with the RST 5.5, 6.5, 7.5 inputs but is not compatible with the RST 7 generated by the 8228. (Figure 5) To maintain this compatibility it can be achieved by adding a latch which will force a RST 7 instruction into the bus upon interrupt acknowledge (INTA). (Figure 6)

RESTART	VECTOR LOCATION
RST 7	38_{16}
RST 5.5	$2C_{16}$
RST 6.5	34_{16}
RST 7.5	$3C_{16}$
TRAP	24_{16}

FIGURE 5. ADDITIONAL 8085A INTERRUPTS

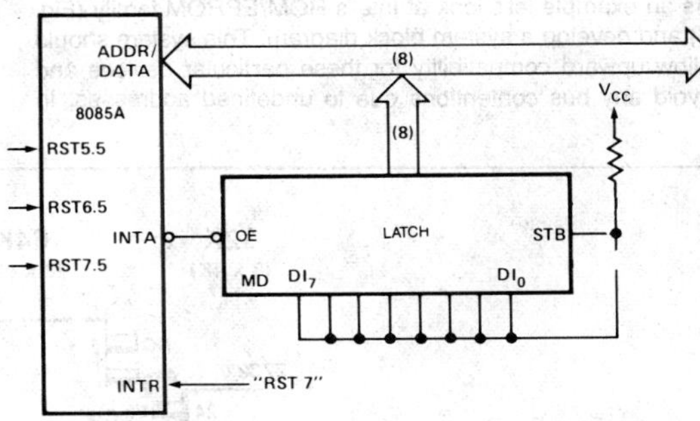

FIGURE 6. 8085A "RST 7" IMPLEMENTATION

SECTION 2
DETAILED APPLICATION EXAMPLES

Memory Addressing

One of the necessary functions of the microprocessor bus is to interface with the memory where the program is stored. ROM and EPROM memories are typically used to store programs while static and dynamic RAMS are generally used for data memory. The following discussions cover the interfacing to be used for these types of memory.

ROM - EPROM ADDRESSING

Later in this Appendix a section is devoted to an approach for developing a chart showing memory device compatibility for the 8085A. However, there is one area not included that will be discussed here, that is, unbuffered interfacing to standard ROM or EPROM memories. To use an unbuffered interface to ROM or EPROM it is necessary to understand a particular characteristic of the 8085A.

The 8085A has a period of time, T4 through T6 of the op code fetch cycle and certain instructions, where addresses A8 through A15 are undefined. Be careful about this. Not having addresses stable and using an address select method that would randomly turn on memory devices will cause bus contention and reliability problems in the unbuffered system. In the memory compatibility section of this Application Note, a minimum (unbuffered 8085 Family and medium system, at least one level of buffering) configurations are considered. These configurations do not have bus contention problems. In the minimum system only 8085 Family components will be discussed where addresses are latched on the falling edge of ALE, thus ignoring any extraneous address transitions. The medium system is assumed to have data buffers that are enabled only at the proper time, thus again preventing any bus contention problems. What about the user who wants to use standard ROM or EPROM without buffering?

As an example let's look at Intel's ROM/EPROM family (Fig. 7) and develop a system block diagram. This system should allow upward compatibility for these particular devices and avoid any bus contentions due to undefined addresses. In Figure 8 a traditional decoding scheme is shown that uses the time difference between tacc (address access) and tco (chip select access) to allow for decoding of the EPROM/ROM to be selected. Connecting only these signals, however, in an unbuffered system will result in data contention because of the spurious addresses during opcode fetch. The proper interconnect for this type of interface is shown in Figure 9 where an output enable ($\overline{OE}$) signal will prevent any bus contention. This output enable is controlled by the read control signal, $\overline{RD}$, of the 8085A. This signal only occurs after addresses have stabilized.*

Note also that a PROM is recommended for the decoding function vs. an 8205 (1 of 8 decoder). Why? This PROM allows the user to easily upgrade his system to 64K version with minimum rewiring. As seen in Figure 7, only 4 pins are being altered (18-21) in the Intel ROM/EPROM family to allow for this upward compatibility. All a user would need to do is initially design his layout for 28 pin devices, thereby allowing total flexibility from 32K to 64K with the ease of changing a decoding PROM and a few wires.† Application Note AP-30 can be ordered at no charge which fully discusses the application of Intel's 5 Volt EPROM and ROM family for microprocessor systems.

STATIC MEMORIES

The same consideration must be applied to standard static memories as with the ROMs/EPROMs in an unbuffered system memory device selection must be qualified by a memory read or write to prevent spurious selection. Some Intel static RAM devices have an Output Enable for this purpose. For other standard static RAMs, the chip selects must be qualified by $\overline{RD}$, $\overline{WR}$ or ALE to prevent random selection.

*Both $\overline{RD}$ and $\overline{WR}$ signals should be pulled up to +5V through a resistor to avoid random selection during 3-state.

†Another method is shown later in Figure 15 that facilitates the use of a decoder, such as the Intel 8205.

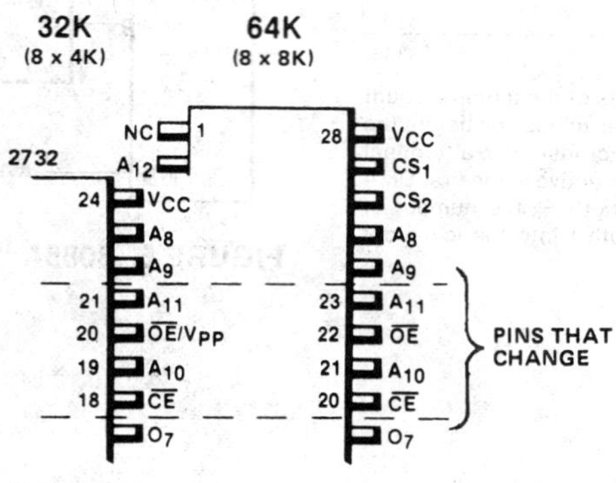

Figure 7. Intel® EPROM/ROM Compatible Family

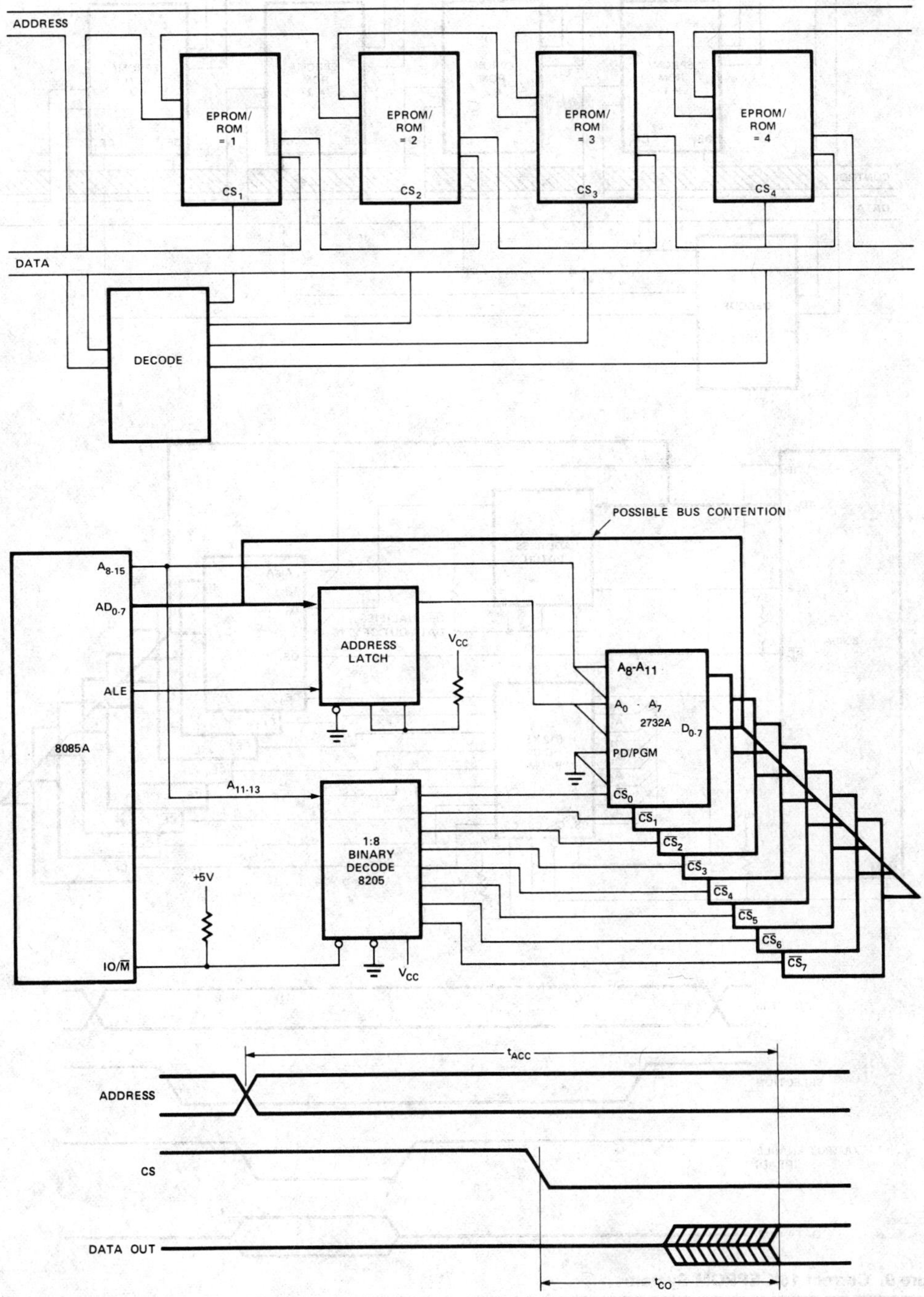

Figure 8. Traditional 16K EPROM System

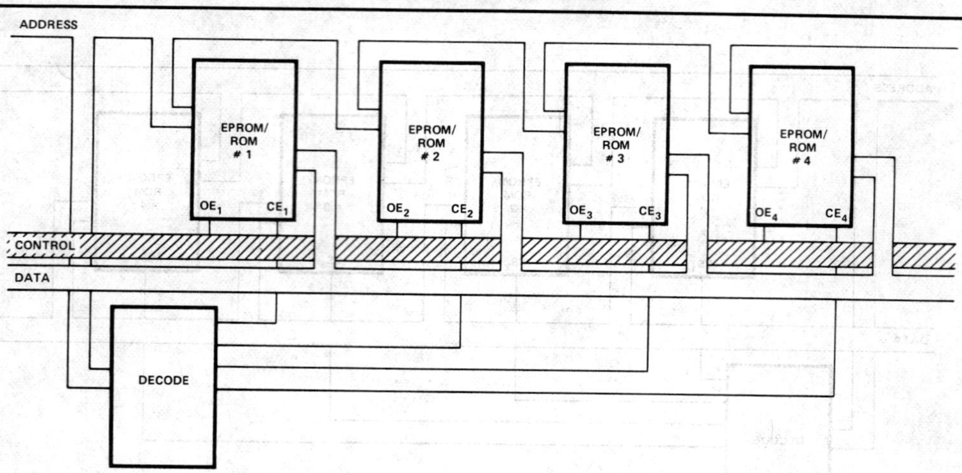

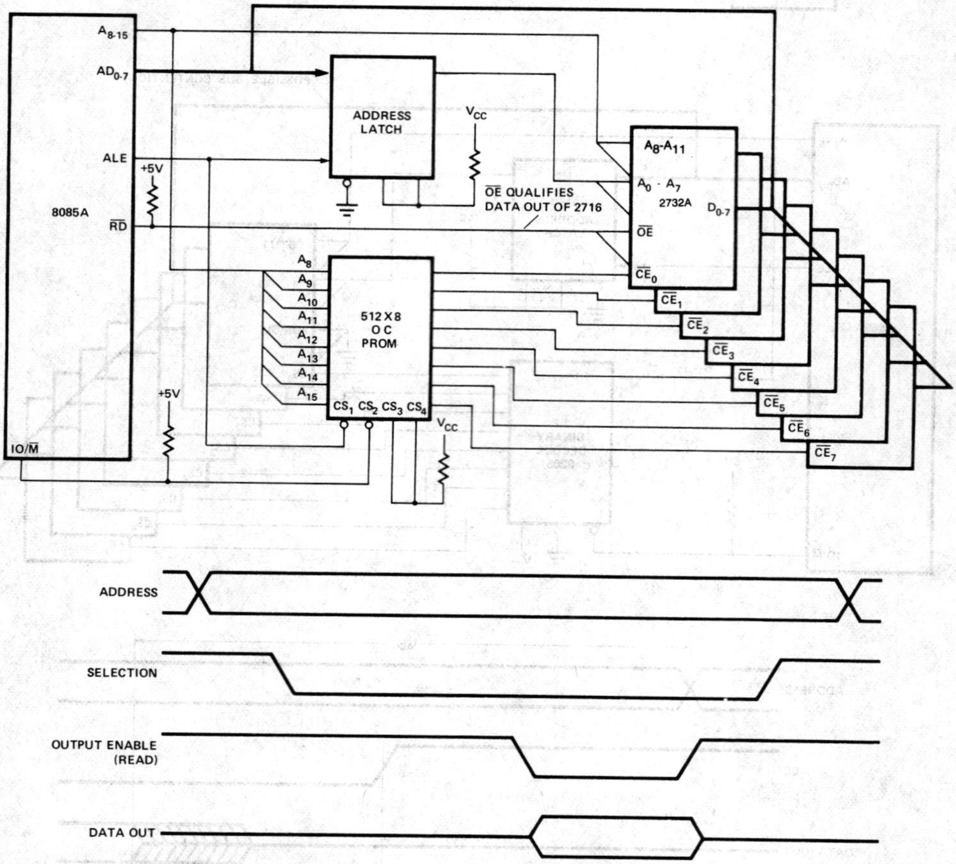

Figure 9. Correct 16K EPROM System

SYSTEM TIMINGS

8085A CLK-IN vs. CLK-OUT vs. Control Timings

This section shows timing characteristics which relate the input clock to the control signals and the output clock. These timings can be treated as constants, that is, within the normal operative range of the processor, they are cycle or 8085A, A-2 speed independent.

Be careful about manipulating the timings given in this section with the specifications in the data sheet. The specifications on the 8085A, A-2 are *not* mutually exclusive; that is, you can't add minimums to minimums and obtain a valid minimum for some other timing parameter. Where the timing parameter is specified directly, this takes precedence over any other method you come up with to find that specification (through adding and subtracting others). This was not done to confuse the user, but to provide the most optimal timings for his system!

To understand the timing parameters in this section it would be helpful to understand how the internal signals are generated in the 8085A. Referring to Figure 13, it is seen that the rising edge of the X1 input causes flip-flop A to toggle. From this flip-flop two internal signals are generated that drive all functions in the 8085A, A-2 and produce the output control signals and clock. Referring to Figure 15, it is seen that clock output is derived from the internal $\phi 1$ signal in the schematic of Figure 14. This output signal is a MOS output unlike the bipolar outputs of the 8224 in the 8080A system. This restricts the user to the loading limitations of a MOS driver (for further details see bus loading section). The rest of the output control signals with their respective internal controlling edges are also shown in Figure 14.

Since the path between the X1 input and the clock output can have a considerable amount of variance, the relationships of these two clocks vary significantly. Figures 15 and 16 are a set of timing diagrams illustrating the relationship of the clock input to the clock output to the various control signals. For designs that require these relationships to synchronize different systems, components, etc; the designer must allow for these variances in the relationships.

Parameter	Description	Min	Max	Units
$t_{\phi AL}$	Time from C.F. to next Address valid (A_0 - A_7)		130	ns
$t_{\phi ALU}$	Time from C.F. to next Address valid (A_8 - A_{15} only)		70	ns
$t_{\phi AT}$	Time from C.F. to present Address remaining valid (A_8 - A_{15} only)	−20		ns
$t_{\phi CL}$	Time from C.F. to control low (L.E.)	−10	60	ns
$t_{\phi CT}$	Time from C.R. to control low (T.E.)	−10	60	ns
$t_{\phi DL}$	Time from C.F. to Data Out becoming valid		65	ns
$t_{\phi DT}$	Time from C.F. to Data Out remaining valid	−20		ns
$t_{\phi DS}$	Data-in set up time to C.R.	100		ns
$t_{\phi DH}$	Data-in hold time to C.R.	0		ns
$t_{\phi LL}$	Time from C.F. to ALE high (L.E.)	−60	0	ns
$t_{\phi LT}$	Time from C.R. to ALE high (T.E.)	0	70	ns
t_{XKF}	Time from X_1 input to C.F.	30	150	ns
t_{XKR}	Time from X_1 input to C.R.	30	120	ns

C.F. = Clock Falling, C.R. = Clock Rising, L.E. = Leading Edge, T.E. = Trailing Edge

NOTE: These numbers are guaranteed by design and are not tested by Intel.

8085A, 8085A-2 Clock Parameters

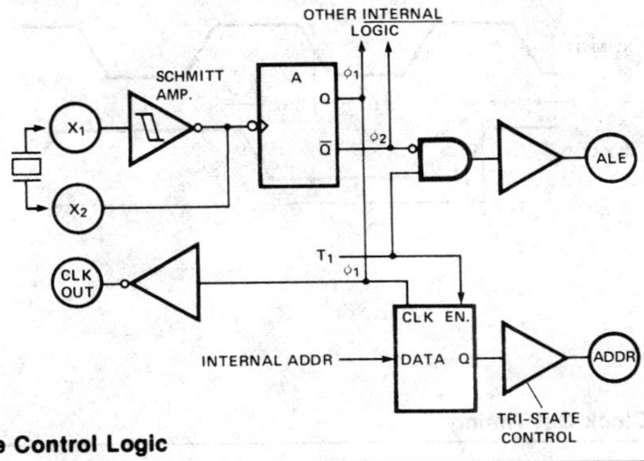

Figure 13. Clock and Sample Control Logic

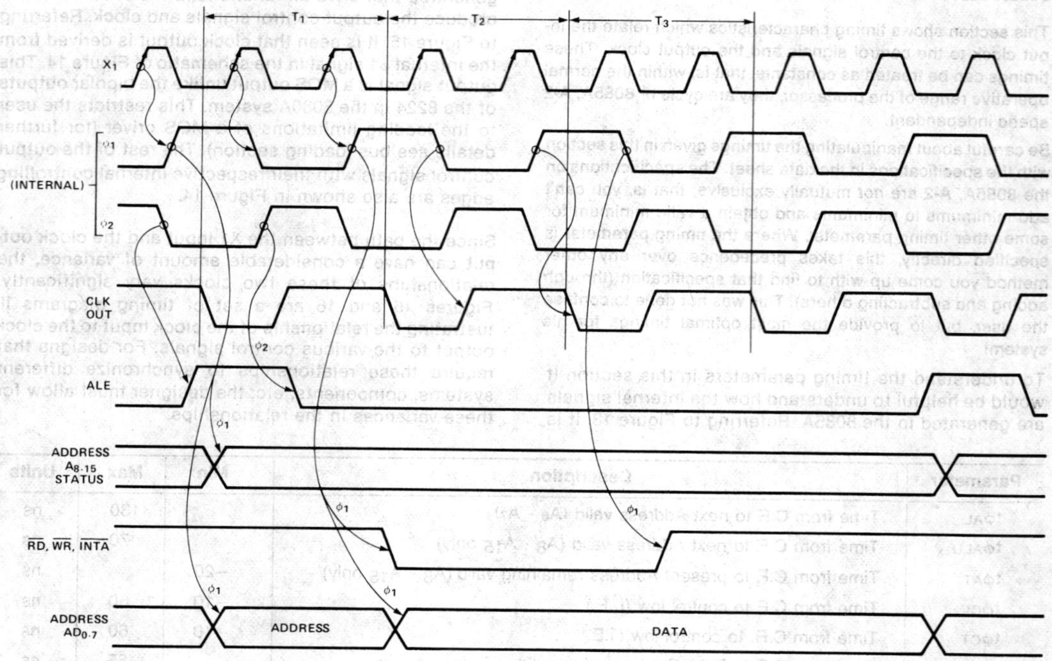

Figure 14. Clock In (X1) to Output Relationship

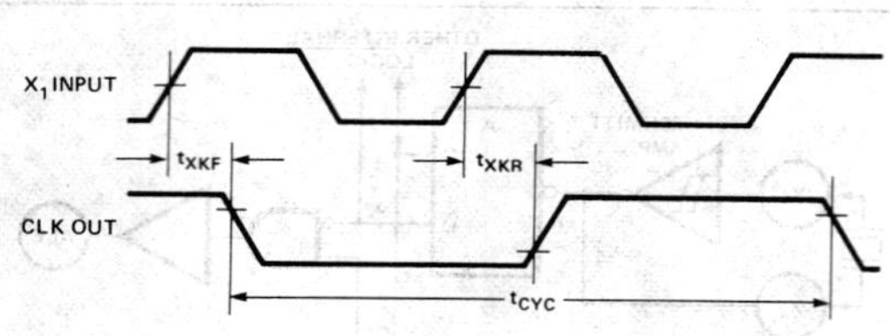

Figure 15. 8085A-2 Clock In/Clock Out Timing

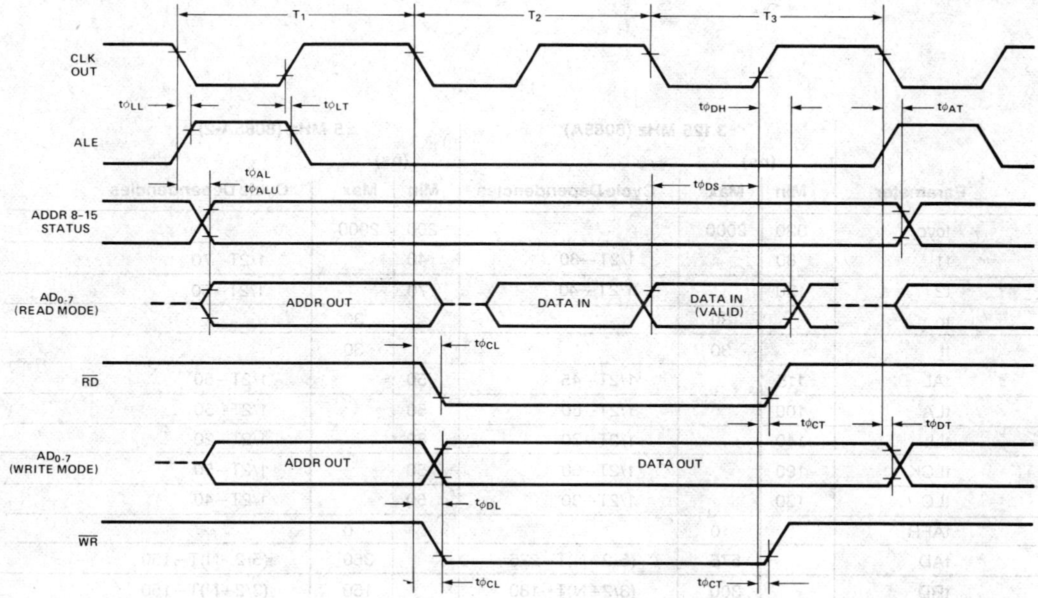

Figure 16. 8085A-2 Clock Related Timing

3.125 vs. 5 MHz Considerations

The 8085A (with maximum internal clock frequency of 3.125 MHz) and 8085A-2 (5 MHz) have some differences in their bus operation. There are two sets of peripherals that can be used with both the 8085A and 8085A-2. There are the dedicated peripherals in the 8085 Family that directly interface with the 8085A, 8085A-2 bus and the standard 8080 Family peripherals that Intel also provides. The standard peripherals that are denoted 825X-5 (also the 8251A and 827X peripherals) are peripherals that can be used with an 8085A or 8085A-2. In the 8085A-2 system a wait state is required for proper I/O operation, but even with this wait state system speed is still 30% higher than the 8085A without wait states. An example wait state generator for this purpose is shown at the end of the peripheral compatibility section in this Application Note (Figure 19).

The main timing differences to consider when using an 8085A vs. an 8085A-2 are listed in Table 1.

Cycle dependent timings are listed in Table 2. These are very useful when the user is not operating at the full bus speed. Remember that each 8085A, A-2 device divides its clock input frequency by 2. Therefore, a 10 MHz crystal will produce a 200ns output cycle (denoted as T in the cycle dependent timings). A timing diagram showing the relationships of the timing parameters given in Table 2 can be found on the data sheets.

—Clock (crystal) requirements. The 8085A, A-2 requires the following crystal specifications to run at top bus speed:

8085A	6.25 MHz frequency, parallel resonant, fundamental, 10 mwatt drive level, RS < 75 ohms, CL = 20-35 pf, and CS < 7 pf.
8085A-2	10 MHz frequency, all other specifications the same as 8085A.

—Memory and Peripheral Compatibility - Discussed in detail in upcoming sections.

—Cycle dependent timings (Table 2)

Table 1. 8085A vs. 8085A-2.

Parameter	3.125 MHz (8085A) (ns) Min	Max	Cycle Dependencies	5 MHz (8085A-2) (ns) Min	Max	Cycle Dependencies
tcyc	320	2000		200	2000	
t1	80		1/2T—80	40		1/2T−70
t2	120		1/2T—40	70		1/2T−50
tr		30			30	
tf		30			30	
tAL	115		1/2T−45	50		1/2T−50
tLA	100		1/2T−60	50		1/2T−50
tLL	140		1/2T−20	80		1/2T−20
tLCK	100		1/2T−60	50		1/2T−50
tLC	130		1/2T−30	60		1/2T−40
tAFR		0			0	
tAD		575	(5/2+N)T−225		350	(5/2+N)T−150
tRD		300	(3/2+N)T−180		150	(3/2+N)T−150
tRDH	0			0		
tRAE	150		1/2T−10	90		1/2T−10
tCA	120		1/2T−40	60		1/2T−40
tDW	420		(3/2+N)T−60	230		(3/2+N)T−70
tWD	100		1/2T−60	60		1/2T−40
tCC	400		(3/2+N)T−80	230		(3/2+N)T−70
tCL	50		1/2T−110	25		1/2T−75
tARY		220	3/2T−260		100	3/2T−200
tRYS	110			100		
tRYH	0			0		
tHACK	110		1/2T−50	40		
tHABE		210	1/2T+50		150	1/2T+50
tRV	400		3/2T−80	220		3/2T−80
tAC	270		T−50	115		T−85
tHDS	170			120		
tHDH	0			0		
tINS	360		1/2T+200	150		1/2T+50
tINH	0			0		
tLDR		460	2T−180		270	4/2T−130

Where T = tcyc and N = the number of wait states that are incorporated.
All mathematical operations in Table 2 are performed from left to right, except where qualified with parenthesis.

Table 2. 8085A and 8085A-2 Cycle Dependencies

Memory Device Compatibility

Determining What Memory to Select For Your Application

When developing a system which will use sufficient memory to require buffering (see the capacitive loading section to determine when it is needed), it is important to understand how to select the slowest, lowest cost memory and still be compatible with the bus timings with minimum wait states. A generalized procedure has been developed in the following section for determining the memory access needed for different applications and the number of wait states required (if any). In general the amount of time available for accessing the memory can be obtained from the following formula:

Available memory access = 8085A access time (from control signal of interest) - Buffering/Decoding delay (to and from memory)

The three main "control" signals of interest which determine memory access are that of t_{RD} (read to valid data in), t_{AD} (valid address to valid data in) and t_{LDR} (address latch enable to valid data in). When dealing with different types of memories, one or more of these signals becomes important.

Even though memory access compatibility is probably one of the most important parameters to consider, as this is directly reflected in the price of the memory, it is not the only parameter that is important. Some of the other major timing considerations are as follows:

WRITE ENABLE - Is the write enable signal sufficiently long to guarantee a write?

Is data set up properly with respect to this write to be compatible with the memory's requirements?

Is data held long enough?

DATA FLOAT - Does your system have sufficient margin to prevent bus contention?

(i.e., Does the memory let go of the data bus in time for the processor to use it? Remember that the 8085A shares its Data Bus with the lower 8 addresses.)

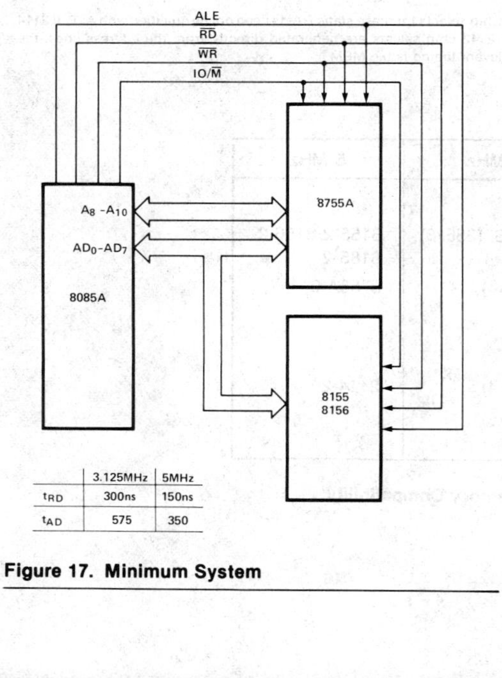

	3.125MHz	5MHz
t_{RD}	300ns	150ns
t_{AD}	575	350

Figure 17. Minimum System

We will first go through the minimum system which can be represented by the dedicated set of components Intel has developed for the 8085A (Fig. 17). The two timing specs were taken from the data catalog for t_{RD} and t_{AD} (t_{LDR} is irrelevant here). Looking at the 8155/6 and 8355/8755A, a comparison can be made for the access times:

	8085A (3.125 MHz)	8155/6	8755A
t_{RD}	300 (max)	170 (max)	170 (max)
t_{AD}	575 (max)	400 (max)	400/450 (max)

This shows that there is plenty of bus margin for the 3.125 MHz minimum application of the 8085A. Access time for the processor can be interpreted as the time from when the control signal is presented on the bus to the time when the processor will expect the data to be valid so it can sample it. Conversely, memory access times show the amount of time that will elapse between when it is told to present its information to when it actually does it. As long as the memory access spec is less than the processor access spec (minus appropriate buffering delays) the memory is access time compatible.

In more complicated systems where one level of data, address and control buffering is required (such as the case when there are many signal paths and device loading on one card), the delays of the latches and bidirectional drivers must be taken into consideration.

First consider a ROM, EPROM or static RAM configuration as shown in Figure 18. Using the generalized available memory access formula, t_{AD}, t_{RD} and t_{LDR} for the memory can be determined using the data sheet timing delays for the buffers.

	3.125MHz	5MHz
T_{RD}	250	100
T_{AD}	500	275
T_{LDR}	390	200

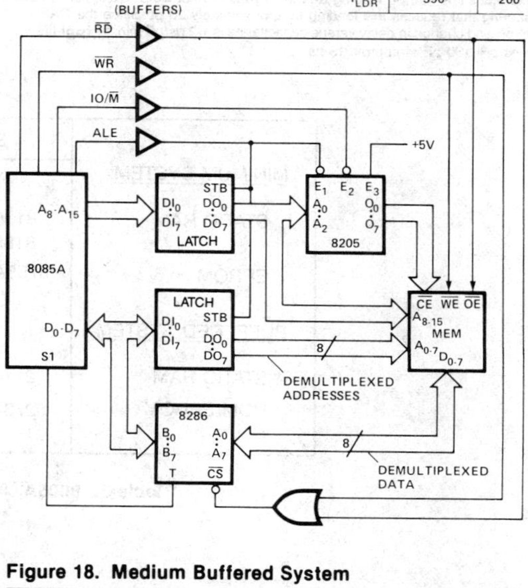

Figure 18. Medium Buffered System

t_{AD} MEMORY = t_{AD}8085A − (8282 + 8205 delay) − (8286 delay) + transitional gain due to buffering*

= t_{AD}85 − (T_{IVOV} + t--) − (T_{IVOV}) + t_{CAPB}*

= (5/2+N)T − 225 − 55 − 35 + 15

= (5/2+N)T − 300 (for 8085A)

(5/2+N)T − 225 (for 8085A-2)

where N = number of wait states and T = cycle time,

For minimum 8085A timing 500ns = t_{AD} memory

8085A-2 timing 275ns = t_{AD} memory

The 8085A timing parameter t_{AL} was not taken into consideration as the 8282 transfers information directly through without concern of the address latch enable. t_{RD} can be obtained in a similar manner.

The read signal $\overline{RD}$ goes through a buffer before it reaches the memory. This must be taken into consideration when calculating effective t_{RD} for the memory.

t_{RD} MEMORY = t_{RD} 8085A − (buffer delay) − (8286 delay) + transitional gain due to buffering

= t_{RD} 85 − (delay) − (T_{IVOV}) + t_{CAPB}

= (3/2+N)T − 180 − 30 − 35 + 15

= (3/2+N)T − 230 (for 8085A)

(3/2 + N)T − 200 ns (for 8085A-2)

*t_{CAPB} is additional time thrown back in for improvement in signal transitions. This is because buffering the signals reduces the capacitive loading considerably. The data sheet gives timings for maximum capacitive loading. Characterization has shown change in delay versus capacitive loading as .12 ns/pf min (under 20 pF loading) and .24 ns/pF max (under 150 pF loading). To take into consideration the effects of this loading two parameters are defined:

t_{CAPA} - delay for a signal to leave the old logic level

t_{CAPB} - delay for a signal to complete the transition from the old to new logic level

where t_{CAPA} = 1/2 t_{CAPB}

	MIN	MAX
t_{CAPA}	7 ns	15 ns
t_{CAPB}	15 ns	30 ns

In the memory compatibility calculations tCAPB min is added on as spec sheet values assume 150 pF loading and this system is not worst case, i.e., it has buffering that reduces this loading to approximately 20 pf. Since the CAP = 130 pF and change in delay versus capacitance is 1/2 ns/pF min, t_{CAPB}MIN = (.1 ns/pF) 130 pF = approx. 15 ns.

For minimum 8085A timing 250ns = t_{RD} memory

8085A-2 timing 100ns = t_{RD} memory

Therefore for t_{LDR}:

t_{LDR} MEMORY = t_{LDR} 8085 − (buffer delay) − (8205) − (8286) + t_{CAPB}

= t_{LDR} − (delay) − (t--) − (T_{IVOV}) + t_{CAPB}

= 2T −180 −30 −20 −35 +15

= 2T −250 for 8085A

= 2T −200 for 8085A-2

For minimum 8085 timing = 390ns

8085A-2 timing = 200ns

To obtain memory access parameters for a multicard system (which would have buffering at both ends of the system bus), it is a simple matter of subtracting off the additional buffering delays.

With these timings a memory compatibility table can be developed from the data sheets (Table 3). With most of these memories it is relatively straightforward to determine the controlling signal used to select and enable the device. To illustrate this, listed below are the controlling signals of interest for the different memories as they are used in a typical configuration:

		Relevant Control Signal
RAM		
2114		
	Address access	- t_{AD} MEM
	Chip select access	- t_{LDR} MEM**
ROM		

**Chip selects for these static RAMs need not be qualified with ALE. If 2114 or 2142 chip selects are generated directly from the address lines, the relevant timing is t_{AD} MEM.

	3.125 MHz	5 MHz
MINIMUM SYSTEM:		
STATIC RAM	8155/8156, (256x8) 8185 (1Kx8)	8155-2/8156-2 8185-2
EPROM	8755A (2Kx8)	8755A-2
BUFFERED SYSTEM:		
STATIC RAM	2114 (1Kx4)	2114-2
ROM/EPROM	2732 (4Kx8)	

Table 3. 8085A, A-2 Memory Compatibility.

In general, t_{AD} MEM and t_{LDR} MEM are the parameters needed for chip enabling, selection and address access times, and probably are the most important considerations when determining which memory device to use. When there is an output enable, tRD MEM is also used. All relevant access times must be met by the resulting system configuration to be compatible.

Peripheral Compatibility - 3.125 and 5 MHz

Intel supports its processors with many LSI peripheral components that do a wide range of functions to simplify circuit design. The 8085A compatible peripherals have been denoted the "−5" notation to show compatibility. The "−5" notation also signifies that these devices are compatible with the 8085A-2 with one wait state interjected. This wait state is produced by taking the ready line low at the proper time as shown in Figure 19.

A list of these peripherals is shown in Table 6 with corresponding relevant specifications to illustrate 8085A-2 compatibility. The analysis for determining the resulting timings is similar to the analysis in the previous memory compatibility section.

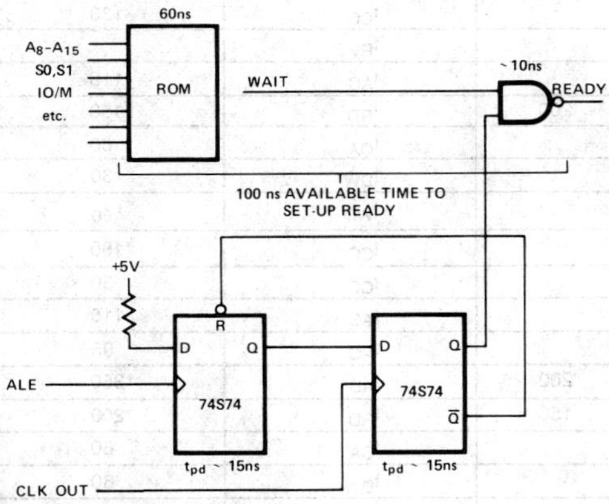

Figure 19. 8085A-2 Wait State Generator

Taking note of asterisked margins shown on the comparison sheet: t_{AD}, t_{RD}, t_{RR} and t_{DW}, it is seen that they are all taken care of by introducing a wait state. The double asterisked margins deal with the t_{RV} spec on the 8255A-5, 8253-5 and 8279-5 peripherals. t_{RV} is the time from the rising edge of $\overline{WR}$ or $\overline{RD}$ to the next falling edge. To allow sufficient time for this spec it is necessary to delay the commands sent to these three peripherals. Enough dead time must occur to make up for the entire negative portion of the margin (for example: 790ns in the 8253-5 medium system). Since in the 8085A-2 every machine cycle is at least 200ns long, 4 machine cycles are sufficient time to allow peripheral control signal recovery (t_{RV}).

One may notice that all of the 8085A instructions take at least 4 T-states (providing a minimum of 800ns) giving ample time to meet this requirement, just by programming one instruction in between every command sent to the peripheral. I/O mapped I/O, which results in using the Input, Output instructions has this delay time built in when moving the data to be transferred into the accumulator. With memory mapped I/O, any instruction that accesses memory for data will provide the time necessary to not violate t_{RV} as a second fetch is performed.

Bus · Loading Considerations · Decoupling

For the cost conscious designer it is always helpful to know when buffering is needed and when it is not. How much can I load the 8085A output pins down? To answer this it is helpful to first list the DC requirements of the common types of logic loading and compare this to the capabilities of the 8085A.

	Maximum High-Level Input Current	Maximum Low-Level Input Current
TTL (single load)	40μA	1.6mA
Schottky or HTTL	40μA	2.0mA
MOS	10μA	10μA
LSTTL (single load)	20μA	400μA

The 8085A is capable of an IOL of 2mA (low) and IOH of − 400μA. With this spec it is easy to come up with the possible combinations of D.C. loading that the designer can use without buffering:

LOADS	8085A, A-2 limiting factor (level)
1 TTL + 1 LSTTL	LOW
1 TTL + 36 MOS*	HIGH
1 SCHOTTKY or 1 HTTL	LOW
40 MOS (various combinations possible)*	HIGH
5 LS TTL	LOW

* Exceeds capacitive loading limit, to be discussed

If a user exceeds these DC loading limitations he must buffer that particular signal. Another factor that the designer **must** consider is the capacitive load that is seen by the 8085A outputs, which may very well be excessive even if DC loading is not. One may note that even though the 8085A can handle a DC load of 40 MOS devices or 36 MOS + 1 TTL, their collective input capacitances exceed the 150 pF max spec.

Part No.	AC. Parameter	Min. (ns)	Max. (ns)	8085A-2 AC. Parameter	Margin vs. −2 Spec. (ns)
8251A	t_{RD}		200	t_{RD}	*150
	t_{RA} & t_{WA}	0		t_{CA}	60
	t_{DW}	150		t_{DW}	80
	t_{WD}	0		t_{WD}	60
	t_{RR} & t_{WW}	250		t_{CC}	*180
	t_{AR} & t_{AW}	0		t_{AC}	
8253-5	t_{RD}		200	t_{RD}	*150
	t_{RA}	5		t_{CA}	55
	t_{WA}	30		t_{CA}	60
	t_{DW}	250		t_{DW}	*180
	t_{WD}	30		t_{WD}	30
	t_{RR} & t_{WW}	300		t_{CC}	*130
	t_{RV}	1000		t_{RV}	**
	t_{AR} & t_{AW}	50		t_{AC}	65
8255A-5	t_{RD}		200	t_{RD}	*150
	t_{RA}	0		t_{CA}	60
	t_{WA}	20		t_{CA}	40
	t_{DW}	100		t_{DW}	130
	t_{WD}	30		t_{WD}	30
	t_{RR} & t_{WW}	300		t_{CC}	*130
	t_{RV}	850		t_{RV}	**
	t_{AR} & t_{AW}	0		t_{AC}	115
8257-5	t_{RD}		200	t_{RD}	*150
	t_{RA} & t_{WA}	0		t_{CA}	60
	t_{DW}	200		t_{DW}	30
	t_{WD}	0		t_{WD}	60
	t_{RR}	250		t_{CC}	*180
	t_{WW}	200		t_{CC}	30
	t_{AR}	0		t_{AC}	115
	t_{AW}	20		t_{AC}	95
8271 & 8273	t_{AD}		200	t_{AD}	*350
	t_{RD}		150	t_{RD}	*200
	t_{CA}	0		t_{CA}	60
	t_{DW}	150		t_{DW}	80
	t_{WD}	0		t_{WD}	80
	t_{RR} & t_{WW}	250		t_{CC}	*180
	t_{AC}	0		t_{AC}	115
8275	t_{RD}		200	t_{RD}	*150
	t_{RA} & t_{WA}	0		t_{CA}	60
	t_{DW}	150		t_{DW}	80
	t_{WD}	0		t_{WD}	60
	t_{RR} & t_{WW}	250		t_{CC}	*180
	t_{AP} & t_{AW}	0		t_{AC}	115
8279-5	t_{AD}		250	t_{AD}	300
	t_{RD}		150	t_{RD}	200
	t_{RA} & t_{WA}	0		t_{CA}	60
	t_{DW}	150		t_{DW}	80
	t_{WD}	0		t_{WD}	60
	t_{RR} & t_{WW}	250		t_{CC}	*180
	t_{RCY}	1000		t_{RV}	**
	t_{AP} & t_{AW}	0		t_{AC}	115

*With 1 "Wait State"
**Must allow for in Software

Table 6. Peripherals vs. 8085A-2

The timing specs of the 8085A are guaranteed as long as the 150 pF maximum loading is not exceeded, which includes the wires, components and parasitics. If the user exceeds this value and wants to guarantee his system timing he must either derate the system timings or use buffering.

What if you choose to ignore this limit and say you can live with the performance degradation? First the timing performance is not all that would degrade, a user must be willing to give up some reliability of his components (All MOS devices have this restraint). This is caused by the excessive switching currents that are needed for this extra loading capacitance. If reliability is not an important consideration, the user can load up to 300 pF on the 8085A bus, but the following correction factors must be used to adjust the timings:

for 150 pF < 300 pF add .13 ns/pF

conversely if less than 150 pF:

for 25 < CL < 150 pF you can subtract .1/ns/pF.

What happens after 300 pF? If the user exceeds this, the noise levels become excessive and problems will result. How much is to much noise? 350 mvolts zero to peak. Prudent designers will always buffer when noise approaches this level, especially in the case of going from one board to another.

The above takes into consideration the actual specification considerations of when to buffer, but there are also transmission line and noise effects that must be considered. When working with dynamic RAMs small (20-30 ohm) resistors are commonly put in series in the address lines to help match impedance levels and reduce reflections. Note that this resistor should be chosen such that it does not severely degrade the voltage levels of the signal. Long parallel board traces with signals that could adversely affect each other should also be avoided to prevent cross talk problems.

By-passing is very important to prevent intermittent problems which often plague the board designer. Large bulk capacitors should be used at strategic locations on the board to prevent power supply droop. This becomes a major factor when there are many devices that can turn on at once and produce a considerable drain from the power supply (such as burst refresh in dynamic RAM).

To help smooth out the current spikes that naturally occur when devices turn on and off, it is recommended to liberally use small capacitors such as the monolithic and other ceramic capacitors which have low inherent inductance. Cutting corners here will often times turn around and bite you.

Proper layout is an important consideration. Power supply lines should be well gridded to supply sufficient current to all areas of the board. A strong ground layout is advised to offset noise problems. Remember if the ground plane moves up in voltage because of excessive charge dumping in a particular area, the supply will drift up correspondingly. Sensing low levels often becomes an intermittent problem when proper ground is not provided.

APPLICATION EXAMPLE 1

MINIMUM SYSTEM APPLICATION AS A TEMPERATURE SENSOR

Overview

Following is an application example that illustrates the use of the interrupt and SOD pins on the 8085A, software for a block search routine, and the procedure for using and reading the 8155 counter. It is a simple application showing the use of the small but powerful 3-chip 8085 system as a temperature sensor (SDK-85 board used). This example can be modified to be an accurate industrial temperature controller, for several locations if desired.

The basic operation behind this application is a monostable multivibrator having its timing pulse duration controlled by a thermistor. The counter in the 8155 converts this timing pulse to a decimal count that is software mapped into a temperature and displayed in degrees C in the address field of the display in the SDK-85 Kit. For the purpose of keeping the software relatively simple, many approximations were incorporated into the code.

Detailed Hardware

The basic SDK kit was used for the initial hardware. This Kit provides for everything necessary to develop and debug a program through the use of the SDK-85 monitor, keyboard and display board. The kit provides for 256 bytes of RAM resident in the 8155 and 2K bytes of ROM or EPROM where the SDK-85 monitor is placed. (See the Intel SDK-85 User's Manual for copy of monitor software code.)

Figure 20 is a schematic of the SDK-85 Kit with only one 8155 and 8355. There is no buffering in this system as all components are on the same board and far below the maximum component loading. A monostable multivibrator (74121) is also shown with a thermistor connected to RE/CE.

The SOD output pin from the 8085A is used for the purpose of starting the monostable multivibrator in generating its temperature controlled timing pulse. This pulse is created by the RC time constant provided for by the thermistor acting as a variable resistor and a .1μF capacitor to put the timing pulse in the desired timing range.

The inverted output of the monostable multivibrator (one shot) has been directly connected to the RST 6.5 pin on the 8085A. Since this pin is high level sensitive, it is necessary to disable interrupts in the program until after the pulse from the one shot goes low.

The hardware addressing in the configuration shown allows for several code spaces that could be used. The RST and TRAP interrupt lines on the 8085A also have hardware start addresses but many of these are altered by the SDK monitor. Table 7 should be useful in understanding the addresses used in the software that follows. Each memory/I/O component in the basic SDK-85 system is enabled by a signal coming from the 8205 address decoder. Since no expansion chips are used, output enables 00 (8355 monitor ROM), 03 (8279 Keyboard) and 04 (8155 RAM) were the only ones needed. Additional memory and/or I/O could have been incorporated using other output enables from the 8205.

Memory/I/O Device	Function	Output from 8205	code space
8155	RAM space	04	2000 - 20FF (20 - 20FF are reserved for monitor RAM locations)
8355	ROM space	00	0000 - 07FF
8279	Keyboard/display controller	03	1800 - 1FFF

stack pointer

Since the monitor uses locations 10C8 through 20FF, the stack pointer must be initialized to 20C8 or less.

	8085A jump address	Usage	monitor mapped address
trap	24H	$\overline{T0}$ of 8155	0157
RST 5.5	2CH	8279 interrupt	028E
RST 6.5	34H	oneshot interrupt	20CE
RST 7.5	3CH	vector interrupt	

I/O ports address	Function
00	Monitor ROM Port A (8355)
01	Monitor ROM Port B (8355)
02	Monitor ROM Port A (8355) Data direction register
03	Monitor ROM Port B (8355) Data direction register
20	Basic command/status register
21	Basic RAM Port A
22	Basic RAM Port B
23	Basic RAM Port C
24	Basic RAM LOW order byte of timer count
25	Basic RAM HIGH order byte of timer count

Table 7. Addressing

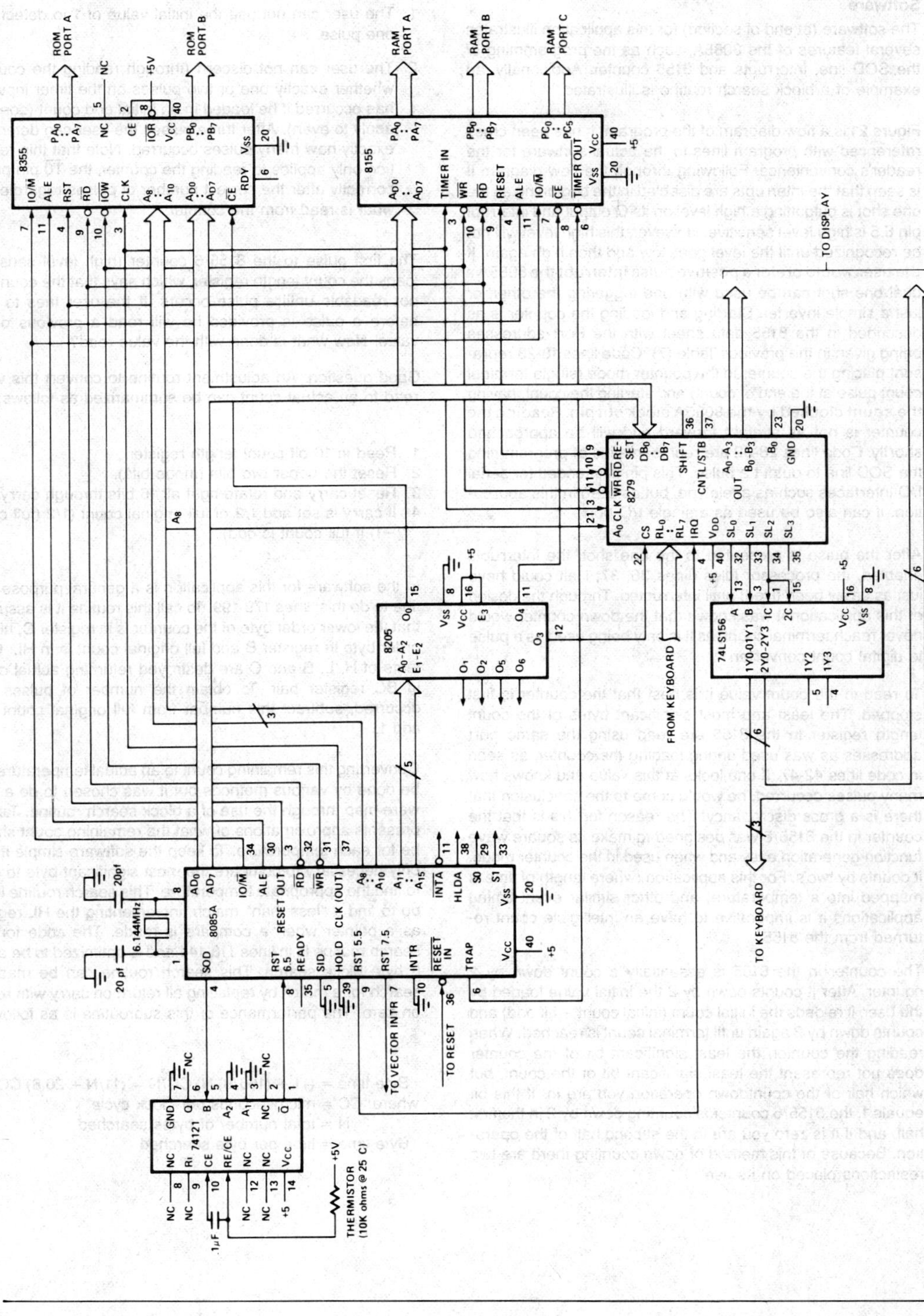

Figure 20. Detailed SDK-85 Kit with Temperature Sensor

Software

The software (at end of section) for this application illustrates several features of the 8085A, such as the programming of the SOD line, interrupts and 8155 counter. Additionally, an example of a block search routine is illustrated.

Figure 21 is a flow diagram of the program. It has been cross referenced with program lines to the actual software for the reader's convenience. Following through the flow diagram it is seen that the interrupts are disabled in the beginning as the one shot is outputting a high level on its Q output and interrupt pin 6.5 is high level sensitive. However, this high level will not be recognized until the level goes low and then high again. If the user would prefer a positive pulse interrupt the 8085A a dual one shot can be used with one triggering the other, or just a simple inverter. Starting and loading the counter is as described in the 8155 data sheet with the Port addresses being given in the previous Table (7). Code lines 18-23 represent placing the counter in the counter mode (single terminal count pulse at the end of count) and starting the count, having the count clocked by the 8085A clock out pin. Reading the counter is not as straight forward and will be approached shortly. Code lines 28-32 are representative of programming the SOD line to output a pulse. This pin is intended for serial I/O interfaces such as a teletype, but as seen in this application, it can also be used as a single I/O port.

After the pulse is presented to the one shot, the interrupts enabled, the processor idles (lines 36, 37; Halt could have just as easily been used) until interrupted. Through the design of this application it was known that the down counter would never reach terminal count, as it is only being used as a pulse to digital count converter.

To read in the count value it is best that the counter is first stopped. The least and most significant bytes of the count length register in the 8155 are read using the same port addresses as was used during loading the counter, as seen in code lines 42-47. If one looks at this value and knows how many pulses occurred, he would come to the conclusion that there is a gross discrepancy! The reason for this is that the counter in the 8155/6 was designed to make its square wave function generation easy and when used in the counter mode, it counts by two's. For this application (where length of time is mapped into a temperature) and other similar event timing applications it is imperative to have an intelligible count returned from the 8155.

The counter in the 8155 is essentially a count down by 2 counter. After it counts down by 2 the initial value loaded by the user, it reloads the initial count (initial count −1 if odd) and counts down by 2 again until terminal count is reached. When reading the counter, the least significant bit of the counter does not represent the least significant bit of the count, but which half of the countdown operation you are in. If this bit equals 1, the 8155/6 counter is counting down by 2 in the first half, and if it is zero you are in the second half of the operation. Because of this method of down counting there are two restrictions placed on its use:

1. The user can not use the initial value of 1 to detect only one pulse.

2. The user can not discern (through reading the counter) whether exactly one or two pulses on the timer input pin has occurred if he loaded in an initial odd count (does not apply to even). After three pulses the user can determine exactly how many pulses occurred. Note that this restriction only applies to reading the counter, the $\overline{\text{TO}}$ pin pulses correctly after the correct number of pulses regardless of what is read from the counter.

The first pulse to the 8155/6 counter (high level sensitive) loads the count length register, which says that the counter is not readable until a pulse occurs. If the user tries to read before a pulse is provided he will read a previous or old value. Now what is done with the value read?

Good question. An adjustment routine to convert this value read to an actual count can be summarized as follows:

1. Read in 16 bit count length register.
2. Reset the upper two bits (mode bits).
3. Reset carry and rotate right all 16 bits through carry.
4. If carry is set add 1/2 of full original count (1/2 (full count −1) if full count is odd).

In the software for this application is a general purpose routine to do this; lines 179-199. To call this routine it is assumed that the lower order byte of the counter is in register C, higher order byte in register B and full original count is in HL. Contents of H, L, B and C are destroyed returning actual count in BC register pair. To obtain the number of pulses that occurred, subtract this number from full original count and add 1.

Converting this remaining count to an actual temperature can be done by various methods but it was chosen to do a software map through the use of a block search routine. Table 8 presents approximations of what the remaining count should be for each temperature. To keep the software simple it was only necessary to compare the most significant byte to a list to find the appropriate temperature. This search routine is set up to find a "less than" match, incrementing the HL register as a pointer when a compare is made. The code for this search routine is in lines 118-144 and is optimized to be a fast 8 byte block search. This search routine can be made to search for a match by replacing all return on carry with return on zero. The performance of this subroutine is as follows:

Byte time = (11 + (166/8) N) CC/N = (11/N + 20.8) CC
where: CC = microseconds per clock cycle
N = total number of bytes searched
Byte time = time per byte searched

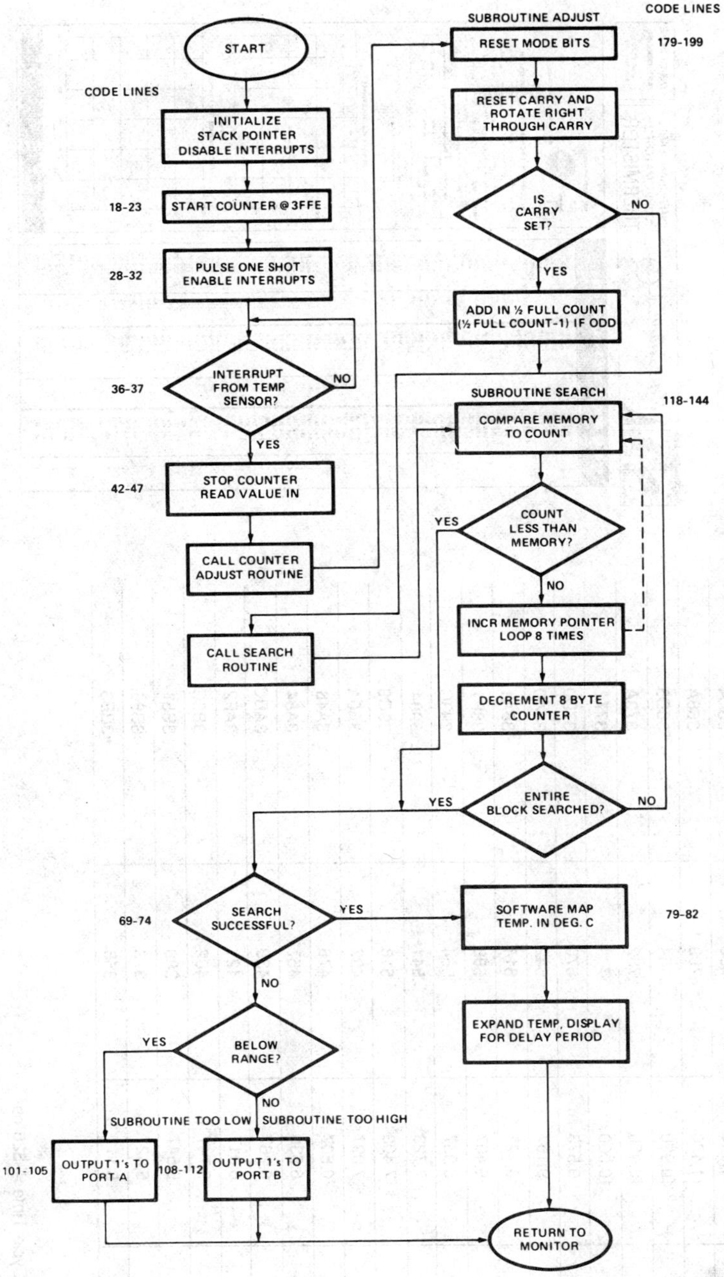

Figure 21. Temperature Sensor Flow Diagram

DEG. C	THERMISTOR OHMS	(.7) (.1μ) (R_T) APPROX. TIME (ms)	START WITH $3FFE_H$ APPROX. COUNT LEFT (HEX)
20	12,490	.874	3585
21	11,940	.836	35FA
22	11,420	.799	366A
23	10,920	.764	36D5
24	10,450	.732	373A
25	10,000	.7	3772
26	9,573	.670	37D0
27	9,167	.642	384D
28	8,777	.614	38A1
29	8,407	.588	38F1
30	8,057	.564	393C
31	7,723	.541	3984
32	7,403	.518	39C8
33	7,097	.497	3A0A
34	6,807	.476	3A48
35	6,530	.457	3A84
36	6,267	.439	3ABC
37	6,017	.421	3AF2
38	5,747	.402	3B2C
39	5,547	.388	3B57
40	5,327	.373	3B86
41	5,117	.358	3BB3

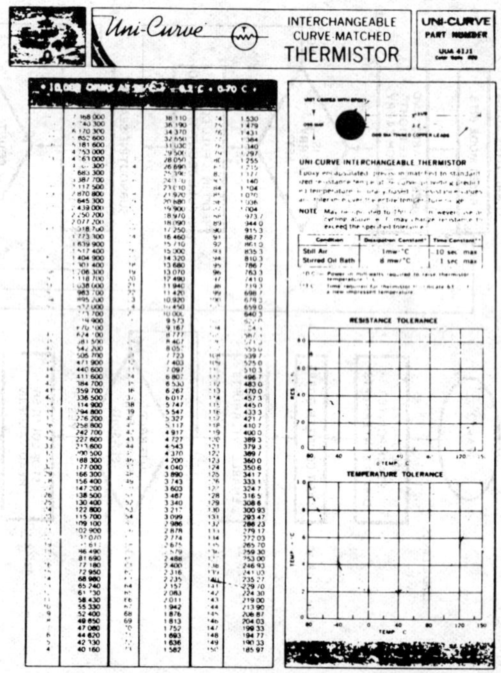

8085A Cycle Time = 326 ns

Oneshot Approx. Time =

L_{N2} (CEXT) (REXT)

$\approx$ (.7) (.1μ) $R_{THERMISTOR}$

Table 8. Thermistor Resistance Mapping

For an example with N = 256, CC = .32 μsec at 3.125 MHz; Byte time = 6.7 μsec. A match search routine with minimum memory usage is given below:

```
Search  Cmp M          compare byte
        RZ             return if match
        INX H          else increment pointer
        DCR C          has the entire
        JNZ search     block been searched?
        STC            If so set no match flag
        RET            and return.
```

In this application, a user may want to have several temperature ranges which can be swapped in and out with a block move subroutine. Similar code can be developed for this as shown below for a 4 byte move group:

```
BLKMV   LXI H, 000H    clear HL
        DAD SP         move SP to HL
        SHLD SAVESP    save sP
        MOV H, B       move Block move
        MOV L, C       Source address
        SPHL           To SP
        XCHG           Move Block move
                       address to HL
Loop    POP B          fetch four bytes from
        POP D          source store 1st byte
        MOV M, C       at destination
        INX H
        MOV M, B       2nd
        INX H
        MOV M, E       3rd
        INX H
        MOV M, D       4th
        INX H
        DCR A          check for end of
        JNZ Loop       Block move
        LHLD SAVESP    return old
        SPHL           SP
        RET            return
```

Once the count less than match is found in the application the HL register has 10 added to it which points it at the corresponding temperature (lines 79-82). This temperature is then displayed in the address field of the SDK 85 display using user available monitor routines. If the temperature is out of range the code detects it (lines 69-74) and outputs 1's on Port A or Port B if the temperature was too low or too high respectively (lines 101-105 "too low" and lines 108-112 "too high").

APPLICATION EXAMPLE 2

CRT INTERFACE

Most microprocessor systems require some sort of serial communications. This may be selected for reasons of economy (to reduce the number of interconnections required in a distributed system), or it may be necessary in order to communicate with such common peripherals as CRT's or teletypewriters.

These peripherals all use a standard convention for transmitting serial ASCII code. Each data byte is transmitted as a series of 10 or 11 bits. The uniform time per bit corresponds to the data transmission rate. For example, if the transmission rate is to be 2400 baud (2400 bits per second), each bit time must be 1/2400 bps = 416.7 μsec/bit. The standard 10-bit sequence consists of a logically zero "Start" bit, 8 data bits (least significant bit first), and one or more stop bits (logic 1). An 11-bit sequence with two stop bits is used for 110 baud TTY's. The logic one level continues until the start bit of the next byte to ensure that each 10-bit sequence is initiated with a one-to-zero transition. The 8 bits transferred might be raw binary data or alphanumeric characters using the standard ASCII code. In this case, the most significant bit – the last data bit transmitted – will depend on the parity convention being used. This sequence is illustrated for the ASCII "space" character in Figure 22.

The algorithm for receiving serial code involves sampling the incoming data at the middle of each bit time. The eight sampled values are shifted into a serial byte corresponding to the data originally transmitted. The one-to-zero transition at the beginning of each byte makes it possible to synchronize the sampling points relative to the start of each data sequence.

Hardware Interface

In general, any serial communications system will require both hardware and software interfaces. Since the SOD line can drive only one TTL load, additional current and voltage buffering is required to be compatible with the RS-232C interface standard used by most peripherals. A schematic for achieving this buffering is shown in Figure 23. The MC1488 and MC1489 circuits interface positive logic TTL signals with the RS-232 high voltage inverted logic levels.

Software Package

The software needed to drive the CRT interface is divided into three parts. All three use software timing and delay loops, with fixed and variable parameters. In conjunction, they are able to identify incoming signals at any rate from below 110 to over 9600 baud and respond at the same rate.

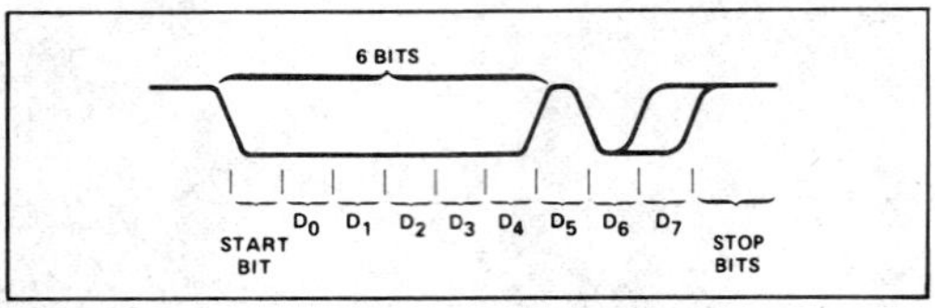

Figure 22. ASCII Space Character

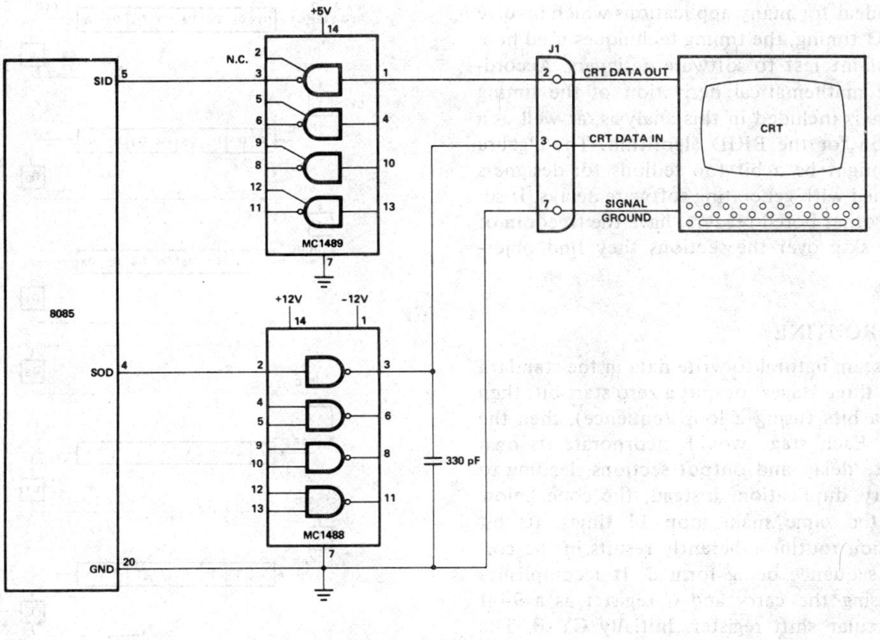

Figure 23. RS-232C Interface Schematic

Upon power-up or reset, or when the console device baud rate is changed, the baud rate identification subroutine (BRID) is called. This routine waits until an ASCII space character (20H) is received from the console. (Any other character will result in a case of mistaken identification.) When a space character is received, two time parameters are computed which correspond to the bit time and one-half the bit time of the baud rate being used. These are stored as variables BITTIME and HALFBIT. To output a character to the console, the character code is placed in register C, and the subroutine COUT is called. This routine uses BITTIME as a parameter for the software delay loop which determines the baud rate. To accept a character from the keyboard, CIN is called. CIN returns after the next key is typed, with the corresponding character code in register C. CIN uses both parameters BITTIME and HALFBIT.

Since COUT and CIN use time parameters computed by BRID, they will function at a rate the same as that of the initial space character input. Because of the nature of the software, the rate does not depend on the CPU clock frequency. This results in additional flexibility in the following respects:

1. The software does not need to be modified if the 8085 crystal frequency is changed or Wait states are added.
2. Since the time base is no longer critical, the quartz crystal could be replaced by a less expensive RC network, provided the frequency does not drift by more than a few percent during a session. Additional drift can be accommodated by periodically recalling the BRID routine.
3. Communication is possible at non-standard baud rates which relaxes the constraints on system peripherals.

It should be noted, though, that slowing down the CPU clock will decrease its throughput proportionately. In addition, it will degrade the maximum resolution of the delay loops, with the result that the highest baud rates may no longer be achievable.

A more detailed analysis of the CRT interface routines will be presented in the order of increasing complexity: COUT, CIN, and BRID. Since SID and

SOD are ideal for many applications which involve critical I/O timing, the timing techniques used here may be of interest to software designers. Accordingly, the mathematical derivation of the timing parameters is included in this analysis, as well as a justification for the BRID algorithm. The algebra involved might be a bit too tedious for designers unconcerned with generating software delays. If so, they (and other bored readers) have the freedom of choice to skip over the sections they find objectionable.

OUTPUT ROUTINE

It would seem natural to write data in the standard format in three stages: output a zero start bit, then the 8 data bits (using a loop sequence), then the stop bits. Each stage would incorporate its own appropriate delay and output sections, leading to unnecessary duplication. Instead, the code below executes the same main loop 11 times. Its bit manipulation routine inherently results in the correct data sequence being formed. It accomplishes this by using the carry and C register as a 9-bit pseudo-circular shift register. Initially CY=0. The algorithm outputs CY, waits one bit time, sets CY=1, and then rotates the pseudo-register right one bit. This repeats for 11 cycles. On the tenth and all subsequent loops, the output bit will be a logical one, since that bit had been set nine loops earlier while in the CY (see Figure 24).

When COUT is called the registers to be used must be preserved and interrupts disabled so the timing loop will not be disrupted. Clear the CY in preparation for outputting the start bit, and set the loop counter for 11 bits (if 110 baud will never be used, the counter could be set to 10):

```
COUT:   PUSH    B
        PUSH    H
        DI
        XRA     A
        MVI     B,11
```

Output of the contents of the CY:

```
C01:    MVI     A,80H       <7>
        RAR                 <4>
        SIM                 <4>
```

The numbers in brackets indicate how many macine cycles are required for each instruction. They will be referred to in the timing analysis section.

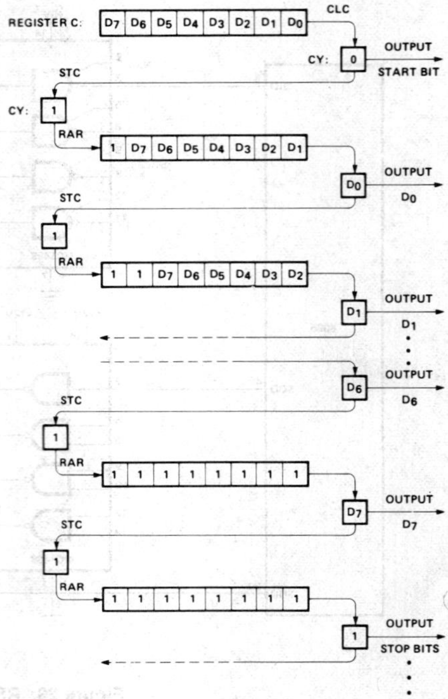

Figure 24. Data Serialization Algorithm

Get stuck in a loop for the appropriate time (don't worry for now how "BITTIME" is determined):

```
        LHLD    BITTIME     <16>
C02     DCR     L           [illegible]
        JNZ     C02         [illegible]
        DCR     H           [illegible]
        JNZ     C02         [illegible]
```

Rotate the contents of register C right into the CY, while moving a one into the left end. Continue until all bits have been transmitted:

```
        STC                 <4>
        MOV     A,C         <4>
        RAR                 <4>
        MOV     C,A         <4>
        DCR     B           <4>
        JNZ     C01         <10>
```

Restore processor status and return:

```
        POP     H
        POP     P
        EI
        RET
```

INPUT ROUTINE

The console input routine uses the opposite procedure; instead of moving a bit from register C to the CY, then to A_7, then to SOD, CIN loads a bit from SID into A_7, then moves it to CY, then into register C.

First, set up the CPU as before:

```
CIN:    PUSH    H
        DI
        MVI     B,9
```

When a start bit transition arrives, the first sampling should not be taken until the middle of the first data bit, one and one-half bit times after the transition. Await the start bit transition, then set up the delay parameter for one-half bit time:

```
CI1:    RIM                     <4>
        ORA     A               <4>
        JM      CI1             <7>
        LHLD    HALFBIT         <16>
```

Loop for one-half bit time before starting to sample data:

```
CI2:    DCR     L               (D)
        JNZ     CI2             (D)
        DCR     H               (D)
        JNZ     CI2             (D)
```

Wait until the middle of the next bit before sampling SID, then move the data bit into CY:

```
CI3:    LHLD    BITTIME         <16>
CI4:    DCR     L               (D)
        JNZ     CI4             (D)
        DCR     H               (D)
        JNZ     CI4             (D)
        RIM                     <4>
        RAL                     <4>
```

Decrement the bit counter. If this is the ninth cycle, the 8 data bits are in register C, so quit (the first stop bit will already have been received, and be in CY):

```
        DCR     B               <4>
        JZ      CI5             <7>
```

Otherwise, continue. Rotate the data bit right into register C, and repeat the cycle:

```
        MOV     A,C             <4>
        RAR                     <4>
        MOV     C,A             <4>
        NOP                     <4>
        JMP     CI3             <10>
```

(A NOP is needed to make the COUT and CIN loops exactly equal in number of machine cycles, so that each can use the same delay parameter.) Restore status and return.

```
CI5     POP     H
        EI
        RET
```

TIMING ANALYSIS

COUT and CIN now need to be provided with parameters for BITTIME and HALFBIT. It can be seen from the above code that each routine uses 61 + D machine cycles per input or output bit, where D is the number of cycles spent in either four line delay segment. If $\langle H \rangle$ and $\langle L \rangle$ are the contents of the H and L registers going into this section of code, then:

$$D = 22 + (\langle L \rangle - 1) \times 14 + (\langle H \rangle - 1) \times [(255 \times 14) + 25] \quad (1)$$

If $\langle H \rangle' \equiv \langle H \rangle - 1$, $\langle L \rangle' \equiv \langle L \rangle - 1$, and

$$\langle HL \rangle' \equiv 256\,\langle H \rangle' + \langle L \rangle' \quad (2)$$

then

$$D = 22 + 14\,\langle L \rangle' + 3595\,\langle H \rangle' \quad (3)$$

This can be approximated by:

$$D = 22 + 14\,\langle HL \rangle' \quad (4)$$

This approximation is exact for $\langle H \rangle' = 0$; otherwise, it is accurate to within 0.3%. Thus each loop of COUT or CIN uses a total of:

$$C = 61 + D = 83 + 14\,\langle HL \rangle' \text{ machine cycles} \quad (5)$$

Each machine cycle uses two crystal cycles in the 8085, so the resulting data rate is:

$$B = \frac{\text{cycle frequency}}{C} = \frac{(\text{crystal frequency}) \div 2}{83 + 14\,\langle HL \rangle'} \quad (6)$$

For a typical calculation, see the example below.

EXAMPLE

To produce 2400 baud with the standard 6.144 MHz crystal:

$$2400 = \frac{(6.144 \times 10^6) \div 2}{83 + 14 \langle HL \rangle'}$$

$$14 \langle HL \rangle' = \left(\frac{6.144 \times 10^6 \div 2}{2400}\right) - 83$$

$$\langle HL \rangle' = \left[\left(\frac{6.144 \times 10^6 \div 2}{2400}\right) - 83\right] \div 14 = 85.5 \cong 86$$

$$\langle HL \rangle' = 86_{10} = 0056H$$

$$\langle HL \rangle = 0157H = \text{BITTIME}$$

To determine the true data rate this parameter will produce, substitute into equation (6):

$$\text{Date Rate} = \frac{6.144 \times 10^6 \div 2}{83 + 14(86)}$$

$$= 2387 \text{ baud, which is } 0.54\% \text{ slow.}$$

For 9600 baud, the same calculations will yield $\langle HL \rangle'$ = 17, which is actually 0.3% slow; a sizzling 19200 baud or 38400 baud could each be generated to within 5% if $\langle HL \rangle'$ = 6 or 0! Table 9 presents the parameters for several standard baud rates.

Notice that the resolution of the delay algorithm – the difference between bit times resulting from parameters which differ by one – is 14 machine cycles. As a result, the true bit delay produced can always manage to be within ±2.3 μsec of the delay desired. This guarantees that at rates up to 9600 baud, where each bit time is at least 104 μsec wide, some value of BITTIME can be found which will be accurate to within 2.2%.

BAUD RATE IDENTIFICATION ROUTINE

The function of BRID is to compute the appropriate parameters BITTIME and HALFBIT. It accomplishes this by observing the data pattern received when the space bar is pressed on the console device. Since a space character has the ASCII code 20H = 00100000B, the pattern represented back in Figure 4 is transmitted. Notice that the initial zero level is 6 bits wide. Suppose it could be determined that this corresponds to M machine cycles. Then one bit would correspond to (M÷6) machine cycles. The reason for dividing down a space several bits long is so that any distortion caused by the signal rise and fall times, or any lack of precision in detecting the two transitions, will be reduced by a factor of six. Since the bit period of COUT and CIN is 83 + 14 $\langle HL \rangle'$, BRID must generate a value $\langle HL \rangle'$ such that:

$$M \div 6 = 83 + 14 \langle HL \rangle' \quad (7)$$

$$\langle HL \rangle' = \frac{(M \div 6) - 83}{14} \quad (8)$$

$$\langle HL \rangle' = \frac{M}{84} - 6 \text{ (approximately)} \quad (9)$$

This value can be determined by setting register pair HL to –6, then incrementing it once every 84 machine cycles during the period that the incom-

Table 9

DELAY PARAMETERS FOR STANDARD BAND RATES USING 6.144 MHz CRYSTAL

TARGET BAUD RATE	$\langle HL \rangle'_{10}$ (See Text)	$\langle HL \rangle'_{16}$ (See Text)	⟨HL⟩ or BITTIME (See Text)	HALFBIT	ACTUAL BAUD RATE PRODUCED	% ERROR
110	1989	07C5	08C6	04E3	109.99	-0.006
150	1457	05B1	06B2	03D9	149.99	-0.005
300	726	02D6	03D7	026C	299.80	-0.068
600	360	0168	0269	01A5	599.65	-0.059
1200	177	00B1	01B2	0159	1199.5	-0.039
2400	86	0056	0157	012C	2386.9	-0.547
4800	40	0028	0129	0115	4777.6	-0.469
9600	17	0011	0112	0109	9570.1	-0.312
19200	6	0006	0107	0104	18395.2	-4.37

ing signal is zero. BITTIME is then obtained by individually incrementing registers H and L. To obtain HALFBIT, divide the value of ⟨HL⟩′ determined above by two before incrementing each register.

In order to implement this algorithm, set HL to −6, verify that the incoming signal is a logic one, then wait for the start bit transition.

```
BRID:   MVI     A,0C0H
        SIM
        LXI     H,-6H
BRI1:   RIM
        ORA     A
        JP      BRI1
BRI2:   RIM
        ORA     A
        JM      BRI2
```

Increment register pair HL, then delay so that each cycle will require 84 machine cycles:

```
BRI3:   INX     H           <6>
        MVI     E,04H       <7>
BRI4:   DCR     E           (53)
        JNZ     BRI4        [illegible]
```

Check if SID is still low. If so, repeat:

```
        RIM                 <4>
        ORA     A           <4>
        JP      BRI3        <10>
```

Otherwise continue. Store HL temporarily for the HALFBIT calculation. Obtain and store BITTIME:

```
        PUSH    H
        INR     H
        INR     L
        SHLD    BITTIME
```

Restore HL, calculate HALFBIT, and return:

```
        POP     H
        ORA     A
        MOV     A,H
        RAR
        MOV     H,A
        MOV     A,L
        RAR
        MOV     L,A
        INR     H
        INR     L
        SHLD    HALFBIT
        RET
```

The assembled listings for these subroutines, along with a simple test program, is presented in the CRT and Cassette Code.

APPLICATION EXAMPLE 3

CASSETTE RECORDER INTERFACE

There are many situations where data has to be transmitted through a non-ideal medium. To give three typical examples, a system with electrically isolated elements might require that signals be AC coupled, communications through an audio network (such as telephone or radio) are greatly bandwidth limited, and some applications (such as a distributed network in an industrial environment) must tolerate random electrical noise. Attempting to record data on a cheap cassette recorder (the one used for this note cost $17.00) will reveal all of these shortcomings, plus one: The tape speed fluctuates significantly and varies as the batteries run down, hence the data rate is inconsistent.

The recording scheme used here makes very few demands on the transmission medium. It makes no attempt to transmit DC voltage levels. Instead, data is transmitted by a series of variable length tone bursts. The dominant frequency of the tone used can be selected to be within the passband of the particular medium. Data is transmitted with each bit composed of a tone burst followed by a pause. The first third of a bit period is always a tone burst, the middle third is either a tone burst continuous with the first or a pause corresponding to, respectively, a one or zero, and the final third is always a pause, as shown in Figure 25. Thus, data is distinguished by the burst/pause ratio.

Hardware Design

These tone bursts are obtained from the 8085 SOD line, using analog signal conditioning to eliminate the DC component of the waveform. (This low frequency component is due to the single-ended nature of the SOD line: it's deviations from ground are all positive, which unbalances the capacitive input stage of the recorder.) A suggested interface circuit is shown in Figure 26, using one LM324 quad op amp and a few standard value discrete components which should be available in even a digital design laboratory. On playback, analog circuitry is again used to detect the presence of a tone burst. In Figure 26, A2 buffers the incoming signal, and A3 inverts it. The peaks of these two signals are transmitted through D1 or D2 and are filtered by an RC network. Comparator A4 then squares up the output and produces the logic signal read by the SID pin. Since the op amps are powered by the single 5-volt supply, a 2.0-volt reference level is obtained from a resistive voltage divider. The waveforms present at several points in the circuit are shown in Figure 27.

Software

The algorithm for reading a data bit off the tape is simple and straightforward: If the tone burst is longer than the pause, the bit is a one. Otherwise, it is a zero. Since only the time ratio is considered, any variation in tape speed will not affect the data determination.

> **VOLUME CONTROL**
>
> A question that arises with any audio cassette interface is how to set the volume control. (Recording level is usually determined internally.) When the playback level is correct, the logic signal output from A4 will have either a one-third or two-thirds duty cycle. This can be readily observed with an oscilloscope. In the field, an old-fashioned mechanical-type voltmeter could be connected to the A4 output, and the volume adjusted until the meter needle hovered somewhere between 1/3 and 2/3 the high level output voltage. With random data, the reading would be about 2 volts. There will be a fairly wide range of acceptable volume settings. (Since the quivering meter needle is being used here for inertial signal averaging, a digital voltmeter would not be very helpful in this application.)

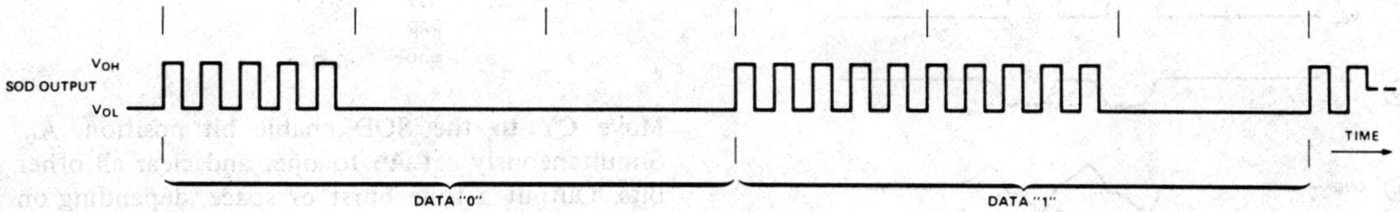

Figure 25. Tape Interface Data Recording Scheme

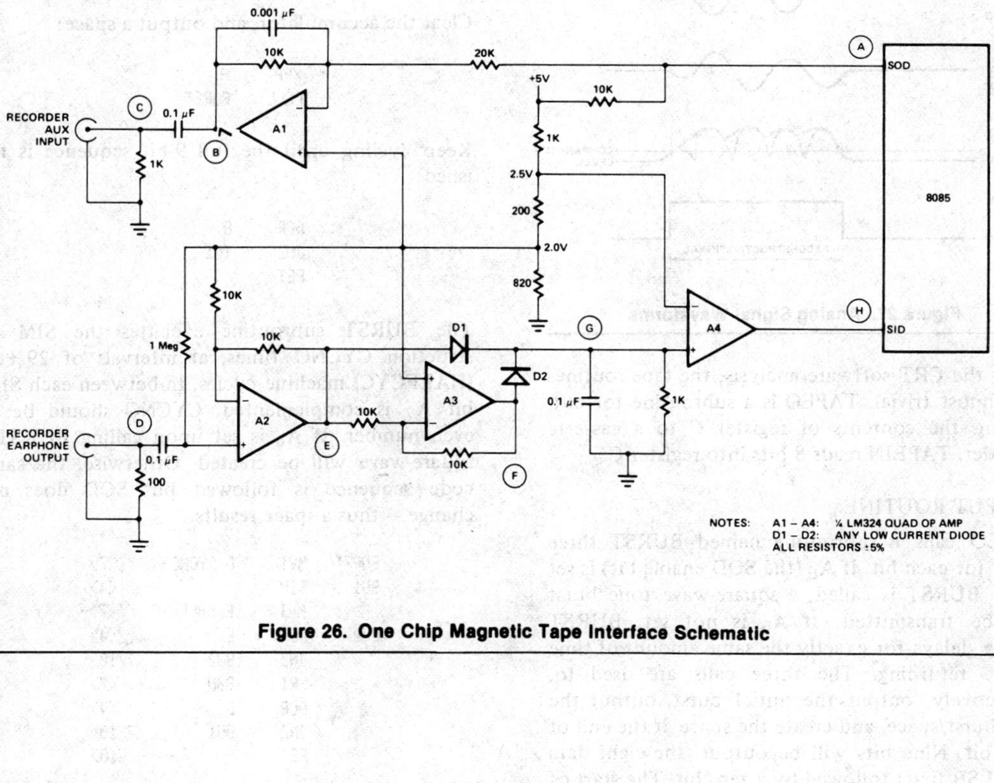

Figure 26. One Chip Magnetic Tape Interface Schematic

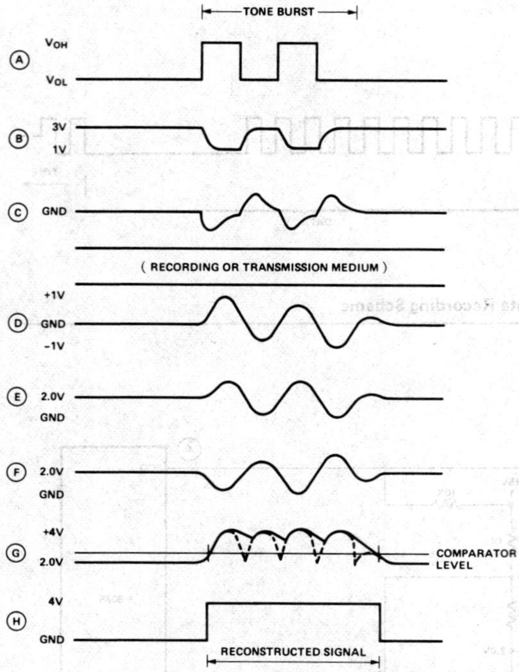

Figure 27. Analog Signal Waveforms

After the CRT software analysis, the tape routines are almost trivial. TAPEO is a subroutine for outputting the contents of register C to a cassette recorder. TAPEIN reads 8 bits into register C.

OUTPUT ROUTINE

TAPEO calls a subroutine named BURST three times for each bit. If A_6 (the SOD enable bit) is set when BURST is called, a square-wave tone burst will be transmitted. If A_6 is not set, BURST simply delays for exactly the same amount of time before returning. The three calls are used to, respectively, output the initial burst, output the data burst/space, and create the space at the end of each bit. Nine bits will be output: the eight data bits (LSB first) followed by a zero bit. The start of the initial burst of the trailing zero is needed to mark the end of the final space of the preceding data bit.

Start each bit by outputting a tone burst:

```
TAPEO:  MVI     B,9
TO1:    MVI     A,0C0H
        CALL    BURST
```

Rotate register C through CY:

```
        MOV     A,C
        RAR
        MOV     C,A
```

Move CY to the SOD enable bit position, A_6. Simultaneously set A_7 to one, and clear all other bits. Output a tone burst or space, depending on the previous contents of CY:

```
        MVI     A,01H
        RAR
        RAR
        CALL    BURST
```

Clear the accumulator, and output a space:

```
        XRA     A
        CALL    BURST
```

Keep cycling until the full 9-bit sequence is finished:

```
        DCR     B
        JNZ     TO1
        RET
```

The BURST subroutine executes the SIM instruction CYCNO times, at intervals of 29 + 14 ⟨HALFCYC⟩ machine cycles. In between each SIM, bit A_7 is complemented. CYCNO should be an even number. If A_6 is set upon calling BURST a square-wave will be created. Otherwise, the same code sequence is followed but SOD does not change – thus a space results.

```
BURST:  MVI     D,CYCNO         <7>
BU1     SIM                     <4>
        MVI     E,HALFCYC       <7>
BU2     DCR     E               <4>
        JNZ     BU2             <7/10>
        XRI     80H             <7>
        DCR     D               <4>
        JNZ     BU1             <7/10>
        RET                     <10>
```

INPUT ROUTINE

TAPEIN uses a subroutine called BITIN to move the data at the SID pin into the CY. The maximum rate at which SID is read is limited by a delay loop in BITIN.

Initialize the bit counter and the register D, which will keep track of the tone burst time. If a tone burst is being received when TAPEIN is called, wait until the burst is over:

```
TAPEIN: MVI     B,8
        MVI     D,00H
TI1:    CALL    BITIN
        JC      TI1
        CALL    BITIN
        JC      TI1
```

(Throughout this subroutine, a level transition is recognized only after it has been read once initially and then verified on the next reading. This provides some degree of software noise immunity.) Now await the start of the next burst:

```
TI2     CALL    BITIN
        JNC     TI2
        CALL    BITIN
        JNC     TI2
```

The next burst has now arrived. Keep reading the SID pin, decrementing register D (thus making it more negative), each cycle until the pause is detected:

```
TI3     DCR     D
        CALL    BITIN
        JC      TI2
        CALL    BITIN
        JC      TI2
```

Now continue reading the SID pin, incrementing the D register (back towards zero), each cycle until the next burst is received:

```
TI4     INR     D
        CALL    BITIN
        JNC     TI4
        CALL    BITIN
        JNC     TI4
```

Now, if the burst lasted longer than the space, D was not incremented all the way back to zero; it is still negative. If the space was longer, D was incremented up through zero; it is now positive. In other words, the sign bit of D will now correspond to the data bit that would lead to each of these results. Move the sign bit into the CY, then rotate it into register C:

```
        MOV     A,D
        RAL
        MOV     A,C
        RAR
        MOV     C,A
        MVI     D,00H
```

Continue until the last bit has been received:

```
        DCR     B
        JNZ     TI3
        RET
```

(Notice that the first half of this subroutine is incorporated in the second half. In fact, the assembled listing included in the Appendix makes use of this fact to eliminate 24 bytes of duplicated code.)

BITIN waits a short time in order to regulate the sampling rate, then reads SID and moves the data bit into the CY:

```
BITIN:  MVI     E,CKRATE    <7>
BI1:    DCR     E           <4>
        JNZ     BI1         <7/10>
        PIM                 <4>
        RAL                 <4>
        RET                 <10>
```

The tone burst frequency and duration, and the TAPEIN sampling rate are determined by HALFCYC, CYCNO, and CKRATE. Tables 10 and 11 give typical values.

Table 10

EXAMPLE COMBINATIONS OF HALFCYC AND CYCNO. ALL VALUES IN DECIMAL

APPROXIMATE TONE FREQUENCY	CORRESPONDING HALFCYC VALUE	RESULTING DATA RATE			
		8 4	20 10	100 50	CYCNO CYC/BURST
500 Hz	217	42	17	3.3	bps
1 kHz	108	83	33	6.6	bps
2 kHz	53	166	66	13	bps
5 kHz	20	414	166	33	bps
10 kHz	9	826	330	66	bps

Table 11

MAXIMUM SAMPLING RATES FOR VARIOUS VALUES OF CKRATE

CKRATE VALUE	SAMPLING RATE (INCLUDING CALL & RET)
1	17.6 μsec
20	104 μsec
80	378 μsec
250	1.14 msec

The CRT and Cassette Code also includes a simple block record routine utilizing TAPEO. Before calling BLKRCD, HL must be set to the start of the desired block, and the recorder turned on manually. Successive bytes will be recorded until the end of that page, i.e., until L is incremented to zero. The playback routine requires presetting HL to the target address and turning on the recorder before PLAYBK is called. These routines incorporate a long tone burst before each data block to allow a recorder with Automatic Gain Control to stabilize before the data starts.

ADDITIONAL COMMENTS

The two design examples given so far were built up using an SDK-85 System Design Kit. Both hardware interfaces were wire-wrapped on the ample breadboarding area provided on the board. The connections between SID and SOD and the onboard TTY interface were broken, so as not to affect the 8085 I/O electrical characteristics.

The CRT interface was tested with a Beehive Mini-Bee II Terminal in the full duplex mode at each of its 14 possible transmission rates, from 110 to 9600 baud. It was also checked out at 19200 baud using a Beehive B-100 terminal. In addition, the software was exercised using an SBC 80/20 system as a variable baud rate character generator and receiver.

An additional advantage to having software selectable communications rates is that it would be possible to communicate with several system peripherals, each at its own preferred rate, without having to duplicate hardware. For example, the addition of a single 7408 AND gate and an output port (such as on the 8155) would make it possible to use the same two RS-232 circuits to interface with up to seven I/O devices (see Figure 28). Three of the MC1488 drivers have Enable inputs which can be controlled by the output port. One AND gate can be used to buffer the SOD line and drive the MC1488 Data inputs. The rest of the 7408 can be configured as a four input AND gate. This would act as an inverted logic OR gate to reduce the four MC1489 receiver outputs to a single line, which could be read by the SID. This assumes that only one input device (CRT, PTR) at a time will be used (which is usually the case in a non-time shared, interactive application), and that the unused devices are transmitting a logic one level (which should also be the case).

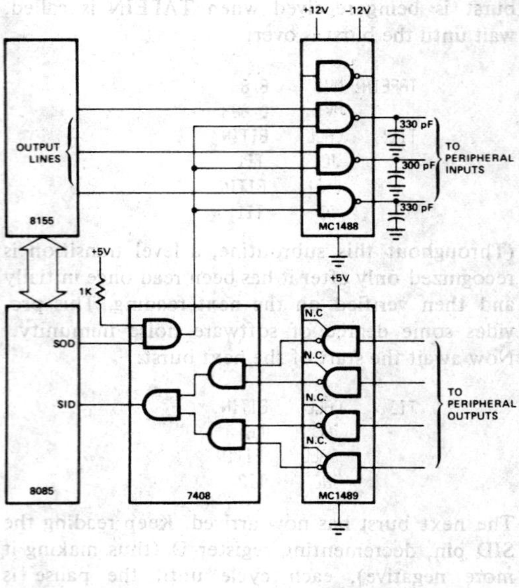

Figure 28. Interfacing 8085 to Multiple Peripherals

The software needed to support additional peripherals would be simple and straightforward. A routine intended to dump a section of memory to a paper tape punch, for example, would first have to store BITTIME and HALFBIT somewhere (perhaps on stack), load the variables with new parameters corresponding to the paper tape punch rate, and then write a bit pattern to the output port which would disable the console driver and enable the punch (and perhaps a typewriter). After the dump was over, the original time parameters and driver status would be restored.

As explained before, the BRID routine computed rate parameters based on the fact that an ASCII "space" character resulted in a zero level 6 bits long. Conceivably, some obscure peripherals might produce a transient between successive zero bits. (This might be the case, for example, if the signal was produced by mechanical rather than electronic means.) If so, the BRID algorithm used here probably would not work reliably. Once the two time parameters were identified, though, COUT and CIN could still be used. An alternate algorithm for baud rate identification would require a table in ROM (note the fifth and final R/S-I/O-M/D permutation). This table would contain a list of delay parameters corresponding to the standard transmission rates, as computed for the selected crystal frequency. Initialization would require the operator to hit a specific key several times (usually the "U" key, which generates a pattern of alternating ones and zeros). The identification routine would attempt to "read" this pattern at each baud rate, in turn, until finding the rate at which the read was successful.

The cassette recorder used to develop the tape interface was a Lloyd's push-button model which cost $17 in 1972. Empirical testing has indicated that for this application, the quality of the cassette recorder is less critical than the quality of the tape itself. In other words, some 33¢ cassettes were not very reliable, even when used with more expensive recorders.

When using a cassette at the beginning of a side, allow the tape to run for about 10 seconds until the leader has passed before starting to write data. Otherwise, data will be lost to the leader.

Depending on the recorder quality, the tone burst frequency and duration can be optimized for higher data rates by modifying HALFCYC and CYCNO. If so, CKRATE should also be reduced, so that between about 10 and 80 data samplings are made during a single (one-third width) tone burst. At greatly increased frequencies, some of the components in the analog interface might also be modified.

The two simple routines for recording and playing back blocks of data were intended to illustrate one way of using TAPEIN and TAPEO, and therefore do not contain any provisions for error detection or correction. Depending on the nature of a particular application, these routines could be augmented with parity bit or checksum comparison, or an error correcting code technique.

Funny things happen when recording and playing back a page of RAM which includes the subroutine stack. Eventually, PLAYBK will start writing over the data at the top of the stack, destroying the subroutine traceback sequence. The next RET instruction will then cause a jump to a place where you'd rather not be.

The printout reproduced in the CRT Code includes the assembled listings for the CRT and magnetic tape interfaces discussed in this application note. The object code produced was programmed into an 8755 EPROM, which was installed in the expansion PROM socket of the SDK-85 board. Some very minor differences exist between this listing and the code segments presented earlier, which were written for maximum clarity.

Temperature Sensor Code

```
ASM80 :F1:TEST.SRC MOD85

ISIS-II 8080/8085 MACRO ASSEMBLER, V2.0        MODULE  PAGE   1

LOC  OBJ          SOURCE STATEMENT

                  ;
                  ;
026C              HXDSP   EQU   026CH          ;EXPAND HEX TO DISPLAY, SDK MONITOR ROUTINE
02B7              OUTPUT  EQU   02B7H          ;OUTPUT TO DISPLAY, SDK MONITOR ROUTINE
05F1              DELAY   EQU   05F1H          ;DELAY DISPLAY, SDK MONITOR ROUTINE
                  ;
2000              ORG     2000H
                  ;
                  ;
                  ;
                  ;
2000 31C820               LXI   SP,20C8H       ;INITIALIZE STACKPOINTER
2003 F3                   DI                   ;DISABLE INTERRUPTS
                  ;
                  ;  INITIALIZE COUNTER IN 8155 FOR COUNTDOWN MODE. LOAD COUNTER
                  ;  WITH HIGHEST VALUE (3FFF).
                  ;
2004 3EBF                 MVI   A,0BFH
2006 D325                 OUT   25H            ;ADDRESS FOR TOP HALF OF COUNTER
2008 3EFF                 MVI   A,0FFH
200A D324                 OUT   24H            ;  "   "  LOWER HALF OF COUNTER
200C 3EC0                 MVI   A,0C0H
200E D320                 OUT   20H            ;COUNT DOWN MODE START
                  ;
                  ;  PULSE THE ONE SHOT WITH A POSITIVE GOING PULSE ON THE SOD
                  ;  OUTPUT PIN OF THE 8085.
                  ;
2010 3EC8                 MVI   A,0C8H
2012 30                   SIM                  ;OUTPUT A HIGH ON SOD LINE
2013 3E48                 MVI   A,48H
2015 30                   SIM                  ;OUTPUT A LOW ON SOD LINE
2016 FB                   EI                   ;ENABLE INTERRUPTS(AFTER PULSE)
                  ;
                  ;  IDLE UNTIL ONESHOT INTERRUPTS THE RST 6.5 PIN ON THE 8085.
                  ;
2017 00           NPO     NOP
2018 C31720               JMP   NPO            ;IDLE UNTIL INTERRUPT
                  ;
                  ;  AFTER INTERRUPT, STOP COUNTER AND READ IN FINAL COUNT FROM
                  ;  8155. STORE IN REGISTER PAIR BC.
                  ;
201B 3E40         CNTU    MVI   A,40H
201D D320                 OUT   20H            ;STOP COUNTER
201F DB24                 IN    24H
2021 4F                   MOV   C,A            ;STORE LOWER ORDER BYTE IN C
2022 DB25                 IN    25H
2024 47                   MOV   B,A            ;STORE HIGHER ORDER BYTE IN B
2025 263F                 MVI   H,3FH          ;LOAD HL WITH FULL START COUNT
2027 2EFF                 MVI   L,0FFH
                  ;
                  ;  ADJUST THE COUNT VALUE IN REGISTER BC TO REPRESENT ACTUAL
                  ;  COUNT  (SEE TEXT FOR EXPLANATION)
```

Temperature Sensor Code (Cont'd)

```
ISIS-II 8080/8085 MACRO ASSEMBLER, V2.0        MODULE   PAGE   2

LOC  OBJ         SEQ        SOURCE STATEMENT

                       ;
2029 CD6820                 CALL    ADJUST          ;CONVERTS 8155 COUNT TO ACTUAL COUNT
                       ;
                       ;  SETUP INITIALIZATION FOR SEARCH ROUTINE. ROUTINE LOOKS FOR TEMPERATURE
                       ;  RANGE OF COUNT (SEE TEXT). SEARCH ONLY FOR UPPER HALF TO SIMPLIFY CODE.
                       ;
202C 2E80                   MVI     L,80H           ;SET HL TO BEGINNING OF SEARCH
202E 2620                   MVI     H,20H           ;STRING IN MEMORY.
2030 B0                     ORA     B               ;CLEAR CARRY FOR ROUTINE.
2031 78                     MOV     A,B             ;PLACE B INTO ACCUMULATOR
2032 0E01                   MVI     C,1H            ;SET TIMES THROUGH SEARCH
2034 CD9220                 CALL    SEARCH          ;LOOKS FOR TEMP RANGE COUNT IS IN
                       ;
                       ;  CHECK IF SEARCH WAS SUCCESSFUL. IF NOT THEN OUTSIDE ACCEPTABLE
                       ;  RANGE.
                       ;
2037 3E80                   MVI     A,80H           ;DID L FIND LESS THAN AT
2039 AD                     XRA     L               ;AT BEGINNING OF STRING?
203A CAAF20                 JZ      TLOW            ;TEMP BELOW ALLOWED LIMITS, SET PORT A
203D 3E00                   MVI     A,00H           ;DID C GET DECREMENTED?
203F B9                     CMP     C               ;IF SO,SEARCH DID NOT FIND
2040 CAB820                 JZ      THIGH           ;TEMP ABOVE LIMITS, SET PORT B
                       ;
                       ;  SOFTWARE MAP THE MATCH TO A TEMPERATURE IN DEGREES C BY ADDING
                       ;  10 TO SEARCH ADDRESS. PLACE TEMPERATURE IN REGISTER E.
                       ;
2043 3E0A                   MVI     A,0AH           ;SHIFT HL BY 10 (SOFTWARE MAP)
2045 85                     ADD     L
2046 6F                     MOV     L,A
2047 5E                     MOV     E,M             ;READ IN TEMPERATURE
                       ;
                       ;  SET UP INITIALIZATION FOR DISPLAYING TEMPERATURE USING SDK
                       ;  MONITOR ROUTINES. FIRST EXPAND DE REGISTER AND THEN DISPLAY
                       ;  FOR DELAY PERIOD.
                       ;
2048 0600                   MVI     B,00H           ;CLEAR DOT AT ADDRESS FIELD
204A CD6C02                 CALL    HXDSP           ;CALL EXPAND
204D 3E00                   MVI     A,00H
204F CDB702                 CALL    OUTPUT          ;OUTPUT TO SDK DISPLAY
2052 11FF00                 LXI     D,0FFH          ;SET DELAY PERIOD
2055 CDF105                 CALL    DELAY           ;DISPLAY FOR DELAY PERIOD
2058 CF                     RST     1               ;SOFTWARE RESTART
                       ;
                       ;  SUBROUTINES
                       ;
20AF                      ORG   20AFH
                       ;
                       ;
20AF 3E03                 TLOW  MVI     A,03H
20B1 D320                   OUT     20H
20B3 3EFF                   MVI     A,0FFH          ;SET PORT A AS 1'S
20B5 D321                   OUT     21H
20B7 CF                     RST     1
                       ;
                       ;
```

Temperature Sensor Code (Cont'd)

```
ISIS-II 8080/8085 MACRO ASSEMBLER, V2.0        MODULE   PAGE    3

LOC  OBJ         SEQ         SOURCE STATEMENT

20B8 3E03            THIGH:  MVI     A,03H
20BA D320                    OUT     20H
20BC 3EFF                    MVI     A,0FFH          ;SET PORT B AS 1'S
20BE D322                    OUT     22H
20C0 CF                      RST     1
                     ;
                     ;
2092                 ORG     2092H
                     ;
                     ;
2092 BE              SEARCH: CMP     M
2093 D8                      RC
2094 23                      INX     H               ;ELSE INCREMENT POINTER
2095 BE                      CMP     M               ;COMPARE 2ND BYTE
2096 D8                      RC
2097 23                      INX     H
2098 BE                      CMP     M               ;COMPARE 3RD BYTE
2099 D8                      RC
209A 23                      INX     H
209B BE                      CMP     M               ;COMPARE 4TH BYTE
209C D8                      RC
209D 23                      INX     H
209E BE                      CMP     M               ;COMPARE 5TH BYTE
209F D8                      RC
20A0 23                      INX     H
20A1 BE                      CMP     M               ;COMPARE 6TH BYTE
20A2 D8                      RC
20A3 23                      INX     H
20A4 BE                      CMP     M               ;COMPARE 7TH BYTE
20A5 D8                      RC
20A6 23                      INX     H
20A7 BE                      CMP     M               ;COMPARE 8TH BYTE
20A8 D8                      RC
20A9 23                      INX     H
20AA 0D                      DCR     C               ;HAS ENTIRE BLOCK BEEN
20AB C29220                  JNZ     SEARCH          ;SEARCHED? IF SO SET NO
20AE C9                      RET                     ;LESS THAN AND RETURN.
                     ;
                     ;  RESTART 6.5 JUMP ADDRESS
                     ;
20CE                 ORG     20CEH
                     ;
                     ;
20CE C31B20                  JMP     CNTU
                     ;
                     ;
                     ;
                     ;
                     ;
                     ;
                     ;  SEARCH COMPARE DATA STRING (SEE TEXT)
                     ;
                     ;
2080                 ORG     2080H
                     ;
```

Temperature Sensor Code (Cont'd)

```
ISIS-II 8080/8085 MACRO ASSEMBLER, V2.0        MODULE   PAGE   4

 LOC  OBJ          SOURCE STATEMENT

                   ;
2080 35                     DB      35H,36H,37H,38H,39H,3AH,3BH,3CH
2081 36
2082 37
2083 38
2084 39
2085 3A
2086 3B
2087 3C
                   ;
                   ;  SOFTWARE MAP TO TEMPERATURE
                   ;
208B               ORG      208BH
                   ;
                   ;
208B 21                     DB      21H,23H,25H,28H,31H,35H,39H
208C 23
208D 25
208E 28
208F 31
2090 35
2091 39
                   ;
                   ;
2060               ORG      2060H
                   ;
                   ;
                   ;  SUBROUTINE ADJUST FOR COUNT IN 8155
                   ;
2060 78            ADJUST: MOV     A,B          ;LOAD ACCUMULATOR WITH UPPER HALF
2061 E63F                  ANI     3FH          ;RESET UPPER TWO BITS,CLEAR CARRY
2063 1F                    RAR                  ;ROTATE RIGHT THROUGH CARRY
2064 47                    MOV     B,A          ;STORE SHIFTED VALUE BACK IN B
2065 79                    MOV     A,C          ;LOAD ACCUMULATOR WITH LOWER HALF
2066 1F                    RAR                  ;ROTATE WITH CARRY RIGHT
2067 4F                    MOV     C,A          ;STORE SHIFTED VALUE IN C
2068 D0                    RNC                  ;1ST HALF OR SECOND? IF SECOND RETURN
2069 3F                    CMC                  ;CLEAR CARRY
206A 7C                    MOV     A,H          ;OBTAIN ONE HALF OF FULL COUNT
206B 1F                    RAR                  ;IF HL IS ODD THIS CONTAINS
206C 67                    MOV     H,A          ;ONE HALF(FULL COUNT-1), WHICH
206D 7D                    MOV     A,L          ;IS CORRECT
206E 1F                    RAR
206F 6F                    MOV     L,A
2070 09                    DAD     B            ;DOUBLE PRECISION ADD
2071 44                    MOV     B,H          ;RESTORE BC REGISTERS WITH COUNT
2072 4D                    MOV     C,L
2073 C9                    RET
                   ;
                   ;
                           END

PUBLIC SYMBOLS


EXTERNAL SYMBOLS


USER SYMBOLS



ISIS-II 8080/8085 MACRO ASSEMBLER, V2.0        MODULE   PAGE   5

ADJUST A 2060   CNTU   A 201B   DELAY  A 05F1   HXDSP  A 026C   NPO    A 2017   OUTPUT A 02B7   SEARCH A 2092
THIGH  A 20B8   TLOW   A 20AF

ASSEMBLY COMPLETE,  NO ERRORS
```

CRT and Cassette Code

```
ISIS-II 8080/8085 ASSEMBLER, V1 0       MODULE                PAGE    1

 LOC  OBJ         SEQ          SOURCE STATEMENT

                     0 $   MOD85 TITLE('8085 SERIAL I/O NOTE APPENDIX')
```

CRT and Cassette Code (Cont'd)

```
ISIS-II 8080/8085 ASSEMBLER, V1.0        MODULE                    PAGE    2
8085 SERIAL I/O NOTE APPENDIX

 LOC  OBJ         SOURCE STATEMENT

                 ;      THE FOLLOWING PROGRAMS AND SUBROUTINES ARE DESCRIBED IN DETAIL
                 ;      IN INTEL CORPERATION'S APPLICATION NOTE AP-29, "USING THE 8085
                 ;      SERIAL I/O LINES".  THE FIRST SECTION IS A GENERAL PURPOSE CRT
                 ;      INTERFACE WITH AUTOMATIC BAUD RATE IDENTIFICATION; THE SECOND
                 ;      SECTION IS A MAGNETIC TAPE INTERFACE FOR STORING DATA ON CASSETTE
                 ;      TAPES.  THE CODE PRESENTED HERE IS ORIGINED AT LOCATION 800H,
                 ;      AND MIGHT BE PART OF AN EXPANSION PROM IN AN INTEL SDK-85
                 ;      SYSTEM DESIGN KIT.
                 ;
20C8             BITTIME EQU     20C8H   ;ADDRESS OF STORAGE FOR COMPUTED BIT DELAY
20CA             HALFBIT EQU     20CAH   ;ADDRESS OF STORAGE  FOR HALF BIT DELAY
000B             BITSO   EQU     11      ;DATA BITS PUT OUT (INCLUDING TWO STOP BITS)
0009             BITSI   EQU     9       ;DATA BITS TO BE RECIEVED (INCLUDING ONE STOP BIT)

0800                     ORG     800H    ;STARTING ADDRESS OF SDK-85 EXPANSION PROM

                 ;CRTTST CRT INTERFACE TEST.  WHEN CALLED, AWAITS THE SPACE BAR BEING PRESSED ON
                 ;       THE SYSTEM CONSOLE, AND THEN RESPONDS WITH A DATA RATE VERIFICATION
                 ;       MESSAGE.  THERE AFTER, CHARACTERS TYPED ON THE KEYBOARD ARE ECHOED
                 ;       ON THE DISPLAY TUBE.  WHEN A BREAK KEY IS TYPED, THE ROUTINE IS
                 ;       RE-STARTED, ALLOWING A DIFFERENT BAUD RATE TO BE SELECTED ON THE CRT.
0800 31C020      CRTTST: LXI     SP,20C0H
0803 3EC0        CRT1:   MVI     A,0C0H  ;SOD MUST BE HIGH BETWEEN CHARACTERS
0805 30                  SIM
0806 CD1A08              CALL    BRID    ;IDENTIFY DATA RATE USED BY TERMINAL
0809 CD4708              CALL    SIGNON  ;OUTPUT SIGNON MESSAGE AT RATE DETECTED
080C CD8A08      ECHO:   CALL    CIN     ;READ NEXT KEYSTROKE INTO REGISTER C
080F 79                  MOV     A,C
0810 B7                  ORA     A       ;CHECK IF CHARACTER WAS A <BREAK> (ASCII 00H)
0811 CA0308              JZ      CRT1    ;IF SO, RE-IDENTIFY DATA RATE
                                         ;THIS ALLOWS ANOTHER RATE TO BE SELECTED ON CRT
0814 CD6908              CALL    COUT    ;OTHERWISE COPY REGISTER C TO THE SCREEN
0817 C30C08              JMP     ECHO    ;CONTINUE INDEFINITELY (UNTIL BREAK)

                 ;BRID   BAUD RATE IDENTIFICATION SUBROUTINE
                 ;       EXPECTS A <CR> (ASCII 20H) TO BE RECIEVED FROM THE CONSOLE.
                 ;       THE LENGTH OF THE INITIAL ZERO LEVEL (SIX BITS WIDE) IS MEASURED
                 ;       IN ORDER TO DETERMINE THE DATA RATE FOR FUTURE COMMUNICATIONS.
081A 20          BRID:   RIM             ;VERIFY THAT THE "ONE" LEVEL HAS BEEN ESTABLISHED
081B B7                  ORA     A       ;\ AS THE CRT IS POWERING UP
081C F21A08              JP      BRID
081F 20          BRI1:   RIM             ;MONITOR SID LINE STATUS
0820 B7                  ORA     A
0821 FA1F08              JM      BRI1    ;LOOP UNTIL START BIT IS RECIEVED
0824 21FAFF              LXI     H,-6    ;BIAS COUNTER USED IN DETERMINING ZERO DURATION
0827 1E04        BRI3:   MVI     E,04H
0829 1D          BRI4:   DCR     E       ;53 MACHINE CYCLE DELAY LOOP
082A C22908              JNZ     BRI4
082D 23                  INX     H       ;INCREMENT COUNTER EVERY 84 CYCLES WHILE SID IS LOW
082E 20                  RIM
```

CRT and Cassette Code (Cont'd)

```
ISIS-II 8080/8085 ASSEMBLER, V1.0      MODULE        PAGE    3
8085 SERIAL I/O NOTE APPENDIX

 LOC  OBJ         SEQ        SOURCE STATEMENT

 082F B7                     ORA     A
 0830 F22708                 JP      BRI3
                             ;(HL) NOW CORRESPONDS TO INCOMING DATA RATE
 0833 E5                     PUSH    H       ;SAVE COUNT FOR HALFBIT TIME COMPUTATION
 0834 24                     INR     H       ;BITTIME IS DETERMINED BY INCREMENTING
 0835 2C                     INR     L       ;\ H AND L INDIVIDUALLY
 0836 220820                 SHLD    BITTIME
 0839 E1                     POP     H       ;RESTORE COUNT FOR HALFBIT DETERMINATION
 083A B7                     ORA     A       ;CLEAR CARRY
 083B 7C                     MOV     A,H     ;ROTATE RIGHT EXTENDED (HL)
 083C 1F                     RAR             ;\ TO DIVIDE COUNT BY 2
 083D 67                     MOV     H,A
 083E 7D                     MOV     A,L
 083F 1F                     RAR
 0840 6F                     MOV     L,A
 0841 24                     INR     H       ;PUT H AND L IN PROPER FORMAT FOR DELAY
 0842 2C                     INR     L       ;\ SEGMENTS (INCREMENT EACH)
 0843 220A20                 SHLD    HALFBIT ;SAVE AS HALF-BIT TIME DELAY PARAMETER
 0846 C9                     RET
                     ;
                     ;  SIGNON WRITES A SIGN-ON MESSAGE TO THE CRT AT WHAT SHOULD BE THE CORRECT RATE.
                     ;  IF THE MESSAGE IS UNINTELLIGIBLE. . . . WELL, SO IT GOES.
 0847 215508          SIGNON: LXI    H,STRNG ;LOAD START OF SIGN-ON MESSAGE
 084A 4E              S1:     MOV    C,M     ;GET NEXT CHARACTER
 084B AF                      XRA    A       ;CLEAR ACCUMULATOR
 084C B1                      ORA    C       ;CHECK IF CHARACTER IS END OF STRING
 084D C8                      RZ             ;RETURN IF SIGN-ON COMPLETE
 084E CD6908                  CALL   COUT    ;ELSE OUTPUT CHARACTER TO CRT
 0851 23                      INX    H       ;INDEX POINTER
 0852 C34A08                  JMP    S1      ;ECHO NEXT CHARACTER
                     ;
 0855 0D              STRNG:  DB     0DH,0AH ;<CR><LF>
 0856 0A
 0857 42415544                DB     'BAUD RATE CHECK'
 085B 20524154
 085F 45204348
 0863 45434B
 0866 0D                      DB     0DH,0AH ;<CR><LF>
 0867 0A
 0868 00                      DB     00H     ;END-OF-STRING ESCAPE CODE
                     ;
                     ;  COUT  CONSOLE OUTPUT SUBROUTINE
                     ;        WRITES THE CONTENTS OF THE C REGISTER TO THE CRT DISPLAY SCREEN
 0869 F3              COUT    DI
 086A C5                      PUSH   B
 086B E5                      PUSH   H
 086C 060B                    MVI    B,BITSO ;SET NUMBER OF BITS TO BE TRANSMITTED
 086E AF                      XRA    A       ;CLEAR CARRY
 086F 3E80            CO1:    MVI    A,80H   ;SET WHAT WILL BECOME SOD ENABLE BIT
 0871 1F                      RAR            ;MOVE CARRY INTO SOD DATA BIT OF ACC
 0872 30                      SIM            ;OUTPUT DATA BIT TO SOD
 0873 2A0820                  LHLD   BITTIME
 0876 2D              CO2:    DCR    L       ;WAIT UNTIL APPROPRIATE TIME HAS PASSED
```

CRT and Cassette Code (Cont'd)

```
ISIS-II 8080/8085 ASSEMBLER, V1.0        MODULE                  PAGE    4
8085 SERIAL I/O NOTE APPENDIX

LOC  OBJ              SOURCE STATEMENT

0877 C27608                JNZ    CO2
087A 25                    DCR    H
087B C27608                JNZ    CO2
087E 37                    STC               ;SET WHAT WILL EVENTUALLY BECOME A STOP BIT
087F 79                    MOV    A,C        ;ROTATE CHARACTER RIGHT ONE BIT,
0880 1F                    RAR               ;\ MOVING NEXT DATA BIT INTO CARRY
0881 4F                    MOV    C,A
0882 05                    DCR    B          ;CHECK IF CHARACTER (AND STOP BIT(S)) DONE
0883 C26F08                JNZ    CO1        ;IF NOT, OUTPUT CURRENT CARRY
0886 E1                    POP    H          ;RESTORE STATUS AND RETURN
0887 C1                    POP    B
0888 FB                    EI
0889 C9                    RET

                  ;CIN    CONSOL INPUT SUBROUTINE WAITS FOR A KEYSTROKE AND
                  ;       RETURNS WITH 8 BITS IN REG C.
088A F3           CIN:     DI
088B E5                    PUSH   H
088C 0609                  MVI    B,BITSI    ;DATA BITS TO BE READ (LAST RETURNED IN CY)
088E 20           CI1:     RIM               ;WAIT FOR SYNC BIT TRANSITION
088F B7                    ORA    A
0890 FA8E08                JM     CI1
0893 2ACA20                LHLD   HALFBIT
0896 2D           CI2:     DCR    L          ;WAIT UNTIL MIDDLE OF START BIT
0897 C29608                JNZ    CI2
089A 25                    DCR    H
089B C29608                JNZ    CI2
089E 2AC820       CI3:     LHLD   BITTIME    ;WAIT OUT BIT TIME
08A1 2D           CI4:     DCR    L
08A2 C2A108                JNZ    CI4
08A5 25                    DCR    H
08A6 C2A108                JNZ    CI4
08A9 20                    RIM               ;CHECK SID LINE LEVEL
08AA 17                    RAL               ;DATA BIT IN CY
08AB 05                    DCR    B          ;DETERMINE IF THIS IS FIRST STOP BIT
08AC CAB608                JZ     CI5        ;IF SO, JUMP OUT OF LOOP
08AF 79                    MOV    A,C        ;ELSE ROTATE INTO PARTIAL CHARACTER IN C
08B0 1F                    RAR               ;ACC HOLDS UPDATED CHARACTER
08B1 4F                    MOV    C,A
08B2 00                    NOP               ;EQUALIZES COUT AND CIN LOOP TIMES
08B3 C39E08                JMP    CI3
08B6 E1           CI5:     POP    H
08B7 FB                    EI
08B8 C9                    RET               ;CHARACTER COMPLETE

                  ;**********************************************************************

                  ;       THE FOLLOWING CODE IS USED BY THE CASSETTE INTERFACE.
                  ;       SUBROUTINES TAPEO AND TAPEIN ARE USED RESPECTIVELY
                  ;       TO OUTPUT OR RECEIVE AN EIGHT BIT BYTE OF DATA.  REGISTER C
                  ;       HOLDS THE DATA IN EITHER CASE.  REGISTERS A,B,&C ARE ALL DESTROYED.
0010              CYCNO    EQU    16         ;TWICE THE NUMBER OF CYCLES PER TONE BURST
001E              HALFCYC  EQU    30         ;DETERMINES TONE FREQUENCY
```

CRT and Cassette Code (Cont'd)

```
ISIS-II 8080/8085 ASSEMBLER, V1.0      MODULE                     PAGE    5
8085 SERIAL I/O NOTE APPENDIX

 LOC  OBJ           SOURCE STATEMENT

0016           CKRATE  EQU    22      ;SETS SAMPLE RATE
00FA           LEADER  EQU    250     ;NUMBER OF SUCCESIVE TONE BURSTS COMPRISING LEADER
00FA           LDRCHK  EQU    250     ;USED IN PLAYBK TO VERIFY PRESENCE OF LEADER

               ;BLKRCD                OUTPUTS A VERY LONG TONE BURST (<LEADER> TIMES
               ;                      THE NORMAL BURST DURATION) TO ALLOW RECORDER ELECTRONICS
               ;                      AND AGC TO STABILIZE.  THEN OUTPUTS THE REMAINDER OF THE
               ;                      256 BYTE PAGE POINTED TO BY <H>, STARTING AT BYTE <L>.
08B9 0EFA      BLKRCD: MVI    C,LEADER;SET UP LEADER BURST LENGTH
08BB 3EC0              MVI    A,0C0H  ;SET ACCUMULATOR TO RESULT IN TONE BURST
08BD CDF008    BR1:    CALL   BURST   ;OUTPUT TONE
08C0 0D                DCR    C
08C1 C2BD08            JNZ    BR1     ;SUSTAIN LEADER TONE
08C4 AF                XRA    A       ;CLEAR ACCUMULATOR & OUTPUT SPACE, SO THAT
08C5 CDF008            CALL   BURST   ;\ START OF FIRST DATA BYTE CAN BE DETECTED
08C8 4E        BR2:    MOV    C,M     ;GET DATA BYTE TO BE RECORDED
08C9 CDD108            CALL   TAPEO   ;OUTPUT REGISTER C TO RECORDER
08CC 2C                INR    L       ;POINT TO NEXT BYTE
08CD C2C808            JNZ    BR2
08D0 C9                RET            ;AFTER BLOCK IS COMPLETE


               ;TAPEO                 OUTPUTS THE BYTE IN REGISTER C TO THE RECORDER.
               ;                      REGISTERS A,B,C,D,&E ARE ALL USED.
08D1 F3        TAPEO:  DI
08D2 D5                PUSH   D       ;D&E USED AS COUNTERS BY SUBROUTINE BURST
08D3 0609              MVI    B,9     ;WILL RESULT IN 8 DATA BITS AND ONE STOP BIT
08D5 AF        TO1:    XRA    A       ;CLEAR ACCUMULATOR
08D6 3EC0              MVI    A,0C0H  ;SET ACCUMULATOR TO CAUSE A TONE BURST
08D8 CDF008            CALL   BURST
08DB 79                MOV    A,C     ;MOVE NEXT DATA BIT INTO THE CARRY
08DC 1F                RAR
08DD 4F                MOV    C,A     ;CARRY WILL BECOME SOD ENABLE IN BURST ROUTINE
08DE 3E01              MVI    A,01H   ;SET BIT TO BE REPEATEDLY COMPLEMENTED IN BURST
08E0 1F                RAR
08E1 1F                RAR
08E2 CDF008            CALL   BURST   ;OUTPUT EITHER A TONE OR A PAUSE
08E5 AF                XRA    A       ;CLEAR ACCUMULATOR
08E6 CDF008            CALL   BURST   ;OUTPUT PAUSE
08E9 05                DCR    B
08EA C2D508            JNZ    TO1     ;REPEAT UNTIL BYTE FINISHED
08ED D1                POP    D       ;RESTORE STATUS AND RETURN
08EE FB                EI
08EF C9                RET

08F0 1610      BURST:  MVI    D,CYCNO ;SET NUMBER OF CYCLES
08F2 30        BU1:    SIM            ;COMPLEMENT SOD LINE IF SOD ENABLE BIT SET
08F3 1E1E              MVI    E,HALFCYC
08F5 1D        BU2:    DCR    E       ;REGULATE TONE FREQUENCY
08F6 C2F508            JNZ    BU2
08F9 EE80              XRI    80H     ;COMPLEMENT SOD DATA BIT IN ACCUMULATOR
08FB 15                DCR    D
08FC C2F208            JNZ    BU1     ;CONTINUE UNTIL BURST (OR EQUIVILENT PAUSE) FINISHED
```

CRT and Cassette Code (Cont'd)

```
ISIS-II 8080/8085 ASSEMBLER, V1.0       MODULE                  PAGE    6
8085 SERIAL I/O NOTE APPENDIX

  LOC  OBJ          SOURCE STATEMENT

 08FF C9                   RET

                ;PLAYBK         WAITS FOR THE LONG LEADER BURST TO ARRIVE, THEN CONTINUES
                ;               READING BYTES FROM THE RECORDER AND STORING THEM
                ;               IN MEMORY STARTING AT LOCATION <HL>.
                ;          CONTINUES UNTIL THE END OF THE CURRENT PAGE (<L>=0FFH) IS REACHED.
 0900 0EFA      PLAYBK:    MVI      C,LDRCHK   ;<LDRCHK> SUCCESSIVE HIGHS MUST BE READ
 0902 CD3D09    PB1:       CALL     BITIN      ; \ TO VERIFY THAT THE LEADER IS PRESENT
 0905 D20009               JNC      PLAYBK     ; \ AND ELECTRONICS HAS STABILIZED
 0908 0D                   DCR      C
 0909 C20209               JNZ      PB1
 090C CD1509    PB2:       CALL     TAPEIN     ;GET DATA BYTE FROM RECORDER
 090F 71                   MOV      M,C        ;STORE IN MEMORY
 0910 2C                   INR      L          ;INCREMENT POINTER
 0911 C20C09               JNZ      PB2        ;REPEAT FOR REST OF CURRENT PAGE
 0914 C9                   RET

                ;TAPEIN CASSETTE TAPE INPUT SUBROUTINE.   READS ONE BYTE OF DATA
                ;          FROM THE RECORDER INTERFACE AND RETURNS WITH THE BYTE IN REGISTER C.
 0915 0609      TAPEIN:    MVI      B,9        ;READ EIGHT DATA BITS
 0917 1600      TI1:       MVI      D,00H      ;CLEAR UP/DOWN COUNTER
 0919 15        TI2:       DCR      D          ;DECREMENT COUNTER EACH TIME ONE LEVEL IS READ
 091A CD3D09               CALL     BITIN
 091D DA1909               JC       TI2        ;REPEAT IF STILL AT ONE LEVEL
 0920 CD3D09               CALL     BITIN
 0923 DA1909               JC       TI2
 0926 14        TI3:       INR      D          ;INCREMENT COUNTER EACH TIME ZERO IS READ
 0927 CD3D09               CALL     BITIN
 092A D22609               JNC      TI3        ;REPEAT EACH TIME ZERO IS READ
 092D CD3D09               CALL     BITIN
 0930 D22609               JNC      TI3
 0933 7A                   MOV      A,D
 0934 17                   RAL                 ;MOVE COUNTER MOST SIGNIFICANT BIT INTO CARRY
 0935 79                   MOV      A,C
 0936 1F                   RAR                 ;MOVE DATA BIT RECIEVED (CY) INTO BYTE REGISTER
 0937 4F                   MOV      C,A
 0938 05                   DCR      B
 0939 C21709               JNZ      TI1        ;REPEAT UNTIL FULL BYTE ASSEMBLED
 093C C9                   RET

 093D 1E16      BITIN:     MVI      E,CKRATE
 093F 1D        BI1:       DCR      E
 0940 C23F09               JNZ      BI1        ;LIMIT INPUT SAMPLING RATE
 0943 20                   RIM                 ;SAMPLE SID LINE
 0944 17                   RAL                 ;MOVE DATA INTO CY BIT
 0945 C9                   RET

                           END

PUBLIC SYMBOLS
```

CRT and Cassette Code (Cont'd)

```
ISIS-II 8080/8085 ASSEMBLER, V1.0        MODULE                    PAGE    7
8085 SERIAL I/O NOTE APPENDIX


EXTERNAL SYMBOLS


USER SYMBOLS
BI1    A 093F   BITIN  A 093D   BITSI  A 0009   BITSO  A 000B   BITTIM A 20C8   BLKRCD A 08B9   BR1    A 08BD
BR2    A 08C9   BRI1   A 091F   BRI3   A 0927   BRI4   A 0929   BRID   A 081A   BU1    A 08F2   BU2    A 08F5
BURST  A 08F0   CI1    A 088E   CI2    A 0896   CI3    A 089E   CI4    A 08A1   CI5    A 08B6   CIN    A 088A
CKRATE A 0016   CO1    A 086F   CO2    A 0876   COUT   A 0869   CRT1   A 0803   CRTTST A 0800   CYCNO  A 0010
ECHO   A 080C   HALFBI A 20CA   HALFCY A 001E   LDRCHK A 00FA   LEADER A 00FA   PB1    A 0902   PB2    A 090C
PLAYBK A 0900   S1     A 084A   SIGNON A 0847   STRNG  A 0855   TAPEIN A 0915   TAPEO  A 08D1   TI1    A 0917
TI2    A 0919   TI3    A 0926   TO1    A 08D5

ASSEMBLY COMPLETE, NO ERROR(S)
```

CRT and Cassette Code (Cont'd)

```
ISIS-II ASSEMBLER SYMBOL CROSS REFERENCE V1.0                     PAGE   1

BI1      249#   250
BITIN    215    230    222    235    227    248#
BITSI     16#   120
BITSO     15#    95
BITTIM    13#    60    100    129
BLKRCD   163#
BR1      165#   167
BR2      170#   173
BRI1      45#    47
BRI3      49#    55
BRI4      50#    51
BRID      28     42#    44
BU1      201#   207
BU2      203#   204
BURST    165    169    184    191    193    200#
CI1      121#   123
CI2      125#   126    128
CI3      129#   142
CI4      130#   131    133
CI5      137    143#
CIN       30    118#
CKRATE   155#   248
CO1       97#   110
CO2      101#   102    104
COUT      25     81     92#
CRT1      26#    33
CRTTST    25#
CYCNO    153#   200
ECHO      30#    36
HALFBI    14#    71    124
HALFCY   154#   202
LDRCHK   157#   214
LEADER   156#   163
PB1      215#   218
PB2      219#   222
PLAYBK   214#   216
S1        77#    83
SIGNON    29     76#
STRNG     76     85#
TAPEIN   219    227#
TAPEO    171    179#
TI1      228#   245
TI2      229#   231    233
TI3      234#   236    238
TO1      182#   195

CROSS REFEPENCE COMPLETE
```

DOMESTIC SALES OFFICES

ALABAMA

Intel Corp.
5015 Bradford Drive
Suite 2
Huntsville 35805
Tel: (205) 830-4010

ARIZONA

Intel Corp.
11225 N. 28th Drive
Suite 214D
Phoenix 85029
Tel: (602) 869-4980

Intel Corp.
1161 N. El Dorado Place
Suite 301
Tucson 85715
Tel: (602) 299-6815

CALIFORNIA

Intel Corp.
21515 Vanowen Street
Suite 116
Canoga Park 91303
Tel: (818) 704-8500

Intel Corp.
2250 E. Imperial Highway
Suite 218
El Segundo 90245
Tel: (213) 640-6040

Intel Corp.
1510 Arden Way, Suite 101
Sacramento 95815
Tel: (916) 920-8096

Intel Corp.
4350 Executive Drive
Suite 105
San Diego 92121
(619) 452-5880

Intel Corp.*
2000 East 4th Street
Suite 100
Santa Ana 92705
Tel: (714) 835-9642
TWX: 910-595-1114

Intel Corp.*
San Thomas 4
2700 San Thomas Expressway
Santa Clara, CA 95051
Tel: (408) 986-8086
910-338-0255

COLORADO

Intel Corp.
3300 Mitchell Lane, Suite 210
Boulder 80301
Tel: (303) 442-8088

Intel Corp.
4445 Northpark Drive
Suite 100
Colorado Springs 80907
Tel: (303) 594-6622

Intel Corp.*
650 S. Cherry Street
Suite 915
Denver 80222
Tel: (303) 321-8086
TWX: 910-931-2289

CONNECTICUT

Intel Corp.
26 Mill Plain Road
Danbury 06810
Tel: (203) 748-3130
TWX: 710-456-1199

EMC Corp.
222 Summer Street
Stamford 06901
Tel: (203) 327-2934

FLORIDA

Intel Corp.
242 N. Westmonte Drive
Suite 105
Altamonte Springs 32714
Tel: (305) 869-5588

Intel Corp.
6363 N.W. 6th Way, Suite 100
Ft. Lauderdale 33309
Tel: (305) 771-0600
TWX: 510-956-9407

FLORIDA (Cont'd)

Intel Corp.
11300 4th Street North
Suite 170
St. Petersburg 33702
Tel: (813) 577-2413

GEORGIA

Intel Corp.
3280 Pointe Parkway
Suite 200
Norcross 30092
Tel: (404) 449-0541

ILLINOIS

Intel Corp.*
300 N. Martingale Road, Suite 400
Schaumburg 60172
Tel: (312) 310-8031

INDIANA

Intel Corp.
8777 Purdue Road
Suite 125
Indianapolis 46268
Tel: (317) 875-0623

IOWA

Intel Corp.
St. Andrews Building
1930 St. Andrews Drive N.E.
Cedar Rapids 52402
Tel: (319) 393-5510

KANSAS

Intel Corp.
8400 W. 110th Street
Suite 170
Overland Park 66210
Tel: (913) 345-2727

MARYLAND

Intel Corp.*
7321 Parkway Drive South
Suite C
Hanover 21076
Tel: (301) 796-7500
TWX: 710-862-1944

Intel Corp.
7833 Walker Drive
Greenbelt 20770
Tel: (301) 441-1020

MASSACHUSETTS

Intel Corp.*
Westford Corp. Center
3 Carlisle Road
Westford 01886
Tel: (617) 692-3222
TWX: 710-343-6333

MICHIGAN

Intel Corp.
7071 Orchard Lake Road
Suite 100
West Bloomfield 48033
Tel: (313) 851-8096

MINNESOTA

Intel Corp.
3500 W. 80th Street
Suite 360
Bloomington 55431
Tel: (612) 835-6722
TWX: 910-576-2867

MISSOURI

Intel Corp.
4203 Earth City Expressway
Suite 131
Earth City 63045
Tel: (314) 291-1990

NEW JERSEY

Intel Corp.*
Parkway 109 Office Center
328 Newman Springs Road
Red Bank 07701
Tel: (201) 747-2233

Intel Corp.
75 Livingston Avenue
First Floor
Roseland 07068
Tel: (201) 740-0111

NEW MEXICO

Intel Corp.
8500 Menual Boulevard N.E.
Suite B 295
Albuquerque 87112
Tel: (505) 292-8086

NEW YORK

Intel Corp.*
300 Vanderbilt Motor Parkway
Hauppauge 11788
Tel: (516) 231-3300
TWX: 510-227-6236

Intel Corp.
Suite 2B Hollowbrook Park
15 Myers Corners Road
Wappinger Falls 12590
Tel: (914) 297-6161
TWX: 510-248-0060

Intel Corp.*
211 White Spruce Boulevard
Rochester 14623
Tel: (716) 424-1050
TWX: 510-253-7391

NORTH CAROLINA

Intel Corp.
5700 Executive Center Drive
Suite 213
Charlotte 28212
Tel: (704) 568-8966

Intel Corp.
2700 Wycliff Road
Suite 102
Raleigh 27607
Tel: (919) 781-8022

OHIO

Intel Corp.*
6500 Poe Avenue
Dayton 45414
Tel: (513) 890-5350
TWX: 810-450-2528

Intel Corp.*
Chagrin-Brainard Bldg., No. 300
28001 Chagrin Boulevard
Cleveland 44122
Tel: (216) 464-2736
TWX: 810-427-9298

OKLAHOMA

Intel Corp.
6801 N. Broadway
Suite 115
Oklahoma City 73116
Tel: (405) 848-8086

OREGON

Intel Corp.
10700 S.W. Beaverton
Hillsdale Highway
Suite 22
Beaverton 97005
Tel: (503) 641-8086
TWX: 910-467-8741

PENNSYLVANIA

Intel Corp.
1513 Cedar Cliff Drive
Camphill 17011
Tel: (717) 737-5035

Intel Corp.*
455 Pennsylvania Avenue
Fort Washington 19034
Tel: (215) 641-1000
TWX: 510-661-2077

Intel Corp.*
400 Penn Center Boulevard
Suite 610
Pittsburgh 15235
Tel: (412) 823-4970

PUERTO RICO

Intel Microprocessor Corp.
South Industrial Park
Las Piedras 00671
Tel: (809) 733-3030

TEXAS

Intel Corp.
313 E. Anderson Lane
Suite 314
Austin 78752
Tel: (512) 454-3628

TEXAS (Cont'd)

Intel Corp.*
12300 Ford Road
Suite 380
Dallas 75234
Tel: (214) 241-8087
TWX: 910-860-5617

Intel Corp.*
7322 S.W. Freeway
Suite 1490
Houston 77074
Tel: (713) 988-8086
TWX: 910-881-2490

Industrial Digital Systems Corp.
5925 Sovereign
Suite 101
Houston 77036
Tel: (713)988-9421

UTAH

Intel Corp.
5201 Green Street
Suite 290
Murray 84123
Tel: (801) 263-8051

VIRGINIA

Intel Corp.
1603 Santa Rosa Road
Suite 109
Richmond 23288
Tel: (804) 282-5668

WASHINGTON

Intel Corp.
110 110th Avenue N.E.
Suite 510
Bellevue 98004
Tel: (206) 453-8086
TWX: 910-443-3002

Intel Corp.
408 N. Mullan Road
Suite 102
Spokane 99206
Tel: (509) 928-8086

WISCONSIN

Intel Corp.
450 N. Sunnyslope Road
Suite 130
Chancellory Park I
Brookfield 53005
Tel: (414) 784-8087

CANADA

BRITISH COLUMBIA

Intel Semiconductor of Canada, Ltd.
301-2245 W. Broadway
Vancouver V6K 2E4
Tel: (604) 738-6522

ONTARIO

Intel Semiconductor of Canada, Ltd.
2650 Queensview Drive
Suite 250
Ottawa K2B 8H6
Tel: (613) 829-9714
TELEX: 053-4115

Intel Semiconductor of Canada, Ltd.
190 Attwell Drive
Suite 500
Rexdale M9W 6H8
Tel: (416) 675-2105
TELEX: 06983574

QUEBEC

Intel Semiconductor of Canada, Ltd.
620 St. Jean Blvd.
Pointe Claire H9R 3K3
Tel: (514) 694-9130
TWX: 514-694-9134

*Field Application Location

intel

DOMESTIC DISTRIBUTORS

ALABAMA

Arrow Electronics, Inc.
1015 Henderson Road
Huntsville 35805
Tel: (205) 837-6955

†Hamilton/Avnet Electronics
4812 Commercial Drive N.W.
Huntsville 35805
Tel: (205) 837-7210
TWX: 810-726-2162

†Pioneer/Technologies Group Inc.
4825 University Square
Huntsville 35805
Tel: (205) 837-9300
TWX: 810-726-2197

ARIZONA

†Hamilton/Avnet Electronics
505 S. Madison Drive
Tempe 85281
Tel: (602) 231-5100
TWX: 910-950-0077

Kierulff Electronics
4134 E. Wood Street
Phoenix 85040
Tel: (602) 437-0750
TWX: 910-951-1550

Wyle Distribution Group
17855 N. Black Canyon Highway
Phoenix 85023
Tel: (602) 866-2888

CALIFORNIA

Arrow Electronics, Inc.
19748 Dearborn Street
Chatsworth 91311
Tel: (818) 701-7500
TWX: 910-493-2086

Arrow Electronics
9511 Ridgehaven Court
San Diego 92123
Tel: (619) 565-4800
TLX: 888064

†Arrow Electronics, Inc.
521 Weddell Drive
Sunnyvale 94086
Tel: (408) 745-6600
TWX: 910-339-9371

Arrow Electronics, Inc.
2961 Dow Avenue
Tustin 92680
Tel: (714) 838-5422
TWX: 910-595-2860

†Avnet Electronics
350 McCormick Avenue
Costa Mesa 92626
Tel: (714) 754-6051
TWX: 910-595-1928

Hamilton/Avnet Electronics
1175 Bordeaux Drive
Sunnyvale 94086
Tel: (408) 743-3300
TWX: 910-339-9332

†Hamilton/Avnet Electronics
4545 Viewridge Avenue
San Diego 92123
Tel: (619) 571-7500
TWX: 910-595-2638

†Hamilton/Avnet Electronics
20501 Plummer Street
Chatsworth 91311
Tel: (818) 700-6271
TWX: 910-494-2207

†Hamilton/Avnet Electronics
4103 Northgate Boulevard
Sacramento 95834
Tel: (916) 920-3150

Hamilton/Avnet Electronics
3002 G Street
Ontario 91311
Tel: (714) 989-9411

Hamilton/Avnet Electronics
19515 So. Vermont Avenue
Torrance 90502
Tel: (213) 615-3909
TWX: 910-349-6263

Hamilton Electro Sales
9650 De Soto Avenue
Chatsworth 91311
Tel: (818) 700-6500

†Hamilton Electro Sales
10950 W. Washington Boulevard
Culver City 90230
Tel: (213) 558-2458
TWX: 910-340-6364

Hamilton Electro Sales
1361 B West 190th Street
Gardena 90248
Tel: (213) 558-2131

CALIFORNIA (Cont'd)

†Hamilton Electro Sales
3170 Pullman Street
Costa Mesa 92626
Tel: (714) 641-4150
TWX: 910-595-2638

Kierulff Electronics
10824 Hope Street
Cypress 90430
Tel: (714) 220-6300

Kierulff Electronics, Inc.
1180 Murphy Avenue
San Jose 95131
Tel: (408) 947-3471
TWX: 910-379-6430

Kierulff Electronics, Inc.
14101 Franklin Avenue
Tustin 92680
Tel: (714) 731-5711
TWX: 910-595-2599

†Kierulff Electronics, Inc.
5650 Jillson Street
Commerce 90040
Tel: (213) 725-0325
TWX: 910-580-3666

Wyle Distribution Group
26560 Agoura Street
Calabasas 91302
Tel: (818) 880-9000
TWX: 818-372-0232

†Wyle Distribution Group
124 Maryland Street
El Segundo 90245
Tel: (213) 322-8100
TWX: 910-348-7140 or 7111

†Wyle Distribution Group
17872 Cowan Avenue
Irvine 92714
Tel: (714) 843-9953
TWX: 910-595-1572

†Wyle Distribution Group
11151 Sun Center Drive
Rancho Cordova 95670
Tel: (916) 638-5282

†Wyle Distribution Group
9525 Chesapeake Drive
San Diego 92123
Tel: (619) 565-9171
TWX: 910-335-1590

†Wyle Distribution Group
3000 Bowers Avenue
Santa Clara 95051
Tel: (408) 727-2500
TWX: 910-338-0296

Wyle Military
17810 Teller Avenue
Irvine 92750
Tel: (714) 851-9958
TWX: 310-371-9127

Wyle Systems
7382 Lampson Avenue
Garden Grove 92641
Tel: (714) 851-9953
TWX: 910-595-2642

COLORADO

Arrow Electronics, Inc.
1390 S. Potomac Street
Suite 136
Aurora 80012
Tel: (303) 696-1111

†Wyle Distribution Group
451 E. 124th Avenue
Thornton 80241
Tel: (303) 457-9953
TWX: 910-936-0770

†Hamilton/Avnet Electronics
8765 E. Orchard Road
Suite 708
Englewood 80111
Tel: (303) 740-1017
TWX: 910-935-0787

CONNECTICUT

†Arrow Electronics, Inc.
12 Beaumont Road
Wallingford 06492
Tel: (203) 265-7741
TWX: 710-476-0162

†Hamilton/Avnet Electronics
Commerce Industrial Park
Commerce Drive
Danbury 06810
Tel: (203) 797-2800
TWX: 710-456-9974

†Pioneer Northeast Electronics
112 Main Street
Norwalk 06851
Tel: (203) 853-1515
TWX: 710-468-3373

FLORIDA

†Arrow Electronics, Inc.
350 Fairway Drive
Deerfield Beach 33441
Tel: (305) 429-8200
TWX: 510-955-9456

†Arrow Electronics, Inc.
1001 N.W. 62nd Street
Suite 108
Ft. Lauderdale 33309
Tel: (305) 776-7790
TWX: 510-955-9456

†Arrow Electronics, Inc.
50 Woodlake Drive W., Bldg. B
Palm Bay 32905
Tel: (305) 725-1480
TWX: 510-959-6337

†Hamilton/Avnet Electronics
6801 N.W. 15th Way
Ft. Lauderdale 33309
Tel: (305) 971-2900
TWX: 510-956-3097

†Hamilton/Avnet Electronics
3197 Tech. Drive North
St. Petersburg 33702
Tel: (813) 576-3930
TWX: 810-863-0374

Hamilton/Avnet Electronics
6947 University Boulevard
Winterpark 32792
Tel: (305) 628-3888
TWX: 810-853-0322

†Pioneer Electronics
221 N. Lake Boulevard
Suite 412
Alta Monte Springs 32701
Tel: (305) 834-9090
TWX: 810-853-0284

†Pioneer Electronics
674 S. Military Trail
Deerfield Beach 33442
Tel: (305) 428-8877
TWX: 510-955-9653

GEORGIA

†Arrow Electronics, Inc
3155 Northwoods Parkway, Suite A
Norcross 30071
Tel: (404) 449-8252
TWX: 810-766-0439

Hamilton/Avnet Electronics
5825 D. Peachtree Corners
Norcross 30092
Tel: (404) 447-7500
TWX: 810-766-0432

Pioneer Electronics
5835B Peachtree Corners E
Norcross 30092
Norcross 30092
Tel: (404) 448-1711
TWX: 810-766-4515

ILLINOIS

†Arrow Electronics, Inc.
2000 E. Alonquin Street
Schaumberg 60195
Tel: (312) 397-3440
TWX: 910-291-3544

†Hamilton/Avnet Electronics
1130 Thorndale Avenue
Bensenville 60106
Tel: (312) 860-7780
TWX: 910-227-0060

†Pioneer Electronics
1551 Carmen Drive
Elk Grove Village 60007
Tel: (312) 437-9680
TWX: 910-222-1834

INDIANA

†Arrow Electronics, Inc.
2495 Directors Row, Suite H
Indianapolis 46241
(317) 243-9353
TWX: 810-341-3119

Hamilton/Avnet Electronics
485 Gradle Drive
Carmel 46032
Tel: (317) 844-9333
TWX: 810-260-3966

†Pioneer Electronics
6408 Castleplace Drive
Indianapolis 46250
Tel: (317) 849-7300
TWX: 810-260-1794

KANSAS

†Hamilton/Avnet Electronics
9219 Quivera Road
Overland Park 66215
Tel: (913) 888-8900
TWX: 910-743-0005

KENTUCKY

Hamilton/Avnet Electronics
1051 D. Newton Park
Lexington 40511

MARYLAND

Arrow Electronics, Inc.
8300 Guilford Road #H
Rivers Center
Columbia 21046
Tel: (301) 995-0003
TWX: 710-236-9005

†Hamilton/Avnet Electronics
6822 Oak Hall Lane
Columbia 21045
Tel: (301) 995-3500
TWX: 710-862-1861

†Mesa Technology Corporation
16021 Industrial Drive
Gaithersburg 20877
Tel: (301) 948-4350
TWX: 710-828-9702

†Pioneer Electronics
9100 Gaither Road
Gaithersburg 20877
Tel: (301) 948-0710
TWX: 710-828-0545

MASSACHUSETTS

†Arrow Electronics, Inc.
1 Arrow Drive
Woburn 01801
Tel: (617) 933-8130
TWX: 710-393-6770

†Hamilton/Avnet Electronics
10D Centennial Drive
Peabody 01960
Tel: (617) 532-3701
TWX: 710-393-0382

Pioneer Northeast Electronics
44 Hartwell Avenue
Lexington 02173
Tel: (617) 863-1200
TWX: 710-326-6617

MICHIGAN

Arrow Electronics, Inc.
755 Phoenix Drive
Ann Arbor 48104
Tel: (313) 971-8220
TWX: 810-223-6020

†Hamilton/Avnet Electronics
32487 Schoolcraft Road
Livonia 48150
Tel: (313) 522-4700
TWX: 810-242-8775

Hamilton/Avnet Electronics
2215 29th Street S.E.
Space A5
Grand Rapids 49508
Tel: (616) 243-8805
TWX: 810-273-6921

†Pioneer Electronics
13485 Stamford
Livonia 48150
Tel: (313) 525-1800
TWX: 810-242-3271

MINNESOTA

†Arrow Electronics, Inc.
5230 W. 73rd Street
Edina 55435
Tel: (612) 830-1800
TWX: 910-576-3125

Hamilton/Avnet Electronics
10300 Bren Road East
Minnetonka 55343
Tel: (612) 932-0600
TWX: (910) 576-2720

†Pioneer Electronics
10203 Bren Road East
Minnetonka 55343
Tel: (612) 935-5444
TWX: 910-576-2738

MISSOURI

†Arrow Electronics, Inc.
2380 Schuetz
St. Louis 63141
Tel: (314) 567-6888
TWX: 910-764-0882

†Microcomputer System Technical Demonstrator Centers

DOMESTIC DISTRIBUTORS

MISSOURI (Cont'd)

†Hamilton/Avnet Electronics
13743 Shoreline Court
Earth City 63045
Tel: (314) 344-1200
TWX: 910-762-0684

NEW HAMPSHIRE

†Arrow Electronics, Inc.
3 Perimeter Road
Manchester 03103
Tel: (603) 668-6968
TWX: 710-220-1684

Hamilton/Avnet Electronics
444 E. Industrial Drive
Manchester 03104
Tel: (603) 624-9400

NEW JERSEY

†Arrow Electronics, Inc.
6000 Lincoln East
Marlton 08053
Tel: (609) 596-8000
TWX: 710-897-0829

†Arrow Electronics, Inc.
2 Industrial Road
Fairfield 07006
Tel: (201) 575-5300
TWX: 710-998-2206

†Hamilton/Avnet Electronics
1 Keystone Avenue
Bldg. 36
Cherry Hill 08003
Tel: (609) 424-0110
TWX: 710-940-0262

†Hamilton/Avnet Electronics
10 Industrial
Fairfield 07006
Tel: (201) 575-3390
TWX: 710-734-4388

†Pioneer Northeast Electronics
45 Route 46
Pinebrook 07058
Tel: (201) 575-3510
TWX: 710-734-4382

†MTI Systems Sales
383 Route 46 W
Fairfield 07006
Tel: (201) 227-5552

NEW MEXICO

Alliance Electronics Inc.
11030 Cochiti S.E.
Albuquerque 87123
Tel: (505) 292-3360
TWX: 910-989-1151

Hamilton/Avnet Electronics
2524 Baylor Drive S.E.
Albuquerque 87106
Tel: (505) 765-1500
TWX: 910-989-0614

NEW YORK

†Arrow Electronics, Inc.
25 Hub Drive
Melville 11747
Tel: (516) 694-6800
TWX: 510-224-6126

†Arrow Electronics, Inc.
3375 Brighton-Henrietta Townline Road
Rochester 14623
Tel: (716) 427-0300
TWX: 510-253-4766

Arrow Electronics, Inc.
7705 Maltage Drive
Liverpool 13088
Tel: (315) 652-1000
TWX: 710-545-0230

Arrow Electronics, Inc.
20 Oser Avenue
Hauppauge 11788
Tel: (516) 231-1000
TWX: 510-227-6623

Hamilton/Avnet Electronics
333 Metro Park
Rochester 14623
Tel: (716) 475-9130
TWX: 510-253-5470

Hamilton/Avnet Electronics
103 Twin Oaks Drive
Syracuse 13206
Tel: (315) 437-2641
TWX: 710-541-1560

†Hamilton/Avnet Electronics
933 Motor Parkway
Hauppauge 11788
Tel: (516) 231-9800
TWX: 510-224-6166

NEW YORK (Cont'd)

†MTI Systems Sales
38 Harbor Park Drive
P.O. Box 271
Port Washington 11050
Tel: (516) 621-6200
TWX: 510-223-0846

†Pioneer Northeast Electronics
1806 Vestal Parkway East
Vestal 13850
Tel: (607) 748-8211
TWX: 510-252-0893

†Pioneer Northeast Electronics
60 Crossway Park West
Woodbury, Long Island 11797
Tel: (516) 921-8700
TWX: 510-221-2184

Pioneer Northeast Electronics
840 Fairport Park
Fairport 14450
Tel: (716) 381-7070
TWX: 510-253-7001

NORTH CAROLINA

Arrow Electronics, Inc.
5240 Greendairy Road
Raleigh 27604
Tel: (919) 876-3132
TWX: 510-928-1856

†Hamilton/Avnet Electronics
3510 Spring Forest Drive
Raleigh 27604
Tel: (919) 878-0819
TWX: 510-928-1836

Pioneer Electronics
9801 A-Southern Pine Boulevard
Charlotte 28210
Tel: (704) 524-8188
TWX: 810-621-0366

OHIO

Arrow Electronics, Inc.
7620 McEwen Road
Centerville 45459
Tel: (513) 435-5563
TWX: 810-459-1611

†Arrow Electronics, Inc.
6238 Cochran Road
Solon 44139
Tel: (216) 248-3990
TWX: 810-427-9409

†Hamilton/Avnet Electronics
954 Senate Drive
Dayton 45459
Tel: (513) 433-0610
TWX: 810-450-2531

†Hamilton/Avnet Electronics
4588 Emery Industrial Parkway
Warrensville Heights 44128
Tel: (216) 831-3500
TWX: 810-427-9452

†Pioneer Electronics
4433 Interpoint Boulevard
Dayton 45424
Tel: (513) 236-9900
TWX: 810-459-1622

†Pioneer Electronics
4800 E. 131st Street
Cleveland 44105
Tel (216) 587-3600
TWX: 810-422-2211

OKLAHOMA

Arrow Electronics, Inc.
4719 S. Memorial Drive
Tulsa 74145
Tel: (918) 665-7700

OREGON

†Almac Electronics Corporation
1885 N.W. 169th Place
Beaverton 97006
Tel: (503) 629-8090
TWX: 910-467-8746

Hamilton/Avnet Electronics
6024 S.W. Jean Road
Bldg. C, Suite 10
Lake Oswego 97034
Tel: (503) 635-7848
TWX: 910-455-8179

Wyle Distribution Group
5250 N.E. Elam Young Parkway
Suite 600
Hillsboro 97124
Tel: (503) 640-6000
TWX: 910-460-2203

PENNSYLVANIA

†Arrow Electronics, Inc.
650 Seco Road
Monroeville 15146
Tel: (412) 856-7000

Pioneer Electronics
259 Kappa Drive
Pittsburgh 15238
Tel: (412) 782-2300
TWX: 710-795-3122

†Pioneer Electronics
261 Gibralter Road
Horsham 19044
Tel: (215) 674-4000
TWX: 510-665-6778

TEXAS

†Arrow Electronics, Inc.
3220 Commander Drive
Carrollton 75006
Tel: (214) 380-6464
TWX: 910-860-5377

†Arrow Electronics, Inc.
10899 Kinghurst
Suite 100
Houston 77099
Tel: (713) 530-4700
TWX: 910-880-4439

Arrow Electronics, Inc.
10125 Metropolitan
Austin 78758
Tel: (512) 835-4180
TWX: 910-874-1348

†Hamilton/Avnet Electronics
2401 Rutland
Austin 78757
Tel: (512) 837-8911
TWX: 910-874-1319

†Hamilton/Avnet Electronics
2111 W. Walnut Hill Lane
Irving 75062
Tel: (214) 659-4100
TWX: 910-860-5929

†Hamilton/Avnet Electronics
8750 West Park
Hosuton 77063
Tel: (713) 780-1771
TWX: 910-881-5523

Pioneer Electronics
9901 Burnet Road
Austin 78758
Tel: (512) 835-4000
TWX: 910-874-1323

Pioneer Electronics
13710 Omega Road
Dallas 75234
Tel: (214) 386-7300
TWX: 910-850-5563

Pioneer Electronics
5853 Point West Drive
Houston 77036
Tel: (713) 988-5555
TWX: 910-881-1606

UTAH

†Hamilton/Avnet Electronics
1585 West 2100 South
Salt Lake City 84119
Tel: (801) 972-2800
TWX: 910-925-4018

Wyle Distribution Group
1959 South 4130 West, Unit B
Salt Lake City 84104
Tel: (801) 974-9953

WASHINGTON

†Almac Electronics Corporation
14360 S.E. Eastgate Way
Bellevue 98007
Tel: (206) 643-9992
TWX: 910-444-2067

Arrow Electronics, Inc.
14320 N.E. 21st Street
Bellevue 98007
Tel: (206) 643-4800
TWX: 910-444-2017

Hamilton/Avnet Electronics
14212 N.E. 21st Street
Bellevue 98005
Tel: (206) 453-5874
TWX: 910-443-2469

WISCONSIN

†Arrow Electronics, Inc.
430 W. Rausson Avenue
Oakcreek 53154
Tel: (414) 764-6600
TWX: 910-262-1193

WISCONSIN (Cont'd)

†Hamilton/Avnet Electronics
2975 Moorland Road
New Berlin 53151
Tel: (414) 784-4510
TWX: 910-262-1182

CANADA

ALBERTA

Hamilton/Avnet Electronics
2816 21st Street N.E.
Calgary T2E 6Z2
Tel: (403) 230-3586
TWX: 03-827-642

Zentronics
Bay No. 1
3300 14th Avenue N.E.
Calgary T2A 6J4
Tel: (403) 272-1021

BRITISH COLUMBIA

Hamilton/Avnet Electronics
105-2550 Boundry Road
Burmalay V5M 3Z3
Tel: (604) 272-4242

Zentronics
108-11400 Bridgeport Road
Richmond V6X 1T2
Tel: (604) 273-5575
TWX: 04-5077-89

MANITOBA

Zentronics
590 Berry Street
Winnipeg R3H OS1
Tel: (204) 775-8661

ONTARIO

Arrow Electronics Inc.
24 Martin Ross Avenue
Downsview M3J 2K9
Tel: (416) 661-0220
TELEX: 06-218213

Arrow Electronics Inc.
148 Colonnade Road
Nepean K2E 7J5
Tel: (613) 226-6903

†Hamilton/Avnet Electronics
6845 Rexwood Road
Units G & H
Mississauga L4V 1R2
Tel: (416) 677-7432
TWX: 610-492-8867

†Hamilton/Avnet Electronics
210 Colonnade Road South
Nepean K2E 7L5
Tel: (613) 226-1700
TWX: 05-349-71

†Zentronics
8 Tilbury Court
Brampton L6T 3T4
Tel: (416) 451-9600
TWX: 06-976-78

Zentronics
564/10 Weber Street North
Waterloo N2L 5C6
Tel: (519) 884-5700

Zentronics
155 Colonnade Road
Unit 17
Nepean K2E 7K1
Tel: (613) 225-8840
TWX: 06-976-78

QUEBEC

Arrow Electronics Inc.
4050 Jean Talon Quest
Montreal H4P 1W1
Tel: (514) 735-5511
TELEX: 05-25596

Arrow Electronics Inc.
909 Charest Blvd.
Quebec 61N 269
Tel: (418) 687-4231
TLX: 05-13388

Hamilton/Avnet Electronics
2795 Rue Halpern
St. Laurent H4S 1P8
Tel: (514) 335-1000
TWX: 610-421-3731

Zentronics
505 Locke Street
St. Laurent H4T 1X7
Tel: (514) 735-5361
TWX: 05-827-535

†Microcomputer System Technical Demonstrator Centers

EUROPEAN SALES OFFICES

BELGIUM

Intel Corporation S.A.
Parc Seny
Rue du Moulin a Papier 51
Boite 1
B-1160 Brussels
Tel: (02)661 07 11
TELEX: 24814

DENMARK

Intel Denmark A/S*
Glentevej 61 - 3rd Floor
DK-2400 Copenhagen
Tel: (01) 19 80 33
TELEX: 19567

FINLAND

Intel Finland OY
Ruosilantie 2
000390 Helsinki
Tel: (0) 544 644
TELEX: 123 332

FRANCE

Intel Paris
1 Rue Edison, BP 303
78054 Saint-Quentin en Yvelines
Tel: (33) 1 30 64 60 00
TELEX: 69901677

FRANCE (Cont'd)

Intel Corporation, S.A.R.L.
Immeuble BBC
4 Quai des Etroits
69005 Lyon
Tel: (7) 842 40 89
TELEX: 305153

WEST GERMANY

Intel Semiconductor GmbH*
Seidlstrasse 27
D-8000 Munchen 2
Tel: (89) 53891
TELEX: 05-23177 INTL D

Intel Semiconductor GmbH*
Mainzerstrasse 75
D-6200 Wiesbaden 1
Tel: (6121) 70 08 74
TELEX: 04168183 INTW D

Intel Semiconductor GmbH
Bruckstrasse 61
7012 Fellbach
Stuttgart
Tel: (711) 58 00 82
TELEX: 7254826 INTS D

Intel Semiconductor GmbH*
Hohenzollernstrasse 5*
3000 Hannover 1
Tel: (511) 34 40 81
TELEX: 923625 INTH D

ISRAEL

Intel Semiconductors Ltd.*
Atidim Industrial Park
Neve Sharet
Dvora Hanevia
Bldg. No. 13, 4th Floor
P.O. Box 43202
Tel Aviv 61430
Tel: 3-491099/8
Telex: 371215

ITALY

Intel Corporation Italia Spa*
Milanofiori, Palazzo E
20094 Assago (Milano)
Tel: (02) 824 40 71
TELEX: 315183 INTMIL

NETHERLANDS

Intel Semiconductor Nederland B.V.*
Alexanderpoort Building
Marten Meesweg 93
3068 Rotterdam
Tel: (10) 21 23 77
TELEX: 22283

NORWAY

Intel Norway A/S
P.O. Box 92
Hvamveien 4
N-2013
Skjetten
Tel: (2) 742 420
TELEX: 18018

SPAIN

Intel Iberia
Calle Zurbaran
28-1-IZQDA
28010 Madrid
Tel: (34) 1410 40 04
TELEX: 46880

SWEDEN

Intel Sweden A.B.*
Dalvagen 24
S-171 36 Solna
Tel: 8/7340100
TELEX: 12261

SWITZERLAND

Intel Semiconductor A.G.*
Talackerstrasse 17
8152 Glattbrugg postfach
CH-8065 Zurich
Tel: (01) 829 29 77
TELEX: 57989 ICH CH

UNITED KINGDOM

Intel Corporation (U.K.) Ltd.*
Pipers Way
Swindon, Wiltshire SN3 1RJ
Tel: (793) 696 000
TELEX: 444447 INT SWN

*Field Application Location

EUROPEAN DISTRIBUTORS/REPRESENTATIVES

AUSTRIA

Bacher Elektronische Geraete GmbH
Rotenmuehlgasse 26
A 1120 Wien
Tel: (222) 83 56 46
TELEX: 11532 BASAT A

W. Moor GmbH
Storchengasse 1/1/1
A-1150 Wien
Tel: 222-85 86 46

BELGIUM

Inelco Belgium S.A.
Ave. des Croix de Guerre 94
B1120 Brussels
Tel: (021) 216 01 60
TELEX: 25441

DENMARK

ITT MultiKomponent A/S
Naverland 29
DK-2600 Gloskrup
Tel: (02) 45 66 45
TX: 33355

FINLAND

Oy Fintronic AB
Melkonkalu 24 A
SF-00210 Helsinki 21
Tel: (0) 692 60 22
TELEX: 124 224 Ftron SF

FRANCE

Generim
Z.I. de Courtaboeuf
Avenue de la Baltique
F-91943 Les Ulis Cedex-B.P.88
Tel: (1) 907 78 78
TELEX: F691700

Jermyn S.A.
16, Avenue de Jean-Jaures
F-94600 Choisy-Le-Roi
Tel: (1) 853 12 00
TELEX: 260 967

Metrologie
La Tour d' Asnieres
4, Avenue Laurent Cely
F-92606-Asnieres
Tel: (1) 790 62 40
TELEX: 611-448

FRANCE (Cont'd)

Tekelec Airtronic
Cte des Bruyeres
Rue Carle Vernet B.P. 2
F-92310 Sevres
Tel: (1) 534 75 35
TELEX: 204552

WEST GERMANY

Computer 2000
Garmischer Strasse 4-6
D-8000 Munchen 2
Tel: (089) 519-96-0
TELEX: 5214562

Electronic 2000 Vertriebs A.G.
Stahlgruberring 12
D-8000 Munich 82
Tel: (89) 42 00 10
TELEX: 522561 EEC D

Jermyn GmbH
Postfach 11 80
Schulstrasse 84
D-6277 Bad Camberg
Tel: (06434) 231
TELEX: 484426 JERM D

CES Computer Electronics Systems GmbH
Gutenbergstrasse 4
D-2359 Henstedt-Ulzburg
Tel: (04193) 4026
TELEX: 2180260

Metrologie GmbH
Hansastrasse 15
D-8000 Munich 21
Tel: (89) 57 30 84
TELEX: 5213189

Proelectron Vertriebs GmbH
Max Planck Strasse 1-3
D-6072 Dreieich
Tel: (6103) 33564
TELEX: 417983

IRELAND

Micro Marketing
Glenageary Office Park
Glenageary
Co. Dublin
Tel: (1) 85 62 88
TELEX: 31584

ISRAEL

Eastronics Ltd.
11 Rozanis Street
P.O. Box 39300
Tel Aviv 61390
Tel: (3) 47 51 51
TELEX: 33638

ITALY

Electra 3S S.P.A.
Viale Elvezia, 18
I 20154 Milano
Tel: (2) 34 97 51
TELEX: 332332

Intesi
Milanofiori Pal. E/5
I-20090 Assago
Milano
Tel: (2) 82470
TELEX: 311351

NETHERLANDS

Koning & Hartman
Koperwerf 30
P.O. Box 43220
2544 EN's Gravenhage
Tel: 31 (70) 210.101
TELEX: 31528

NORWAY

Nordisk Elektronic (Norge) A/S
Postoffice Box 122
Smedsvingen 4
1364 Hvalstad
Tel: (2) 846 210
TELEX: 17546

PORTUGAL

Ditram
Componentes E Electronica LDA
Av. Miguel Bombarda, 133
P-1000 Lisboa
Tel: (19) 545 313
TELEX: 14182 Brieks-P

SPAIN

ITT SESA
Miguel Angel 21, 6 Piso
Madrid 10
Tel: (34) 14 1954 00
TELEX: 27461

Diode Espana
Avenida De Brasil 5
28020 Madrid
Tel: 455 36 86
TELEX: 42148

SWEDEN

Nordisk Electronik AB
Huvudstagatan 1
Box 1409
S-171 27 Solna
Tel: (8) 734 97 70
TELEX: 10547

SWITZERLAND

Industrade AG
Hertistrasse 31
CH-8304 Wallisellen
Tel: (01) 830 50 40
TELEX: 56788 INDEL CH

UNITED KINGDOM

Bytech Ltd.
Unit 57
London Road
Early, Reading
Berkshire RJ 12 1W
Tel: (0734) 61031
TELEX: 848215

Comway Microsystems Ltd.
Market Street
Bracknell
Berkshire RJ 12 IQP
Tel: (344) 55333
TELEX: 847201

Jermyn Industries Vestry Estate
Oxford Road
Seven Oaks
Kent TN 14 5EU
Tel: (0732) 450144
TELEX: 95142

M.E.D.L.
East Lane Road
North Wembley
Middlesex HA9 7PP
Tel: (190) 49307
TELEX: 28817

Rapid Recall, Ltd.
Rapid House/Denmark St
High Wycombe
Bucks HP11 2ER
Tel: (494) 26 271
TELEX: 837931

YUGOSLAVIA

H. R. Microelectronics Enterprises
P.O. Box 5604
San Jose, California 95150
Tel: 408/978-8000
TELEX: 278-559

intel

INTERNATIONAL SALES OFFICES

AUSTRALIA

Intel Australia Pty. Ltd.*
(Mailing Address)
P.O. Box 571
North Sydney NSW, 2060

(Shipping Address)
Spectrum Building
200 Pacific Highway
Level 6
Crows Nest, NSW, 2065
Tel: 011-61-2-957-2744
TELEX: 790-20097
FAX: 011-61-2-957-2744

CHINA

Intel PRC Corporation
15/F, Office 1, Citic Bldg.
Jian Guo Men Wai Avenue
Beijing, PRC

HONG KONG

Intel Semiconductor Ltd.*
1701-3 Connaught Centre
1 Connaught Road
Tel: 011-852-5-215-311
TWX: 60410 ITLHK

JAPAN

Intel Japan K.K.
5-6 Tokodai, Toyosato-machi
Tsukuba-gun, Ibaraki-ken 300-26
Tel: 029747-8511
TELEX: 03656-160

Intel Japan K.K.*
Komeshin Bldg.
2-1-15 Naka-machi
Atsugi, Kanagawa 243
Tel: 0462-23-3511

Intel Japan K.K.*
Daiichi Mitsugi Bldg.
1-8889 Fuchu-cho
Fuchu-shi, Tokyo 183
Tel: 0423-60-7871

Intel Japan K.K.*
Bldg. Kumagaya
2-69 Hon-cho
Kumagaya, Saitama 360
Tel: 0485-24-6871

Intel Japan K.K.*
Ryokuchi-Station Bldg.
2-4-1 Terauchi
Toyonaka, Osaka 560
Tel: 06-863-1091

JAPAN (Cont'd)

Intel Japan K.K.
Shinmaru Bldg.
1-5-1 Marunouchi
Chiyoda-ku, Tokyo 100
Tel: 03-201-3621

Intel Japan K.K.*
Flower-Hill Shin-machi East Bldg.
1-23-9 Shinmachi
Setagaya-ku, Tokyo 154
Tel: 03-426-2231

Intel Japan K.K.*
Mitsui-Seimei Musashi-Kosugi Bldg.
915-20 Shinmaruko, Nakahara-ku
Kawasaki-Shi, Kanagawa 211
Tel: 044-733-7011

Intel Japan K.K.
Mishima Tokyo-Kaijo Bldg.
1-1 Shibahon-cho
Mishima-shi
Shizuoka-Ken 411
Tel: 0559-72-4121

KOREA

Intel Semiconductor Asia Ltd.
Singsong Bldg. 8th Floor #906
25-4 Yoido-Dong, Youngdeungpo-Ku
Seoul 150
Tel: 011-82-2-784-8186 or 8286
TELEX: K29312 INTELKO

SINGAPORE

Intel Semiconductor Ltd.
101 Thomson Road
21-06 Goldhill Square
Singapore 1130
Tel: 011-65-250-7811
TWX: RS 39921

TAIWAN

Intel Semiconductor Ltd.
Rm. 808, Min Chi Bldg.
746 Min Sheng East Road
Taipei

*Field Application Location

INTERNATIONAL DISTRIBUTORS/REPRESENTATIVES

ARGENTINA

VLC S.R.L Bartalome Mitre 1711
3 Piso
1037 Buenos Aires
Tel: 011-54-1-49-2092
Telex: 17575 EDARG-AR

Agent:
Soimex International Corporation
15 Park Row, Room #1730
New York, New York 10038
Tel: (212) 406-3052

AUSTRALIA

Total Electronics
(Mailing Address)
Private Bag 250
Burwood, Victoria 3125

(Shipping Address)
9 Harker Street
Burwood
Victoria 3125
Tel: 011-61-3-288-4044
TELEX: AA 31261

Total Electronics
P.O. Box 139
Artamon, N.S.W. 2064
Tel: 011-61-02-438-1855
TELEX: 26297

BRAZIL

Elebra Microelectronica S/A
R. Florida, 1821-8 ander
04571 - Sao Paulo-SP
Tel: 011-55-11-533-9977
TELEX: 1125957

CHILE

DIN
(Mailing Address)
Av. VIC, MacKenna 204
Casilla 6055
Santiago
Tel: 011-56-2-277-564
TELEX: 352-0003

(Shipping Address)
A102 Greenville Center
3801 Kennett Pike
Wilmington, Delaware 19807

CHINA

Novel Precision Machinery Co., Ltd.
Flat D 20 Kingsford Ind. Bldg.
Phase 1 26 Kwai Hei Street NT
Hong Kong
Tel: 011-852-5-223222
TWX: 39114 JINMI HK

CHINA (Cont'd)

Schmidt & Co. Ltd.
18/F. Great Eagle Centre
Wanchai
Hong Kong
Tel: 011-852-5-822-0222
TWX: 74766 SCHMC HK

HONG KONG

Schmidt & Co. Ltd.
18/F. Great Eagle Centre
Wanchai
Tel: 011-852-5-822-0222
TWX: 74766 SCHMC HK

INDIA

Micronic Devices
65 Arun Complex
D V G Road
Basavan Gudi
Bangalore 560 004
Tel: 011-91-812-600-631
TELEX: 011-5947 MDEV

Micronic Devices
104/109C Nirmal Industrial Estate
Sion (E)
Bombay 400 022
Tel: 011-91-22-48-61-70
TELEX: 011-71447 MDEV IN

Micronic Devices
R-694 New Rajinder Nager
New Delhi 110 060

Ramlak International, Inc. (Agent)
465 S. Mathilda Avenue
Suite 302
Sunnyvale, CA 94086
Tel: (408) 733-8767

S & S Corporation
P.O. Box 20160
San Jose 95160-0160

JAPAN

Asahi Electronics Co. Ltd.
KMM Bldg. Room 407
2-14-1 Asano, Kokurakita-Ku
Kitakyushu City 802
Tel: (093) 511-6471
TELEX: AECKY 7126-16

C. Itoh Micronics Corp.
OS 85 Bldg. 2-6-5 Suda-Cho
Kanda Chiyoda-Ku, Tokyo 101
Tel: (03) 256-2211
TELEX: (03) 252-3774

JAPAN (Cont'd)

Ryoyo Electric Corporation
Shuwa Sakurabashi Bldg.
4-5-4 Hatchobori
Chuo-Ku, Tokyo 104
Tel: (03) 555-4811

Tokyo Electron Ltd.
Shinjuku Nomura Bldg.
1-26-2 Nishi-Shinjuku
Shinjuku-Ku, Tokyo 160
Tel: (03) 343-4411
TELEX: 232-2220 LABTEL J

KOREA

J-TEK Corporation
2nd Floor, Government Pension Bldg.
24-3 Yoido-Dong
Youngdungpo-Ku
Seoul 150
Tel: 011-82-2-782-8039
TELEX: KODIGIT K25299

Koram Digital USA (Agent)
14066 East Firestone Boulevard
Sante Fe Springs, CA 90670
Tel: (714) 739-2204
TELEX: 194715 KORAM DIGIT LSA

Samsung
23rd Fl. Dong Bang Bldg.
1502-KA Taepyung-RU
Chung-Ku
Seoul
Tel: 777-78
TELEX 27970 KORSST K

Tristar Semiconductor (Agent)
5150 Great America Parkway
Santa Clara, CA 95050
(408) 980-1630

MEXICO

DICOPEL S.A.
Tochtli 368 Fracc. Ind. San. Antonio
Azcapotzalco
C.P. 02760-Mexico, D.F.
Tel: 90115255613211
TELEX: 1773790 DICOME

NEW ZEALAND

Northrup Instruments & Systems Ltd.
459 Kyber Pass Road
P.O. Box 9464, Newmarket
Auckland 1
Tel: 011-64-9-501-219, 501-801, 587-037
TELEX: NZ21570 THERMAL

Northrup Instruments & Systems Ltd.
P.O. Box 2406
Wellington 856658
TELEX: NZ3380

PAKISTAN

Computer Applications Ltd.
7D Gizri Boulevard
Defence
Karachi-46
Tel: 011-92-21-530-306
TELEX: 24434 GAFAR PK

Horizon Training Co., Inc. (Agent)
1 Lafayette Center
1120 20th Street N.W.
Suite 530
Washington, D.C. 20036
Tel: (202) 887-1900
TWX: 248890 HORN

SINGAPORE

General Engineers Corporation Pty. Ltd.
203 Henderson Road
1102 Henderson Industrial Park 0315
Tel: 011065-271-3163
TELEX: RS23987 GENERCO

SOUTH AFRICA

Electronic Building Elements, Pty. Ltd.
(Mailing Address)
P.O. Box 4609
Pretoria 0001
Tel: 011-27-12-469921
TELEX: 3-22786 SA

(Shipping Address)
Pine Square, 18th Street
Hazelwood Pretoria

TAIWAN

Mitac Corporation
No. 585 Ming Sheng E. Road
Taipei
Tel: 011-96-2-501-8231
TELEX: 11942 TAIAUTO

Mectel International, Inc. (Agent)
3385 Viso Court
Santa Clara, CA 95050
Tel: (408) 988-4513
TWX: 910-338-2201
FAX: 408-980-9742

YUGOSLAVIA

H. R. Microelectronics Enterprises
P.O. Box 5604
San Jose, California 95150
Tel: (408) 978-8000
TELEX: 278-559

*Field Application Location

DOMESTIC SERVICE OFFICES

CALIFORNIA

Intel Corp.
21515 Vanowen
Suite 116
Canoga Park 91303
Tel: (818) 704-8500

Intel Corp.
2250 E. Imperial Way
Suite 218
El Segundo 90245
Tel: (213) 640-6040

Intel Corp.
1350 Shorebird Way
Mt. View 94043
Tel: (415) 968-8211
TWX: 910-339-9279
910-338-0255

Intel Corp.
2000 E. 4th Street
Suite 110
Santa Ana 92705
Tel: (714) 835-5577
TWX: 910-595-2475

Intel Corp.
4350 Executive Drive
Suite 150
San Diego 92121
Tel: (619) 452-5880

COLORADO

Intel Corp.
650 South Cherry
Suite 720
Denver 80222
Tel: (303) 321-8086
TWX: 910-931-2289

CONNECTICUT

Intel Corp.
26 Mill Plain Road
Danbury 06811
Tel: (203) 748-3130

FLORIDA

Intel Corp.
1500 N.W. 62nd Street
Suite 104
Ft. Lauderdale 33309
Tel: (305) 771-0600
TWX: 510-956-9407

FLORIDA (Cont'd)

Intel Corp.
242 N. Westmonte
Suite 105
Altamonte Springs 32714
Tel: (305) 869-5588

GEORGIA

Intel Corp.
3280 Pointe Parkway
Suite 200
Norcross 30092
Tel: (404) 441-1171

ILLINOIS

Intel Corp.
300 N. Martingale Rd.
Suite 300
Schaumburg 60194
Tel: (312) 310-8034
Dispatch: (312) 310-1803

KANSAS

Intel Corp.
8400 W. 110th Street
Suite 170
Overland Park 66210
Tel: (913) 642-8080

MARYLAND

Intel Corp.
5th Floor Product Service
7833 Walker Drive
Greenbelt 20770
Tel: (301) 441-1020

MASSACHUSETTS

Intel Corp.
27 Industrial Avenue
Chelmsford 01824
Tel: (617) 256-1800
TWX: 710-343-6333

MICHIGAN

Intel Corp.
7071 Orchard Lake Road
Suite 100
West Bloomfield 48033
Tel: (313) 851-8905

MISSOURI

Intel Corp.
4203 Earth City Expressway
Suite 143
Earth City 63045
Tel: (314) 291-2015

NEW JERSEY

Intel Corp.
385 Sylvan Avenue
Englewood Cliffs 07632
Tel: (201) 567-0820
TWX: 710-991-8593

Intel Corp.
Raritan Plaza III
Raritan Center
Edison 08817
Tel: (201) 225-3000

NORTH CAROLINA

Intel Corp.
2306 W. Meadowview Road
Suite 206
Greensboro 27407
Tel: (919) 294-1541

OHIO

Intel Corp.
Chagrin-Brainard Bldg.
Suite 305
28001 Chagrin Boulevard
Cleveland 44122
Tel: (216) 464-6915
TWX: 810-427-9298

Intel Corp.
6500 Poe
Dayton 45414
Tel: (513) 890-5350

OREGON

Intel Corp.
10700 S.W. Beaverton-Hillsdale
Highway
Suite 22
Beaverton 97005
Tel: (503) 641-8086
TWX: 910-467-8741

OREGON (Cont'd)

Intel Corp.
5200 N.E. Elam Young Parkway
Hillsboro 97123
Tel: (503) 681-8080

PENNSYLVANIA

Intel Corp.
201 Penn Center Boulevard
Suite 301 W
Pittsburgh 15235
Tel: (313) 354-1540

TEXAS

Intel Corp.
313 E. Anderson Lane
Suite 314
Austin 78752
Tel: (512)454-3628
TWX: 910-874-1347

Intel Corp.
12300 Ford Road
Suite 380
Dallas 75234
Tel: (214) 241-8087
TWX: 910-860-5617

WASHINGTON

Intel Corp.
110 110th Avenue N.E.
Suite 510
Bellevue 98004
Tel: 1-800-525-5560
TWX: 910-443-3002

WISCONSIN

Intel Corp.
450 N. Sunnyslope Road
Suite 130
Brookfield 53005
Tel: (414) 784-8087